The Road

The Road

Indian Tribes and Political Liberty

Russel Lawrence Barsh
and James Youngblood Henderson

University of California Press

BERKELEY · LOS ANGELES · LONDON

University of California Press
Berkeley and Los Angeles, California
University of California Press, Ltd.
London, England
© 1980 by
The Regents of the University of California
ISBN 0-520-03629-8
Library of Congress Catalog Card Number: 77-91777
Printed in the United States of America

1 2 3 4 5 6 7 8 9

An earlier version of part three of this book previously appeared in R. L. Barsh, "The Omen: Three Affiliated Tribes v. Moe and the Future of Tribal Self-Government," 5 *American Indian Law Review* 1 (1977).

Contents

Prologue

This book is about the rights of Indian tribes on tribal reservations. It is addressed to a great riddle: the political relationship between these sovereign American tribes and *the other* sovereign American government, that is, the government of the United States. We will not consider the rights of the individual Indians, as members of tribal governments or the national government, except where the nature of these individual rights elucidates the political status of tribes collectively.

Indian tribes are a common mental experience and natural fact for most Indians. Birth into a family, a territory, a spiritual world, and a race is a fact, but it is less significant than the mental experience that tribal people share. The essence of this mental experience is a world view—a warm, deep and lasting communal bond among all things in nature in a common vision of their proper relationship. This consciousness cements a collective culture that has proved resilient in modern society. Among members of the community it assumes the form of an interpersonal spiritual communion which has never been and may never be destroyed by outside forces. It continues to be the center of the tribal circle—the foundation of the whispering ideology of tribalism in this land. In combination with the natural fact of birth into a tribe, it has always kept tribal government the hope and road for the future of Indian people.

In the face of fickle federal policy, war and genocide, tribes have endured on the strength of their common experience. The community has at times resembled the scattering trees of a storm-swept prairie, but, with the aid of an unbroken communion with their ancestors' spirits, Indian people have never allowed their tribes to perish. Tribalism has always been *the Road*, that is, the heart and spirit of the Indian people. Tribalism is not an association of interest but a form of consciousness which faithfully reflects the experience of Indians. It is a normative system. The entire history of the federal relationship with tribes is a history of attempts to subvert this consciousness and replace it with the naked, alienated individualism and formal equality of contemporary American society. Indian people have resisted and endured, but the poverty and hate which follow upon failure to assimilate obligingly into the American "melting pot" are the high price they have paid for it. Indeed, poverty is ample evidence that mere communal property interests are not the glue that binds the tribal fabric, as some have argued.

The precise legal status of Indian tribes remains a source of confusion. Fundamental to this confusion is the basic fact of the survival of tribes as the only *consensual* government of Indian people—a fact which defies the anticipated disintegration of tribes and submersion of tribal Indians in white society. The legacy of judicial principles, rules and assumptions devised by *the other* government in the nineteenth century to explain the tribal-federal relationship was predicated on a theory of inevitable political evolution from "primitive" tribalism to "civilized" society. The Tribe, as a form of organization, was supposed to be as vanishing as the buffalo. Although Indian tribes have survived, notwithstanding a century of coercive government intervention, the legal system appears content to quibble over the details of the old rules rather than abandon them. The more the American courts strive to resolve tribal status from precedental principles, the more their opinions cast doubt upon the meaningfulness of the legal legacy.

In constitutional law today, the United States is a tripartite society. The citizens of the states enjoy all of the personal (or civil) and political liberties afforded by our system of delegated and limited powers. The residents of the territories and possessions are somewhat less secure, because in theory their political franchise may be altered, or even extinguished, if Congress chooses. Citizens of Indian tribes, by contrast, have little civil or political liberty. Their use of property is completely regulated, they are subject to separate laws and administration, and their self-governing powers have been altered at Congress's pleasure. No direct challenge to the constitutionality of this division has been heard in the Supreme Court for sixty years.

The current situation of tribal members evokes the whole course of political liberty in American history. While eminent jurists have attempted to brush the issue aside by referring to it as ''unique'' or ''anomalous,'' it is in reality as fundamental and ancient as the existence of human society. It is the same issue that sparked the colonists to rebel against the British empire: the legitimacy of subordinating a community's economic and political rights to the pleasure of a powerful majority. In this respect, tribal citizens stand in the same position today as the colonists did in 1776.

The significance of this similarity lies in the fact that the architecture of the Constitution was intended to prevent a recurrence of the tyranny suffered by the colonies. The framers of the Constitution sought to accomplish their purpose by establishing a perpetual, dynamic equilibrium between central and local powers. Participation of all the people on both sides of this balance was expected to check accumulations of power by the few. However, as American society adjusted to the reality, unanticipated by the framers, of coexistence with Indian tribes, these essential requirements of political liberty were forgotten. A euphoria of national greatness blurred the vision of a road of political liberty which began in the colonial experience, and replaced this vision with submission to the law of economic expediency.

To us, political liberty means an effective voice in national government, *and* the right of the people to establish local governments to exercise any or all of the powers they have reserved to themselves. By this test, Indian tribes and tribal citizens have been systematically deprived of their constitutional rights for at least one hundred years. In the succeeding chapters we will attempt to define the constitutional guarantee of political liberty more fully, to explain the historical process by which tribal citizens have come to be deprived of their political liberty, and to develop a conceptual strategy for legal restoration of their right to a government of their choice. By not breaking completely with the deeper layers of American constitutional jurisprudence, we hope to transform, rather than negate, the consciousness of non-Indian Americans and preserve the continuity of both tribal and national government.

ON METHOD

We will often have recourse in the chapters that follow to matters of historical causality, but merely as a point of departure. The use of history is always fraught with difficulties and limitations. Law and history have a certain similitude in social theory. Lawyers seek evidence of the future in past events. Charles Miller, a historian, has written in his book, *The Supreme Court and the Uses of History*:

[H]istory may be defined as that which, in the opinion of the Supreme Court, is. believed to be true about the past—about past facts and past thoughts. . . . For purposes of analysis it may again be divided into two categories: history internal to the law and history external to the law. This distinction, like many distinctions, is blurred at the boundaries but clear at the center. History internal to the law con-sists of precedents . . . and legal history. Legal history pertains to the history of legal terms and doctrines. . . . Somewhere on the borderline between legal history, which is internal to the law, and general political history, which is external to the law, lies the history used in . . . litigation involving Indian tribes. In no other fields of public law does history play so decisive a role, a role and a decisiveness accepted by all parties to the litigation as well as the court.[1]

Professor Miller may have overstated the point when he referred to "all parties." Indian tribes have usually disagreed with the history invoked in the course of particular disputes, yet Miller concludes that "beyond an appeal to conscience and legal documents the best evidence in most Indian cases is the testimony of history, especially the use, possession, practice and expectations concerning the lands."[2] This has proved the tribes' undoing. It is important to bear in mind the differences between *general history* which "includes political, social, economic and cultural history,"[3] and may be understood as empirical reality, and *borderline history*, which may be described as institutionalized or conventionalized reality.

The use of borderline history by the federal courts poses profound

1. Charles Miller, *The Supreme Court and the Uses of History* 24 (Cambridge, Mass.: 1969).
2. *Id.*
3. *Id.* 25.

problems in legal method for tribal advocates. The main problem is that it vindicates past generations of lawyers' subjective selections of facts, and receives new facts, whether historical or contemporary, only to the extent that they are *familiar*, that is, consistent with old facts. Every community of people holds in common a certain set of assumptions about reality, called a *paradigm* by the philosopher Thomas Kuhn. A paradigm is the shared conception of *what is possible*, the boundaries of acceptable inquiry, the list of limiting cases.[4] Courts are a kind of community, and the set of past judicial actions—precedent—constrains future initiative. What judges have said before is accepted as probably true, fossilizing antiquated prejudices, poor judgment and personal idiosyncrasies. Legal theory supposes that precedent guarantees *continuity*, which we equate with *justice*, at least if it is fair to define justice as relative certainty of outcomes. But precedent makes it quite difficult for courts to alter their data even in the face of compelling evidence of injustice or absurdity. Tribes pay a particularly high price for judicial conservatism and judicial resistance to new ideas and information, because they are trapped, unlike others, by both precedents of law and precedents of fact. If the courts continue to accept nineteenth-century assumptions regarding the transitory nature of tribalism, their inquiry will continue to be too narrow to arrive at viable solutions tolerable to the Indian people. "One element of the past intrudes quite unnecessarily upon the present," laments Charles Curtis in his book *Lions Under the Throne*. "We try to make the most of the consequences of what our forefathers did, but there is no reason why we should feel we have to carry out their plans for us. Were they so wise they didn't need to know the facts?"[5]

Borderline history is biased history. The legal legacy does not conform either to modern historical scholarship or to the continuing existence of tribalism. The accumulation of past doctrines, policies and practices designed to accelerate tribal disintegration has become the reality of the legal system. Past comments of judges are accepted over facts which illustrate the failure of their expectations to materialize in society. These conditions might be bearable if they lent certainty and consistency to tribal affairs, in keeping with the jurisprudential justification of the use of

---

4. Thomas Kuhn, *The Structure of Scientific Revolutions* 43 (2nd ed. Chicago: 1970).
5. Charles Curtis, Jr., *Lions Under the Throne* 2 (Boston: 1947).

precedent. Unfortunately, as we will demonstrate, uncertainty plagues the law of tribal status, because the judges are slaves of a borderline history now grown so complex that few if any are aware of it all, and fewer still can recognize its accumulating self-contradictions. Our objective, then, must be to replace borderline history with elementary constitutional principles: to replace an artificial history that conceals false assumptions and unacceptable values with an explicit normative framework more consistent with general American political philosophy.

The remarkable thing about the conventional wisdom of tribal political status is its self-contradiction. If we are to believe the United States Supreme Court, the only general principle of tribal-federal law is that there are no general principles.[6] We believe this to be false. General principles *can* be constructed to rationalize the status of tribes. Admittedly, such principles cannot be slavishly deduced from legal history. This is obvious: a judiciary convinced that there can be no generalities creates none. It has thus been necessary for us to go beyond rigorous legal analysis and examine the inconsistencies between our social ideals and law, politics and administration. We have concluded that a new conceptualization of the federal-tribal relationship, which we call the *federal-tribal compact* or *treaty federalism*, is necessary to reconcile the status of tribes with American society's essential social and political values.

The current ideological situation is dangerous. Courts' denial of general principles increases their opportunities to act capriciously. This represents, in fact, one of those inconsistencies between general American ideals and the law of tribes. Common law embodies the use of the precedent because we value consistency and equate it with justice. What is the logic of the exception for tribes? To reconcile this problem, lawyers have expended much paper and ink learnedly struggling to discover some elegant and hitherto obscure common denominator among the courts' products. Like medieval theologians, they avoid confrontation with their system's fatal paradoxes by immersing their thoughts in trivial comparisons and nice distinctions. We do not believe that there exists some subtle logic by which the apparent negation of American political values in tribal affairs can be made to disappear. Our approach has therefore been to construct a principle, sufficiently agreeable to the legacy of familiar case law to be intellectually acceptable, yet so freed from historical constraints and

---

6. *McClanahan v. Arizona Tax Comm'n*, 411 U.S. 164, 172 (1973); *Mescalero Apache Tribe v. Jones*, 411 U.S. 145, 148 (1973).

technical distinctions as to be capable of providing an understandable and practical guide for future conduct.

In other areas of constitutional litigation, historians and lawyers are equally reluctant to concede the legitimacy of the past as a source of new institutions. In fact, although the framers of the Constitution themselves studied history to detect the political errors of the past and avoid them in the future, they did not conceive of themselves as limited by precedent.[7] They compared notes on the Iroquois Confederacy and classical republics, and argued the relative merits of the Swiss cantons and Dutch States-General, but did not pretend that the whole range of legitimate possibility for the new nation could be so discovered. As Alexander Hamilton observed, "the sacred rights of mankind are not to be rummaged for among old parchments or musty records."[8] Americans criticized those English jurists who "sought to establish right by appeal to precedent and to an unbroken tradition evolving from time immemorial, and . . . assumed . . . that the accumulation of the ages, the burden of inherited custom, contained within it a greater wisdom than any man or group of men could devise by the power of reason."[9]

The American Constitution does in fact embody much earlier law, especially the English Bill of Rights. At the same time its draftsmen recognized that they confronted difficulties unknown to the ancients or to their own European ancestors. As scholars they were capable of drawing upon history and science as tools to deduce appropriate new forms of government with reasonable hope for success, relying on observable similarities in causes and effects. But as politicians they had to communicate the wisdom and desirability of the scheme ultimately arrived at to a suspicious public, educated to different institutions and ideals. To break the shackles of political dogma and familiarity with old institutions, they distilled and disseminated a new framework of political analysis, hoping thereby to bring the people to speak a political language less hostile to the institutions they proposed for ratification.

7. Pauline Maier, *From Resistance to Revolution* 44, 289 (New York: 1972). Ezra Stiles advised "Men of Genius and penetrat[in]g Observation [to] take a large and Comprehensive View of the polities of the States and Countries around the Globe," including the "Lights of Orientals and Asiatics of the World itself both in ancient and modern Ages" (*id*. 290).

8. Bernard Bailyn, *The Ideological Origins of the American Revolution* 188 (Cambridge, Mass.: 1967).

9. *Id*. 33. To Americans of 1776 government was, in the words of "Cato," " a mere Piece of Clockwork," to be designed to "move to the publick Advantage" (Maier, *From Resistance to Revolution* 289).

Like the reconceptualization in this book, the original theory of the Constitution was not solely the product of empirical scholarship. It was philosophy, and that was indispensible. "The Revolution," after all, John Adams would later write, "was in the minds of the people."[10] As the philosophers of science have observed, empirical knowledge accumulates constantly, but real change does not occur until a new framework of analysis is discovered.[11] Systems of knowledge, even the exact sciences, tend to become dogmatic because they rely upon old ideas to analyze new events. In the social sciences the problem is complicated by the subtle interrelationships of different disciplines, such that the dogmatic assumptions of each tend to prove the truth of all the others. When inconsistencies accumulate beyond reasonable toleration, a new system must be organized to reconcile old and new knowledge. This is a qualitative leap, a leap of faith. It is an act of intellectual transcendence. Only by transcending the integration of knowledge and ideas do we find, in Roberto Unger's metaphor, "the key that will allow us to escape from the prison-house, just as it was the chain with which the gates were long ago locked by the builders."[12]

If conceptualization is a prison house, it can only be broken by reconceptualization. However, scholars strive hard to confine themselves to "certain technical riddles notable for their remoteness from our concern with understanding and transformation of society."[13] We have endeavored to analyze and reconceptualize, to transcend the conventional dogma of our field of study and introduce an alternative framework of analysis. We will undoubtedly be criticized for painting too broadly with the brush of imagination. We do not apologize. All law and social theory represent efforts to rationalize an irrational world full of inconsistency and uncertainties. At the margin, the choice among rationalizations is a matter of meaningfulness, not empirical demonstration, a matter of consistency with

10. Bailyn, *Ideological Origins* 1. Governor Pownall's great treatise, *The Administration of the British Colonies* (5th ed. London: 1774), described the English common law as "nothing more but the practice and determination of the courts on points of law, drawn into precedents; where the circumstances of a country and people, and their relation to the statutes and common law differ so greatly [as in America]; the common law of these countries must, in its natural course, become different, and sometimes even contrary, or at least incompatible, with the common law of England" (1 *id.* 105).
11. Kuhn, *Scientific Revolutions* 43.
12. Roberto Mangabeira Unger, *Knowledge and Politics* 4 (Chicago: 1975).
13. *Id.*

consciousness. The English conservatives who concluded from their failure to show the colonists their "error" that all Americans were fools, failed to realize that the "obviousness" of their arguments was a product of nothing more than consistency with their own experience. Pauline Maier has observed that, in the end, the American Revolution became possible because Americans lost their empathy—what we have called a common experience—with other Britons.[14] They could no longer accept being "a free and a great people together," as Jefferson put it.[15] Our goal has been to arrive at a conceptualization consistent with the experience of both tribal and nontribal citizens. If we have succeeded, it may provide *the Road* for political reconciliation.

14. Maier, *From Resistance to Revolution* 269–70.
15. *Id.* 268.

Part One

The Conceptualization of
Political Liberty in America

1

The New Order

Ten years ago, the Supreme Court observed that "[n]o right is more precious in a free country than that of having a voice in the election of those who make the laws under which we, as good citizens, must live. Other rights, even the most basic, are illusory if the right to vote is undermined."[1] It seems obvious that our nation, born in a struggle for political liberty, should guarantee meaningful local self-government and effective national representation to all citizens as the only ultimate security of their lives and property. The right of political liberty is, in the words of the Declaration of Independence, a "self-evident" truth.

James Madison, in fact, proposed an amendment to the Constitution:

that all power is originally vested in, and consequently derived from, the people. That government is instituted and ought to be exercised for the benefit of the people; which consists in the enjoyment of life and liberty, with the right of acquiring and using property, and generally of pursuing and obtaining happiness and safety.[2]

1. *Wesberry v. Sanders*, 376 U.S. 1, 17 (1964).
2. Herman V. Ames, "The Proposed Amendments to the Constitution of the United States during the First Century of its History," 2 *Annual Report of the American Historical Association, 1896* 185 (Washington, D.C.: 1897). It was supported by New York, North Carolina and Virginia. Madison described its principles as "self-evident" when he submitted the amendment to Congress (Bennett Patterson, *The Forgotten Ninth Amendment* 148–49 [Indianapolis: 1955]).

It was never submitted to the people. Both houses of Congress were satisfied that the words "We the People" in the Preamble "speak as much as it is possible to speak; it is a practical recognition of the right of the people to ordain and establish Governments."[3] The Senate nonetheless did respond to Madison by adding the words "or to the people" to the Tenth Amendment,[4] as they hoped to eliminate any risk of future doubt that legitimate power must be traceable to popular consent.

The American Bill of Rights was so similar to British common-law traditions that many opposed ratification as an unnecessary waste of time.[5] The English Bill of Rights, a statute of William III, had already enumerated the "indubitable rights and liberties" of Englishmen: freedom of religion, no standing army, an equal opportunity to hold public office, no excessive bail or fines, jury trial, and no taxation without consent, among other things.[6] The procedural safeguards of Magna Carta, such as habeas corpus, were also included in the common law. By retaining the common law generally, it was argued, the new nation had preserved undiminished all of these liberties.

If the American government was to be "a new order" (to quote from the Great Seal), what essential freedoms did it add to the British foundation? Specific additions were made to the Bill of Rights, such as the separation of Church and State and the right to bear arms, but they had not been key objectives of the Revolution, nor were they altogether foreign to British political thought. The theory of checks and balances had previously been embodied in the tripartite division of the British legislature into King,

3. Patterson, *Ninth Amendment* 144—45, 149.

4. Ames, "Proposed Amendments," 88—89, 186. This compromise was originally suggested by Mr. Carroll as an alternative to inserting Madison's first clause at the beginning of what is now the Tenth Amendment (Patterson, *Ninth Amendment* 193).

5. James Iredell argued that such limitations were unnecessary in a government of limited and delegated powers (*Answers to Mr. Masons objections to the new Constitution* [1788], reprinted in Paul Leicester Ford, *Pamphlets on the Constitution of the United States* [Brooklyn, N.Y.: 1888]; and in 4 *Elliot's Debates on the Confederation and Constitution* 147—49 [Washington, D.C.: 1830—1845]).

6. 1 W. & M. Sess. 2 ch. 2 §6. Another objection to an American Bill of Rights was that any declaration of specific rights necessarily implied that *no other rights* were intended to be preserved. Hamilton shared this view (Patterson, *Ninth Amendment* 9). It was generally agreed that "no man . . . could enumerate all the individual rights not relinquished by this Constitution," as James Iredell put it at the North Carolina ratifying convention (4 *Elliot's Debates* 147—49). Impressed by this reasoning, Madison offered what is now the Ninth Amendment as a remedy (Patterson, *Ninth Amendment* 10—13, 115—16; Ames, "Proposed Amendments," 166—67).

Lords, and Commons, although our Constitution transforms Britain's three social estates into purely functional branches of government. A more securely independent judiciary was established, but that can hardly be the greatest novelty of our system.[7]

The truly radical accomplishments of our Constitution are the mutually reinforcing principles of democratic representation and federalism. Each serves, in a different way, to check the potential for despotism in a government of great size and wealth, and neither had any real counterpart in the British constitution of 1776. The people are secured in the reservation of certain powers to themselves and to their locally constituted, and therefore in principle more accountable, subfederal governments. They are further secured by their direct representation, proportionately and collectively, in the two houses of Congress. As *The Federalist* explained,[8] both measures combine to protect local communities of interest against the majoritarian excesses possible in a large and heterogeneous society. No matter how small, a political community has an equal voice in the Senate. Even if the Senate is so large as to dilute its voice there, a political community enjoys a sphere of exclusive legislation within which to protect the peferences and interests of its members. James Iredell argued that this protection is so complete it renders a Bill of Rights superfluous.[9]

English political economists were astonished by the colonists' demand for direct representation in Parliament, since fewer than five percent of the residents of the British isles themselves were entitled to vote.[10] The House of Commons was still apportioned according to the demography of medieval England, underrepresenting towns and cities that had grown faster than the countryside.

Defenders of the status quo rationalized that "every member of Parliament sits in the House not as representative of his own constituents but as one of that august assembly by which all the commons of Great

7. On the role of an independent judiciary in conservative English political thought, see Bernard Bailyn, *The Ideological Origins of the American Revolution* 74–75 (Cambridge, Mass.: 1967).

8. *The Federalist*, No. 51.

9. Iredell, *Answers to Mr. Masons objections*, Answer No. 1.

10. Josiah Tucker, *Four Tracts on Political and Commercial Subjects* 112–13 (3rd ed. Gloucester, England: 1776); James MacPherson, *The rights of great Britain asserted against the claims of America: being an answer to the declaration of the general congress* 4–7 (London: 1776).

Britain are represented.''[11] Although elected by the few, it was their sacred duty to advance the real welfare of all. James Otis retorted that one could "as well prove that the British House of Commons in fact represent all of the people of the globe.''[12] What principle guaranteed their supposed wisdom and independence of their electors?

"Virtual representation" was somewhat less pernicious in the mother country than in America. English representatives bore the same taxes and regulations as other residents of the British isles, and therefore had their own interest at stake in any increase: "The security of the nonelectors against oppression is that their oppression will fall also upon the electors and the representatives.''[13] On the other hand, members of the Commons were not touched by taxes levied on the colonists, with whom their social and economic associations were more remote than with fellow Britons.[14] The root of the evil was Parliament's making laws with special applications to the colonies, legally externalizing the consequences of its actions.

The Georgian Parliament was not organized along functional lines, but divided into social classes: the King, Lords, and Commons. Each of these estates was presumed selfish, and, if not checked, inherently disposed to despotism. However, "each estate, armed with a power of self-defense against the encroachments of the other two, by being enabled to put a negative upon any or all of their resolves, neither the King, Lords, or Commons could be deprived of their rights or properties but by their own consent.''[15] The supreme legislature was conceived to be a perfect mix of

11. Thomas Whately, quoted in Bailyn, *Ideological Origins* 166; *id.* generally, 166−70. Also Thomas Pownall, 1 *The Administration of the British Colonies* 152 (5th ed. London: 1774); Tucker, *Four Tracts* 116, 178−79. This resembles our own theory that senators, owing to their longer tenures of office, tend to develop a broader perspective. See Noah Webster, *An Examination into the leading principles of the Federal Constitution . . . By a Citizen of America* (Philadelphia: 1787), reprinted in Ford, *Pamphlets*.

12. James Otis, *Considerations On Behalf of the Colonists in a letter to a Noble Lord* 9 (London: 1765).

13. Daniel Dulaney, quoted in Bailyn, *Ideological Origins* 167. See also Richard Price, *Observations on the Nature of Civil Liberty, the Principles of Government, and the Justice and Policy of the War with America* 24 (5th ed. London: 1776). "We might have flattered ourselves," Arthur Lee suggested, "that a *virtual obedience* would have exactly corresponded with a *virtual representation*" (Bailyn, *Ideological Origins* 168).

14. Dean Tucker argued that the colonists did *in fact* enjoy an equal opportunity to vote for Parliament: they were free to emigrate to England, purchase freeholds, and vote there! (Tucker, *Four Tracts* 109−111).

15. Moses Mather, quoted in Bailyn, *Ideological Origins* 73. See Pauline Maier, *From Resistance to Revolution*, 291−95 (New York: 1972), regarding the popular theory of an inherent tendency in the king to corrupt Parliament.

monarchy, aristocracy and democracy, operating by consensus.

The flaw lay in treating the vast majority of the population as a single, homogeneous estate. As it approached the industrial age. Britain diversified, straining the Georgian idealization of the Commons. The rise of the British middle class within this estate rendered the ideal of homogeneity untenable. In America the distortion was even more severe. There was no American peerage. Consequently, the king was represented in absentia in two of the three branches of colonial government, the council and the governorship. Even conservative observers would find in this a dangerous, unconstitutional imbalance. Some suggested as a remedy that an American peerage of sorts be established to moderate the colonial assemblies, but this innovation was completely unacceptable to most Americans.[16]

Although Americans rejected the theory of three estates, they did not believe that theirs was a homogeneous society, or that it could be governed without balancing competing interests. On the contrary, they assumed a far greater diversity of legitimate competing interests than merely three. Each point of view was entitled to be heard, such that the legislature "should be in miniature an exact portrait of the people at large."[17] Unlike the conservatives, who believed that diversity in a democratic state inevitably results in perpetual turmoil, American radicals trusted that democratic participation of all interests, however great or small, would unite a diverse society.

More than separation, British conservatives thus feared a "Contagion" of republican ideology spreading from the colonies to the mother country.[18] Americans were circulating a theory of government absolutely subversive of Parliament's legitimacy, and it strengthened the embattled English republican movement's demands for a sweeping reapportionment of the Commons.[19] Dr. Richard Price, once accused of being Britain's "republican goliah," took his countrymen to task for criticizing the Americans' demand for a proportional representation. "It is saying that we

16. Bailyn, *Ideological Origins* 276, 278–79, 292.

17. Quoted in Bailyn, *Ideological Origins* 172.

18. Josiah Tucker, *A series of Answers to certain popular objections, against separating from the Rebellious Colonies and discarding them entirely: being the Concluding Tract of the Dean of Gloucester on the subject of American Affairs* xii, 71–73, 76, 99 (Gloucester, England: 1776).

19. Bailyn, *Ideological Origins* 47. The American movement also owed a great deal to the English, which they admired greatly (Maier, *From Resistance to Revolution* 204–5, 250–60).

want liberty; and therefore, they ought to want it. . . . Ought we not rather to wish earnestly, that there may at least be ONE FREE COUNTRY left upon earth, to which we may fly, when venality, luxury, and vice have completed the ruin of liberty here?''[20]

Federalism was as dangerous to the ruling coalitions in eighteenth-century British government as proportional representation. Britain had once been a federation of sorts. Notwithstanding the efforts of the Norman administrators to unify their conquests, local legislative prerogatives survived and grew in the first five centuries of the new kingdom, commonly by royal initiative, often for a price, and protected by Article 16 of Magna Carta. Local jurisdictions, such as manors, towns and ports, merchant associations and fairs, guilds, and chartered companies (including the two great universities), passed laws and enforced them in their own courts.[21] The City of London was the greatest of all of these legislative franchises; the Jewish Exchequer perhaps the most particular. New jurisdictions, such as the great overseas trading companies, were formed well into the age of expansion.[22]

Following the Civil War, Parliament made a concerted effort to establish its legislative supremacy against both king and corporations. The prerogative of the king to grant monopolies and franchises was denied, and the right of local jurisdictions to resist parliamentary alterations of their charters was exploded. The whole system of medieval British federalism, so profitable to the king, was replaced by a single central bureaucratic administration of law and revenue. Jacobite absolutism was crushed by

20. Price, *Observations* 24. ''The liberty of America might have preserved our liberty . . . the means of restoring our almost lost constitution'' (*id*. 41, 61). A number of American and English writers joined Price in predicting that America would become a refuge for uncorrupted Britons. Samuel Ward wrote in 1773 that ''the Liberty of America is the life of Britain, and if Slavery takes place in this Country, Britain will fall a sacrifice to her own tyranny'' (Maier, *From Resistance to Revolution* 246–48; see also *id*. 260–65, and Bailyn, *Ideological Origins* 89, 138–43). ''If America is an humble instrument of the salvation of Britain,'' Joseph Warren warned, ''it will give us the sincerest joy; but if Britain must lose her liberty, she must lose it alone'' (Maier, *From Resistance to Revolution* 265). See also Otis, *Considerations* 7.

21. See *Dr. Bonham's Case*, 8 Co. Rep. 113b, 77 Eng. Rep. 646 (Hil. 7 Jac. 1, 1609), regarding constitutional limitations on the adjudicative powers of corporations; and of limitations on corporations' monopoly privileges, see *The Case of Monopolies*, 11 Co. Rep. 84b, 77 Eng. Rep. 1260 (Trin. 44 Eliz. 1, 1602), and *An Act Concerning Monopolies*, 21 Jac. 1 c. 3 (1623).

22. Especially instructive of the nature of these institutions is Sigmund Diamond, ''From Organization to Society: Virginia in the Seventeenth Century,'' in Stanley Katz, ed., *Colonial America* (Boston: 1970). On the enforceability of corporation law in royal courts see *The City of London's Case*, 8 Co. Rep. 122a, 77 Eng. Rep. 658 (Hil. 7 Jac. 1, 1609), overturned by *The Printers' Case* (1770), discussed in Maier, *From Resistance to Revolution* 186.

stripping the king of the power to create corporate fiefs independent of Parliament.

Concurrent with the demise of local franchise, Parliament denied the responsibility of its members to advocate the interests of their respective districts of election. Parliament would no longer be, in Burke's memorable phrase, "a *congress* of ambassadors from different and hostile interests, which interest each must maintain, as an agent and advocate, against other agents and advocates; but Parliament is a *deliberative* assembly of *one* nation, with *one* interest, that of the Whole."[23] To admit that its members sat as representatives of collectivities would recognize local sovereignties, a result no conservative would allow. For the safety and stability of the state, some "supreme, irresistible, absolute, and uncontrollable authority," must exist.[24] Any distribution of power to local subdivisions was believed factious and dangerous, a process that would continue ad absurdum.[25] Indeed, English commentators were so confident of this that they declared the existence of a "sovereignty with a sovereignty" an obvious self-contradiction.[26]

American radicals were unconvinced. They shared a long experience of sui generis federalism at both the provincial and imperial levels. Particularly in New England, where individual towns exercised substantial self-governing powers themselves, colonial assemblies were congresses of local interest. The colonies fully appreciated their differences in economy and culture. They negotiated individually with the imperial government through agents or lobbyists and exercised almost unrestricted powers of domestic legislation and taxation through the 1760s.[27] The practicality of such a government was a reality, not a mere theory. Colonial radicals readily assumed that the solution to their problems was formalization of this de facto federal union with Britain.[28]

Once it is understood, however, that centralization of authority in Par-

---

23. Bailyn, *Ideological Origins* 163. Appropriately our American federal legislature is called a "Congress."

24. Bailyn, *Ideological Origins* 200—202; Maier, *From Resistance to Revolution* 46−47.

25. If we treated sovereignty "like matter, divisible *ad infinitum*" Joseph Galloway feared, "and under this profound mistake, you began with splitting and dividing it, until by one slice after another, you have hacked and pared it away to less than an atom" (Bailyn, *Ideological Origins* 223). Compare James Otis, *The Rights of the British Colonies Asserted and proved* 48 (Boston: 1764).

26. Bailyn, *Ideological Origins* 206, 220, 222−23.

27. *Id.* 164−65, 203−4, 208−9.

28. Americans idealized medieval federalism and argued that centralization represented a corrupting innovation (Bailyn, *Ideological Origins* 80−81).

liament was regarded by Britons as the great triumph of England's seventeenth-century turmoil, it is easy to imagine the horror with which they viewed the prospect of a federal union with America. Any permanent division of authority between the colonies and Parliament marked a return to a medieval state of affairs. The national commercial and proprietary interests which controlled Parliament were unlikely to benefit from a return to local regulation, nor was the revenue system, which nationalized had served to finance commercial expansion overseas, likely to survive unscathed. The colonists' repeated appeals to the king for relief against Parliament's exactions at that time, combined with their frequent argument that they were subject to the power of the king alone, did little to assuage Parliament's apprehensions of a revival of royal absolutism.

The Revolution can also be understood as a reaction to overextended bureaucracy. Most Englishmen were satisfied with the Restoration's balancing of a moderate king with a more jealous and powerful Parliament. However, the eighteenth-century Hanovers sought to reenlarge the crown through the instrument of the ministry. "Robinarchy" is what Bolingbroke called this mutated constitution, alluding to the alleged machinations of Robert Walpole.[29] The "ministerial engine" had, it was argued, become a virtual fourth estate, "[f]or their power and interest is so great that they can and do procure whatever laws they please, having (by power, interest, and application of the people's money to *placemen* and *pensioners*) the whole legislative authority at their command."[30] Its interests being the increase of salaries and pensions, the civil service was popularly assumed to constitute an *illegitimate* social rank differentiable from the admittedly selfish but traditionally institutionalized interest groups of King, Lords and Commons. If the ministry was corrupt, moreover, it was at least in large part owing to the lack of adequate popular representation in

29. *Id.* 49–50. Maier, *From Resistance to Revolution* 102–7, 171–74, 177, 183–85, 200–203, 205–12, 239–41, has shown how this evolved and ultimately implicated the king himself as chief conspirator. Bailyn contends that it was all, in the final analysis, merely paranoia (*Ideological Origins* 148–50).

30. Bailyn, *Ideological Origins* 125; also 103–4, 124–27, 129–31, 144–59. John Trenchard and Thomas Gordon ("Cato") described the process as (1) the ministry insulating the king from the people; (2) constant foreign wars to keep the people distracted from corruption at home; (3) appointment of incompetents to civil posts; and (4) instigation of civil disorders to provide an excuse for domestic repression (Maier, *From Resistance to Revolution* 45). Many colonists read the Stamp Act as a foot-in-the-door precedent of no real economic hurt standing by itself, but which the ministry hoped might stir up a violent reaction justifying the dispatch of troops (Bailyn, *Ideological Origins* 100–101).

Parliament. However, the civil service was a more visible and vulnerable target than the constitution itself. Thus while at first the colonists vigorously defended the constitution there was no limit to their fury against administrative incompetence and oppression.[31]

Americans were perhaps more sensitive to this issue because, having been left largely to their own devices for more than a century, they were suddenly beset in 1763 with the full measure of Grenvillean bureaucracy. They adopted a number of ingenious explanations for this phenomenon. Having sucked England dry, a popular argument ran, the civil service was emigrating, and henceforth "new offices will be constituted and new officers palmed upon us until the number is so great that we cannot by our constant labor and toil maintain any more."[32] The English people themselves, under the baleful influences of contagious corruption and national prosperity, had been lulled into submissiveness and debauchery.[33] They were not as aware as the colonists that bureaucratic government is tantamount to *slavery,* for it is nothing less than "being wholly under the power and control of another as to our actions and properties."[34] Bureaucratic regulation places power in the hands of appointed, rather than elected officials. Since the civil servant is not accountable to his charges, he is no more concerned for their welfare than a slaveowner, that is, to see that they are productive of revenue.

Overextension of bureaucracy is interlinked with direct representation and federalism. Representatives are unlikely to vote their own lives and fortunes into the hands of civil servants, at least not without comprehensive safeguards, just as they are unlikely to tax themselves without good reason. Representatives must, moreover, assume visible responsibility for their own constituents to remain in office, while they can afford to transfer responsibility for unrepresented or inadequately represented groups to appointed officials. To the extent that responsible representatives do find sound reason to delegate authority to administrators, federalism provides a framework for decentralization of bureaucratic activities.

31. Maier, *From Resistance to Revolution* xii, 4−7, 100.

32. Bailyn, *Ideological Origins* 128−29, 131. Colonial officials bore the brunt of the conspiracy allegations (*id.* 99−100, 122; Maier, *From Resistance to Revolution* 149, 154−57, 171.

33. Bailyn, *Ideological Origins* 86−92, 132−37; Maier, *From Resistance to Revolution* 221−24, 250−51, 260−65.

34. The definition is Moses Mather's, quoted in Bailyn, *Ideological Origins* 233.

2

The Inheritors of Locke and Filmer

The accession of William of Orange in 1688 was by election rather than inheritance, and on the condition that he guarantee certain fundamental rights of Englishmen.[1] John Locke's *Two Treatises of Government* supported the legitimacy of the new king by arguing that *all* governments originate in the free consent of the people according to such rules and conditions as they may choose for themselves and their rulers.[2] William's election was therefore nothing more than the establishment of a new compact to replace the failed and broken compact of the ancient line of British sovereigns.

Tucked away near the end of Locke's *Second Treatise* was an argument far more radical than his idealization of the contractual origin of governments:

Whenever the legislators endeavor to take away and destroy the property of the people, or to reduce them to slavery under arbitrary power, they put themselves into a state of war with the people who are thereupon absolved from any further obedience. . . . Whensoever, therefore, the legislative shall . . . by ambition, fear, folly, or corruption, endeavor to grasp themselves, or put into the hands of any other an absolute power over the lives, liberties, and estates of the people, by

1. Discussed in James Otis, *The Rights of the British Colonies Asserted and proved* 15−22, 64−65 (Boston: 1764).
2. See John Locke's Preface to his *Two Treatises of Government* (London: 1690).

12

this breach of trust they forfeit the power the people had put into their hands for quite contrary ends, and it devolves to the people, who have a right to resume their original liberty and, by the establishment of a new legislative, such as they shall think fit, provide for their own safety and security, which is the end for which they are in society.[3]

Whatever the original form of a society, the people have an antecedent right to some minimum degree of liberty and order. Should their rulers transgress, the legitimacy of the constitution terminates automatically and laws enacted pursuant to it cease to have any morally or legally binding force. "For a people thus abused to rise unanimously and to resist their prince, even to dethroning him, is not criminal, but a reasonable way of vindicating their liberties and just rights," wrote an American admirer and disciple, Jonathan Mayhew, half a century later.[4] It is the government, not the people, who dissolve the constitution in such cases, for "the moment that . . . they attempt to render themselves independent of the people, that moment their authority ceases, they themselves break the compact with the people, and from that moment the people . . . have a constitutional right to form their government anew."[5] A vicious king is not deposed; he "un-kings" himself by his acts of despotism.[6] Indeed, the people have not only a right, but a moral duty to reassume powers abused by their rulers.[7]

The reception of Locke's *Two Treatises* made it clear that the Restoration government would not condone the theories of Robert Filmer, a Stuart absolutist whose works enjoyed a wide circulation before the Civil War at the instigation of King James. Liberty, in Filmer's view, is a mere privilege granted to the people from time to time at the pleasure of their king. The king's right to rule is divine and absolute, analogous to and coextensive with the power of a father over the family, and of God over all mankind. Filmerism may be reduced to a thesis that all citizens are wards of the State, in perpetual pupilage and dependence.[8] Thus the form or constitution

3. *Id.* C. 19 §222.
4. Quoted in Bernard Bailyn, *The Ideological Origins of the American Revolution* 93 (Cambridge, Mass.: 1967).
5. *The Massachusetts Spy* (newspaper), quoted in Pauline Maier, *From Resistance to Revolution* 219 (New York: 1972); see also *id.* 27—28, 238. Thus when the Sons of Liberty were formed they assumed many of the responsibilities of local administration left untended by the Crown (*id.* 135—37, 139—40).
6. Maier, *From Resistance to Revolution* 41.
7. Bailyn, *Ideological Origins* 311—18.
8. An excellent discussion of Filmerism and the American reaction to it is found in Edwin Burroughs and Michael Wallace, "The Ideology and Psychology of National Liberation," 6 *Perspectives in American History* 167 (1972).

of the State is not a matter of human design or will, but an inescapable dictate of God and nature. It is discovered, not made. It is invariable and it is the *moral duty* of citizens to obey.

The Glorious Revolution vindicated the power of the people to create new government and should have put this doctrine to rest. However, eighteenth-century American radicals encountered a reactionary backlash of Filmerism.[9] Their critics referred to America as a "spoiled child" in need of "correction," and characterized the taxes imposed upon the colonies by Parliament as gratitude due the royal "indulgent parent."[10] Obedience to royal authority was a moral and filial duty, regardless of the justice of the king's acts.[11] Former Governor Pownall of New York, in a widely-read treatise on colonial administration, stated the imperial position this way:

> While the circumstances of a community such, either from any natural incapacity in its infancy, or from any political incapacity, by its holding principles that *refer to a foreign jurisdiction*—there such Colonies cannot be trusted with their own will. They remain therefore *under pupillage or regency, governed* ab extra.[12]

Dr. Price was not alone in wondering at the logic of the paternal analogy in words paraphrased from Locke, "But there is a period when, having acquired . . . a capacity of judging for themselves, [children] become independent agents."[13] The colonists justly feared that their "childhood"

---

9. Bailyn, *Ideological Origins* 311−18.

10. James MacPherson, *The Rights of great Britain asserted against the claims of America: being an answer to the declaration of the general congress* 12−14, 70−71, 77, 79−80 (London: 1776); Josiah Tucker, *Four Tracts on Political and Commercial Subjects* 119 (3rd ed. Gloucester, England: 1776). Filmerism played an important part in the early propaganda on the Irish question. John Cary, answering Molyneux's defense of Irish nationalism, argued at length that the Irish were too primitive to properly maintain their own government (Dedicatory to Cary, *An Answer to Mr. Molyneux His case of Ireland's being bound by acts of Parliament in England, Stated: and his dangerous notion of Ireland's being under no subordination to the Parliamentary authority of England, Refuted* [London: 1698]). Ireland was given its own parliament notwithstanding, leading several supporters of American rights to offer Ireland as a precedent (Otis, *Rights of the British Colonies* 45, 53−54, 75−76; Arthur Lee, *An Appeal to the Justice and Interest of the people of Great Britain, in the present disputes with America* 34 [London: 1775]; Richard Price, *Observations on the Nature of Civil Liberty, the Principles of Government, and the Justice and Policy of the War with America* 59 [5th ed. London: 1776]).

11. Bailyn, *Ideological Origins* 311−18.

12. Thomas Pownall, 2 *The Administration of the British Colonies* 59−60 (5th ed. London: 1774).

13. Price, *Observations* 21−22; similarly Pownall, 2 *Administration* 15−16. More seriously, many believed that social rank conduced to public order by fixing interpersonal relationships and chilling ambition and mobility (Bailyn, *Ideological Origins*, 311−18).

would be perpetuated as long as they took no hand in the parliamentary process of regulating it.

What had happened was simple. The revolutionary principles adopted to legitimize the Restoration constitution had since become a political embarrassment to the crown. King William's government had become the establishment, and the political science of the deposed Stuart absolutists now provided arguments for the Hanovers' right to rule. The colonists naturally responded by imagining themselves defenders of the constitution of their grandfathers, and by describing the official crown position as a dangerous innovation. By resisting, the colonists were "not attempting any change of Government—only a preservation of the Constitution" of 1688 "according to its true form and original texture."[14]

Americans' use of the slogan *liberty* also met with reactionary arguments, chiefly resurrected from the works of Hobbes. Hobbes defined *liberty* as a state of boundless free will or anarchy, in contrast with *civil society*.[15] Americans agreed instead with Locke that "[t]he liberty of man in society, *is to be under no other legislative power, but that established by consent* . . . not . . . for every one to do what he lists, to live as he pleases, and not to be tied by any laws."[16] What Hobbes had described was not liberty, but "licentiousness," an altogether different matter.[17] "Civil Liberty is the power of a *Civil Society* or State to govern itself . . . by laws of its own making."[18] Without it, man "is a poor and abject animal," regardless of his material wealth.[19] Being so fundamental to

14. Maier, *From Resistance to Revolution* 96, 101; also 47–48. In other words, they hoped to preserve the revolutionary constitution of 1688, not the Stuart one.

15. Hobbes, like many others, presented the Indians as examples of the poverty and despair supposedly attendant upon a lack of absolute centralized government. Richard Ashcraft, "Hobbes' Natural Man: A Study in Ideology Formation," 33 *Journal of Politics* 1076 (1971). Similarly Pownall, 2 *Administration* 116, 214–15; William Douglass, *A Summary, Historical and Political, of the First Planting, Progressive Improvements, and Present State of the British Settlements in North America* 154, 160 (London: 1760). Compare Edmund Burke's "Liberty in its fullest extent is the darling passion of the Americans," referring to *native* Americans, in his monograph on the progress of the colonies (Burke, 1 *An Account of the European Settlements in America* 175–76 [3rd ed. London: 1760]).

16. James Otis, *A Vindication of the Conduct of the House of Representatives of the Province of the Massachusetts-Bay* 17 (Boston: 1762), and *Considerations On Behalf of the Colonists in a letter to a Noble Lord* 13 (London: 1765); Lee, *Appeal* 34.

17. Price, *Observations* 7–8.

18. *Id.* 2, Levi Hart described political liberty as "a power of acting agreeable to the laws which are made and enacted by the consent of the PEOPLE, and in no ways inconsistent with the natural rights of a single person, or the good of society" (Quoted in Bailyn, *Ideological Origins* 77).

19. Price, *Observations* 3.

civilized life, liberty is no more alienable than life itself.[20]

But how is liberty to be created and preserved? Here, for both strategic and ideological reasons, the American position was ambivalent. On the one hand, radicals were not prepared to limit their immediate demands to the realization of those few specific rights enumerated in existing laws and agreements. On the other they were impressed with the tactical possibilities of setting up their colonial charters as evidence of irrevocable covenants with the sovereign which Parliament lacked power to alter. Eventually these alternatives would have to be reconciled.

Americans' political or "civil liberty" was, after all, not a set of rights or limitations, but a *process of participation.* It must therefore arise in the first instance not from the enumeration of specific rights but from the establishment of a form of government lacking power to oppress.[21] A government created by the people themselves should act only in furtherance of the general good,[22] which is the securing of "life, liberty, and property."[23] But the people cannot rely upon the intent of the original political compact and public trust to guarantee these rights. The preservation of liberty requires a fair representation at every level of the government, a continuing participation in all decisions.[24] Thus "*Civil Liberty*, in its most perfect degree, can be enjoyed only in small states, where every member is capable of giving his suffrage in person, and of being chosen into public offices."[25] In large states, some form of representation is dictated by necessity, but the actual consent of the people may be preserved if they are guaranteed an *equal opportunity to vote* for members of the legislature.[26] Conversely, "no one community can have any power over the property or legislation of another community, which is not incorporated with it by a just and adequate representation."[27] "Parliament must be in part constituted by the people over whom its laws have sway in all cases whatsoever,"

---

20. Otis, *Considerations* 17, and *Rights of the British Colonies* 9; Price, *Observations* 15.

21. Bailyn, *Ideological Origins* 78–79, 181–83.

22. Otis, *Rights of the British Colonies* 30; Price, *Observations* 4, 7. Pownall was also agreeable to this principle (1 *Administration* 138ff, 176–78).

23. Otis, *Rights of the British Colonies* 10; similarly, "security, liberty, property" (*id.* 70; and Price, *Observations* 3–4, 61). This phrase, of course, found its way into Mr. Jefferson's Declaration of Independence.

24. Otis, *Rights of the British Colonies* 35, 62–63; Bailyn, *Ideological Origins* 173–75, 299.

25. Price, *Observations* 4; Bailyn, *Ideological Origins* 282–84, 287–88.

26. Otis, *Considerations* 4–6.

27. Price, *Observations* 11; also 6, 16. For a detailed critique of the colonial tax issue see Otis, *Rights of the British Colonies* 36–39, 59–61; Lee, *Appeal* 7–15; Pownall, 1 *Administration* 138–40.

Arthur Lee concluded, ''or else it is not a constitutional power.''[28]

In a diversified state, moreover, government must also be hierarchical to best serve the general welfare. ''It would be impossible for the parliament to judge so well, of their [the colonies'] abilities to bear taxes, impositions on trade, and other duties and burdens, or of the local laws that might be really needful, as a legislature here.''[29] Ideally the empire should consist of a federal union guaranteeing the authority of each of the local legislatures in their respective orbits.[30]

Advocates of direct representation and federalism argued that liberty maximizes public order and allegiance.[31] Laws made by representative legislatures need no compulsion in their execution.[32] The citizen of a free state, ''having his property secure, and knowing himself his own governor, possesses a consciousness of dignity in himself, and feels incitements to emulation and improvement.''[33] But all of this was conjectural, conservatives replied. If these were features of the frame of government the people themselves would choose, why was there nothing in the documentary record to substantiate it? Where was the original political compact? The oft-cited charters of the colonies did not purport to be irrevocable compacts of sweeping dimensions, but mere acts of convenience, and being acts of Parliament were subject to repeal at any time.[34] Since everyone knew that the British constitution was nothing more than an accumulation of laws from time to time modified by parliamentary additions and subtractions, it seemed nonsense to suppose that charters could bind the supreme legislature, even where they were explicit.[35]

The radicals never conceded that charters were analogous in either form

28. Lee, *Appeal* 36.
29. Otis, *Rights of the British Colonies* 35.
30. E.g., Franklin's plan (Pownall, 2 *Administration* 144); the Pennsylvania plan (*id.* 89); Pownall's own plan (*id.* 37, 77); the Earl of Shelburne's plan (Price, *Observations* 62−63); the Galloway plan (5 *Elliot's Debates on the Confederation and Constitution* 176−77 [Washington, D.C.: 1830−1845]). All were received coolly by the defenders of imperialism (Tucker, *Four Tracts* 172; Maier, *From Resistance to Revolution* 288−89, 245; Bailyn, *Ideological Origins* 209−17, 224).
31. Otis, *Vindication* 19, 51−55; Lee, *Appeal* 35; Franklin, quoted in Pownall, 2 *Administration* 117; also 1 *Administration* 86, 167.
32. This thesis was revived after the war by Richard Henry Lee in his ''Letters of a Federal Farmer,'' Nos. 2 and 3, reprinted in Paul Leicester Ford, *Pamphlets on the Constitution of the United States* (Brooklyn, N.Y.: 1888). See also James Winthrop's ''Letters of Agrippa,'' No. 13, reprinted in Paul Leicester Ford, *Essays on the Constitution of the United States* (Brooklyn, N.Y.: 1892).
33. Price, *Observations* 10, 30−31.
34. MacPherson, *Rights of great Britain* 9, 43−44; Pownall, 1 *Administration* 87−88, 2 *Administration* 304; Price, *Observations* 27−28.
35. Bailyn, *Ideological Origins* 175.

or intent to other legislative acts. Nonetheless they admitted that their arguments proceeded in large part from the deep structure or "spirit" of charters, of the national constitution itself, and from universal rights antecedent to them, rather than express language.[36] Indeed, it had to be so. All of the particular rights of man could never be precisely codified, being too numerous.[37] All charters and bills of rights were merely declaratory of some of these fundamental rights, and did not create them.[38]

Here they found some small comfort in the common law. In *Dr. Bonham's Case,* Lord Coke observed "that in many cases, the common law will controul Acts of Parliament, and sometimes adjudge them to be utterly void: for when an Act of Parliament is against common right and reason, or repugnant, or impossible to be performed, the common law will controul it, and adjudge such Act to be void."[39] Was this "common right and reason" the deep structure of the constitution? Unfortunately, what survived of the case was its narrow rule that an act of Parliament cannot be construed to make a man a judge of his own cause, rather than its devastating hint that Parliament may be subject to judicial supremacy and unwritten fundamental principles in all cases whatsoever. After the Revolution even American jurists read it to mean simply "that the courts are to give the statute a reasonable construction [and] will not readily presume, out of respect and duty to the lawgiver, that any very unjust or absurd consequence was within the contemplation of the law."[40]

The search for a source of rights consistent with American objectives and political realities ultimately resolved itself in a complex paradigm. *Political* liberty is to be assumed regardless of the documentary record, because it is natural, inalienable, and antecedent to all political compacts.

36. *Id.* 176. This drew the contempt of Tories who regarded history as the best source of law (MacPherson, *Rights of great Britain* 3–4; Tucker, *Four Tracts* 101–2). The colonists denied the relevancy of history, arguing that a long reign of oppression cannot vindicate itself (Otis, *Rights of the British Colonies* 12, 25–26; Price, *Observations* 18–19). Liberty was a natural right antecedent to the constitution (Otis, *Vindication* 17 and *Rights of the British Colonies* 9, 30–31; Price, *Observations* 15; Dr. Priestley, quoted in Josiah Tucker, *A series of Answers to certain popular objections, against separating from the Rebellious Colonies and discarding them entirely* 63–66 [Gloucester, England: 1776]; Lee, *Appeal* 23).
37. Otis, quoted in Bailyn, *Ideological Origins* 188.
38. *Id.* 69 n.13, 176, 184–88.
39. 8 Co.Rep. 113b, 118a, 77 Eng. Rep. 646, 652 (Hil. 7 Jac. 1, 1609). As a foundation for the use of this argument, however, the colonists were forced to admit their allegiance and subjection to the British constitution (Otis, *Rights of the British Colonies* 15, 32, 34, 40–41, 49, 69; Otis, *Considerations* 13–14, 19).
40. James Kent, 1 *Commentaries on American Law* 419–20 (New York: 1826). As Lord Holt put it most charitably, "an Act of Parliament can do no wrong, though it may do several

The absence of an appropriate vehicle for the exercise of political rights in a written constitution merely demonstrates the tyranny of the government. Charters or compacts identify legitimate political bodies and irrevocably recognize particular personal rights, but they do not and cannot create or destroy political liberty. Accordingly the express provisions of the colonial charters were enforceable, and their silence as to representation in Parliament was no evidence against the existence of that right.

Americans were not overly concerned, then, that the British constitution lacked a sufficiency of specific personal rights, nor did they expand considerably on those rights in their own Constitution. Rather, the contest was over the ability of the British government, as a process and as then structured, to secure and preserve these and other personal rights. Americans believed the absence of local and direct national representation had demonstrably rendered the government incapable of resisting English interest groups and corrupt ministries where American affairs were involved. As Dr. Price observed, the situation was not such that a purge of the ministry, and enlightened, benevolent colonial administration, could suffice as a remedy, but only an irrevocable structural reorganization of the government itself, tending to a proper balance of interests, arising from the consent of both peoples.[41] Refusal of the establishment to yield any power by means of a federalized or decentralized empire[42] made separation unavoidable.

---

things that look pretty odd'' (*City of London v. Wood*, 12 Mod. 669, 77 Eng. Rep. 1592 [1796]). Lord Ellesmere casts serious doubt on the real legal significance of *Dr. Bonham's Case* when he writes in his *Observations* (77 Eng. Rep. 652 n.c.):

And for novelty in *Dr. Bonham's case*, the Chief Justice having no precedent for him, but many judgments against him, yet doth he strike in sunder the bars of government of the College of Physicians: and, without any pausing on the matter, frustrate the patent of King Henry VIII., whereby the college was erected, and tramples upon the Act of Parliament, 14&15 H.8 whereby that patent was confirmed, blowing them both away as vain, and of no value, and this in triumph of himself being accompanied but with the opinion of one Judge only for the matter in law where three other Judges were against him, which case possesseth a better room in the press than is deserved.

41. Price, *Observations* 26.
42. Tories frequently complained that *any* number of American M.P.'s would intolerably dilute the power of the old English (Tucker, *Four Tracts* 114–15; Pownall, 1 *Administration* 170). It was also feared that American representation would eventually shift the seat of the empire to an American city (letter of Pownall to Franklin, in W. T. Franklin, ed., *The Private Correspondence of Benjamin Franklin* 303 [London: 1817]). Franklin was, ironically, accused by Tucker of conspiring to such a scheme (*id.* 296). Under the Galloway plan of union, for example, Americans would have taken one-third of the seats in the Commons (5 *Elliot's Debates* 176–77). Franklin himself was agreeable in principle to a voteless delegation, as a wedge for debate and filibuster, at least in his early writings (letter to Governor Shirley, in Pownall, 2 *Administration* 117).

3

The Federal System

As hope of a constitutional resolution disappeared, the colonists sought in a new government the structural safeguards they had been unable to win in the old. The Declaration of Independence echoes the fundamental axiom of the colonial radicals that, to secure liberty, "governments are instituted among men, deriving their just powers from the consent of the governed," which consent must of necessity be exercised through representatives chosen by all of the people. As James Lincoln cried out at the South Carolina Ratifying Convention, "What have you been contending for these ten years past? Liberty! What is Liberty! *The power of governing yourselves.*"[1]

Federalists and antifederalists disagreed over the precise form of the new republic, especially the extent to which centralized power could be recognized without a return to parliamentary-style absolutism, but shared a common belief that sovereign power ought only to serve and defend the persons and property of the people. "Civil liberty consists in the consciousness of that security, and is best guarded by political liberty,

1. 4 *Elliot's Debates on the Confederation and Constitution* 214, 313 (Washington, D.C.: 1830—1845).

which is the share that every citizen has in the government."[2] A perfect democratic society would be small enough to avoid the dangers of mediate representation, but in a larger community in which representation is a necessity, it is essential that it be equal, so that the general legislature will reflect "the same interests, feelings, opinions, and views the people themselves would were they all assembled."[3] The power of the jury to acquit for political reasons, and the system of proportional representation, were often described as the two best checks against despotism.[4]

As Noah Webster observed, "were the United States one indivisible interest," proportional representation "would be a perfect rule."[5] However, the history of the country had led to "some separate interests—some local institutions, which they [the people] will not resign." To prominent federalists, the reservation of local powers to the states and their direct representation in the Senate served more than the purpose of preserving socioeconomic diversity. According to James Madison, the Bill of Rights would not stand alone. "Besides this security . . . the State Legislatures will jealously and closely watch the operations of this Government, and be able to resist with more effect every assumption of power, than any other power on earth can do; and the greatest opponents of the Federal Government admit the State Legislatures to be sure guardians of the people's liberty."[6]

It was Madison's belief that the greatest practical danger in a democratic republic would prove to be unchecked majority rule.

It is of great importance in a republic not only to guard the society against the oppression of its rulers, but to guard one part of the society against the injustice of the other part. Different interests necessarily exist in different classes of citizens. If a majority be united by a common interest, the rights of the minority will be insecure. There are but two methods of providing against this evil; the one by creating a will in the community independent of the majority—that is of the society itself; the other, by comprehending in the society so many separate discriptions of

2. "Agrippa," in Morton Borden, *The Antifederalist Papers* 27 (Ann Arbor, Mich.: 1965). See also David Ramsay, *An Address to the Freemen of South Carolina, on the subject of the Federal Constitution* (Charleston, S.C.: 1787), reprinted in Paul Leicester Ford, *Pamphlets on the Constitution of the United States* (Brooklyn, N.Y.: 1888).

3. "Cato," in Borden, *Antifederalist Papers* 37; "Federal Farmer," No. 3, reprinted in Ford, *Pamphlets;* Noah Webster, *An Examination into the leading principles of the Federal Constitution . . . By a Citizen of America* 7–8 (Philadelphia: 1787).

4. "Federal Farmer," No. 2, reprinted in Ford, *Pamphlets* 288; *Federal Farmer*, No. 4.

5. Webster, *Examination* 19.

6. Bennett Patterson, *The Forgotten Ninth Amendment* 116 (Indianapolis: 1955).

citizens as will render an unjust combination of a majority of the whole very improbable, if not impracticable. . . . [T]he second method will be exemplified in the federal republic of the United States.[7]

In the constitutional scheme, "[t]he sovereignty, the independence, and the rights of the States are intended to be guarded by the Senate,"[8] in which the "collision" of state interests will serve as a check on majoritarian excesses.[9]

There were already those like Henry Knox, who argued that "the vile State governments are sources of pollution, which will contaminate the American name perhaps for ages. Machines that must produce ill, but cannot produce good, smite them in the name of God and the people."[10] However, ratification of the Constitution, and later the Tenth Amendment, in principle opposed a nationalization of political power by which the states might "eventually be absorbed by our *grand continental vortex,* or dwindle into petty corporations, and have power over little else than *yoaking hogs* or determining the width of *cart wheels.*"[11] As much as the federalists may have been mistaken as to the practical ability of the Constitution to guarantee against it, centralization was to be avoided.

Our mixed form of government recognizes most significantly the fundamental social *and commercial* argument of the revolution: that a heterogeneous society cannot be fairly ruled by one body, nor can such achieve the greatest possible prosperity. In modern terminology, the administration of government and the making of critical choices must take place, for maximum efficiency, at those levels which optimize diversity and coordination. The orchestration of different local preferences and outputs in federalism avoids two errors of extremism. Complete unity would frustrate local preferences and lead to a state of general dissatisfaction and lack of cooperation. Productivity would decline, and force would become necessary to enforce the laws. On the other hand we learned all too well during the thirteen years of association and confederation that complete decen-

---

7. *The Federalist,* No. 51; Patterson, *Ninth Amendment* 114.
8. Theodore Sedgwick, cited in Patterson, *Ninth Amendment* 174.
9. Dickinson, in 5 *Elliot's Debates* 168; Pinckney in 4 *Elliot's Debates* 330.
10. Samuel Bannister Harding, *The Contest over the Ratification of the Federal Constitution in the States of Massachusetts* 12 (New York: 1896).
11. "Montezuma," in Borden, *Antifederalist Papers* 20–22; also *id.* 7–8 and 13–18, and "Federal Farmer," No. 2, reprinted in Ford, *Pamphlets.*

tralization tends to result in such a profusion of local protectionist laws that no economic benefit or political strength is gained from union, and the members could as well remain independent republics. If, as the "Federalist Farmer," Richard Henry Lee, so eloquently expressed it, we hold sufficient goals in common to be prepared to sacrifice some of our local preferences and prerogatives to further them, then and only then are we truly prepared to benefit from aggregation into one nation.[12]

The significance of the American form of government is therefore not in its ability to generate greater *power* through unity, but in its capacity for greater *unity* in its balance of centralized power and local power. The greater the differences within a society, the more successful such a plan of government should prove to be, in contrast with centralized governments of any description.

It is of more than merely academic interest to contemplate the forms of government our revolutionary ancestors did *not* choose for themselves. Along with all of the other bits and pieces of the revolutionary dialogue which survived the war to influence the Convention was the idea of an American peerage. Although they had rebelled against a corrupt king and ministry and a malapportioned Parliament, many Americans still admired the British theory of "mixed" government, in which social classes or estates are balanced institutionally. If the new government were to have no king, it would be in danger of becoming an unrestrained democracy unless the third estate, the nobility, or some body of men of analogous function and interest, were interposed to lend to the legislature wisdom, conservatism, and perspective transcending the tides of popular fashions and jealousies.[13] This body, described as a "Senate" long before its composition had been agreed on, could have been organized by providing for election for life or for very long terms, or election out of the wealthy, landed and, therefore, relatively stable existing economic aristocracy of the new republic.[14]

James Madison was deeply troubled and ambivalent over this problem,

---

12. "Federal Farmer," No. 2.

13. "[A] portion of enlightened citizens, whose limited number, and firmness, might seasonably interpose against tempestuous counsels," observed Madison (5 *Elliot's Debates* 242).

14. A property test was supported by Madison, Mason, Dickinson, Gerry, Pinckney, Franklin, Butler, and Baldwin (5 *Elliot's Debates* 166, 246–47, 260, 275–76, 370–71, 402–3).

and corresponded with Jefferson about it during the Convention in an effort to seek vindication in another's conversion.

In all civilized countries the people fall into different classes, having a real or supposed difference of interests. There will be creditors and debtors; farmers, merchants, and manufacturers. There will be, particularly, the distribution of rich and poor. It was true . . . we had not among us . . . hereditary distinctions of rank . . . nor . . . extremes of wealth or poverty. . . . We cannot, however, be regarded at this time, as one homogeneous mass, in which everything that affects a part will affect in the same manner the whole. In framing a system which we wish to last for ages, we should not lose sight of the changes which ages will produce. An increase of population will of necessity increase the proportion of those who will labor under all the hardships of life, and secretly sigh for a more equal distribution of its blessings. These may in time outnumber those who are placed above the feelings of indigence. According to the equal laws of suffrage, the power will slide into the hands of the former. No agrarian attempts have yet been made in this country, but symptoms of a levelling spirit, as we have understood, have sufficiently appeared . . . to give notice of the future danger. How is this danger to be guarded against, on the republican principles; how is danger, in all cases of interested coalitions, to oppress the minority, to be guarded against.?[15]

Since it was obviously true "that an inequality [of wealth] would exist as long as liberty existed and that it would unavoidably result from that liberty itself,"[16] it became necessary "to protect the minority of the opulent against the majority."[17] The political process should prevent popular emotions from overriding natural and, it seems to have been generally assumed, healthy economic forces. Still good Lockeians, the members of the Convention were satisfied that the protection of property is the chief object of men's association in civil society.[18]

Proposals for meeting these concerns envisioned a bicameral legislature comprised of a populist House and aristocratic Senate—nothing more, really, than the British Parliament without the monarch. "In the first place, the checking branch must have a personal interest in checking the other branch," explained Gouverneur Morris.

In the second place, it must have great personal property; it must have the aristocratic spirit; it must love to lord it through pride. . . . The rich will strive to

---

15. 5 *Elliot's Debates* 242−43.
16. 5 *Elliot's Debates* 244 (Hamilton). "From the protection of different and unequal faculties of acquiring property, the possession of different degrees and kinds of property inevitably results" (*The Federalist* No. 10 [Madison]).
17. 1 *Elliot's Debates* 449−50 (Madison).
18. 5 *Elliot's Debates* 278−79, 371.

establish their dominion, and enslave the rest. They always did. They always will. The proper security against them is to form them into a separate interest. The two forces will then control each other.[19]

Madison agreed. "Persons and property being both essential objects of government, the most that either can claim is such a structure of it as will leave a reasonable security for the other. And the most obvious provision, of this double character, seems to be that of confining to the holders of property . . . the right of suffrage for one of the two legislative branches."[20] A somewhat more moderate version suggested by Gouverneur Morris and Elbridge Gerry would have retained the separation of representation of states from the confederation, but apportioned each state's vote on the basis of its relative property.[21]

As the debates wore on, however, even the supporters of these measures became ambivalent. Their doubts were both ideological and practical. Defenders of revolutionary virtue like Dickinson "doubted the policy of interweaving into a republican constitution a veneration for wealth,"[22] anticipating a recurrence of the evils of corruption and submission attributed less than a generation earlier to the class structure of the British constitution. Madison himself gradually retreated from his original militancy on the issue of admitting to greater and greater diversity in the population, and thereby implicitly confessed oversimplification. When he first introduced his plan he seemed to suggest two great estates of wealth and poverty, but when he told the Convention shortly afterwards that "every class of citizens should have an opportunity of making their rights be felt and understood in the public councils," he referred to three classes: landowners, men of commerce, and manufacturers.[23] By the time he wrote *The Federalist*, he described all human society as a veritable circus of factions "incited and actuated by some common impulse or passion, or of interest, adverse to the rights of other citizens," arising often but not solely out of perceived inequalities of wealth.[24] He also began to suspect that interest groups are constantly changing membership owing to economic mobility—the freedom and "universal hope of acquiring property"—

19. 5 *Elliot's Debates* 270–71.
20. 5 *Elliot's Debates* 580.
21. 5 *Elliot's Debates* 280–81, 297.
22. 5 *Elliot's Debates* 371.
23. 5 *Elliot's Debates* 371–72. Similarly, Richard Henry Lee, *An Additional Number of Letters from the Federal Farmer to the Republican* (1788), Letter No. 7.
24. *The Federalist*, No. 10.

making any neat class distinction wholly artificial.[25] His fellow delegates to the Convention could not even agree among themselves how to measure wealthiness.[26]

A more sinister note was struck by the cynical Gouverneur Morris, who, like Madison, quickly became ambivalent over his original proposals. The House, he argued, would never really be a populist body. Since wealth is a major factor in obtaining public notice and winning elections, members of the House will tend to be wealthy. For all practical purposes both houses will be seated with men of property, making the whole bicameral scheme frivolous.[27] Besides being frivolous, any class-based plan would be totally subversive to the political integrity of the states and the survival of federalism, issues which had been so much a part of the Revolution.[28]

Considering how attentively the framers received arguments for class balance and institutionalized class distinctions, it is all the more significant that the Senate was given its present structure, one in which it is the "duty of the senators to preserve distinct, and to perpetuate the respective sovereignties they shall represent."[29] The Senate is a balancing force, but of an entirely different kind than Madison originally conceived. Senators, he wrote in *The Federalist*, would represent such large districts that they would necessarily have a broader perspective and be less susceptible to influence by small interest groups.[30] Even if one state became "tainted" with extremism the remainder would check it.

More fundamentally, the Senate reflects a shift in theories of society. The British view of three fixed and distinct social estates was rejected by the Revolution and again in 1789. It assumes that significant differences among persons arise from inequalities in wealth and power, wealth consisting of land by nature and power being hereditary by law. The American view assumes instead that significant differences among persons arise from differences in political culture and association which are most strongly felt territorially: horizontal rather than vertical organization. Wealth and power are in constant state of flux because of liberty, and provide no reliable measure of interest either within each state or across the nation. The danger

25. 5 *Elliot's Debates* 299–300, 581, 583.
26. 5 *Elliot's Debates* 371, 385–86. As the explicit debate was between land ownership and banked capital, the implicit contest was between planters and merchants.
27. 5 *Elliot's Debates* 386–87; Madison agreed (*id.* 387).
28. See Hamilton's argument in *The Federalist*, No. 9, that federalism is not a new idea, but has many historical precedents—much the same argument made before the war in support of proposals for a British federal system.
29. Lee, *Additional Letters*, Letter No. 11.
30. *The Federalist*, No. 10; see, too, his remarks in 5 *Elliot's Debates* 581.

of majority oppression is not, therefore, from the have-nots making war on the haves, but a majority coalition of political subdivisions taxing the others for idiosyncratic ends.[31]

The contemporary practical significance of federalism among the states is a matter of some debate. There is some evidence that the states retain such a degree of difference in preferences, *especially structural political preferences*, that they remain necessary to the maintenance of a viable union.[32] Studies of federalism in practice suggest that federal policymakers are abandoning a division-of-power or adversary conception of our system of government for one that expressly recognizes its cooperative and creative effects on the general welfare.[33] "In the representative branch," Richard Henry Lee reminds us, "we must expect chiefly to collect *the confidence* of the people, and in it to find almost entirely the force of persuasion."[34] There is no doubt that the official emphasis in Washington for several years has been on a decentralization of federal powers, undoing the possible excesses of New Deal enthusiasm. On the other hand, the national revenue system remains largely dominated by the national budget,[35] and the courts have unquestionably authorized far greater congressional powers over traditionally local matters than the framers seem either to have intended or anticipated.[36]

In this book, however, we are concerned with subfederal entities that are *not* states, and at the same time preserve *as much or more diversity* than the original twelve ratifiers of the Constitution. If a right exists to local self-government, the fact that the states have ceased to exercise it effectively, or no longer really need it, is no answer to tribal demands for sovereignty.

31. This was changed by the Seventeenth Amendment in 1913.
32. Samuel Patterson, "The Political Cultures of the American States," 30 *Journal of Politics* 187 (1968).
33. Richard Leach, *American Federalism* 10ff (New York: 1970).
34. Lee, *Additional Letters*, Letter No. 7 (emphasis ours).
35. Wallace Oates, *Fiscal Federalism* (New York: 1972); George Break, *Intergovernmental Fiscal Relations in the United States* (Washington, D.C.: 1967). Manipulation of local subdivisions through the national budget is also familiar from India's federal system (H.C.L. Merillat, *Land and the Constitution in India* [New York: 1970]) and Canada's (Richard Simeon, *Federal-Provincial Diplomacy* [Toronto: 1972]).
36. Their intent is not only evident from contemporary personal documents such as *The Federalist*, but from the character of the Revolution as, in part, a challenge to mercantilist regulatory excesses and the high taxes and enforcement costs associated with interstate shipping (Arthur Schlesinger, *The Colonial Merchants and the American Revolution: 1763–1776* [New York: 1918]). See William Letwin, *Law and Economic Policy in America* (New York: 1965), and Richard Hofstadter, *The Age of Reform* (New York: 1955), for the political history of the growth of federal regulation in the first half of this century.

Part Two

The Historical Development of the Doctrine of Tribal Sovereignty

4

Discovery, Entitlement, and Tribal Property, 1700-1823

We' mapi mak' o' 'kawih ahi' yayapi.
[Flag around the earth / they carry it along][1]

The Constitution was the written manifestation of the beliefs of its authors. It embodied a fundamental commitment to the universal potential of political liberty as the basis of organized society. But, like a constellation in the winter sky, the constitutional idea lived only in the minds of believers.

Once they had achieved the power to rule, the revolutionary idealists must have been haunted by doubts. Could natural rights and popular consent be recognized and preserved in a workable government? Would political liberty prove a bond or a cleavage in real society? The first generation of the Revolution was challenged to demonstrate the practicality of governing according to its announced principles. The challenge was intensified by European monarchs' initial reluctance to extend diplomatic status to a republic born in rebellion, and lacking either a familiar form of government or any claim to historical or cultural antiquity.[2]

1. Loosely, "They carry their institutions around the world" (Ben Kindle's Winter Count for the year 1791, from Martha Warren Beckwith, "Mythology of the Oglala Sioux," 43 *Journal of American Folklore* 339–442 [1930]).

2. We attribute early nineteenth-century Americans' intense interest in prehistory to the need for a sense of historical legitimacy. As in Cooper's novels, the American frontiersmen were ambivalently imaged as the Indians' conquerors and as their *rightful heirs and descendants.*

Like slavery, relations with Indian tribes tested American idealism to the limit, and attracted the most critical European scrutiny. If the Americans expected recognition from the international community on the basis of their sui generis political sovereignty, they would have to recognize in turn the ancient sovereignty of Indian peoples already admitted to the family of nations—or else discover some profound political distinction between white and Indian societies theretofore unsuspected.

Indian nations themselves responded to the continental revolution with hesitancy. Already recognized as sovereign by European states, and in alliance with many of them, they were as reluctant as other nations to stake their future on an untried, radical "new order." Great western nations and confederacies such as the Cherokee, Delaware and Iroquois had, moreover, pledged by treaty to aid and protect the British interest.

British law was explicit in its regard for tribal sovereignty. In the case of the *Mohegin Indians* the Privy Council upheld a 1743 Court of Commissioners' ruling that restricted colonial land purchases to treaties with legitimate tribal officers. The commissioners' report explained that

The Indians, though living amongst the king's subjects in these countries, are a separate and distinct people from them, they are treated with as such, they have a policy of their own, they make peace and war with any nation of Indians when they think fit, without controul from the English.[3]

Twenty years later a Royal Proclamation of George III reaffirmed the policy of *Mohegin Indians* and forbade provincial officers from purchasing or interfering with the territory of the western tribes.[4]

It is not surprising, then, that the Cherokees not only fought on the British side in the Revolutionary War, but refused to surrender *without a separate treaty of peace* with the United States. They recognized neither the British surrender at Yorktown nor the Treaty of Paris as binding on them, and continued hostilities until congressional representatives agreed to a mutual demobilization at Hopewell in 1785.[5] It is instructive that there

3. *The Governor and Company of Connecticut and Moheagan Indians* (London: 1769), in the collection of the Houghton Library, Harvard University; 5 *Acts of the Privy Council of England, Colonial Series* 218 (London: 1912); Joseph Henry Smith, *Appeals to the Privy Council from the American Plantations* 418 (New York: 1950); J. Y. Henderson, "Unraveling the Riddle of Aboriginal Title," 5 *American Indian Law Review* 75, 96–102 (1977).

4. The full text in the original is available in William Waller Hening, 7 *The Statutes at Large: Being a Collection of All the Laws of Virginia* 663 (Richmond, Virginia: 1819–1823).

5. Charles Joseph Kappler, ed., 2 *Indian Affairs: Laws and Treaties* 8 (Washington, D.C.: 1904).

is no reference to capitulation or surrender in that document.

The Delawares, on the other hand, eventually succumbed to the revolutionary ideal and, amidst General Washington's promises of a great alliance, joined the war on the American side. In 1778 the Delawares became the first Indian nation to conclude a treaty with the United States. The text of that treaty tells us a great deal about the application of revolutionary principles to tribal affairs for, in addition to guaranteeing the Delawares' "territorial rights," it invites them, with other tribes, "to join the present confederation, and to form a state, whereof the Delaware nation shall be the head, and have a representation in Congress."[6]

The end of the war itself in no way settled the status of tribes. Some allied themselves with the new republic, typically agreeing to make no agreements with other European powers. Others continued to treat with Great Britain. Both Britain and the United States continued to be competitors for tribal trade and commerce.[7]

There was no question on either side of the Atlantic that Indian affairs were to be conducted by treaty in accordance with the law of nations, as they had been conducted before the war. The precise institutional repository of the treaty power, as well as its scope, were nevertheless to remain at issue in the United States. Controversies over the nature of the United States' power to treat with tribes under its new and untested Constitution would gradually become confused with the tribes' power to treat with other nations, which had never before been questioned.

The Articles of Confederation authorized Congress to "manage the affairs" of tribes but did not forbid states to make international treaties. Congress interpreted this as delegating to itself exclusive power to make treaties of trade and alliance with Indian nations. The states disregarded it in dealing with tribes situated within their boundaries. As a result it happened in some cases that one tribe concluded treaties with the United States and one or more individual states.[8]

---

6. *Id.* 3.

7. The United States was somewhat more attractive to the tribes as an ally at first because its political culture was more familiar. R. L. Barsh, "Native American Loyalists and Patriots," 10 (3) *Indian Historian* 9 (summer 1977).

8. Madison observed in his notebook that "the Fedl authy was violated by Treaties & wars with Indians, as by Geo: by troops, raised & kept up. witht. the consent of Congs. as by Massts by compacts witht. the consent of Congs. as between Pena. and N. Jersey. and between Virga. & Maryd. From the Legisl: Journals of Virga. it appears, that a vote to apply for a sanction of Congs. was followed by a vote agst. a communication of the Compact to

The framers of the Constitution sought to avoid this result by lodging a supreme and exclusive treaty power in Congress.[9] The treaty power does not distinguish between Indian nations and other nations, nor does the Commerce Clause, which refers to "Commerce with foreign nations . . . and with the Indian tribes."[10] Presumably, then, a treaty of foreign commerce is no different constitutionally than a treaty of Indian commerce.

There was a serious defect, however, in the constitutional assignment of treaty power, for it did not specify whether a treaty could be used to enlarge the nation. In a letter to John Breckenridge regarding the purchase of Louisiana, President Jefferson explained, "The Constitution has made no provision for our holding foreign territory, still less for incorporating foreign nations into our Union,"[11] and recommended an amendment.

The settlement and admission of states in the old Northwest posed no problem. The land not occupied by Indians had been acquired from Britain in the Revolution and settled by American citizens. On the contrary Florida, Louisiana, and Indian tribes were foreign sovereignties. Any merger was to be consensual and by treaty, not war. Had the president power irrevocably to internalize and subject to domestic federal control, a foreign territory? A treaty turned to such a purpose was no longer, in truth, a treaty. It would deal with the internal police, rather than the external relations, of the nation, and unless the merged territory were consolidated

---

Congs" (Max Farrand, ed., 3 *Records of the Federal Convention of 1787* 548 [New Haven, Conn.: 1911]). In 1777 Georgia and South Carolina forced the Cherokees to agree to a cession (the so-called Treaty of DeWitt's Corner) under which both states subsequently claimed the same tract of land (John Pendleton Kennedy, 2 *Memoirs of the Life of William Wirt* 241 [rev. ed. Philadelphia: 1850]).

9. The Pinckney plan included "exclusive Power . . . of regulating Indian Affairs." This was omitted in the first draft of the Constitution. Pinckney then resubmitted the article as "To regulate affairs with the Indians as well within as without the limits of the United States." The Committee of Detail rewrote this as "To regulate commerce . . . with Indians, within the Limits of any State, not subject to the laws thereof," and the Committee of Eleven finally reduced it to its present state, "To regulate commerce . . . with the Indian tribes" (Farrand, 2 *Records* 143, 159, 321, 324, 367, 481, 495, 497, 499, 503, 595, 610). Obviously the chief concern was making plain Congress's power to deal with tribes located *within* state boundaries, and therefore not clearly "foreign nations."

10. Art. I, §8, cl. 3.

11. Andrew A. Lipscomb, ed., 10 *The Writings of Thomas Jefferson* 411 (Washington, D.C.: 1903). During the Convention Pinckney proposed to enumerate in Article I congressional power to dispose of public lands and to erect territorial governments, *at the same time* that he proposed a power "To regulate affairs with the Indians as well within as without the limits of the United States." Both proposals went to the Committee of Detail, but only the latter was reported out (Farrand, 2 *Records* 321, 324).

immediately with an existing state, it would alter the political geography of the country and relative influence of the states.

If the president only had constitutional power to deal with tribes by treaty, it seemed he could not, without amendment, exercise that power for territorial acquisition. Nor did the Constitution contain any direct authority for the federal government to acquire land, except from the states.[12]

When early nineteenth-century federal courts came to grips with the legality of federal land acquisitions from tribes, what authority could they produce? The revolutionary generation of American lawyers had struggled to extirpate any vestiges of monarchism embedded in the common law. Blackstone's painstaking deductions of land tenures and rights from the positive authority of a sole and indivisible national sovereign were admired but discarded.[13] The feudal heritage of confusing ownership with the authority to govern, already crumbling in practice on both sides of the Atlantic, was officially laid to rest by the revolutionary bar.[14]

This reform was not extended to the analysis of tribal rights and powers, however, for it was entirely a reform of the United States' domestic law and policy in keeping with revolutionary principles. Tribes were external to the United States and its Revolution, and were connected to the Union, when at all, through the exercise of Congress's external powers in foreign affairs—war and treaties. When confronted with issues of Indian law, American lawyers returned to eighteenth-century English interpretations of the law of nations which perpetuated the prerevolutionary, monarchic notion of sovereign authority flowing from the absolute ownership of land by a prince.[15]

The confusion of property and sovereignty in English law can be traced to the writings of James Harrington and John Locke. Harrington, a man of ingenious and farsighted interest in the mechanism of representative government, failed to become influential in his own time, but found a following a century later in revolutionary America among men such as John Adams, James Madison, and James Otis.[16] In *Oceana*,[17] he argued

12. Art. I, §8, cl. 17 ("Exclusive Legislation").

13. Perry Miller, *The Life of the Mind in America from the Revolution to the Civil War* 223–30 (New York: 1965).

14. *Id.* 223 ff.; Morton J. Horwitz, "The Emergence of an Instrumental Conception of American Law, 1780–1820," 5 *Perspectives in American History* 285, 309–13 (1971).

15. For a more thorough discussion of these principles see Henderson, "Aboriginal Title."

16. Theodore W. Dwight, "Harrington and his Influence upon American Political Institutions," 2 *Political Science Quarterly* 1 (1887).

17. *The Commonwealth of Oceana* (London: 1656).

that the distribution of political power in society evolves naturally out of the distribution of land. If most of a society's property is owned by one man, a monarchy tends to emerge. If a small group of men controls most of the land, either an aristocracy or mixed monarchy evolves. And if the great majority of the people own land, then a popular form of government will tend to be established. Harrington's work, like Locke's, was largely justificatory. Dedicated to Cromwell, *Oceana* built a rather feudal theory of human society into apparent consistency with the seventeenth-century, land-based Parliament. However, its generalizations influenced later liberal theorists, such as Locke, into making subtle concessions to feudalism in their expositions of popular sovereignty.

Although Locke strenuously denied that wealth could establish *legitimate authority*, he agreed with Harrington that the chief end of any political society should be the preservation of property.[18] More importantly, Locke suggested that ownership serve as a manifestation of consent. If a man loses faith in his government, he can forswear his allegiance to it and leave it for a more hospitable community. But as long as he continues to own land under the protection of that government, he implicitly accepts its authority.[19] This ironically supported the arguments of eighteenth-century apologists for the malapportioned Parliament. By continuing to own property under British rule, Americans and unrepresented Britons implicitly consented to be taxed and regulated.[20]

It had been the practice of the colonies to purchase tribal territory piecemeal, sometimes by proper cessions, but more often by selling patents to selected individuals and leaving it to these patentees to settle with the occupant Indians. Eighteenth-century litigation established that the validity of tribal and individual Indian deeds was conditional on the authority of the seller to sell as a matter of tribal law, and the authority of the purchaser to purchase as a matter of English law.[21] No court specified what rights, if any, existed if one or the other element was lacking in the transaction, nor,

18. John Locke, *Two Treatises of Government*, Second Treatise, ch. 9, §124 (London: 1690).
19. *Id.* ch. 8, §§119-20.
20. Then we always have Dean Tucker's argument (ch. 1, fn. 14, above) that all Britons enjoyed an equal opportunity to purchase those freeholds that did carry the franchise with them.
21. As in the case of the Mohegin Indians, *op. cit.* For early examples of cancellation of deeds obtained from Indians in contravention of tribal law see, John Cox, Jr., ed., 1 *Oyster Bay Town Records* 520, 676 (New York: 1916); Maryland Historical Society, 1 *Archives of Maryland* 431 (Baltimore: 1885-).

even more importantly, what effect the transaction could have on the jurisdiction of the tribe. It was often assumed as a matter of practice that a simple sale by deed, silent as to jurisdiction, conveyed not only the use of the soil but political dominion as well. But this assumption was not universally accepted.

Locke had argued that property is the form by which the consensus of men in society is established. Men are free to abandon a political community, but by continuing to hold property within it they implicitly or "operationally" consent to its power to regulate their behavior. By purchasing land lying within tribal territory, individual Europeans therefore consented to tribal political authority—*according to European political principles.* To avoid the implications of operational consent, first the Crown, and later Congress, forbad the purchase of tribal land without license.[22] It was hoped that the requirement of public authority would convert the private sale into a cession between sovereigns—or at least rebut the presumption that the purchaser had incorporated himself with the tribal seller.

The major part of the territory of the United States was held either under the assumption that simple deeds conveyed dominion, or under crown and congressional licenses to purchase, or both. Frequently a single tract was claimed by two or more grantees under conflicting theories. A collision was inevitable and necessary, and on its outcome rested the distribution of most of the wealth in the country.

It came in 1810 in the case of *Fletcher v. Peck.*[23] The legislature of Georgia had patented a strip of land in what is now Alabama and Mississippi to a development company. Subsequently the legislature repented of its liberality, revoked the patent, and resold the tract on different terms to another party. Purchasers from the original patentees appealed to the Supreme Court for a ruling that the revocation and resale had been unconstitutional. The Court agreed, concluding that a state legislature is prohibited from disturbing vested property rights by the Constitution and by the "general principles which are common to our free institutions."

The most important issue in the case was avoided, however. The disputed tract lay in territory claimed by Georgia (on the basis of crown

22. Proclamation of 1763, note 4; Article 3 of the Ordinance of 1787 ("Northwest Ordinance"); and the Indian Intercourse Acts of 1793, 1 Stat. 329, and 1834, 4 Stat. 729 (1834), as amended now 24 U.S.C. 177.
23. 10 U.S. (6 Cranch) 87.

patents), by the United States, and by Spain, and still in the exclusive occupation of Indian tribes. Both Congress and the Spanish Crown asserted exclusive rights to purchase from the natives, and neither nation had delegated any authority over the tract to the state of Georgia. How, then, could Georgia have patented the land to anyone in the first place?

In his majority opinion the chief justice, John Marshall, remarked almost casually in closing that it was unnecessary to consider whether the land had ever been purchased from the Indians.[24] He neither denied the state's power to grant a fee simple estate in land it had not purchased, nor the tribe's right to continue to occupy that land undisturbed until it chose to sell it. He simply asserted that there was *no inconsistency* between state ownership and tribal occupancy. The state, he explained, could have and convey fee simple title, but the Court would ''respect'' the Indians' absolute right to the use.

Marshall's exercise in redefining the legal significance of the words ''fee simple'' left the tribe in effective possession of all that had ever before been regarded as a perfect legal title. Whatever it was called, the state of Georgia had nothing but the exclusive right to authorize certain persons to purchase from the Indians, since, according to Marshall, a patentee from the state could not remove tribal occupants without tribal consent. Why, then, asked Justice Johnson in his separate opinion, didn't Marshall simply give words their usual legal meaning? Surely the Indians, as exclusive possessors, and ''absolute proprietors'' of the soil enjoyed the title, while Georgia's right amounted to ''only an exclusion of all competitors from their market.''[25] The state's patentees had bought ''a mere possibility,'' an interest in the land should the Indians ever choose to dispose of it, and Georgia's patent operated against the state as nothing more than ''a covenant to convey'' following an Indian sale. In Johnson's view, Marshall's use of the phrase, ''fee simple title'' was an absurdity. ''Can, then, one nation be said to be seized in lands, the rights of soil of which is in another nation?''

Like Marshall, Johnson struggled to force the facts into familiar concepts and terminology. Someone must have fee title, but who? Johnson's approach was functional. Fee title means exclusive possession, he reasoned, therefore tribes, which have the possession, must have the title.

24. *Id*. 142–43.
25. *Id*. 146.

Marshall, on the other hand, took a political view of the matter. He intimated that tribes could not have a fee or any other kind of Anglo-American legal title, being foreign to our laws and external to our authority. Yet they could have their own kind of ownership under their own laws, which the courts, under the laws of nations, would be compelled to recognize and respect. Though differing in semantics, Marshall and Johnson agreed on the essential point: unrelinquished tribal rights, however named, were superior to any rights conveyed by a state to its citizens. Marshall's choice of language would later prove unfortunate, however.

Two years later, in *New Jersey v. Wilson*,[26] the Court first evidenced a deeper confusion of property and sovereignty. In return for liberal cessions of land, New Jersey agreed not to tax a tribe's reserved territory. Some years later, *with the consent of the state legislature*, the tribe sold its tax-exempt land. Subsequently the state legislature repealed the tax exemption and the non-Indian purchasers appealed to the courts.

Marshall's Court held that purchasers from a tribe stand, with respect to the land, in precisely the same position as the tribe. The tax exemption being contractual in nature, the state repeal was repugnant to the Constitution as an impairment of the obligation of contracts.[27] By this device, the Court cleverly avoided any suggestion that the tribe might be exempt from taxation because of its political independence from New Jersey, the original act of exemption being merely declaratory of preexisting rights.[28] The Court did not distinguish between the tribe as a sovereign and the tribe as a mere landowner, implicitly accepting New Jersey's pretension that, but for its grant of exemption, it could have taxed the tribe. It was as if the Court believed that New Jersey held the ultimate fee or dominion of the tribe's territory.

The changing temper of law and public opinion was nowhere better illustrated than in the negotiation of the Treaty of Ghent with Great Britain in 1814. Tribes had fought on both sides and occupied much of the dis-

---

26. 11 U.S. (7 Cranch) 164 (1812).

27. The Court did suggest that New Jersey could have conditioned its authorization of the sale that the purchasers release the tax exemption to the state (*id.* 167).

28. We know of no case of tribal lands being taxed by the colonies. Individual Indian lands were sometimes taxed, e.g., Beverly Fleet, ed., 21 *Virginia Colonial Abstracts* 20, 22, 58 (Richmond, Va.: 1938–1948), but even these fee lands escaped taxation when the tribe survived as a self-governing and self-financing organization, e.g., John Russell Bartlett, ed., 6 *Records of the Colony of Rhode Island and Providence Plantations, in New England* 14 (Providence, R.I.: 1856–1865).

puted territory. The original British proposal for the meetings did not mention Indian affairs.[29] However, it was at once apparent to the American ministers upon their arrival that the Crown was prepared to make tribal status the threshold issue. It was to be, in fact, as Lord Gambier took pleasure in repeating, the "sine qua non" of any settlement,[30] and its consideration consumed the better part of two months.

John Quincy Adams and his colleagues insisted that the future of Indian tribes was no proper concern in a treaty between Britain and the United States, since the tribes were not represented[31] and were, he argued moreover, "subjects" of the United States rather than nations,[32] incapable of treating with a foreign power. Indeed, the War of 1812 having been "wholly of a maritime nature" the Americans had not been instructed by the president to discuss Indian matters.[33] Nevertheless, they would discuss the issue if only to dispel the "erroneous impressions" Great Britain evidently harbored regarding federal Indian policy.[34]

The Americans painted a rosy picture. The British delegation was told, Adams later wrote to Secretary of State Monroe, "that no nation observed a policy more liberal and humane towards the Indians than that pursued by the United States; that our object has been, by all practicable means, to introduce civilization amongst them; [and] that their possessions were secured to them by well-defined boundaries."[35]

This failed to satisfy His Britannic Majesty's representatives. They accused the United States of a policy of "aggrandisement" demonstrated "by their progressive occupation of the Indian territories," as well as by

29. 3 *American State Papers, Foreign Relations* 706, 711 (Washington, D.C.: 1832).
30. *Id.* 705, 706, 707, 708, 709, 712.
31. *Id.* 720.
32. *Id.* 712, 716, 720. Making a subentity of a nation party to an international treaty, Adams protested, would be "contrary to the acknowledged principles of public law, and to the practice of all civilized nations" (*id.* 711). The British delegation responded by pointing out the provisions for certain individual German states stipulated by France in its Treaty of Munster with the German Empire (*id.* 722). "Can it be necessary to prove that there is no sort of analogy between the political situation of these civilized communities and that of the wandering tribes of North American savages?" Adams retorted (*id.* 724). In other words, a treaty between two nations can provide for special treatment of a substate only if that substate is "civilized"! Later, however, Adams argued that Britain's *failure* to provide specially for tribes in the 1783 Treaty of Paris proved they were not independent nations (*id.* 722, 724, 712). The Treaty may be found in Clive Parry, ed., 48 *Consolidated Treaty Series* 489, 491 (Dobb's Ferry, N.Y.: 1969).
33. 3 *American State Papers, Foreign Relations* 706, 711.
34. *Id.* 706.
35. *Id.* 706; also 712.

their abortive efforts to seize Canada and their purchase of Louisiana,[36] a charge the American ministers naturally denied.[37] As the British conceived it, the United States had adopted a policy "that all the territory which these Indian nations occupy is at the disposal of the United States; that the United States have a right to dispossess them of it; to exercise that right whenever their policy or interests may seem to them to require it; and to confine them to such spots as may be selected, not by the Indian nations, but by the American Government."[38] Under the circumstances, Great Britain was unprepared to "abandon the Indian nations to their fate."[39] As British allies, they were entitled to be accorded territorial integrity, "permanent tranquility and security."[40] "However reluctant His Royal Highness the Prince Regent may be to continue the war, that evil must be preferred if peace can only be obtained on such conditions."[41]

To be sure, the Crown harbored an ulterior motive, for its solution to the problem of tribal security was for both the United States and Great Britain to abstain from further purchases of tribal land, creating thereby a permanent "neutral power" or "barrier" between them.[42] This, it was proposed, would obviate future territorial wars and pacify the hemisphere.

The Americans' response was vigorous and not entirely sincere. Supposing such a buffer state were recognized, they argued, the American people would never accept it as just and would attempt to reconquer it at the earliest fit opportunity.[43] Including it in the treaty would prove futile. Indeed, the major thrust of the American position was to concede, obliquely, the truth of the British accusations.

It may be the interest of Great Britain to limit her settlements in Canada to their present extent, and to leave the country to the west a perpetual wilderness, to be forever inhabited by scattered tribes of hunters; but it would inflict a vital injury on the United States to have a line run through their territory, beyond which their

36. *Id.* 713, 721.
37. *Id.* 715, 723.
38. *Id.* 722. "[I]n effect," the British delegation concluded, the United States had "declared that all Indian nations within its line of demarcation are its subjects, living upon sufferance on lands which it also claims the exclusive right of acquiring, thereby menacing the final extinction of those nations" (*id.* 712). A generation later the Cherokee Removal would vindicate this cynical assessment.
39. *Id.* 714.
40. *Id.* 710.
41. *Id.* 722.
42. *Id.* 706, 708, 709, 715.
43. *Id.* 713, 716.

settlements should forever be precluded from extending; thereby arresting the natural growth of their population and strength.[44]

The Americans confidently predicted that the Indians would be co-beneficiaries of territorial expansion.

[T]he United States, while intending never to acquire lands from the Indians otherwise than peaceably, and with their free consent, are fully determined, in that manner, progressively, and in proportion as their growing population may require, to reclaim from the state of nature, and to bring into cultivation every portion of the territory contained within their acknowledged boundaries. In thus providing for the support of millions of civilized beings, they will not only give to the few thousand savages scattered over that territory an ample equivalent for any right they may surrender, but will always leave them the possession of lands more than they can cultivate, and more than adequate to their subsistence, comfort, and enjoyment, by cultivation. If this be a spirit of aggrandizement, the undersigned are prepared to admit, in that sense, its existence. . . . They will not suppose that [Great Britain] will avow, as the basis of their policy towards the United States, the system of arresting their natural growth within their own territories, for the sake of preserving a perpetual desert for savages.[45]

The American delegation was not satisfied, however, to rest its case solely upon considerations of humane policy, but proceeded, in the words of Lord Gambier, to "advance the novel and alarming pretension that all the Indian nations living within the boundaries of the United States must in effect be considered their subjects, and, consequently, if engaged in war against the United States, become liable to be treated as rebels."[46] The American position embraced a claim to both "sovereignty and soil."[47]

It was here that the so-called *doctrine of preemption* was first explained. "No maxim of public law has hitherto been more universally established among the Powers of Europe possessing territories in America," the Americans suggested without hesitation, "and there is none to which Great Britain has more uniformly and inflexibly adhered."

44. *Id.* 717; also 718.
45. *Id.* 710. We wonder whether Adams or Gambier had read that part of Caesar where he describes the Britons as bearded savages stained blue with woad (*Gallic War* V. 14). See also *id.* VI, 13–28, on the Germans, who, Caesar was distressed to discover, held land in common (*id.* VI.22). The idea that European savages could, given time, become civilized, but American savages could not, was a very pernicious, racist conceit. See, too, 3 *American State Papers, Foreign Relations* 717, where Adams argues that leaving the tribes to themselves will "doo[m] them to perpetual barbarism."
46. *Id.* 722.
47. *Id.* 706, 712, 715, 716, 720.

Without the admission of this principle there would be no intelligible meaning attached to stipulations establishing boundaries between the dominions in America of civilized nations, possessing territories inhabited by Indian tribes. Whatever may be the relations of Indians to the nations in whose territory they are thus acknowledged to reside, they cannot be considered as an independent Power.[48]

Having relied upon this principle to justify colonization of the Atlantic seaboard, it was not for Great Britain to now deny its validity.[49] The tribes themselves had acknowledged it in the Treaty of Greenville (1795), by which they agreed to sell their lands only to the United States, and "acknowledge[d] themselves to be under protection of the . . . United States, and of no other Power whatever."[50]

The United States had, moreover, organized preemption into a unique "political system."

Under that system the Indians residing within the United States are so far independent that they live under their own customs, and not under the laws of the United States; that their rights upon the lands where they inhabit or hunt, are secured to them by boundaries defined in amicable and voluntary treaties between the United States and themselves; and that whenever those boundaries are varied, it is also by amicable and voluntary treaties, by which they received from the United States ample compensation for every right they have to the lands ceded by them. They are so far dependent as not to have the right to dispose of their lands to any private persons, nor to any Power other than the United States, and to be under their protection alone, and not under that of any other Power.[51]

In short, the tribes retained all of their *domestic* sovereignty, losing only the rights to cede land to and ally themselves with the nation or nations of their choice. According to Adams, tribes' *"right of exercising exclusive jurisdiction within the boundary line assigned"* to them in their treaties was not a grant from the United States, the treaties being *"merely declaratory* of the public law . . . founded on principles previously and universally recognized."[52] A clearer admission that, under the laws of

---

48. *Id*. 711–12.

49. *Id*. 716.

50. *Id*. 712; 52 *Consolidated Treaty Series* 442, Article V. In Article IV the United States relinquished all of its "claims" to tribal lands not peviously purchased. "Claims" reasonably comprehend both sovereignty and the soil.

51. 3 *American State Papers, Foreign Relations* 716. And at 720: "The right of the United States to the protection of the Indians . . . was not acquired by . . . treaty; it was a necessary consequence of the sovereignty and independence of the United States."

52. *Id*. (emphasis ours). Indeed, the Treaty of Greenville recognized the tribes' authority to "punish" Americans found within their boundaries (Article VI, 52 *Consolidated Treaty Series* 442).

nations, Congress lacked power to intervene in tribes' domestic government could scarcely be imagined.

The American position nevertheless conveniently confused this moderate theory with true national absorption. Adams repeatedly denied that tribes were "sovereign," and protested that any recognition of them in the Ghent treaty would deprive the United States of sovereignty.[53] But it was not uncommon for nations to cede or limit some of their international powers without any suspicion that in so doing they had ceased to be sovereign; what else is comprised in an ordinary treaty? Whether the powers of tribes in matters of foreign relations had been limited by cession or the operation of international law, there was no precedent to infer extinction of sovereignty from that fact alone.

Surely, the British delegation reasoned, the continuing practice of the United States in making treaties with individual tribes proved that they remained sovereign.[54] Moreover, any voluntary commitment by the tribes to recognize American supremacy had been completely abrogated by the war, which constituted in public law a bilateral repudiation of all previous treaty obligations.[55] When the United States rebelled against the king, it had dissolved all political dependency and made itself sovereign; could it be different for the tribes that took up arms against the United States?

Of course, the United States could not afford to admit these propositions, for to do so would have encouraged British agents to instigate tribal rebellions as excuses for subsequent British military intervention within the boundaries of the United States—precisely what had in part occurred during the last war. But if the American position was understandable in terms of national self-interest, that did not make it just or consistent with international law, nor for that matter consistent with the American Constitution itself. For some unidentifiable reason, however, the British ministers suddenly backed off from their original demands in late September and proposed that the United States merely restore the tribes to their prewar rights.[56] Adams interpreted this as requiring only that the United

53. 3 *American State Papers, Foreign Relations* 720.
54. *Id*. 706, 722.
55. *Id*. 714, 718.
56. *Id*. 710, 718, 723. The proposal to restore to the tribes all of their "possessions, rights, and privileges" was incorporated in the treaty without further discussion or amendment (Article IX, 63 *Consolidated Treaty Series* 429). The British retreat is puzzling since it came so soon after the tide of events in Europe had freed more of His Majesty's troops for the North American theatre.

States commit itself to a prompt and general Indian pacification "of the nature of amnesty" for tribes who had borne arms against Americans.[57] The Treaty of Spring Wells (1815) was made in precise compliance with this agreement.[58]

The British position, albeit never reduced to agreement, was not without influence in American executive policy. In an 1821 opinion of the attorney general of the United States, we find the statement that

So long as a tribe exists and remains in possession of its land, its title and possession are sovereign and exclusive. . . . Although the Indian title continues only during their possession, yet that possession has been held sacred, and can never be disturbed but by their consent. They do not hold under the states, nor under the United States; their title is original, sovereign, and exclusive.[59]

Two years later the Supreme Court reconsidered the issues finessed in *Fletcher v. Peck* and *New Jersey v. Wilson,* and left unresolved by the treaty commissioners at Ghent. In *Johnson v. M'Intosh*[60] the non-Indian plaintiffs derived their title from direct tribal grants obtained by them without the consent of the United States. The non-Indian defendants based their claims on subsequent federal land patents, issued after the whole area had been ceded to the United States by a tribal treaty. The issue was not the extent of the tribe's property rights prior to the cession, but rather whether federal courts were required to respect interests in foreign land obtained by American citizens without the sanction, if not indeed in violation, of federal laws. Analogous questions would be raised a few years later in conflicts over Florida lands between grantees of the Spanish Crown and patentees of the United States.[61]

Consistent with international law and Locke's principle of operational consent, the Court unanimously agreed that individual rights in tribal land were exclusively governed by tribal law. "The person who purchases lands from the Indians, within their territory," the chief justice explained,

incorporates himself with them, so far as respects the property purchased; holds their title under their protection, and subject to their laws. If they annul the grant,

---

57. 3 *American State Papers, Foreign Relations* 720, 724.
58. 65 *Consolidated Treaty Series* 170. See especially Articles II, III, and IV.
59. 1 Op. Atty. Gen. 465 ("The Seneca Lands").
60. 21 U.S. (8 Wheat.) 543 (1823).
61. E.g., *Foster & Elam v. Neilson,* 2 Pet. 253 (1829); *Arrendondo v. United States,* 6 Pet. 691 (1832); *U.S. v. Percheman,* 7 Pet. 51 (1833). The strands of Indian and Spanish land-grant law finally came together in *Mitchel v. United States,* 9 Pet. 711 (1835).

we know of no tribunal [of the United States] which can revise and set aside the proceeding.[62]

The tribal land tenure system was separate and distinct from that of the United States. In the exercise of its commerce power, Congress might have punished American citizens for dealing with tribes for land or goods without license, but the mere fact that an American citizen had purchased an interest in tribal land gave Congress and the courts no power over the land itself. The situation would be no different if, today, an American citizen were to purchase land in Canada or Mexico.

After cession of tribal territory to the United States by treaty, however, international law provided that interests in land be governed by the land tenure system of the new sovereign. Rights acquired before the cession might be lost unless saved by the treaty itself or guaranteed against expropriation by the new sovereign's laws. The chief justice was careful to point out that in *M'Intosh* the tribal grantees' interests were *not* reserved by the treaty of cession, while the patentees' claims were, of course, supported by federal legislation. Although Marshall made no mention of it in his opinion, it was common practice in that era for tribal grantees *to be individually named* in subsequent treaties of cession whenever their interests were agreed to be reserved.[63]

But where did the national government acquire constitutional power to accept these cessions of foreign territory, and then patent them out to individual citizens? International law supported the claims of federal patentees in the territories, but did federal law? The Louisiana Purchase had established an historical precedent, but no legal precedent as yet. Marshall was well aware of the necessity of settling this question in a time

---

62. 21 U.S. 593—94. See also *Jackson v. Porter*, 1 Paine 457 (N.Y. 1825); Henderson, "Aboriginal Title," 75, 87—96.

63. There are many examples among the treaties of this period of provisions for non-Indians' lands. In some cases the treaty expressly validated prior purchases (treaty with the Caddo, Supplementary Articles, 1835, 2 Kappler, *Indian Affairs* 433). In others, named whites were granted preemptive rights to purchase ceded land from the United States (treaty with the Menominee, Art. IX, 1848, *id.* 572). Most frequently the treaty directed the president to patent specified tracts to whites described as having aided the tribes in one way or another—typically traders and interpreters (treaty with the Seneca, Art. XI, 1831, *id.* 325; treaty with the Seneca, 1831, Arts. XII—XIV, *id.* 327; treaty with the Shawnee, Art. XI, 1831, *id.* 331; treaty with the Creeks, Art. VI, 1832, *id.* 341; treaty with the Ottawa, Art. II, 1833, *id.* 392; treaty with the Chickasaw, Art. X, 1834, *id.* 418; treaty with the New York Indians, Arts. IX—X, 1838, *id.* 502).

of frequent and extensive tribal land cessions in the West. Embarrassingly, the Court had held in *Fletcher* eleven years earlier that *the states* could convey the fee in western lands without waiting for federal action.

Marshall sought the power of Congress to purchase and reconvey tribal lands in the two-centuries-old convention among European nations that discovery vested in the discoverer an exclusive or "preemptive" entitlement to deal with the natives as against other European crowns.[64] The British Crown's preemptive rights in America had been conveyed implicitly to the federal government by the Treaties of Paris and Ghent in the articles fixing the exterior boundaries of the United States. This did not really solve the problem, however; how could Congress acquire powers in excess of the Constitution merely as the heir to an international agreement predating the American Revolution? Besides, if national authority over the western territories depended upon a convention among Britain, France and Spain, what would happen if those countries, all still guarding territorial footholds in North America, were to revise their arrangement and parcel out the rest of the continent among themselves?

To avoid these problems Marshall reasoned that discovery had given the United States much more than the sole right to treat for native title: it had given the United States *title itself*. As legal owner of all western Indian lands prior to the adoption of the Constitution, Congress could dispose of them without additional authorization from the states. The original states of the Union had, moreover, ceded their western claims to the United States, an act consistent with Marshall's theory—the act of cession being a recognition of congressional power to accept and dispose, if not of a prior or preemptive federal ownership.

This, too, was an incomplete answer. Needless to say the preemptive

---

64. 21 U.S. 572–74. Among European monarchs discovery was "acknowledged as the law by which the right of acquisition should be regulated *as between themselves*" (*id.* 573 [emphasis ours]). Justice Johnson had earlier developed this thesis in *Fletcher v. Peck* (10 U.S. [6 Cranch] 87, 146 [1810]): "What then, practically, is the interest of the states in the soil of the Indians within their boundaries? Unaffected by particular treaties, it is nothing more than what was assumed at the first settlement of the country, to wit, a right of conquest, or of purchase, exclusively of all competitors, within certain defined limits." The boundary agreement in the peace treaty of 1783 between the United States and Britain for the most part apportioned this right, rather than the soil itself. Most of the line ran west of the extant European settlements through the territories of tribes not yet even treated with. The western boundaries of the first states included considerable tribal land. The various state cessions to the United States between 1783 and 1802 merely quitclaimed any "right of discovery" they might have had to western tribal lands.

right of discovery brought down the price of tribal land,[65] like any other international trade cartel among purchasers, but Marshall's contemporaries were in agreement that nations lose sovereignty only in just wars or by their consent.[66] The United States' monopoly power to sell interests in lands occupied by Indians was simply not enough to give it sovereignty. Marshall was forced to take one more step. He fictionalized discovery into conquest. This was, he freely confessed, an unjust but expedient solution.

However extravagant the pretension of converting the discovery of an inhabited country into conquest may appear; if the principle has been asserted in the first instance, and afterwards sustained; if a country has been acquired and held under it; if the property of the great mass of the community originates in it, it becomes the law of the land, and cannot be questioned. . . . However this restriction may be opposed to natural right, and to the usages of civilized nations, yet, if it be indispensable to that system under which the country has been settled, and be adapted to the actual condition of the two people, it may, perhaps, be supported by reason, and certainly cannot be rejected by courts of justice.[67]

European nations recognized this principle when they defended their colonial boundaries against one another's armies. By continuing to coexist with the United States rather than appealing to the sword, tribes implicitly also recognized the legitimacy of this pretension.[68]

Marshall nevertheless resisted the implications of his own creation, realizing that it was neither consistent with the American ideal of contractual government nor an honest characterization of the country's history. He emphasized that discovery impaired only the *external* powers of tribes—the powers of war and peace, and of international trade. Although tribes' "rights to complete sovereignty, as independent nations, were necessarily diminished," they "were, in no instance, entirely disregarded."[69] Marshall painstakingly demonstrated the extent to which

65. For example, our study of the Oyster Bay land records in Cox, *Oyster Bay Town Records*, indicates that tribal acreage sold to individual Englishmen could be resold within a year to other Englishmen for twice as much or more.

66. E.g., Henry Wheaton, *Elements of International Law* (Dana ed. Boston: 1866), especially sections 20−27.

67. 21 U.S. 591−92.

68. *Id.* 589−91; also see Henderson, "Aboriginal Title," 91−93, 115−16. If tribes went to war they stood little practical chance of success; if they remained at peace, the law regarded them as conquered anyway.

69. 21 U.S. 594. To further confuse the Court's reference to conquest as a source of title, the word "conqueror" meant "purchaser" in feudal English and Scotch Gaelic law (Sir William Blackstone, *Commentaries on the Laws of England* ch. 15, 1029−31 [Oxford: 1765−69]). Also see Sir Henry Spelman, *Glossarium Archaiologicum* (3rd ed. London: 1687)

the United States had actually purchased Indian lands by treaty instead of relying on discovery or conquest to justify confiscation. But his almost feudal characterization of the federal-tribal relationship—tribes merely "occupying" land owned by the United States in fee just as medieval tenant farmers occupied their lands at the sufferance of "lords of the fee"[70]—together with the seductive analogy between the foundation of the British nation on the Norman conquest and the foundation of the American nation on the "conquest" of the Indians, were powerful over-simplifications. Although self-consciously fictitious, they were to influence all subsequent thinking.

---

under *conquestus*; Henry John Stephen, 1 *New Commentaries on the Laws of England* 355 (London: 1841−45); and Edward Augustus Freeman, 2 *The History of the Norman Conquest of England* 626−27 (3rd ed. Oxford: 1877).

70. 21 U.S. 592. Compare the situation in *Penn v. Lord Baltimore*, 1 Ves. Sen. 444, 451−52, 27 Eng. Rep. 1132, 1137 (1750), where it was decided that the Crown had not been defrauded by Penn's statement in his application for a patent to Pennsylvania that the territory was inhabited only by Indians. In fact both Dutch and Swedes had settled there previously, but the court deemed them no more than "some stragglers" which "if not recognized by the Crown . . . is not a settlement."

5

The Conceptualization of Tribal Sovereignty, 1823-1836

[N]o court has ever achieved perfection in its reasoning in its first, or indeed in its twentieth opinion on the same subject. . . . [T]his characteristic of law must be true, even for our greatest and most insightful judges. They grapple with a new problem, deal with it over and over again, as its dimensions change. They settle one case, and find themselves tormented by its unanticipated progeny. They back and fill, zig and zag, groping through the mist for a line of thought which will in the end satisfy their standards of craft and their vision of the policy of the community they must try to interpret. The opinions written at the end of such a cycle rarely resemble those composed at the beginning. Exceptions emerge, and new formulations of what once looked like clear principle. If we take advantage of hindsight, we can see in any line of cases and statutes a pattern of growth, and of response to changing conditions and changing ideas. There are cases that lead nowhere, stunted branches and healthy ones. Often the judges who participate in the process could not have described the tree that was growing. Yet the felt necessities of society have their impact, and the law emerges, gnarled, asymmetrical, but very much alive—the product of a forest, not of a nursery garden, nor of the gardener's art.[1]

The southern states were not content with Marshall's fictions. Tribes' federally protected rights of permanent "occupancy" and internal sovereignty posed a clear and inescapable legal bar to state purchases and settlement of Indian territory. Convinced that Congress would not move quickly enough to treat with tribes for cessions, and infuriated by federal financing of some tribes' establishment of permanent towns, roads and farms,[2] state legislatures took matters into their own hands. Within five years Georgia, Tennessee, Alabama and Mississippi unilaterally extended their political

1. Eugene V. Rostow, "American Legal Realism and the Sense of the Profession," 34 *Rocky Mountain Law Review* 123, 141–42 (1962).
2. Memorial of Georgia, 18th Congress, 1st Session, Document No. 205 (1834), in 2 *American State Papers, Indian Affairs* 490 (Washington, D.C.: 1832).

authority over tribes located within their boundaries. In Georgia the state assembly incorporated the lands of the Cherokee nation, instituted state courts and police, annulled all tribal laws and imprisoned tribal officials.[3]

In its haste to avoid the constitutional question of Congress's exclusive power to purchase and reconvey tribal lands, the Supreme Court had raised a delicate issue of states' rights. As long as tribes remained "foreign" to the United States, it was clear they could be dealt with by treaty alone—by the president. However, *M'Intosh* characterized tribes as a part of the land mass of the United States and under their political authority. How, then, was it proper for Indian matters to continue to be handled by the chief executive, rather than by Congress and the state legislatures in the exercise of their domestic police powers? The states could not conceive how the president could constitutionally exercise a part of the United States' *external* sovereignty over *internal* affairs.

The states moreover believed the president's power to preemptively purchase tribal lands had been delegated to him by individual state-federal agreements subsequent to the Constitution, not by the Constitution itself. In 1802, for example, Georgia relinquished its western claims to the United States on two conditions: first, that the United States purchase for Georgia all tribal lands lying within that state's chartered boundaries, at federal expense and "as soon as it could be done peaceably and on reasonable terms"; and second, that any new states formed out of the balance of the purchased tribal lands conform to all but certain selected provisions of the Northwest Ordinance. Why, Georgians asked, had it been necessary to make this agreement if Congress was already the legal owner and sovereign of that territory?

Georgia's actions and theory came to a test when George Corn Tassels, a Cherokee citizen, was indicted for the murder of another Cherokee within formerly Cherokee territory, by a Hall County, Georgia, grand jury.[4] On a jurisdictional challenge the state superior court ruled that savages can have no lawful government competent to make or keep treaties, or to govern

---

3. Act No. 545 of 20 December 1828, and Act No. 546 of 19 December 1829 (William C. Dawson, ed., *A Compilation of the Laws of the State of Georgia* 198 [Milledgeville, Ga.: 1831]).

4. *State v. Tassels*, Dud. (Ga.) 229 (1830). For the background of the case see *The Richmond Enquirer* for 19 December 1830, p. 4, col. 1. For a more personal view see Joseph Story's letter to his wife, 28 January 1831, quoted in Leonard Baker, *John Marshall: A Life in Law* 736 (New York: 1974).

territory. In language unmistakably influenced by *Fletcher v. Peck*, the state court continued,

Indeed, it seems strange that an objection should now be made to that [Georgia's] jurisdiction. That a government should be seized in fee of a territory, and yet have no jurisdiction over that country, is an anomaly in the science of jurisprudence; but it may be contended that although the State of Georgia may have jurisdiction over the Cherokee territory, yet it has no right to exercise jurisdiction over the persons of the Cherokee Indians who reside upon the territory of which the State of Georgia is seized in fee. Such distinctions would present a more strange anomaly than that of a government having no jurisdiction over territory of which it was seized.[5]

In *Fletcher*, Marshall had distinguished tribal "occupancy" from fee title to reconcile states patenting land with the actual use of the land by tribes. Now the same distinction was being used to argue that no subsequent sale was necessary. Having the fee and the power to patent, the state had complete dominion; the national government nothing but what the state had given it—a duty to negotiate tribal removal at its own expense.[6]

The Cherokee Nation appealed Tassels's conviction to the Supreme Court, but the state assembly ordered him executed as soon as the writ of error was served.[7] With Tassels's case moot, counsel for the tribe moved the Court for a general injunction against Georgia.[8] It was generally reputed that Congress and the president sympathized with the state, so much so that Cherokee counsel Wirt warned the Court in his oral argument against being intimidated by the very real likelihood of presidential contempt of its decree.[9] The state was so set on defying any adverse order that it did not bother to put in an appearance in its own defense.

5. Dud. 229, 236.
6. Similar arguments were made in *State v. Foreman*, 16 Tenn. 256 (1835).
7. "Resolutions of the Legislature Relative to the Case of George Tassels," Acts of Georgia 282–83 (23 December 1830); 29 *Niles Weekly Register* 338 (1830). For an informative statement of Georgia's position, see "Report and Remonstrance of the Legislature of Georgia," Sen. Doc. No. 98, 21st Congress, 1st Session (1830). See also *The Richmond Enquirer* for 8 January 1831, p. 3, col. 6.
8. 30 U.S. (5 Pet.) 1 (1831). The Cherokees took this action on the advice of Daniel Webster, among others in Congress, only after President Jackson refused to intervene on their behalf with the governor of Georgia (John Pendleton Kennedy, 2 *Memoirs of the Life of William Wirt* 252–54, 156).
9. Richard Peters, ed., *The Case of the Cherokee Nation Against the State of Georgia. Argued and Determined at the Supreme Court of the United States* 153–56 (Philadelphia: 1831). See also Wirt's letter to Judge Carr, in Kennedy, 2 *Memoirs* 255. Wirt had grave misgivings, apparently, regarding the ethics and patriotism of his prosecuting the case (*id.* 255, 259, 261–62).

Deftly sidestepping a constitutional crisis, the Court disposed of the case on purely jurisdictional grounds. Article III of the Constitution limits the judicial power of the United States to "Controversies between two or more States;—between a State and Citizens of another State;—between citizens of different States;— . . . and between a State, or the Citizens thereof, and foreign States, Citizens or Subjects." The majority concurred that the Cherokee Nation was not, strictly speaking, either a state of the Union or a "foreign State," and was therefore ineligible to apply to the courts of the United States for relief.[10] The merits of the Cherokees' claims were scrupulously avoided, however, leaving open the possibility of a fresh suit with some other, constitutionally eligible plaintiff.

To justify the Court's rather tedious construction of the language of the Constitution, the Chief Justice was at pains to completely analyze and describe the Cherokee Nation. As in *M'Intosh*, he was convinced of tribes' right of internal self-government, but had great difficulty divorcing his consideration of sovereignty from discovery and ownership.

Though the Indians are acknowledged to have an unquestionable, and heretofore, unquestioned right to the lands they occupy, until that right shall be extinguished by a voluntary cession to our government; yet it may well be doubted whether those tribes which reside within the acknowledged boundaries of the United States can, with strict accuracy, be denominated foreign nations. They may, more correctly, perhaps be denominated domestic dependent nations. They occupy a territory to which we assert a title independent of their will, which must take effect in point of possession when their right of possession ceases. Meanwhile they are in a state of pupillage. Their relation to the United States resembles that of a ward to his guardian.[11]

10. Wirt feared this would happen; he even asked Judge Carr to sound out the chief justice in confidence on this point before the case was filed (Kennedy, 2 *Memoirs* 257). Marshall declined to discuss it (*id.* 258). Compare the *Nabob of Arcot's Case (Nabob of Arcot v. East India Co.)*, 1 Ves. Jr. 371, 30 Eng. Rep. 391 (1791), 2 Ves. Jr. 56, 30 Eng. Rep. 521 (1792), which questioned whether a foreign prince in his sovereign capacity is entitled to relief in the civil courts. Indeed in one remarkable passage Marshall argued that the tribes had little equity in invoking the protection of an American court, because it had always been their habit to resort in all disputes "to the tomahawk" alone! (30 U.S. [5 Pet.] 18). Apart from any legal absurdity, this is based on a sweeping fallacy. Colonial court records are replete with tribal and individual Indian claims. See for example, James P. Ronda, "Red and White at the Bench: Indians and the Law in Plymouth Colony, 1620–1691," 10 *Essex Institute Historical Collections* 200 (1974); Yasu Kawashima, "Jurisdiction of the Colonial Courts over the Indians in Massachusetts, 1689–1763," 42 *New England Quarterly* 532 (1969). Marshall knew this full well: he had cited the Mohegin Indians' suit against Connecticut eight years earlier in *Johnson v. M'Intosh* (21 U.S. [8 Wheat.] 543, 598 [1823]).

11. 30 U.S. (5 Pet.) 1, 16–17.

As foreign nations, tribes' external sovereignty could not be restricted except by their consent; as domestic subdivisions they could not be saved from the police power of the states unless they were states of the Union themselves. Marshall tried to suggest the best of both principles: that tribes are so far foreign as to be immune from the internal sovereignty of the states, but so far domestic as to be limited by the internal sovereignty of the United States.

Marshall's use of the phrases "domestic dependent nation," "state of pupilage," and "ward and guardian" caused more problems than it solved. His intent was simply to make it plain that tribes exist outside of the political arrangement between the state and federal governments, yet nonetheless are a part of the national political system. Accordingly he fell back on the language of international rather than constitutional law, as he had done in *M'Intosh*.

Marshall's friend and long-time Supreme Court reporter, Henry Wheaton, explained the general significance of "dependency" in his 1836 treatise on the law of nations.

The sovereignty of a particular State is not impaired by its occasional obedience to the commands of other States, or even the habitual influence exercised by them over its councils. It is only when this obedience, or this influence, *assumes the form of express compact*, that the sovereignty of the State, inferior in power, is legally affected by its connection with the other. Treaties of equal alliance, freely contracted between independent States, do not impair their sovereignty. Treaties of unequal alliance, guarantee, mediation, and protection, may have the effect of limiting and qualifying the sovereignty *according to the stipulations of the treaties*.

States which are thus *dependent* on other States, in respect to the exercise of certain rights, essential to the perfect external sovereignty, have been termed *semi-sovereign* States.[12]

Thus defined, dependency is limited to the *express* and *specific* consent of the dependent nation. It is a means by which one nation may place itself for some purposes under the international brokerage and advocacy of another. Marshall's use of the term was ambiguous, however. Tribes are dependent upon the United States, he explained, because "[t]hey look to our government for protection" and accept its aid and relief.[13] Was he saying that the

---

12. Henry Wheaton, *Elements of International Law* §§33, 34 (Dana ed. Boston: 1866).
13. 30 U.S. (5 Pet.) 17–18. Marshall contrasted this relationship to discovery and preemption, which he said the United States exercised independent of the tribes' will.

tribes had agreed to this, or that it followed from their condition, status or behavior?

Marshall was similarly ambiguous in his use of the wardship analogy. In feudal English law, wardship was an incident of fee ownership. When a tenant died leaving a minor child as heir, the lord of the fee estate was entitled to manage and enjoy the profits of the inheritance until the heir attained the age of twenty-one.[14] Was Marshall suggesting that the United States, as fee owner of tribal land, served as the tribes' "guardian in chivalry" in this sense?

Guardianship also carries with it the more modern meaning of "a temporary parent . . . for so long time as the ward is an infant, or under age,"[15] a custodian of the person and trustee of the estate. As trustee the guardian is subject to an accounting and possible indemnification of the ward; the ward cannot contract or convey without the guardian's approval. This is the kind of relationship between tribes and the United States most readers find in the *Cherokee* case.

However, long before Marshall's time, the jurist Blackstone had declared it a "triumph" of the English common law that *the guardian may never have an interest or inheritance in the ward's estate.* To provide otherwise, American and English commentators agreed, would be *quasi agnum committere lupo, ad devorandum*, like entrusting the lamb to the wolf, to be devoured.[16] Since Marshall was adamant regarding the United States' title to tribal territory and reversionary interest in its use after tribal cession, he could not have had in mind a relationship analogous to Anglo-American guardianship.

Indeed, Marshall's consistent use of the words "tutelage" and "pupilage" suggests he was thinking of guardianship in the Roman rather than the English sense. In Latin *tutela* and *pupilla*, the civil guardian and ward of Roman law, enjoyed a special secondary significance describing small,

14. Sir William Blackstone, 1 *Commentaries on the Laws of England* ch. 17 (Oxford: 1765–69); J. H. Baker, *An Introduction to English Legal History* 126 (London: 1971); S.F.C. Milsom, *The Legal Framework of English Feudalism* 155 (Cambridge: 1976). Guardianship in chivalry was abolished in the seventeenth century (Statute 12 Car. II c. 24).

15. Blackstone, 1 *Commentaries* ch. 17, §1.

16. Blackstone traced this doctrine to Glanville who, shortly after the Norman Conquest, wrote, *Nunquam custodia alienjus de jure alicui remanet de quo habeatur suspicio, quod possii vel velit aliquod jus in ipsa hereditate clamare*—no one may remain guardian in law, in whom there is any suspicion he may claim an inheritance (Blackstone, 1 *Commentaries* ch. 17, §1 n. [h]).

often noncitizen households patronized by politically powerful citizens.[17] This kind of contractual patronage is much more consistent with Marshall's other arguments than any notion of involuntary supervision.

The chief justice himself was deeply troubled by the conflicting implications of his use of language. *At his urging* subsequent to the announcement of his decision, Justice Thompson wrote a vigorous dissent, in which Joseph Story concurred.[18] Chancellor Kent, the other great legal luminary of the day, moreover wrote an extensive brief supporting the Cherokee cause which, together with a transcript of Wirt's oral argument, was published with Marshall's blessings in a special volume by Supreme Court reporter Richard Peters.[19]

Encouraged by the Court's evident misgivings, Wirt returned the following term with a test case that avoided all of the jurisdictional issues raised by their first appeal.[20] Samuel Worcester, a New England missionary, was imprisoned by Georgia for entering formerly Cherokee territory without a pass from the state. Representing Worcester, Wirt repeated most of his previous argument,[21] and this time won a unanimous declaration that Georgia's laws were "repugnant to the Constitution, laws, and treaties of the United States."[22] The chief justice now appeared to have no difficulty with tribal sovereignty as a function of collective political rights. Describing tribes as "distinct people, divided into separate nations, independent of

17. Justinian, 1 *Institutes* chs. 13−26; Charles Reinold Noyes, *The Institution of Property* 80 (New York: 1936); J. Y. Henderson, "Unraveling the Riddle of Aboriginal Title," 5 *American Indian Law Review* 75, 102−5 (1977).

18. Marshall approached Thompson and Story after he discovered, at the reading of the opinions in the case, that Baldwin and Johnson went beyond the jurisdictional issue to discuss the merits of Cherokee sovereignty at great length, both concluding that the tribe lacked sovereign character. Story later wrote that "neither Justice T. nor myself contemplated delivering a dissenting opinion, until the Chief Justice suggested to us the propriety of it, and his own desire that we should do it" (Joseph C. Burke, "The Cherokee Cases: A Study in Law, Politics, and Morality," 21 *Stanford Law Review* 500, 516 [1969]).

19. Marshall wrote Peters, "I should be glad to see the whole case. It is one in which the public takes a deep interest, and of which a very narrow view has been taken in the opinion which is pronounced by the court," i.e., in his own opinion, limited to the jurisdictional issue. Marshall explained that he did not have time to consider the wider ramifications of the holding, and that the case should be interpreted only within "narrow limits." He also expressed concern that the majority and concurring opinions "looked to our side of the question only," rather than the tribes' (Burke, "Cherokee Cases," 518).

20. *Worcester v. Georgia*, 21 U.S. (6 Pet.) 515 (1832).

21. This is evident from Story's notes of the case in his benchbook captioned "Memorandums of Arguments in the Supreme Court of the United States beginning with the Jany Term 1831 & ending with the Jany Term 1832," 288−97, in possession of the Harvard Law School library. The arguments were never printed.

22. 31 U.S. (6 Pet.) 515, 563.

each other, and of the rest of the world, having institutions of their own, and governing themselves by their own laws,"[23] Marshall followed closely Justice Thompson's dissent in the first Cherokee appeal.[24]

To clarify his new position, the chief justice reinterpreted his use of the concept of "dependence" in characterizing the tribal-federal relationship. It was, he implied, a pretense, which tribes had tolerated out of ignorance of its legal implications:

> Not well acquainted with the exact meaning of the words, nor supposing it to be material whether they were called the subjects, or the children of their father in Europe; lavish in professions of duty and affection, in return for the rich presents they received; so long as their actual independence was untouched, and their right to self-government acknowledged, they were willing to profess dependence on the power which furnished supplies of which they were in absolute need, and restrained dangerous intruders from entering their country; and this was probably the sense in which the term was understood by them.[25]

The American experience had consisted of a balance of power between tribes and the United States (or the Crown)—a continuous process of negotiation, alliances, reconciliation and solicitude which had always respected tribal political integrity.[26] Tribes had never been conquered, but together with the Europeans, they had yielded and compromised in matters of mutual economic interest, exemplified by their agreeability to the doctrine of preemption of their lands. Notwithstanding preemption, Marshall noted, tribal lands were still "extra-territorial" with respect to the jurisdiction of the states surrounding them.[27]

The tribes had never voluntarily relinquished their internal political authority, nor could the Constitution, delegating to Congress power "To regulate Commerce . . . with the Indian Tribes," be construed to authorize federal intervention in their affairs. Even in the case of a tribe that had

23. *Id.* 542–43.
24. "[I]t is not perceived how it is possible to escape the conclusion that they form a sovereign State. They have always been dealt with as such by the government of the United States, both before and since the adoption of the present Constitution. They have been admitted and treated as a people governed solely and exclusively by their own laws, usages and customs within their own territory, claiming and exercising exclusive dominion over the same; yielding up by treaty, from time to time, portions of their land, but still claiming absolute sovereignty and self-government over what remained unsold" (Thompson's dissent in 30 U.S. [5 Pet.] 1, 53).
25. 31 U.S. (6 Pet.) 515, 546–47.
26. *Id.* 542–56.
27. *Id.* 542.

expressly consented by treaty that the United States have power of "regulating trade with the Indians, and of managing all their affairs,"

To construe the expression . . . into a surrender of self-government, would be, we think, a perversion of their necessary meaning, and a departure from the construction which has been uniformly put on them. The great subject of the article is the Indian trade. The influence it gave made it desirable that Congress should possess it. The commissioners brought forward the claim, with the profession that their motive was "the benefit and comfort of the Indians, and the prevention of injuries and oppressions." This may be true, as respects the regulation of their trade . . . but cannot be true as respects the regulation of all their affairs. The most important of these are the cession of their lands, and security against intruders on them. Is it credible that they should have considered themselves as surrendering to the United States the right to dictate their future cessions, and the terms on which they should be made? or to compel their submission to the violence of disorderly and licentious intruders? It is equally inconceivable that they could have supposed themselves, by a phrase slipped into an article on another and most interesting subject, to have devested themselves of the *right of self-government* on subjects not connected with trade. Such a measure could not be "for their benefit and comfort" or for "the prevention of injuries and oppression."[28]

The Court evidently rejected the notion, since become popular, that Indian treaties which generally recognize the supremacy of the United States or which delegate specific governmental powers to the United States, *imply* a delegation of *all* governing powers to the United States. The "right of self-government," consistent with the underlying political theory of the Constitution, can be alienated only by specific and express consent. This is a useful principle in dealing with the ambiguities of, for example, the 1825 series of western Indian treaties, which generally began, "It is admitted by the (   ) tribe of Indians, that they reside within the territorial limits of the United States, acknowledge their supremacy, and claim their protection."[29]

Worcester overruled the Court's characterization of tribes in *Cherokee Nation*, making it clear that tribes' relationship to the United States is governed by consent and the concept of dependency in international law, not by any wardship or subordination arising out of Indians' nature or condition. "The Constitution," Marshall explained, "by declaring treaties already made, as well as those to be made, to be the supreme law of the land, has adopted and sanctioned the previous treaties with the Indian

28. *Id.* 553–54.
29. These may be found in Charles Joseph Kappler, ed., 2 *Indian Affairs: Laws and Treaties* 225 ff. (Washington, D.C.: 1904).

nations, and consequently admits their rank among those powers who are capable of making treaties."[30] The treaty relationship "was that of a nation claiming and receiving the protection of one more powerful, not that of individuals abandoning their national character, and submitting as subjects to the laws of a master."[31] The tribes were no different than many small nations of Europe. "A weak State in order to provide for its safety, may place itself under the protection of one more powerful without stripping itself of the right of government, and ceasing to be a State."[32]

Marshall would allow no trace of the ownership/sovereignty confusion in *Fletcher* and *M'Intosh* to survive. To be sure, he wrote in *Worcester*, discovery allocated the "exclusive right to purchase, but did not found that right on a denial of the right of the possessor to sell."[33] Crown charters and other European grants were mere "blank paper, so far as the rights of the natives were concerned."[34] In the absence of tribal consent by treaty, discovery could have no effect whatever on tribes' internal affairs.

By this reasoning tribes are not within the scope of the federal-state compact, but relate to the United States through separate compacts authorized and enforced under the Treaty Clause: treaty federalism, as opposed to constitutional federalism. Beyond specific grants of tribal jurisdiction by treaty, Congress is limited to the regulation of "commerce," a power no greater in regard to Indian tribes than foreign nations.[35] All redefinition of tribes' political relationship to the United States must follow the same course—mutual agreement.[36]

30. 31 U.S. (6 Pet.) 559.
31. *Id*. 555.
32. *Id*. 561.
33. *Id*. 544.
34. *Id*. 546.
35. This receives support from Joseph Story's *Commentaries on the Constitution of the United States* §1065 (5th ed. Boston: 1891); where it is asserted that the word "commerce" in Article I, Section 8 "must carry the same meaning throughout the sentence." Compare the Articles of Confederation, Article IX, Section 4, granting Congress power to "manage the affairs" of tribes provided the "legislative right if any state within its own limits be not infringed or violated." The articles recognized the fact that several colonies had acquired a limited jurisdiction over individual tribes by treaty, e.g., the Articles of Peace with the Susquehannah (3 *Archives of Maryland* 277−78 [1885−], and Articles with the Trasquakins etc. (*id*. 363−64). As far as we can determine, only one tribe ever agreed by treaty to become *completely* subject to the British Crown: the Narragansetts. See their treaty of 1644 in John Russell Bartlett, ed., 1 *Records of the Colony of Rhode Island and Providence Plantations, in New England* 134−36 (Providence, R.I.: 1856−1865); for its strict enforcement by the Crown, see *id*. 36−38, 138−40.
36. Madison confided in Wirt shortly before the case that he feared this theory might arise (Kennedy, 2 *Memoirs* 260). Where, in all of this, is the theory of "conquest" so often attributed to Marshall by modern commentators, and popularized by Felix Cohen in his

In his seventy-seventh year, Marshall had conceived a whole new dimension of federalism and of the American national political system. Justice Story wrote his wife, "It was a very able opinion, in his best manner. Thanks be to God, the Court can wash their hands clean of the iniquity of oppressing the Indians and disregarding their rights."[37] "The Court has done its duty," Story explained to a friend five days after the decision, "Let the nation do theirs. If we have a government let its command be obeyed; if we have not it is well to know it at once, & look to consequences." These were prophetic words. The Court's decision invalidating all execution of Georgia laws in Cherokee territory as repugnant to federal laws, treaties, and the Constitution, was never enforced.[38]

Charles Grover Haines has commented that John Marshall was "adept" at concealing his politics behind a camouflage of legal reasoning, hamstringing the opposition with a display of apparently strict construction of the law.[39] *Worcester* was Marshall's masterpiece. A federalist, he could not have failed to realize that recognition of tribal sovereignty might ultimately detract from federal supremacy and complexify the federal system. On the other hand, the states' seizure of tribal territory was an immediate and open flaunting of federal authority, so far as it had been committed by treaty to safeguard tribal property. He was caught on the horns of a political dilemma. In *Cherokee Nation* he sought to avoid the problem altogether by refusing jurisdiction, a technicality, and scrupulously refusing to comment on the merits. But the presence of the tribes proved to be a persistent, rather than transitory, phenomenon. On second

---

Handbook of Federal Indian Law (Washington, D.C.: 1942), chapters 9 and 21? *Worcester* passes the idea of conquest off as a politically convenient fiction, carefully pointing out that the United States was just as anxious as the tribes to secure peace on the frontier (31 U.S. [6 Pet.] 551). Even granting that there were many Indian wars, the Court has never seen fit to investigate their cause, legality or resolution in a particular case. That the fiction of conquest is a part of the law of tribal status is itself an historical fiction. But the conquest fiction served the purpose of defending American territorial claims to Europeans who knew no better and were constantly bombarded with American dime-novel literature depicting an unending battle for survival against savage interlopers.

37. William Wetmore Story, 2 *Life and Letters of Joseph Story* 87 (Boston: 1851). In fact, Marshall was so anxious to get the opinion out he inadvertently omitted one of the most important jurisdictional points in the form of the appeal: "in the hurry with which the argument was finished it slipped my memory" (letter of Marshall to Supreme Court reporter Richard Peters, 23 March 1832).

38. Wirt never moved the Court to issue Georgia a show-cause order why the officers of that state should not be held in contempt for continuing to exercise power over Cherokee territory (Burke, "The Cherokee Cases," 525, 530). In this way the Court escaped a direct state challenge to its authority.

39. Charles Grover Haines, *The Role of the Supreme Court in American Government and Politics 1789--1835* 622 (Berkeley, Calif.: 1960).

impression he therefore abandoned the technicalities, exceptions, and confusions that had served him well from *Fletcher* to *Cherokee Nation*, and persuaded his fellow justices to join him in a search for fundamental principles consistent with the Constitution and American political theory. In this way he probably hoped to fashion a clear and ideologically acceptable modus vivendi for the tribes, states, and the Union, clearing away the thicket of piecemeal rules he had previously planted.[40]

The thicket, however, survived and grew into a forest. Marshall's unfortunate references to "dependency" and "wardship" were frequently repeated by later Courts, in defiance of the superseding precedent of *Worcester*. Mr. Justice Black observed in *Williams v. Lee* a generation ago that although "the broad principles of that decision came to be accepted as law," there have been departures "where essential tribal relations were not involved."[41] The very statement of events in that manner indicates how far we really have come from *Worcester*. The proper question is not whether an exercise of tribal power is "essential" but whether it is inconsistent with a lawful exercise of Congress's *limited and delegated* powers. The burden, according to *Worcester*, is not on the tribe to show that its activities are "essential," but on the United States to show that the tribe has delegated the power.

For the nearly forty years following *Worcester*, the United States recognized the exclusive domestic sovereignty of tribes in fact, subject only to their delegation of (commerce) powers to the United States by specific consent. The only major Indian legislation during this period regulated traders on tribal lands.[42] Even when Congress in 1836 directed the forcible removal of tribes from the boundaries of the southeastern states, no suggestion was made that the physical power to remove implied a legal power to deny them self-government within or beyond the frontier.[43]

40. The thicket came to include discovery, conquest, historical custom, treaties, wardship, dependency (now "trusteeship"), and ownership or title.

41. 358 U.S. 217, 220 (1958).

42. Chiefly the Indian Intercourse Acts, for which Francis Paul Prucha, *American Indian Policy in the Formative Years* (Cambridge, Mass.: 1962) is an excellent reference. See also Story, *Commentaries* §1099, and Chancellor Kent's discussion in Peters, *Case of the Cherokee Nation*.

43. If anything, the Indians were told that removal far from the states would enhance their ability to govern themselves without interference. See, for example, negotiations with the Cherokees in 1823 (1 *American State Papers, Indian Affairs* 467–77; House Report No. 474, 23rd Congress, 1st Session 14 ff. [1834]). William Wirt and James Madison concurred in this theory (Kennedy, 2 *Memoirs* 260–61).

6

The Emergence of Federal Intervention and the Citizenship Dilemma, 1871-1886

[S]o far as the law is concerned, complete anarchy exists in Indian Affairs.[1]

Beginning in 1871, Congress embarked on a sequence of new policies that marked the end of meaningful tribal self-government. Tribes were defined out of the Treaty Power (1871);[2] prohibited from making contracts without the consent of the secretary of the interior (1871);[3] forced to submit to a federally organized Indian police force (1875);[4] made subject to a code of oppressive rules drafted and executed by the Bureau of Indian Affairs, which sought to regulate their family, religious and economic affairs (1882);[5] and, finally, tribal territories were subdivided without regard for tribal law (1887).[6] The Supreme Court sustained these innovations by introducing some innovations of its own. Indians were held not able to become citizens, notwithstanding the unambiguous language of the Fourteenth Amendment (1884),[7] and they were subjected to the "plenary

1. Former Commissioner of Indian Affairs Francis A. Walker in "The Indian Question," 116 *North American Review* 335 (1873).
2. Act of 3 March 1871, c. 120, §1, 16 Stat. 566; 25 U.S.C. 71.
3. Act of 3 March 1871, c. 120 §3, 16 Stat. 570; 25 U.S.C. 81 as amended. For legislative history see 43 *Congressional Globe* 789 (27 January 1871), and 43 *Congressional Globe* 1483 ff. (22 February 1871).
4. William T. Hagan, *Indian Police and Judges* (New Haven: 1966); R. L. Barsh and J. Y. Henderson, "Tribal Courts, the Model Code, and the Police Idea in American Indian Policy," 40 *Law and Contemporary Problems* 25 (1976).
5. Francis Paul Prucha, ed., *Americanizing the American Indian* 296−305 (Cambridge, Mass.: 1973).
6. D. S. Otis, *The Dawes Act and the Allotment of Indian Lands* (Norman, Okla.: 1972).
7. *Elk v. Wilkins*, 112 U.S. 94.

power'' of Congress in their domestic affairs, without protection of the Bill of Rights (1886).[8] The first of these doctrines was overcome in principle by a 1924 statute.[9] The second, however, has survived, legitimizing increasingly interventionist policies, and demeaning Indian citizenship.[10]

President Grant's Peace (or "Quaker") Policy was enthusiastically supported by the Bureau of Indian Affairs, which called repeatedly for the coercive disruption of tribal governments, allotment in severalty of Indian lands, and subjection of Indians to Anglo-American legal rules of a temporary and "educationally" transitional nature.[11] One commissioner's report stated the objective quite succinctly: reservations were to become "penal" institutions, in which Indians would be carefully rewarded for "civilized" behavior and swiftly punished for traditional activities.[12] Congress was advised that the tribes, left to their own devices by a consistent line of executive policy since *Worcester*, had not progressed quickly enough. Pressure was necessary to accelerate their supposed climb to civilization, and it would have to be exerted directly upon individual Indians wherever they were found. Until the matter reached the Supreme Court eighteen years later, Congress and the bureau proceeded on this course without legal precedent or authority.

Three principal arguments were commonly advanced in support of allotment: it would accelerate economic development,[13] reduce federal welfare

8. *U.S. v. Kagama*, 118 U.S. 375.

9. Act of 2 June 1924; 43 Stat. 253.

10. "Plenary power" is approvingly referred to recently in *McClanahan v. Arizona Tax Commission*, 411 U.S. 164, 172 (1973); *Norvell v. Sangre de Cristo Development Corp.*, 519 F.2d 370 (C.A. N.M. 1975); *Groundhog v. Keeler*, 442 F.2d 674, 678 (C.A. Ok. 1971); *Maryland Gas Co. v. Citizens Nat. Bank*, 361 F.2d 517, 520 (C.A. Fla. 1966) *cert. den'd* 385 U.S. 918; *U.S. v. Blackfeet Tribe*, 364 F.Supp. 192, 194 (D.C. Mt. 1973), *reconsidered* 369 F.Supp. 562, 563−64.

11. See, for example, the *Report of the Commissioner of Indian Affairs, 1872* 11; *1873* 4−5; *1874* 15−16; *1876* ix−x; *1877* 2−3. Even the first Indian commissioner of Indian affairs, Eli S. Parker, remarked of tribal sovereignty, "It is time that this idea should be dispelled and the government cease the cruel farce of thus dealing with its helpless and ignorant wards."

12. *Report of the Commissioner of Indian Affairs, 1872* 11.

13. Otis, *Dawes Act* 9; Prucha, *American Indian* 94−95, 115−16. "Let him feel his individuality and responsibility, and a sense of proprietorship," advised the *Report of the Commissioner of Indian Affairs, 1882* xlii−xliv, "Encourage him to work and earn a living and provide for the future . . . and abandon his shiftless, do-nothing, dependent life." The commissioner conceived that "[t]hese principles apply as well to the Indian as to the white man." However, the argument from economic growth was not always made with a view toward enriching the Indians; the prosperity of whites was also an issue (*Report of the Commissioner of Indian Affairs, 1883* 80; Otis, *Dawes Act* 17−18, 20−32, especially regarding railroad expansion through Indian lands).

expenditures,[14] and the Indians wanted it.[15] Psychological, cultural and political benefits were also anticipated. A system of private ownership was expected "to break up tribal relations . . . [t]hat cohesion, which is bred . . . of a common history, a common purpose, and a common interest, and unites the Indians in a common destiny," and to prepare Indians for assimilation into the political cultures of the states.[16] It would also free "that spirit of rivalry and desire to accumulate property for personal use or comfort which is the source of success and advancement in all white communities."[17]

Many advocates were genuinely appalled by reservation poverty and anxious to help,[18] but their solution belied a fundamental misconception of the problem. When he tried to summarize Indians' reasons for supporting allotment, Commissioner of Indian Affairs Hiram Price explained that the law would assure "a perfect and secure title that will protect him against the rapacity of the white man."[19] What the Indian needed, the federal administration agreed, was "clear and legal standing . . . in the courts of law."[20] If the problem, then, was Indians' inability to protect their land-holdings against individual whites, what was the source of this? Surely the tribes had, or could readily devise, land tenure systems of their own. Would it not be a complete remedy for state and federal courts to recognize and enforce these tribal tenures against non-Indians?

Everyone's failure to see the obvious[21] was a product of cupidity and doctrine. As a matter of policy, the United States was unprepared to tackle Indians' land problems by any means that recognized tribal sovereignty. Federal spokesmen actually attributed Indian land problems *to* tribal sovereignty, arguing, erroneously, that all tribal societies are inescapably

14. Prucha, *American Indian* 80, 85, 89, 95, 101−2. Senator Dawes himself was very fond of this theme. See also Otis, *Dawes Act* 16−17.

15. Prucha, *American Indian* 89−93; Otis, *Dawes Act* 5, 40−46.

16. Prucha, *American Indian* 81, 89, 93, 105. Allotment would "break down chiefdom" (*Report of the Commissioner of Indian Affairs, 1882* 94). Also Otis, *Dawes Act* 9, 15, 45, 48, 55.

17. Prucha, *American Indian* 80, 89, 93, 101−2, 111−12. Senator Dawes referred to this as "making a man of the Indian" (*id.* 102). He, for one, assumed that Christianization would be a part of the process (*id.* 108). See, too, *Report of the Commissioner of Indian Affairs, 1882* xlii−xliv, 94; *Report of the Commissioner of Indian Affairs, 1883* 8−9; Otis, *Dawes Act* 5.

18. Otis, *Dawes Act* 8.

19. Prucha, *American Indian* 93; *Report of the Commissioner of Indian Affairs, 1882* 28−29; *Report of the Commissioner of Indian Affairs, 1883* 31−33; Otis, *Dawes Act* 42.

20. Prucha, *American Indian* 85; also 80, 84, 88−89.

21. The minority report to the 1880 bill did, to its credit, voice faith in the "tribal system" as a means to foster progress (*id.* 129).

"communistic."[22] A private property scheme could only arise therefore by the intervention of civilized, non-Indian government. They were supported in these allegations by some of the careless language in Marshall's opinions: they misread *M'Intosh* as a finding that tribes simply had no land tenure laws, and embraced its dictum that federal courts could not enforce tribal land tenure laws that were inconsistent with federal laws. We suspect the newly formed Bureau of American Ethnology could have readily exposed the fallacy of assumptions about the absence of tribal tenure,[23] and Congress was, of course, entirely free to authorize and require federal courts to recognize tribal land law. It is plain that no one even considered these possibilities seriously. Indeed, the Bureau of Indian Affairs made the astonishing argument that allotment would protect Indian lands from confiscation *by the United States itself*.[24] If Congress was guilty of lusting

22. Otis, *Dawes Act* 10–11. Characteristically these arguments drew on examples from the Plains tribes, who had in fact been hunters aboriginally, and conveniently ignored all of the sedentary, agricultural tribes (Prucha, *American Indian* 89–90, 126; *Report of the Commissioner of Indian Affairs, 1882* 86; *Report of the Commissioner of Indian Affairs, 1883* 51). Everywhere derogatory references to the "reservation system" are used as if it were synonymous with tribal government. Prucha, *American Indian* 109, 120. The "reservation system" was actually under federal control, and its failures were the failures of the United States. See, for example, the *Report* for 1882 at 166, to the effect that the Makah are rich in developable timber but the Bureau of Indian Affairs won't let them cut it. When tribes did develop their lands, the bureau used this as an excuse to terminate its assistance, as noted in the 1883 *Report* at 62. In any case, Senator Dawes apparently cared little whether a particular tribe was economically successful or not:

The head chief [of the Five Civilized Tribes] told us that there was not a family in that whole nation that had not a home of its own. There was not a pauper in that nation, and the nation did not owe a dollar. It built its own capital . . . and built its own schools and hospitals. Yet the defect of the system was apparent. They have got as far as they can go, because they own their land in common. . . . There is no selfishness, which is at the bottom of civilization (Otis, *Dawes Act* 10).

That Dawes did not think his remarks self-contradictory is a tribute to nineteenth-century American market morality. The irritating thing is that the Five Civilized Tribes actually had a very highly developed system of private land ownership, including a homestead policy and a constitutional prohibition against uncompensated governmental takings patterned on the Fifth Amendment (*The Constitution and Laws of the Cherokee Nation* [New Echota: 1840], especially Articles I and VI, sec. 6 of the Act of Union; *The Laws of the Cherokee Nation* [1852]). Dawes could not have been ignorant of these published laws; he disregarded them.

23. Indeed, the evidence was available in the Bureau of Indian Affairs' own official reports (Otis, *Dawes Act* 44–45).

24. Prucha, *American Indian* 80, Allotment "substitutes a personal title evidenced by a patent protected by law for a tribal right of occupancy during the good pleasure of Congress" (*id.* 114–15). See also Otis, *Dawes Act* 13–14; *Report of the Commissioner of Indian Affairs, 1882* 102; *Report of the Commissioner of Indian Affairs, 1883* 70. Fifty years later, when the economic failure of allotment was undeniable, supporters were still defending it as the only way Indians could have "individual rights which would be protected by law and which could not be taken from them by legislation or influences without their consent" ("Hearings, 'To Grant Indians Living Under Federal Tutelage the Freedom to Organize for Purposes of Local

for tribal land, why should it be any more willing to respect allotments than to respect the tribes' exterior boundaries? Would it not have been easier, if Congress were remorseful over its past conduct, simply to stop pressuring tribes for cessions?

Backers of the General Allotment Act made much of the fact that it declared allotted Indians subject to the laws of the state or territory in which they resided.[25] They assumed that this granted Indians national and state citizenship and eliminated the need for the Bureau of Indian Affairs.[26] As it happened, allotment was an economic failure and, while it succeeded in destroying many tribes, it had little effect on citizenship or on the bureau.

Even before the law was passed, critics predicted that Indians would suffer from shortages of capital and skills.[27] Allotment required Indians to acquire capital and assume financial liabilities too quickly.[28] At the same time it encumbered their land and proceeds with burdensome administrative restrictions placing them at a competitive disadvantage.[29] The whole scheme was "experimental" and "theoretical" taken in the most charitable light; more cynically it could be seen to have as its "real aim . . . to get at the Indian lands and open them up to settlement."[30] The bureau—which ironically would be levelling these same criticisms itself in a little less than fifty years[31]—evidently survived the law unharmed on the excuse

Self-Government and Economic Enterprise,' " 133, Senate Committee on Indian Affairs, 73rd Congress, 2nd Session [1934]). Tribes proposed that they make their own provisions for private property, their own land tenure law (Otis, *Dawes Act* 43). Many that were not allotted, did.

25. Prucha, *American Indian* 102, 105, 112. See the text of the act, 25 U.S.C. 348–49, as amended.

26. Prucha, *American Indian* 101–2, 104–6.

27. House minority report, 1880 (*id.* 125); statement of the Indian Rights Association, 1889 (*id.* 116–17).

28. Prucha, *American Indian* 126–27.

29. *Id.* 127.

30. *Id.* 128; Otis, *Dawes Act* 18–19. Even the sale of surplus land was rationalized by advocates of allotment, who argued that it brought the allottees into closer proximity with the "civilizing influence" of white people (*Report of the Commissioner of Indian Affairs, 1883* 52, 54).

31. See especially Commissioner John Collier's memorandum to both Houses of Congress reproduced in "Hearings, 'To Grant Indians . . . Freedom to Organize,' " 16–30, and "Hearings, 'Readjustment of Indian Affairs,' " 15–29, House Committee on Indian Affairs, 73rd Congress, 2nd Session (1934). House Committee Chairman Howard succinctly described the theory of allotment in these words: "The mere issuance of a fee patent would give to the Indians pride of ownership, thrift, industry, and the means of self-support; it would break down the tribal status of the Indians and convert them into typical American citizens; it would,

of managing residual tribal property and restrictions on allotments.[32] This led "friends of the Indian" to demand that Congress liquidate forthwith all tribal assets, as if the only function of tribal property had been to justify the bureau's existence.

And what of citizenship? Let us look back for a moment to 1868, eighteen years before passage of the General Allotment Act. Congress and the courts faced a double constitutional dilemma. The newly ratified Fourteenth Amendment declared that "All persons born or naturalized in the United States, and subject to the jurisdiction thereof, are citizens of the United States and of the State wherein they reside."[33] Indians were unquestionably born within the boundaries of the United States, and regulation of their domestic affairs would seem to qualify as evidence of their subjection to federal authority. If they were citizens, however, they would be entitled to vote and seek the protection of all the limiting clauses of the Constitution and Bill of Rights.

On the other hand, if Indians were not citizens, they would have to be aliens subject only to the Treaty Power. As long as they could be governed solely by the authority of specific treaties, however, the pressure that could be brought to bear upon them to "civilize" would be minimal, since treaties are only made by mutual consent. Congress would have to rely upon the president's ability to persuade tribes to agree to the introduction of "civilizing" institutions. In the past, persuasion had usually involved money, and the cost of making new treaties was beginning to alarm Congress.[34]

The House in 1871 was predominantly Republican, the party of the Peace Policy. Impatient with the treaty process and frustrated by their lack of participation in it, House Republicans instigated a dramatic shift of

---

they said, solve the Indian problem, and in the course of a single generation relieve the Government of the immense and costly burden of caring for its Indian wards" (78 *Congressional Record* 11727 [June 15, 1934]).

32. Prucha, *American Indian* 119, 120–21.

33. Section 2.

34. Subsidies were almost always distributed in goods, at the insistence of the United States. This made it possible for corrupt federal procurement practices to severely affect the quantity and quality of goods reaching the tribes. Indian bureau corruption was a central issue in the Indian appropriations fight in 1871 (43 *Congressional Globe* 730ff [25 January 1871]; *id.* 768ff [26 January 1871]; *id.* 1112 [10 February 1871]; *id.* 1493 [22 February 1871]) and it became evident in the course of the 1875 Belknap impeachment hearings (4 *Congressional Record* Part 7 [1876]) that most of the annuity funds had been absorbed by the federal distributive bureaucracy. As the bureau and the War Department skimmed off more and more of the subsidy, the tribes were forced to demand more payments.

power over Indian affairs. Armstrong of Pennsylvania drafted, and Sargent of California cosponsored, a House compromise amendment to the 1871 Indian treaty appropriations bill.[35] In return for House approval of the next year's treaty appropriations, and withdrawal of a threatened House amendment that would have nullified most of the important treaties with the tribes of the High Plains, the Senate reluctantly agreed to repudiate the power of the president to treat with tribes.[36]

Supporters of the compromise amendment insisted that Congress was merely *defining*, legislatively, what were the "Foreign Nations" referred to in Article II of the Constitution, rather than taking constitutional power away from the president.[37] The Democratic minority was strenuously opposed, but in vain. When Senator Davis of Kentucky tried to debate the legitimacy of Congress's supplanting the Supreme Court's interpretive functions,[38] his Democratic colleague Senator Saulsbury observed sarcastically, that "[s]omehow or other, my honorable and distinguished friend still believes that there is such a thing as the Constitution of the United States . . . While this [the Republican] party continues in power . . . it has no authority whatever."[39]

The most serious consequence of the compromise amendment was

35. 43 *Congressional Globe* 1810–1812, 1821–1825 (1 March 1871).

36. Act of 3 March 1871, c. 120, §1, 16 Stat. 566; 25 U.S.C. 71. The language and legislative history of the act make it clear that the obligations assumed by previous treaties are not to be impaired. Wilson of Minnesota, for example, maintained "[t]hat an Indian treaty stands just as a foreign treaty does; that we are just as much bound to pay sums of money provided to be paid in a treaty with Red Cloud or Spotted Tail, as we are to pay the Czar of Russia the purchase money for Alaska. It is a contract in either case made by departments of our Government recognized as competent by the Constitution and the decisions of our courts thereupon. If there is anything wrong in this it is in *our* system" (43 *Congressional Globe* 766 [26 January 1871]) (emphasis is ours). See also the exchange between McCormick and Eldridge in the House on 28 January 1871 (43 *Congressional Globe* App. 307) and the discussion of tribal sovereignty (*id*. 763 [26 January 1871]). The act was passed within a year after the Supreme Court held in *The Cherokee Tobacco* (78 U.S. 616 [1870]), that a subsequent act of Congress may control a prior Indian treaty. However, consistent with its saving of prior treaties in the act, Congress later compensated the Cherokees for the losses they sustained as a result of the Supreme Court's decision (act of 14 May 1874, 18 Stat. 549, c. 173).

37. See the debate in the Senate on 1 March 1871 in 43 *Congressional Globe* (1821–1825). No one suggested that a constitutional amendment might be necessary. Nor did anyone suggest at the time that it was improper to take such action as an amendment to an appropriation bill without separate hearings, although that issue came up in 1885 when the Major Crimes Act (23 Stat. 385 §9) was tacked on to Indian appropriations (16 *Congressional Record* 2385 [2 March 1885]). This technique of moving interventionist legislation suggests the extent to which Congress acted out of budgetary considerations.

38. 16 *Congressional Record* 1821–22. See also Wilson's remarks, *id*. 767 (26 January 1871).

39. *Id*. 1823.

never openly addressed. Treaties, like contracts, are unenforceable except against those agreeing specifically and expressly to be bound by them. Legislation, however, is presumed to be legitimate when enacted, and enforceable against all persons within the power of the legislature. Consent is neither specific nor express, but general and implied in the right to vote. Tribal Indians in 1871 could not vote. Thus what appeared to be a transfer of responsibility between branches of the federal government, was in actuality an assertion or arrogation of the power to govern tribes without their consent.[40]

Congress's arrogation of domestic powers over Indians threw it back on the other horn of its constitutional dilemma. As Representative Sargent argued on the floor, the amendment presupposed that Indians are "our own subjects, on our own soil, and completely subject to our control."[41] His description placed Indians squarely within the Fourteenth Amendment's classification of persons who are automatically citizens of the United States without naturalization. Congress did not hesitate, however, to coercively deprive tribal members of their political and religious liberties in the twenty years that followed.

The Supreme Court resolved any lingering constitutional doubts by ruling in *Elk v. Wilkins* that a member of an Indian tribe, although born within the United States, was not "subject to the jurisdiction thereof."[42] In view of the facts on public record at the time, either the Court gravely erred, or meant something other than what it said. United States Indian police and courts of Indian offenses were already in operation on most reservations, and Indian agents had been boasting for several years about their forcible suppression of tribal governments and religions. Only the Five Civilized Tribes in Oklahoma and the New York Iroquois were still permitted to retain the form and authority of local self-government.[43]

40. Armstrong himself observed that Congress *could* have limited itself to legislating for tribes on a case-by-case basis, relying in each case upon specific "contractual" arrangements with the tribes. He did not suggest that this kind of procedure was required by the Constitution (43 *Congressional Globe* 1812 [1 March 1871]). In fact, the practice of making "executive agreements" and enacting special legislation for individual tribes now coexists with the general Indian affairs legislation, as a review of 25 U.S.C. and any recent Congress's legislative output will demonstrate.

41. 43 *Congressional Globe* 1811 (1 March 1871).

42. 112 U.S. 94 (1884).

43. On the scope of the police system; see the *Report of the Commissioner of Indian Affairs, 1881* xvii–xviii; *1882* xlii–xlv. On self-regulating tribes, see *Report of the Commissioner of Indian Affairs, 1882* 133–34; *1883* 87–88.

Nothing could have been further from the truth in 1884 than to say that tribal Indians were not subject to federal control.

In fact, Mr. Justice Gray, for the majority, analogized Indians to visiting diplomats, observing that a person *only partially* subject to federal jurisdiction is not automatically a citizen.[44] This implies that Indians in 1884 were as a practical matter also *partly* subject and *partly* immune to United States law. He failed, however, to distinguish between diplomatic status, which is consensual, and Indian status, which Congress imposed on Indians without their consent.

The Court was also careful in its discussion of *Elk* to paraphrase the Fourteenth Amendment, a further indication that it understood the facts quite well. Tribal Indians, the Court said, *owed no allegiance* to the United States. We assume this means that tribal Indians had not yet *voluntarily acceded* to the dismemberment of their governments and the intervention of bureau employees in their domestic affairs. It is true that many Indian leaders continued to resist the bureau. This should have been immaterial. The Fourteenth Amendment only requires that citizens be *subject*, not that they like it.[45]

The Court's decision seems even more irresponsible when it is realized that John Elk was a fully Anglicized farmer living on his own land, and was evidently serious enough about his allegiance to demand his right to vote all the way to the Supreme Court. The Court recognized Elk's special circumstances, but took the position that *only Congress* can decide when an individual Indian is Anglicized *enough* to merit citizenship.[46] In so doing, it vindicated Congress's prior assumption of a power to interpret the Constitution more completely and finally, in matters involving Indians, than would otherwise be consistent with the theory of separation of powers.[47] Moreover, although this proposition took on the appearance of a general rule of justiciability, it was really nothing more than judicial

44. 112 U.S. 94, 110–11, 113–14, 116–17.

45. If criticizing or testing possible abuses of government power were grounds for a denial of citizenship, the First Amendment and judicial review would both be rendered meaningless.

46. This theory was presaged by Judge Deady's remark in *U.S. v. Osborne*, (6 Sawyer 406, 409 [1880]) that "the fact that [an Indian] has abandoned his nomadic life or tribal relations, and adopted the habits and manners of civilized people, may be good reason why he should be made a citizen but does not itself make him one."

47. The Armstrong amendment was never directly challenged as repugnant to the doctrine of separation of powers.

acquiescence in the political reality that Congress was legislatively governing the tribes yet withholding from them the rights of citizens.

Elk was an ideological anachronism, reviving a theory of *subjectship*, as opposed to voluntary allegiance, belonging more properly to monarchical English than American law. As propounded by Sir Edward Coke in *Calvin's Case*,[48] subjectship involved a personal relationship of king and subject, arising out of nature itself, and analogous to the natural bonds between a parent and child. Once born into subjection, or compelled to it, the subject owed a lasting obedience to his king. On the contrary, the Revolution produced a theory of citizenship based upon consent, the founders of the new nation finding it abhorrent that individuals be forced against their wills to submit to political societies of which they did not approve.[49]

In their dissent to *Cherokee Nation*, Justices Thompson and Story had concluded after an examination of their treaties that the Cherokees could not be citizens of the United States, and therefore "must be aliens or foreigners,"[50] citing with approval Chancellor Kent's observation in *Jackson v. Goodell* that "[t]he Indians, though born within our territorial limits, are considered as born under the dominion of their own tribes."[51] This view of the matter was apparently adopted by the majority of the Court in *Worcester*, which denied that individual Indians, by entering into a treaty with the United States, were "abandoning their national charter and submitting as subjects to the laws of a master."[52]

In 1856 Chief Justice Taney contrasted the status of blacks and Indians, concluding in dictum that "if an individual [Indian] should leave his nation or tribe, and take up his abode among the white population, he would be entitled to all the rights and privileges which would belong to an emigrant

48. 77 Eng. Rep. 377 (1608).
49. James H. Kettner, "The Development of American Citizenship in the Revolutionary Area: The Ideal of Volitional Allegiance," 18 *American Journal of Legal History* 208 (1974).
50. 30 U.S. (5 Pet.) 1, 66–67.
51. 20 Johns. 693, 712 (N.Y. 1823), reversing 20 Johns. 188, 193 (1822), and subsequently followed in *Lee v. Glover*, 8 Lowen 189 (N.Y. 1828), *Murray v. Wooden*, 17 Wend. 531 (N.Y. 1837), and *Cornet v. Winton*, 2 Yerg. 143 (Tenn. 1826).
52. 31 U.S. (6 Pet.) 515, 555. In his concurrence, McLean observed that "[n]o one has ever supposed that Indians could commit treason against the United States" (*id.* 583), although he supposed that tribes could be punished under international law for treaty violations. Even in *Cherokee Nation*, Marshall referred to the Cherokees as "a foreign State, not owing allegiance to the United States, nor to any state of the Union, nor to any prince, potentate or state, other than their own" (30 U.S. [5 Pet.] 1,3).

from any other foreign people."[53] Consistent with *Worcester*, the Taney Court continued to maintain the right of Indians to freely choose between tribal and United States allegiance.[54]

While the Fourteenth Amendment was intended principally to remedy the condition of blacks, its language was broad enough to encompass Indians as well. In 1870 the Senate directed its Judiciary Committee "to inquire into and report to the Senate the effect of the fourteenth amendment to the Constitution upon Indian tribes of the country." The committee responded that the amendment "has no effect whatever upon the status of Indian tribes . . . and does not annul the treaties previously made between them and the United States,"[55] reasoning that tribes "have never been subject to the jurisdiction of the United States" in the first place.[56] The report moreover agreed with *Worcester* that the "supremacy" of the United States had had little effect on the tribes except for preemption.[57] In other words, it was the committee's opinion that the amendment could not make Indians citizens *without their consent*.[58]

Thus on the very eve of the Armstrong amendment, both the Senate and the Supreme Court were agreed in principle that Indians' political allegiance was a matter for Indian choice. Although the reason uniformly given for this was that tribes had *not consented* to be assimilated, it had been common to state the rule as one that tribal Indians were "not subject" to federal or state jurisdiction, i.e., not *lawfully* subject to such jurisdiction

53. *Scott v. Sanford*, 112 U.S. (19 How.) 393, 404 (1856). Taney noted elsewhere in his opinion that because of "their untutored and savage state" in 1789, "no one supposed then that any Indians would ask for" citizenship (*id*. 420). This is contradicted by history (Annie Heloise Abel, "Proposals for an Indian State, 1778–1878," *Annual Report of the American Historical Association, 1907* 89).

54. An interesting corollary, if not premonition, of *Elk* was the rule that an American citizen remained subject to federal prosecution even after entering tribal territory (*U.S. v. Rogers*, 4 How. 567 [1846]; *U.S. v. Ragsdale*, 27 Fed. Cas. 684 [U.S.C.C. Ark. 1847]; 2 Op. Atty. Gen. 405 [1930]). This may have been as much directed at fugitive black slaves, who were welcomed by some western tribes, as at fugitive felons.

55. Senate Report No. 268, "Effect of the Fourteenth Amendment upon Indian Tribes," 1, 41st Congress, 3rd Session (1870). However, Justice Harlan in the *Civil Rights Cases* (109 U.S. 3 [1883]), said of the terms of the *Thirteenth* Amendment, "They embrace every race which then was or might thereafter be, within the United States. No race, as such, can be excluded from the benefits or rights thereby conferred" (109 U.S. 33). The majority in that case agreed that the Thirteenth Amendment has the effect of "establishing and decreeing universal civil and political freedom throughout the United States" (109 U.S. 20). Why was this never applied to the Indian context?

56. *Id*. 9–10. See *McKay v. Campbell*, 16 Fed. Cas. 161, 165–66 (D.C.D. Ore. 1871).

57. Senate Report 268, "Effect of the Fourteenth Amendment," 2.

58. Significantly, the report took the position that the Fourteenth Amendment could not annul treaties *because tribes had not ratified it*.

without their consent. The *Elk* Court vindicated the Armstrong amendment by reading this formulation of the rule as a statement of *fact* rather than of *right*. At the same time, *Elk* suggested that even if the *fact* of subjection could be proved, the *right* depended upon the pleasure of Congress. By subtly changing the context of "subjection," the Court succeeded in completely reversing the course of Indian law without appearing to break with precedent.

The dramatic nature of this reversal can best be seen in the case of Pueblo citizenship. Before *Elk*, the Court was inclined to use a two-pronged test of Indian citizenship: consent and capacity. This was analogous to the naturalization of other aliens by examination and oath of allegiance. The Treaty of Guadalupe Hidalgo, which ceded Mexico's northern states to the United States, included a stipulation that United States citizenship be extended to all Mexican citizens in the ceded area. The Pueblos had been Mexican citizens for more than a generation. In *U.S. v. Joseph*, decided eight years before *Elk*, the Court unanimously held that members of this tribe had the same right to sell their private lands to other individuals as citizens of New Mexico.[59] The *ratio* of the case was the treaty, an *act of consent* by the Pueblos as Mexicans, but the Court also found supportive evidence in their "civilized" character, comparing them to the Shakers and Amish who, although "communistic" in political organization, are completely competent to govern themselves and choose to do so.

Mr. Justice Miller reserved the question, not raised by the appeal, whether the Pueblos had a right to enjoy *all* of the benefits of citizenship. He observed, however, "we have no hesitation in saying that their status is not . . . to be determined solely by the circumstance that some officer of the Government has appointed for them an agent," or classified them as a subject people. *Joseph* had been brought by the United States to protect its preemptive interest in Indian lands. The Supreme Court held in effect that it alone would remain the final arbiter of Indians' political rights under the Constitution, not Congress.

After *Elk*, the United States brought another appeal, stemming from the attempted enforcement of special federal Indian regulations in Pueblo territory.[60] This time, the Court upheld the jurisdiction of the United States. Relying almost wholly on Bureau of Indian Affairs sources, Mr. Justice

59. 94 U.S. 614 (1876).
60. *U.S. v. Sandoval*, 231 U.S. 28 (1913).

Van Devanter described the Pueblos as "essentially a simple, uninformed, and inferior people," and concluded that the United States "as a superior and civilized nation [has] the power and duty of exercising a fostering care and protection" over them.[61] The Pueblos had certainly not regressed in a little less than fifty years![62] The cases are distinguishable solely by the later Court's adoption of a position that "[i]n reference to all matters of this kind, it is the rule of this court to follow the action of the executive and other political departments of the government, whose more special duty it is to determine such affairs."[63]

The post-*Elk* Court was scrupulously careful not to concede such extraordinary discretion to Congress without some limitation. "Of course, it is not meant by this that Congress may bring a community or group of people within the range of this power by arbitrarily calling them an Indian tribe," Justice Van Devanter explained. It could only be extended to "distinctly Indian" communities.[64] The principle of volitional allegiance, so central to revolutionary ideology, was therefore entirely overthrown by a racial classification spuriously reconciled with the Fourteenth Amendment, one by which tribes are abandoned to federal despotism.

61. *Id.* 39, 46.
62. Upon reflection, the only way Justice Van Devanter could distinguish *Sandoval* from *Joseph* was by implying that he had better ethnographic data than the earlier Court (*id.* 44). He also intimated that *Joseph* had not involved federal police powers, while *Sandoval* did (*id.* 48–49). This is simply wrong. *Joseph* was an appeal by the United States from dismissal of its action under Section 11 of the Trade and Intercourse Act (94 U.S. 614–15).
63. 231 U.S. 28, 47. This is a quote from *U.S. v. Holliday*, 3 Wall. 407, 419 (1966). *Holliday* held that the United States could prohibit the sale of liquor to Indian *citizens*. Of course, this is distinguishable because the objects of the power had consented to its exercise, explicitly, or implicitly in associating themselves with a nation which at that time discriminated against blacks and Indians as a matter of state and national policy. *Holliday* did not, therefore, abandon the principle of volitional allegiance.
64. 231 U.S. 28, 46.

7

Another Judicial Vindication of Congressional Intervention: The Territorial Analogy, 1854-1886

Elk acquiesced in Congress's prior assumption of "plenary power," but in so doing relied upon the paradoxical fiction that Indians were beyond the authority of the United States. Beginning with *United States v. Kagama* in 1886,[1] the Court laid the groundwork for a more logically consistent vindication of congressional supremacy. *Kagama* reasoned by analogy[2] to the process of territorial incorporation, and expanded it into a theory of domestic colonialism.

Judicial treatment of territorial incorporation changed little over the course of the nineteenth century, despite its association with two great political controversies: slavery and polygamy. Chief Justice Marshall suggested in dictum as early as 1819 that Congress's power to create and regulate territorial governments is beyond dispute and arises from the "all

1. 118 U.S. 375.
2. The analogical mode of thinking by the Court in this case is of a type sometimes described as "irrationalist fallacy logic." Rather than seeking to demonstrate the formal validity of the analogy by testing individual similarities and differences between the two cases, the Court merely indicated that there were good reasons (of policy) for believing it true. An extreme example of this process of well-intentioned self-delusion is found in *People v. Hall* (4 Cal. 399 [1854]), in which the court reasoned by analogy that Asians and Indians were of the same race, and therefore that any restrictive laws referring to "Indians" were also applicable to Asians!

needful Rules and Regulations'' part of the Property Clause.[3] Almost a decade later, he had occasion to discuss this power again in a case involving the validity of congressionally created courts in the Territory of Florida.[4] The treaty of cession of the Floridas had guaranteed American citizenship to their inhabitants, and therefore extended to them "the enjoyment of the privileges, rights, and immunities of the citizens of the United States. . . . They do not, however, participate in political power . . . till Florida shall become a State."[5] Congress could therefore organize their courts and other governing institutions until admission to statehood, but only as a transitional measure, not in violation of the usual rights of citizenship.

In *Benner v. Porter*[6] the Court qualified this rule, holding that Congress could regulate some activities in the territories that ordinarily lay within the scope of reserved state powers guaranteed by the Tenth Amendment. To remain consistent with Marshall's earlier rule, however, *Benner* also attributed a transient, almost emergency character to this extraordinary power: a vacuum-of-power theory. Since territorial settlement proceeded more quickly than the growth of local institutions, federal agencies would have to maintain order temporarily.

The question of limitations on Congress's power to govern the territories was soon embroiled in the slavery controversy. If the Fifth Amendment limited what Congress could demand of new territories, then congressional stipulations that no slaves be transported into those territories would be void as takings of westward immigrants' property without compensation. Chief Justice Roger Taney adopted this argument in the celebrated Dred Scott case. "There is certainly no power given by the Constitution to the Federal Government to establish or maintain Colonies . . . to be ruled and governed at its own pleasure [or] to acquire a Territory to be held and governed permanently in that character."[7] He was emphatic that the Bill of Rights extends to all laws of the United States executed within its boundaries, and that the Constitution as a whole limits the federal

3. *M'Culloch v. Maryland*, 4 Wheat. 316, 422 (1819), in his recitation of the various implied powers of Congress.

4. *American Insurance Co. v. 356 Bales of Cotton*, 1 Pet. 533 (1828).

5. 1 Pet. 542.

6. 9 How. 235, 242 (1850) (validity of federal statute making libel punishable in territorial courts); see also *Cross v. Harrison*, 16 How. 164, 194 (1853).

7. *Scott v. Sanford*, 19 How. 393, 446 (1856).

government's power absolutely, not just its power over the citizens of the states.[8]

After the Civil War, the Court avoided *Scott* as if emancipation had overruled it. In *Late Corporation Church of Jesus Christ v. U.S.*, Mr. Justice Bradley reasoned that when legislating for a territory, Congress "would be subject to those fundamental limitations in favor of personal rights which are formulated in the constitution and its amendments; but these limitations would exist rather by inference and the general spirit of the constitution . . . than by express and direct application of its provisions."[9] This placed the Court in the position of testing federal laws against some undefined and unprincipled "spirit" notion for which there existed no precedent. Bradley's approach gave Congress more leeway in suppressing Mormonism, and in subsequent decisions the Court dispensed with even this minimal obstacle to federal reorganization of Utah: Mormonism and polygamy were held to be universally recognized abominations not entitled to First Amendment protections.[10] Thus the Court could sustain a statute denying polygamists the right to hold public office, and still declare that Congress is "subject . . . to such restrictions as are expressed in the constitution, or are necessarily implied in its terms, or in the purposes and objects of the power itself."[11] All of this may have been a response to a unique political situation, however, for, notwithstanding the *Late Corporation* rule, the Court later held that the First,[12] Sixth[13] and Seventh[14] Amendments are applicable without modification to exercises of Congress's power within the territories.

Following Chief Justice Marshall's theory in *American Insurance*, Mr. Justice Matthews in *Murphy v. Ramsey* drew a distinction between the "right of local self-government" and "personal and civil rights."[15] Only the right of local self-government could be denied to territorial residents.

8. *Id.* 449–50.
9. 136 U.S. 1, 44 (1890); see also *Clinton v. Englebrecht*, 13 Wall. 434, 441 (1871) (territorial legislature has "all powers of self-government consistent with the supremacy and supervision of national authority" per Chase, C.J.). *Late Corporation* introduced the use of the term "plenary power" (136 U.S. 1, 42).
10. *Davis v. Beason*, 133 U.S. 333, 341 (1890).
11. *Murphy v. Ramsey*, 114 U.S. 15, 44 (1885), citing *American Insurance* and *Scott*. See also *First National Bank v. Yankton County*, 101 U.S. 129, 133 (1880).
12. *Reynolds v. U.S.*, 98 U.S. 145, 162 (1878).
13. *Thompson v. Utah*, 170 U.S. 343, 348–49 (1898).
14. *American Publishing Co. v. Fisher*, 166 U.S. 464 (1897).
15. 114 U.S. 15, 44.

Similarly, in *Late Corporation*, the Court observed that ''no government without authority from the United States, express or implied, has any legal right to exist'' on lands owned by the United States.[16] The Court analogized territorial governments' relationship to Congress with the relationship of municipalities to the states.[17] Although limited by its constitution, the state may lawfully authorize, limit and dissolve municipalities at pleasure, and may pass laws that supersede municipal laws.

It is significant, however, that no territorial case brought to the Court involved a formerly self-governing community. All involved lands purchased from European monarchs, many of them colonies subject to military governors.[18] The Mormon state of Deseret was established only after the purchase of Utah by the United States, and before the Territory of Utah was authorized by Congress.[19] In point of fact, the same justices that decided *American Insurance* heard *Worcester* four years later and agreed that tribes had always been self-governing and had a right to remain so. Chief Justice Taney, when he wrote his opinion for *Scott* a generation later, also commented at length on the unique, self-governing status of tribes, relying on the Marshall Court's decisions.[20] Before 1886, then, it was not supposed that the law of territories had any bearing on tribes' political integrity.

Although up to this point the Court had never denied the right of tribes to govern their ''own'' affairs, a certain amount of confusion was developing over the status of *non*-Indians in tribal territory. In 1790, 1802 and 1834, Congress passed Indian Trade and Intercourse Acts[21] purporting to regulate Indian traders and protect Indians from rapacious non-Indians. As part of this scheme, the acts made only the crimes of *whites against Indians* punishable in federal court.[22] They appeared designed to augment, rather

16. 136 U.S. 1, 45.

17. *First National Bank v. Yankton County*, 101 U.S. 129, 133 (1880).

18. See especially in this regard *Cross v. Harrison, op. cit.* Compare Britain's theory of supremacy over the colonies, i.e., that they were collectivities of British subjects residing *in partibus exteris*, who had emigrated there solely at the pleasure of the Crown and *subject to prior conditions* expressed in charters Thomas Pownall, 2 *Administration* 18−23, 26−30 (5th ed. London: 1774), and Josiah Tucker, *Four Tracts on Political and Commercial Subjects* 103−4 (3rd ed. Gloucester, England: 1776).

19. *Murphy v. Ramsey*, 114 U.S. 15, 44 (1885).

20. 19 How. 403−4.

21. 4 Stat. 729.

22. *Id.*, sec. 16, which also provides for the payment of double damages to the Indian victims. The act also provided treaty tribes with a federal remedy against crimes committed by other Indians, *not of the same tribe* (*id.*, sec. 17). This can be understood as execution of the United States' pledge, in its treaties, to ''protect'' tribes.

than to supplant the jurisdiction of tribal governments, to the extent that the latter lacked the institutional machinery to obtain satisfaction from non-members. The unique, international flavor of this arrangement is exemplified by the provision in the acts for federal indemnification of tribes injured by the actions of *unknown* or *fugitive* non-Indians never brought to trial.[23]

The courts were soon called on to explain how the United States could punish persons for acts committed within a concededly foreign jurisdiction. In *United States v. Bailey* Mr. Justice McLean on circuit held an 1817 Act of Congress unconstitutional to the extent that it extended the general criminal laws of the United States to tribal territory.[24] Bailey was convicted of murdering another non-Indian in that part of the Cherokee Nation located in Tennessee.

Consistent with his concurrence in *Worcester* two years earlier, McLean described the Cherokees as "a distinct community, governed by their own laws, and resting for their protection on the faith of treaties and laws of the Union," whose land "can in no sense be considered a territory of the United States." He could find no treaty provision applicable to crimes among non-Indians, authorizing the United States to intervene, although he observed that *state* prosecutions of non-Indians in such cases had never been challenged—a proposition for which he cited no cases or examples.[25]

McLean did not, however, conceive the necessity of deciding as a general principle whether either the states or the United States have a limited jurisdiction in Indian country. The case turned upon the nature of the crime, he concluded, rather than upon a question of territorial jurisdiction. Congress can exercise no greater power over tribal territory in Tennessee than over Tennessee itself. Since murder is not comprehended by Congress's power to regulate commerce among the states and with the Indian tribes, and Bailey's crime was not committed within an area of "exclusive federal legislation" such as the District of Columbia, Congress simply lacked power to punish him *for that act*.[26]

McLean responded critically to the argument of legislative "necessity," i.e., that Congress had acted to fill a jurisdictional vacuum. "The Constitution is no longer the guide, when the government acts from the law of

23. *Id.*, sec. 16.
24. 24 Fed. Cas. 937 (C.C.Tenn. 1834).
25. *Id.* 939. However, the Cherokees had long since agreed to federal jurisdiction of non-Indians' crimes against Indians. Charles Kappler, ed., 2 *Indian Affairs: Laws and Treaties* 8, 29 (Washington, D.C.: 1904).
26. 24 Fed. Cas. 940.

necessity. This law always affords a pretext for usurpation. It exists only in the minds of those who exercise the power, and if followed must lead to despotism."[27]

In *United States v. Rogers*[28] twelve years later, the defendant had been born to non-Indian parents but was later adopted or naturalized according to the forms of Cherokee law. After ruling that Rogers' status as an Indian in a federal prosecution was a matter of federal, not Cherokee law, and that by such a standard he was still white, the Court went on to consider Congress's power to regulate his behavior in Indian country. Distinguishing *Bailey* as having reference to events within a *state* Chief Justice Taney concluded

[W]e think it too firmly and clearly established to admit of dispute, that the Indian tribes, residing within the territorial limits of the United States, are subject to their authority, and when the country occupied by one of them is not within the limits of one of the States, Congress may by law punish any offense committed there, no matter whether the offender be a white man or an Indian.[29]

Rogers and *Bailey* are not inconsistent in the light of *Benner v. Porter* and the evolving doctrine of territorial incorporation. Within the area of the states, Congress's power is strictly limited by Article I of the constitution. Hence in *Bailey* any regulation exceeding those enumerated powers must be void whether exercised within tribal territory *or* on state-controlled lands, so long as the *situs* is within the exterior boundaries of a state. Beyond the states, but still within the territorial boundaries of the United States, the Needful Rules clause of Article IV governs, investing Congress with extraordinary powers.

Certain circumstances render *Rogers* more understandable, but so unique that it should have had no influence on subsequent law. The crime was committed in the Indian Territory, on land *conveyed to the Cherokee Nation by the United States* in fee simple, and subject to federal law.[30] The applicable treaty provided that the land was to be held as a part of the United States, not as original tribal occupancy. For this reason *Rogers* may have reached the right result, but, like *Bailey*, for the wrong reason,

27. *Id.*
28. 4 How. 567 (1846).
29. *Id.* 572.
30. Kappler, 2 *Indian Affairs* 288, 439; see also *id.* 310.

leaving the impression that tribal consent was immaterial in questions of federal authority over Indian country.

Neither case was decided, therefore, with reference to specific tribal-federal agreements consenting to a greater or lesser exercise of federal power. Both cases ruled on the *maximum* constitutional scope of federal power irrespective of any limiting agreement with the tribes. Treaties were not before the Court in either *Bailey* or *Rogers* to rebut the presumption that Congress could exercise the maximum power permitted by the Constitution. At the same time, no tribe could give Congress by treaty more regulatory power than Congress could otherwise exercise pursuant to the Constitution.

Tribes were not parties to these cases, and treaties were not discussed. Both involved non-Indian defendants in federal prosecutions. Neither prosecution ousted a tribal court of jurisdiction, nor did either of the defendants argue that their case belonged more properly in a tribal forum. The Court was therefore unable to properly rule on the extent to which the maximum constitutional power of Congress could not be exercised because of limitations in treaties. That the sweeping language of *Rogers* reflects this procedural dilemma, rather than a rejection of *Worcester*, is clear from the fact that Taney quoted from *Worcester* with unqualified approval in the Dred Scott case several years later.[31]

For almost a generation after *Rogers*, moreover, Congress made no attempt to regulate Indians within tribal territory, although the practice of prosecuting non-Indians' crimes, comfortable to *Bailey* and *Rogers*, continued.[32] Even after the establishment of the Indian Police, Congress was careful to recognize the necessity of tribal consent, and to avoid ousting tribal jurisdiction. The governing federal statute until 1885 provided that no Indian be prosecuted for federal offenses "who has been punished by the local law of the tribe, or . . . where by treaty stipulations the exclusive jurisdiction over such offenses is or may be secured to the Indian tribes respectively."[33]

---

31. *Scott v. Sanford*, 19 How. 393, 404 (1856).

32. After *Rogers* there were two cases involving *state* prosecutions of non-Indians for reservation crimes (*U.S. v. McBratney*, 104 U.S. 622 [1882]; *U.S. v. Draper*, 164 U.S. 240 [1895]). Both involved allotted and surplused reservations in an irreversible process of transition to political incorporation with the state. The tribes having been implicitly dissolved by the allotment process. *Draper* reasoned, the state merely filled a jurisdictional vacuum.

33. 28 R.S. 2146 at that time; discussed and quoted in full in *Ex parte Crow Dog*, 109 U.S. 556 (1883).

In 1885 Congress subjected tribal Indians to federal prosecution for seven enumerated felonies, without qualification.[34] Unfortunately, this experiment in implicitly abrogating treaties was constitutionally tested in a case involving a treatyless tribe. Thus, while the rule may have been correct to the extent of the facts before the Court, as was the case in *Rogers,* it was incorrectly applied by later Courts to situations involving treaty tribes and direct threats to tribal government powers.

United States v. Kagama[35] came to the Supreme Court on a certificate of division between the circuit and district judges who had originally tried it. It involved the murder of one Indian by another on the Hoopa reservation in California. Examining the Constitution for evidence of the scope of Congress's power to intervene in intratribal matters, Mr. Justice Miller expressed perplexity at that document's near silence on the matter.[36] The Apportionment Clause did not, he observed, "shed much light on the power of Congress over the Indians *in their existence as tribes,*"[37] since it dealt only with Indians' enumeration for the apportionment of the House. The only other specific mention of Indians is the Commerce Clause, which he also rejected as a source of authority for the 1885 Act, paraphrasing the Marshall Court's reasoning in *Worcester*:[38]

[W]e think it would be a very strained construction of this clause, that a system of criminal laws for Indians living peaceably on their reservations, which left out the entire code of trade and intercourse laws justly enacted under the provision, and established punishments for the common-law crimes . . . without any kind of commerce, was authorized by the grant of power to regulate commerce with the Indian tribes.[39]

Having thus rejected both express constitutional provisions for Indians and their tribes, the Court sought authority in general principles. Citing both *American Insurance* and *Rogers* with approval, Miller concluded that the Constitution only ordains two levels of sovereignty: state and federal. Being "within the geographical limits of the United States," tribes must

---

34. 23 Stat. 385, §9. Murder, manslaughter, rape, assault with intent to kill, arson, burglary, and larceny were included. Owing to the vague phrasing of the statute there remained some question as to its applicability to Indians off-reservation. See Senator Dawes' remarks in 16 *Congressional Record* 2385 (2 March 1885).
35. 118 U.S. 375 (1886).
36. *Id*. 378.
37. *Id*. 278–79 (emphasis ours).
38. 31 U.S. (6 Pet.) 554.
39. 118 U.S. 375, 378–79.

therefore be subject to either one or the other.[40] This superficially inescapable logic assumes the conclusion, that is, that tribes are a part of the federal system politically and jurisdictionally. It is not difficult to imagine, however, why the Court passed over this problem without discussion. The rule of *M'Intosh* had been that the United States holds the fee in tribal lands, subject to a right of perpetual occupancy. Although originally intended to reconcile formal inconsistencies in our law, rather than to deprive tribes of their rights or property, this rule does imply, however improperly, that tribes are "within the United States" in more than a merely geographical sense.

Perhaps this explains why the Court was careful to note at one point in its argument that Congress's plenary powers arise "not so much from the clause in the Constitution in regard to disposing of and making rules and regulations concerning the territory and other property of the United States, *as from the ownership of the country.*"[41]

Although the Court was correct in that the Constitution itself establishes only two sovereigns, state and federal, it embodies a procedure for recognizing others: the treaty power. By treaty, the United States may delegate power to other nations or councils of nations, or receive delegations of power from them. But in *Kagama* there was no evidence of a treaty arrangement, at least not with the Hoopa tribe. The Court itself observed, however, that the Hoopas had been subjects of Mexico, and their political rights derived from the Treaty of Guadalupe Hidalgo, ceding California to the United States. Strictly construed, therefore *Kagama* applies only in the absence of treaties or analogous forms of limited tribal consent to federal jurisdiction. Loosely interpreted, as it later was, *Kagama* reclassifies all tribal areas as parts of the territory of the United States, and thereby authorizes Congress to abolish tribal governments and create new ones. It provided a sweeping legal theory for a new epoch of federal Indian legislation.

Following the precedent of *American Insurance* and *Murphy*, even this did not justify the extinction of Indians' *personal* liberties guaranteed by the first nine amendments. However, within a year of *Kagama*, Congress passed the General Allotment Act,[42] which directed the secretary of the

---

40. *Id.* 379.
41. *Id.* 379–80 (emphasis ours).
42. Act of 8 February 1887, 24 Stat. 388; 25 U.S.C. 331 *et seq.* as amended.

interior to subdivide reservations, assign plots to individual Indians, and open the "surplus" to homesteading. Allotment should have come as no surprise. During the debates over the Armstrong amendment in 1871, Representative Lawrence of Ohio applauded the demise of the treaty power in these terms: "hereafter the land policy of Congress cannot be broken up and destroyed by Indian treaties."[43]

43. 43 *Congressional Globe* 1812 (1 March 1871).

8

The Doctrine of the Dependent Ward, 1883-1934

In the twenty years following *Kagama*, Congress exercised powers over Indians which, if asserted against state citizens, would not have survived constitutional challenge. Confiscation of property, restrictions on Indians' use of their property, and supervision of tribes' political affairs violated even the somewhat looser First and Fifth Amendment standards applicable to the territories after *American Insurance* and *Murphy v. Ramsey*.[1] The territorial analogy explained how it was that Congress had any power at all within tribal territory, but it did not explain how Congress could exercise that power in conflict with the Bill of Rights.

The Mormon cases could have been read as a general proposition that Congress might suppress "immoral" behavior in the territories notwithstanding the First Amendment.[2] The *Late Corporation* case in particular suggested that this suppression might include confiscation of collective property.[3] It could have been argued that tribal customs attacked by the Indian agents and Indian Police were too abominable to enjoy First

---

1. The earliest comprehensive regulations are printed separately as *Regulations of the Indian Department* (1884). More recent rules appear in Title 25 of the Code of Federal Regulations.
2. *Davis v. Beason*, 133 U.S. 333 (1890).
3. The *Late Corporation* rule.

Amendment protection, and that confiscation of all tribal property was a necessary and lawful step in obliterating them.

However, a much broader and more dangerous doctrine was gaining popularity among scholars at that time. The nineteenth century was the heyday of European imperialism and the debut of the white man's burden. As early as 1837 a special committee advised the British House of Commons to establish special crown protectorates over all native peoples within the empire for their own benefit. It was not only proper, the committee observed, to keep Europeans out of native communities where they might prove destructive, but also to supervise the education and Christianization of the aborigines.

Independently of the obligations of conscience to impart the blessings we enjoy, we have abundant proof that it is greatly for our advantage to have dealings with civilized men rather than with barbarians. Savages are dangerous neighbors and unprofitable customers, and if they remain as degraded denizens of our colonies they become a burden upon the State.[4]

The report was highly critical of the United States for merely "banishing" Indians from settled areas rather than civilizing them.

Americans were impressed. In 1872, the commissioner of Indian affairs observed that "it would be to assume more than would be taken for granted of any white race under the same conditions, to expect that the wild Indians will become industrious and frugal except through a severe course of industrial instruction and exercise, under restraint."[5] The reservation must therefore become a "legalized reformatory" for Indians, a place where they would adopt non-Indian ways "peaceably if they will, forcibly if they must."[6]

The judiciary was a part of the same intellectual movement, and in 1883 it made its debut in the Supreme Court. Crow Dog murdered Spotted Tail on the Brule reservation and was subsequently convicted of murder in federal district court.[7] At that time, the federal criminal code exempted crimes of Indians against other Indians from its general provisions.[8] The United States responded to Crow Dog's habeas corpus, however, on the theory that the tribe had subjected itself to general federal laws by its 1868

4. House of Commons, Select Committee on Aboriginal Tribes, Report (1837).
5. *Report of the Commissioner of Indian Affairs, 1872* 11.
6. *Report of the Commissioner of Indian Affairs, 1889* 3.
7. *Ex parte Crow Dog*, 109 U.S. 556.
8. R.S. 2145, 2146, set out at 109 U.S. 558.

treaty. There was no question but that the treaty superseded all prior inconsistent statutes of the United States.

The solicitor general relied on Article 8 of the treaty, which provided in pertinent part that

congress shall, by appropriate legislation, secure to them an orderly government; they shall be subject to the laws of the United States, and each individual shall be protected in his rights of property, person, and life.[9]

This, he argued, constituted tribal consent to federal regulation, and especially to federal maintenance of law and order. Justice Matthews disagreed.

The pledge to secure to these people, with whom the United States was contracting as a distinct political body, an orderly government . . . necessarily implies . . . that among the arts of civilized life, which it was the very purpose of these arrangements to introduce and naturalize among them, was the highest and best of all,—that of self-government, the regulation by themselves of their own domestic affairs, the maintenance of peace and order among their own members by the administration of their own laws and customs.[10]

Extension of the federal penal code to the reservation would throw off tribal jurisdiction, and apply American standards to

a community separated by race, by tradition, by the instincts of a free though savage life, from the authority and power which seeks to impose upon them the restraints of an external and unknown code, and to subject them to the responsibilities of civil conduct, according to rules and penalties of which they could have no previous warning; which judges them by a standard made by others, and not for them, which takes no account of the conditions which should except them from its exactions, and makes no allowance for their inability to understand it. It tries them not by their peers, nor by the customs of their people, nor the law of their land, but by superiors of a different race, according to the law of a social state of which they have an imperfect conception, and which is opposed to the tradition of their history, to the habits of their lives, to the strongest prejudices of their savage nature; one which measures the red man's revenge by the maxims of the white man's morality.[11]

It was clear, then, that the solicitor's position violated *Worcester's* model of the tribal-federal relationship, since it would permit Congress to regulate internal tribal affairs and individual Indian conduct. Without more precise

9. 109 U.S. 556.
10. 109 U.S. 568–69.
11. 109 U.S. 571.

expression of such an intent in the treaty, the Court was inclined to presume that Congress's power remained purely external. Article 8 could not "have any more extensive meaning than an acknowledgment of their allegiance, as Indians, to the laws of the United States,"[12] analogous perhaps to the allegiance of the states expressed in the Constitution.[13]

Another thread runs though the *Crow Dog* opinion, however, which marks a subtle departure from *Worcester*. Matthews intimated in the two passages quoted above that the "orderly government" secured to the Sioux was to be American-style government, and that the tribe's insulation from federal laws was justified only by their temporary ignorance of them. Could this have been the tribe's intent, to have merely a right to learn the white man's ways?

[I]t is manifest that the provisions had reference to their establishment as a people upon a defined reservation as a permanent home, who were to be urged, as far as it could successfully be done, into the practice of agriculture, and whose children were to be taught the arts and industry of civilized life.[14]

In this transitional capacity, the Indians were to be considered,

as they had always been, as wards, subject to a guardian; not as individuals, constituted members of the political community of the United States, with a voice in the selection of representatives and the framing of the laws, but as a dependent community who were in a state of pupilage, advancing from the condition of a savage tribe to that of a people who, through the discipline of labor, and by education, it was hoped might become a self-supporting and self-governing society.[15]

When he wrote his opinion for *Cherokee Nation v. Georgia* in 1831, John Marshall described tribes as "dependent" because they had voluntarily surrendered their external trade and treaty powers to the United States, and were receiving, at their own request, federal assistance. In Justice Matthews' mind, "dependency" was a voluntary state of education and political transition. In either case, tribal consent was nevertheless an essential element.

Dependency next appeared three years later at the conclusion of *Kagama*'s territoriality argument:

12. 109 U.S. 569.
13. *Cf.* Article IV, sec. 4 and Article VI, cl. 2 of the Constitution.
14. 109 U.S. 569–570.
15. 109 U.S. 569.

The Indian tribes *are* the wards of the nation. They are communities *dependent* on the United States; dependent largely for their daily food; dependent for their political rights.[16]

It had still not risen to the status of a legal principle, but was merely used descriptively. Justice Miller did not even cite *Cherokee Nation* or *Crow Dog* to support it. His point was simply that state governments could not be trusted to assume the responsibilities delegated by tribes to the United States. "Because of local ill feeling, the people of the states where they are found are often their deadliest enemies."[17] But the exclusivity of federal power to deal with tribes had already been established fifty years earlier in *Worcester*, not on any theory of guardianship, but on the solid foundation of the Treaty and Commerce Clauses of the Constitution. It may have been gratuitous, then, for Miller to add that tribes' poverty had been "so largely due to the course of dealing of the federal government with them . . . there arises a duty of protection."[18] *Crow Dog* had mentioned a "duty of protection," but only in the context of express treaty language obligating the United States to undertake some degree of assistance to the tribe.[19] In Justice Miller's hands, this "duty" assumed a general nature arising from equity rather than agreement.

If Miller's remarks in *Kagama* were gratuitous, his associates lost no time in taking advantage of them to forge new doctrine. Six months later Justice Matthews, author of *Crow Dog*, cited *Kagama* to completely upset his earlier formulation of tribes' "peculiar relation" to the United States. The tribal-federal relationship is similar to that

between a superior and inferior, whereby the latter is placed under the care and supervision of the former, and which, while it authorizes the adoption on the part of the United States of such policy as their own public interest may dictate, recognizes, on the other hand, such an interpretation of their acts and promises as justice and reason demand in all cases where power is exerted by the strong over those to whom they owe care and protection.[20]

16. 118 U.S. 375, 383. The Court did not discuss *Worcester* at all. Its use of the "dependency" language from *Cherokee Nation* was, however, only in the context of distinguishing state from federal powers. The Court did not propose that the tribes were actually dependent politically (i.e., subordinate and without independent powers), but argued that the tribes had placed themselves, if at all, under federal rather than state protection.

17. 118 U.S. 383.

18. *Id.*

19. 109 U.S. 569.

20. *Choctaw Nation v. U.S.*, 119 U.S. 1, 27–28 (1886). See, similarly, *Buttz v. No. Pac. R.Co.*, 119 U.S. 55, 66 (1886), to the effect that tribes have "a right to use the land subject to the dominion and control of the government."

The principle of tribal consent had been lost. The United States was to enjoy not only an exclusive power to deal with tribes, but virtually unlimited power to govern them. This power to govern was in fact much greater than the power of a parent or guardian, because it could lawfully be exercised in the United States' "own public interest," not the interest of the "ward," tempered only by some undefined equitable notion of "justice and reason." The reservation could now lawfully be shaped into a "mere educational and disciplinary instrumentalit[y]"[21] in the discretion of Congress.

Four years later, in *Cherokee Nation v. So. Kansas Ry. Co.*, the Court was ready to claim that this had *always* been the law," [f]rom the beginning of the government to the present time."[22]

It is true, as declared in *Worcester v. Georgia* . . . that the treaties and laws of the United States contemplate the Indian Territory as completely separated from the states, and the Cherokee Nation as a distinct community. . . . But that falls far short of saying that they are a sovereign state with no superior within the limits of its territory.[23]

Worcester had been unambiguous, however, that tribes' subordination to Congress is limited to their external affairs. in *So. Kansas Ry.*, the company was defending Congress's power to take tribal land by eminent domain. The wardship idea was being used in its new form, for even supposing that the federal "guardian" had power to dispose of tribal land for the benefit of Indian "wards," no one even bothered to allege that any Indians would actually benefit from the railway.

Rather than seek specific authority for the power of the United States to condemn tribal land, the Court inventively turned the issue around and asked why the United States should *not* be able to condemn tribal land. That the Cherokee Nation alone could exercise the power of eminent domain over tribal land "finds no support in the numerous treaties with the Cherokee Indians, or in the decisions of this court, or in the acts of congress defining the relations of that people with the United States."[24] Whereas even in *Crow Dog* Congress was presumed to have only those

21. *U.S. v. Clapox*, 35 F. 575, 576 (1888).
22. *Cherokee Nation v. So. Kansas Ry. Co.*, 135 U.S. 641, 653, 656 (1890). The Court cited *Cherokee Nation v. Georgia* in support of this generalization.
23. 135 U.S. 654.
24. *Id.*

powers over tribes' domestic affairs that the tribes themselves had consented to, henceforth Congress was to be presumed to have every power of government over Indians it had not *expressly given up to the tribes*.

Tribes' condition of dependency, the Court continued, was original rather than a product of consent. Since no treaty with the Cherokees "evinced any intention to *discharge* them from their condition of pupilage or dependency, and constitute them a separate, independent, sovereign people,"[25] they remained in this original condition. In this way the Court cleverly manipulated Indian treaties, which said nothing about wardship, to serve as evidence that wardship existed. According to the Court's reasoning, tribes never had been sovereign and could become so only by a grant of power from the United States. The application of this principle to the Cherokees was particularly ironic, since they had been industrialized, literate, and completely competitive with their non-Indian neighbors since the time of the *Worcester* decision.[26]

Along with many other tribes, the Cherokees had also been governing their domestic affairs for generations in a very visible manner, through national assemblies, courts, and printed laws. In 1899 the Court dismissed these facts as immaterial in a case upholding the power of Congress to alter the Cherokee Nation's naturalization laws:

It is true that the Indian tribes were for many years *allowed* by the United States to make all laws and regulations for the government and protection of their persons and property, not inconsistent with the constitution and laws of the United States;[27]

but now the policy had changed. Tribes' power to make laws was a matter of federal sufferance or delegation, presumably in advancement of their "education," and could be taken away at any time.

What if Congress had expressly guaranteed certain powers and rights to a tribe? The *So. Kansas Ry.* case seemed to indicate that this would operate as a delegation of power to the "ward." If a delegation, however, the power could be revoked. In *Cherokee Nation v. Hitchcock*[28] and *Lone Wolf*

---

25. *Id.* (emphasis ours), citing *Kagama* and *Rogers* in support.

26. And this was true from a very early date. See, for example, Henry Thompson Malone, *The Cherokees of the Old South: A People in Transition* 137−52 (Athens, Ga.: 1956).

27. *Stephens v. Cherokee Nation*, 174 U.S. 445, 483 (1899) (emphasis ours). Actually, the Court had *never* held that tribal laws had to be consistent with federal law. See *Talton v. Mayes*, 163 U.S. 376 (1896).

28. 187 U.S. 294, 305−6 (1902).

v. Hitchcock[29] the Court took the position that, for the Indians' own good, Congress might alter any of their political or property rights irrespective of applicable treaty stipulations, and even in violation of the Constitution. "It is to be presumed," the Court said, "that in this matter the United States would be governed by such considerations of justice as would control a Christian people in their treatment of an ignorant and dependent race."[30] The discharge of this power was to remain a matter of unreviewable federal "policy," however.

The idea that an act of Congress may supersede an Indian treaty was not new. In 1871 the case of *The Cherokee Tobacco* held that the general revenue laws of the United States control prior inconsistent tax exemptions in an Indian treaty. Congress has power to alter foreign treaties, and Indian treaties "have no higher sanctity; and no greater inviolability or immunity from legislative invasion can be claimed for them."[31] In reaching this conclusion, the Court assumed that treaties with tribes were in all other respects indistinguishable from foreign treaties. Nevertheless it also assumed that Congress can justly enforce federal laws in violation of a tribal treaty *within tribal territory*. Congressional modification of a foreign treaty cannot give the United States authority to enter and alter the laws of that country. That would be an act of war. If the tribes have no right to resist such acts, then they cannot be foreign and their treaties cannot be analogized to foreign treaties. Their situation then resembles that of the states, who cannot resist just federal laws, but whose "treaty" with the United States, the Constitution, is controlling and irrevocable.

Even *Lone Wolf* was unprepared to claim unlimited supremacy for Congress. The exercise of the power to revoke, consistent with the idea of wardship, "presumably . . . will be exercised only when circumstances arise which will not only justify the government in disregarding the stipulations of the treaty, but may demand in the interest of the country and of the Indians themselves, that it should do so."[32] But the obligation was a "moral" one, a matter of "good faith." It was not vulnerable to attack on constitutional grounds. Indians were therefore enough "within" the United States to be as much subject to Congress as citizens, but enough

29. 187 U.S. 553, 565 (1903).
30. *Id*. This phrase was cribbed from dictum in *Beecher v. Wetherby*, 95 U.S. 517, 525 (1877).
31. 11 Wall. 616, 621.
32. 187 U.S. 553, 566.

"outside" the United States to lack constitutional protection. A more ideal legal status for tribes could not have been demanded by those bent on forcing them to be white.

If wardship is a transient state of "pupilage" and education, it is important to determine when wardship ends. Civil guardianship and custody laws must provide, in accordance with the Due Process Clause, opportunities for persons temporarily deprived of their civil rights to demonstrate their competency and be released from supervision. A spendthrift, whose legal status is most comparable to that of an individual Indian, must be given an opportunity to present his own case. Restrictions run against individuals and are extended and removed only after proof of individual facts. Without such protection government would be empowered to imprison individuals or entire groups of dissenters on the mere allegation of their mental insufficiency, a practice we criticize in foreign governments. Under *Lone Wolf*, however, Indian "incompetency" is not a fact to be individually proved. It is presumed from membership in an Indian tribe, as if somehow tribalism itself is the cause. The tribe is not even afforded an opportunity to demonstrate that its collective capability is advanced enough to merit emancipation. All tribes, literate and illiterate, farmers and hunters, educated and uneducated, are thrown together indiscriminately. When *Lone Wolf* was decided, only Congress had authority to remove restrictions against individuals or tribes. In 1906, Congress amended the General Allotment Act to permit the secretary of the interior to certify individual Indians competent "in his discretion."[33] The courts soon concluded that this discretion was unreviewable.[34]

The courts' reception of the wardship idea encouraged statesmen and scholars to embrace it as a general principle for the administration of non-white peoples, especially in the insular Pacific, where the Spanish American War had left the United States a major colonial power. It had been well and proper, Harvard's Dean Langdell argued, to extend constitutional liberties to the white settlers of nineteenth-century, continental territories while they remained subject to exclusive federal jurisdiction, but savage tribes were incapable of "appreciating" such political refinements. They were traditionally cruel, barbaric, and autocratic, therefore to rule them autocratically was merely to give them what they really wanted and

33. Act of May 8, 1906 c. 2348, 34 Stat. 182, now codified as a part of 25 U.S.C. 349.
34. *U.S. v. Lane*, 258 F. 520 (1919); *Mickadiet v. Payne*, 269 F. 194 (1920), *aff'd* 258 U.S. 609 (1920).

understood best.[35] Langdell and others of his persuasion characteristically drew examples from the management of reservations. There was a difference, however. Bureaucrats and reformers always assumed that Indians wanted to be Americanized, but would have to be made to understand Americanism before they could be permitted to enjoy its blessings. Current events suggest that Congress is still not persuaded that the lesson has been learned.[36]

Even after the Indian Reorganization Act put benevolent despotism officially to rest, tribes have been haunted by shadows of the dependency doctrine. Suits by tribes for compensation are one example. At first the Supreme Court upheld the power of the United States to take tribal property without compensation if the purported purpose of the taking was to benefit the Indians, for example, liquidation of tribal lands to establish a school fund.[37] Indians being legally incompetent to make intelligent fiscal choices, their lands could be taken to provide services the government said they really wanted. What the Bureau of Indian Affairs said the Indians really wanted was a matter of unreviewable discretion.

In 1946 the Indian Claims Act required that past uncompensated takings be subjected retroactively to a test of "fair and honorable dealings."[38] The dependency doctrine survived so well, however, that despite the absence of any such provision in the act itself, the courts refused to allow tribes interest on those takings purportedly made *for their benefit*.[39] Tribes claiming compensation for nineteenth-century confiscations have been paid at nineteenth-century land values in twentieth-century, inflated dollars.[40]

35. C. C. Langdell, "The Status of our New Territories," 12 *Harvard Law Review* 365 (1899).

36. See R. L. Barsh and R. L. Trosper, "Title I of the Indian Self-Determination and Education Assistance Act of 1974," 3 *American Indian Law Review* 361 (1975).

37. *Sioux Tribe v. U.S.*, 97 Ct. Cl. 613, 681 (1942).

38. Act of 13 August 1946, c. 959, 60 Stat. 1049; 25 U.S.C. 70.

39. *Fort Berthold v. U:S.*, 390 F.2d 686, 690 (1968); *Klamath and Modoc Tribes v. U.S.*, 436 F.2d 1008, 1015 (Ct.Cl. 1970), *cert. den'd* 404 U.S. 950 *sub nom. Anderson v. U.S.*

40. An assessment of the economic impact of the Indian claims process has yet to be printed. However, the fact that claims were evaluated at the value of the land at the time of taking (almost all before 1900), without interest, should be sufficiently suggestive of the shortcomings of this policy. A recent Interior Department memorandum to Congress indicated that tribes had been awarded only about 2 percent of the total value claimed. About half of all claims suits disposed of by 1971, moreover, were dismissed ("Hearings, 'Extension of the Indian Claims Committee,'" 16, 48, Senate Committee on Indian Affairs, 92nd Congress, 1st Session [1971]). A question may yet arise whether the Indian Claims Act itself was in violation of the Fifth Amendment, by reason of its valuation formula, leading to a second round of compensatory litigation. That would, however, do little to advance the political

Indians therefore receive substantially less compensation than other citizens would be entitled to under the Fifth Amendment. A highway condemnee, for example, does not lose interest on his award because he drives a car and may use the highway.

Lone Wolf brought the process of tribes' legal incorporation to completion. The territorial analogy of *Rogers* and *Kagama* established federal supremacy over their citizens' conduct, and the dependency doctrine freed Congress from constitutional constraints. Yet the authority of tribes to govern themselves, not inconsistent with federal encroachments, had never been repudiated. Tribal domestic sovereignty had been surreptitiously transmogrified, from exclusive to residual, from presumptively inherent to presumptively delegated. All that remained was to deny the authority of tribal governments to exist at all without express federal grant. That final brick was laid, ironically, by an act of Congress which purported to reacknowledge the legitimacy and value of tribal home rule.

---

future of tribes. It is in the nature of claims to settle past accounts, rather than validate future relationships. Indeed, the fact that termination legislation followed the Indian Claims Act by just seven years is suggestive. Moreover, tribes in their governmental capacity today have access to far greater sums through federal assistance, both general and Indian-related, than the prosecution of claims ever produced. Finally, claims awards have always been expended only for such purposes as the United States directs or approves (see 25 U.S.C. 1401−7 [1973], 25 C.F.R. 60). Secretary of the Interior Krug boasted to Congress in 1971 that the application of judgment funds to existing federal programs should obviate any concern that the claims policy would result in a net loss to the United States, and pointed out that the total judgment funds expended have little exceeded the Bureau of Indian Affairs' annual budget.

9

Tribes' "New Deal": The Indian Reorganization Act, 1934

The principle of guardianship reigned supreme for thirty years following the *Lone Wolf* decision. Passage of an act in 1924 to make all Indians United States citizens was no more than a fastidious afterthought, intended, according to the House report, to unify and simplify the multitude of laws extending citizenship to certain tribes or to individual Indians who met specified criteria.[1] In 1931 the chairman of the House Committee on Indian Affairs explained the citizenship act this way:

It would be a great inconsistency for the Government to act as guardian for an alien ward, so in order for our guardianship to be consistent, they had to be made citizens of the United States.[2]

Indians had to be made citizens so that the great experiment in coercive civilization could continue without possible legal impediments. Citizenship was conferred to benefit the government, not the tribes.

A remarkable hearing in the House committee that year showed just how little weight Congress gave to the citizenship act. The chairman intro-

1. House Report No. 222, 68th Congress, 1st Session (1924). See also Senate Report No. 441 of that session. Among the criteria then applicable to Indian citizenship were leaving the reservation, taking a patent in fee, and, for an Indian woman, marrying a non-Indian. The last of these is still on the books (25 U.S.C. 182).

2. "Hearing, 'Emancipated Citizenship for Indians,' " 12, House Committee on Indian Affairs, 71st Congress, 3rd Session (1931).

duced a bill which can only be described as the quintessential expression of the guardianship idea. Disgusted with the "little progress" made in anglicizing Indians since the General Allotment Act, he concluded that Indians were not being taught the right philosophy.[3] To be worthy of citizenship, Indians must learn

Industry, continuity of effort, loyalty, efficiency, perseverance, ambition, economy, business administration, neatness, sobriety, truthfulness, integrity, self-preservation and protection, law observance, self-reliance, self and family support, participation in governmental activities, mental growth and development, and love of country.[4]

This must be accomplished within fifty years, after which all federal bureaucratic supervision would automatically cease, and Indians would become citizens in fact as well as law.[5]

Chairman Sproul recommended that the United States treat Indians the same as "the guardians or parents of white children."[6] Their customs and beliefs, "as foreign and antagonistic to everything in America as that of a Chinaman," must be extirpated.[7] What were these "racial and acquired un-American beliefs"[8] to be challenged?

As a race of people, the Indian is not much inclined to continuous hard work; he is not very ambitious; he specially enjoys fishing, hunting, racing and other sports rather than any kind of hard labor; governmentally he is naturally a tribalist; he is more inclined to tribalism than to individualism; he is not especially interested in acquiring or building for himself a worth while home or residence; he is more interested in the welfare of his race than he is for himself and others individually.[9]

Worst of all, "[a]s long as any Indian upon the reservation has anything to eat, nobody upon the reservation is going to starve."[10] Sproul conceded to his critics that these "communistic" practices were more "altruistic" and

3. *Id.* 2.
4. Section 6 of the bill.
5. Sections 1, 7 and 8 of the bill. Representative Kelly of Pennsylvania observed that continuation of the bureau's supervisory powers had rendered the 1924 act virtually meaningless ("Hearing, 'Emancipated Citizenship,' " 8).
6. "Hearing, 'Emancipated Citizenship,' " 4. "By example you treat him as you teach a child. Let him walk and watch him carefully, help him if he falls, and you make him a citizen" (*id.* 23).
7. *Id.* 13.
8. *Id.* 5.
9. *Id.* 3.
10. *Id.* 12.

more consistent with the Christian religion than the "American" beliefs he sought to substitute for them, but maintained that "you have to teach this communalism out of them," it being "not practicable" in contemporary society.[11]

The Indians themselves had become accustomed to guardianship and, Sproul contended in a brilliant demonstration of what William Ryan calls "blaming the victim," were partly responsible for its continuance.[12] But much of the blame also fell on the Indian Office, which at six thousand employees and a $23 million budget had grown more than fourfold since allotment began.[13] After fifty years, the bureaucracy was larger, Indian population had increased, and tribes still existed.

In 1934 a new administration and reorganized Indian affairs committees brought matters to a head, simultaneously intensifying the attack on the bureau and rejecting altogether the validity of the wardship idea. The first official action taken by Congress was to take away the commissioner of Indian affairs' discretionary power to remove outsiders from reservations, branding it merely an "excuse for arbitrary abuses by bureaucratic officials."[14] At the same time a more sweeping alteration of affairs was hung up in committee. Drafted by the bureau itself[15] and enthusiastically endorsed by President Roosevelt,[16] this bill "to grant Indians . . . the freedom to organize" was confusing to almost everyone else. Even Commissoner of Indian Affairs Collier repeatedly expressed concern that Indians would oppose it out of ignorance and vowed to "persuade" them

11. Colloquoy of Sproul, Williamson and Kelly (*id.* 10−13).

12. *Id.* 4. William Ryan, *Blaming the Victim* (New York: 1972).

13. "Hearing, 'Emancipated Citizenship for Indians,'" 4, 6, 17.

14. See House Report No. 927, 73rd Congress, 2nd Session (1934), at 1. Act of 21 May 1934, c. 321, 48 Stat. 787.

15. "THE CHAIRMAN: I have never been able to find out who in the name of goodness drew up any of this bill.

MR. COLLIER: A good lawyer did it."

"Hearings, 'To Grant Indians Living Under Federal Tutelage the Freedom to Organize for Purposes of Local Self-Government and Economic Enterprise,'" 248, Senate Committee on Indian Affairs, 73rd Congress, 2nd Session (1934). Hereafter referred to as "Senate Hearing."

16. *Id.* 85−86, 145−46; "Hearings, 'Readjustment of Indian Affairs,'" 63, House Committee on Indian Affairs, 73rd Congress, 2nd Session (1934). Hereafter referred to as "House Hearing." On the floor of the House, Chairman Howard quipped, "I do not want anybody to vote against this bill simply because President Roosevelt thinks it is a good bill" (78 *Congressional Record* 11732 [15 June 1934]). In his message to Congress, the president expressed his faith that the bill would encourage Indians to "take an active and responsible part in the solution of their own problems" (House Report No. 1804, 73rd Congress, 2nd Session [1934], at 8).

otherwise if necessary.[17] Representative Rogers of Oklahoma summed it all up when he observed, "Unless the Indians are much more intelligent than the Members of this House here are, they do not understand it."[18] Much of the responsibility for this confusion must be attributed to contradictions in Collier's own committee testimony.

The wardship idea was under attack. "Bear in mind, please," Representative Howard advised the House, "that the status of ward was not of the Indian's seeking. It was forced upon him by our Government."[19] "[T]he incompetency of the Indian . . . is a legal fiction," Collier agreed, "It is a status in law and not a condition of his mind or body."[20] The whole principle was anomalous in our law. "Ordinarily, a guardian is charged with higher responsibility, and a greater degree of care, and with a narrower rather than a broader power by reason of his fiduciary relationship," Senator Steiwer remarked during the hearings, "I am wondering what there is in this particular relationship that we are now dealing with that would give the guardian a greater power than a guardian normally would enjoy."[21] Interior Solicitor Fahy could only answer that "Congress . . . exerts that power constantly."

The Senate committee was disturbed "that the Government can go further in dealing with Indians than in dealing with white people," and demanded to know what the proposed legislation would do to change the situation.[22] Commissioner Collier never offered a satisfactory reply. One day he told the House committee that "[t]he guardianship of the Indian is definitely ended by this plan,"[23] and another he said that the bill would make guardianship "permanent."[24] He also agreed with Representative Christianson that the bill would end federal guardianship of Indians as persons, but not the guardianship of their property.[25] In the end he admitted that "the guardianship of the Government is going to last a long

17. House Hearing 43, 56, 121, 308–9. He did think that Indians were "better informed about this legislation than the mass of the population generally is about important legislation" (*id.* 309). But see the comments of Indian leaders (*id.* 141–43, 265, 299–300) and by the Indian Rights Association (*id.* 502).
18. *Id.* 311, 312–13.
19. 78 *Congressional Record* 11726 (15 June 1934).
20. Senate Hearing 68–69.
21. *Id.* 187.
22. *Id.* 188.
23. House Hearing 65.
24. *Id.* 20.
25. *Id.* 66.

time. It is a thing very profoundly rooted in our political and legal history.''[26] Blaming guardianship on history is a poor excuse for failing to address it in pertinent legislation.

Collier maintained that the bill was primarily economic, not political, in purpose.[27] Title III provided for freezing the allotment process, rationalizing inheritance, and reconsolidating tribal territories by means of free-market purchase, condemnation, and preemptive tribal purchase rights. It also established a revolving credit fund for economic development. In Collier's review, the bill was a three-pronged attack on decreasing reservation per capita land ownership: acquiring more land, making land more productive, and training young Indians to take off-reservation jobs.[28] Capitalization was a key element of the plan,[29] along with more efficient, large-scale management of forestry and range,[30] and keeping lands from being divided into inefficiently small parcels through inheritance.[31] All current economic problems were blamed on allotment, and all of Collier's remedies were designed to undo that policy.[32] Because it would increase reservation output and make Indians wealthier, the land program would mitigate the need for federal subsidies to tribes.[33] "In the long run the policy established by this bill will reduce Federal expenditures, although," Collier admitted, "not immediately."[34]

This may have warmed the committees to the bill, but political issues soon proved to be much more important to its survival. Although the commissioner blamed the General Allotment Act for Indians' problems, Congress was unwilling to accept the onus. Burton Wheeler, chairman of the Senate committee, squarely accused the bureau of subverting that law and complained about congressional reliance on bureau representations of the state of Indian affairs.[35] It was time to end, in House Chairman

26. *Id.*
27. Senate Hearing 62.
28. House Hearing 307−8. Some states may have feared that the land consolidation provision was merely an excuse for expansion of the public domain (Senate Hearing 40).
29. *Id.* 74, 154, 160; House Hearing 31, 109.
30. Senate Hearing 153−54, 158; House Hearing 17, 21, 30−31, 35; see also 78 *Congressional Record* 11729 (15 June 1934).
31. Senate Hearing 91, 151; House Hearing 17−18, 32; 78 *Congressional Record* 11730 (15 June 1934).
32. Senate Hearing 31, 58−61; House Hearing 16, 32.
33. 78 *Congressional Record* 11726, 11728−9 (15 June 1934).
34. House Hearing 60.
35. Senate Hearing 162, 174−75; also 148.

Howard's words, this "sinister . . . bureaucratic absolutism" and free Indians from their status as "Federal peons."[36]

It was impossible for the bureau to proceed without a confession of guilt. Collier described his agency as an "autocrat," a "benevolent despot" with "boundless powers."[37] The proposed legislation, he promised, would end all of this, however,

[T]he unlimited and largely unreviewable exercise of administrative discretion by the Secretary of the Interior and Commissioner of Indian Affairs has been one of the chief sources of complaint on the part of the Indians. It is the chief object of the bill to terminate such bureaucratic authority by transferring the administration of the Indian Service to the Indian communities themselves.[38]

Collier laid the blame for this situation on Congress, however, not the administration.

[T]he bill does not arrogate to the Indian Office or to the Interior Department added power. On the contrary, the bill divests these offices of much arbitrary power; makes them responsible to the Indian whom they serve, and responsible with much greater detail than at present to the courts, and to Congress which has delegated to the Indian Office far too wide a discretion in the past.[39]

How was this reallocation of power to be accomplished? Title I of the proposal declared a policy of authorizing Indians "to organize for the purposes of local self-government and economic enterprise" to promote "civil liberty, political responsibility, and economic independence," and to be accompanied by a "gradual" transfer of power from the bureau to tribal governments.[40] It contemplated the secretary "granting" tribes "such powers of government . . . as may seem fitting in the light of the experience, capacities, and desires of the Indians concerned," in a charter.[41] The charter would provide transition machinery for the gradual transfer of further powers.[42]

The bill enumerated powers the secretary might lawfully grant in a charter, including power to regulate commerce, acquire and dispose of

36. 78 *Congressional Record* 11727, 11729 (15 June 1934).
37. Senate Hearing 31–32, 70, 106, 151.
38. House Hearing 22.
39. *Id*. 20.
40. Title I, sec. 1, H.R. 7902.
41. Title I, sec. 2. Collier testified that the secretary would have to submit his reasons for disapproving a charter to Congress (Senate Hearing 32).
42. Title I, sec. 3.

property, and maintain courts of limited jurisdiction. The charter might also authorize the tribe to compel the transfer of bureau employees.[43] Administrative, regulatory, and service functions of the bureau itself could be delegated to the tribe either on a short-term, experimental basis or for indefinite periods, by contract, subject to "reassumption" by the bureau if the tribe failed to perform satisfactorily.[44]

The worm in the apple was Section 9 of the bill, directing the secretary to "continue to exercise all existing powers of supervision and control over Indian affairs . . . not transferred by charter . . . and . . . to enforce by administrative order or veto, if so provided within the charter, . . . all provisions contained in a charter." This left the secretary with virtually unlimited discretion to retain power through the imposition of "conditions" in charters.

Discussion of these provisions in committee generated more heat than light. Commissioner Collier insisted that the tribe would remain free to choose its own form of government. "The form of organization adopted under the charter is wide open. They could organize into the most ultramodern thing in the world," or remain "traditional."[45] He was forced, however, to meet widespread charges that features of the bill, especially provisions for tribal ownership and cooperative management, inclined tribes towards "communism."[46]

The bill does not introduce any socialistic or communistic idea or device. The facilities which it extends to Indians are those facilities of organization and those modern instrumentalities of business which are the commonplaces of American life and which are indispensible to the prosperity of Americans.[47]

43. Title I, sec. 4. Tribal courts would have been limited to disputes between Indians and to the imposition of fines not to exceed $500 and imprisonment not to exceed six months. An almost identical provision became part of the Indian Civil Rights Act in 1968. See 25 U.S.C. 1302(7).

44. Title I, sec. 7–8. Although these provisions died in committee, the bureau apparently went ahead anyway. In 1975 such transfers were finally given congressional sanction (R. L. Barsh and R. L. Trosper, "The Indian Self-Determination and Education Assistance Act of 1975," 3 *American Indian Law Review* 361 [1975]). In 1934 Collier assured tribes they would receive adequate funding to maintain transferred programs, but the Senate Committee chastized him for holding out such hopes, reminding him that Congress had power to revise appropriations at any time (Senate Hearing 94–97, 105; see also House Hearing 23–24, 27). Although the 1975 act guarantees funding for transferred programs, we are skeptical of the enforceability of that provision (Barsh and Trosper, "Indian Self-Determination," 378).

45. House Hearing 44; also 21, 38.

46. E.g., see House Hearing 178–185; 78 *Congressional Record* 11735–7 (15 June 1934).

47. House Hearing 20; also 44.

Did this foreclose tribes' adopting "un-American" forms of organization? If Collier was implying that the bill's purpose was to lend tribes modern forms of *business* organization, why not simply incorporate them instead of constituting them as local governments?[48]

Collier volunteered a grim picture of tribes' political survival. Under allotment, "not only were they deprived of the right to think and act, but the Government actively prescribed all Indian organization."[49] The bureau still enjoyed discretion . . . over their political thought and political activities."[50] Moreover, "In a great many Indian reservations—more than half of them—the tribal relations have been dissolved, and elsewhere the tribal customs are so vague that nobody knows what they are."[51] Chairman Howard was even more demonstrative when he explained the background of the bill to the House.

Although many thousands of Indians are living in tribal status on the various reservations, their own native tribal institutions have very largely disintegrated or been openly suppressed, and the entire management of Indian affairs has been more and more concentrated in the hands of the Federal Indian Service. The powers of this Bureau over the daily lives and affairs of the Indians have in the past been almost unlimited. It has been an extraordinary example of political absolutism in the midst of a free democracy—absolutism built up on the most rigid bureaucratic line, irresponsible to the Indians and to the public; shackled by obsolete laws; resistant to change, reform or progress.[52]

However, many tribes had preserved their own governments independent of the bureau and had never recognized bureau supremacy.[53] They feared that adoption of a federal charter would constitute recognition of federal

48. As we hope to demonstrate empirically in a future book, the "corporate ideal" survived in bureau administration of the Indian Reorganization Act. The structure of tribal governments mimics corporate organization. Even tribal nomenclature is corporate: e.g., "chairman" of the council, which is often a "business committee" or "board of directors," with "annual meetings." Was this done because Collier admired corporate organization, or to downplay the governmental nature of tribes?
49. Senate Hearing 64. See also Theodore H. Haas, "The Legal Aspects of Indian Affairs from 1887 to 1957," in George E. Simpson and J. Milton Yinger, eds., *American Indians and American Life*; 311 *The Annals of the American Academy of Political and Social Science* 12, 16 (Philadelphia: 1957). Felix Cohen once suggested that the oppression of tribal government was intended to force Indians to take up allotments and sever allegiance to their tribe ("Indian Rights and the Federal Courts," 24 *Minnesota Law Review* 145, 189–90 [1940]).
50. House Hearing 48.
51. *Id.* 316.
52. 78 *Congressional Record* 11729 (15 June 1934).
53. Senate Hearing 119; House Hearing 246, 266.

authority and limitation of their traditional powers.[54] Once a federal charter had been accepted, would that operate as a relinqishment of any source of tribal legitimacy external to the charter? Would subsequent revocation of the charter dissolve the tribe as a body politic?[55]

Collier never answered these fears directly. He did point out, however, that under current laws traditional tribal governments "may be wiped out upon our whim,"[56] but under the proposed legislation "[t]he Secretary could not amend or nullify the charter of self-government." "That is very essential in the bill," he argued, "otherwise the whole thing would be a hoax."[57] Although no legislation could protect tribal government from Congress, this bill at least "eliminates the Bureau's power of termination at will."[58]

This, too, was a contradiction, for elsewhere Collier told Congress that charters could be revoked by the secretary if he determined in his discretion that the tribe had "failed."[59] He was unable to propose a consistent theory of power. At one time he argued that "in a large measure, the charters granted under this bill to Indian communities will be a recognition of tribal powers which Congress has never seen fit to abrogate, rather than a grant of new powers," such that revocation of the charter would simply restore the status quo.[60] At another he analogized the bill to state and federal delegations of power to municipalities and described chartered tribes as federal instrumentalities.[61] He variously described his proposed charter communities as "municipal government," "town government," and "little colonies," with powers limited to "matters of local concern"[62] which might be permitted to be exercised in conflict with state laws[63] and then again might not.[64]

One thing was clear: grants of charter powers "may differ profoundly" in the secretary's discretion.[65] Although he intimated to the Senate

54. Senate Hearing 82−83; 78 *Cong. Rec.* 11736−7 (15 June 1934).
55. Senate Hearing 53, 108 (representatives of the Blackfeet and Arapahoe tribes).
56. *Id.* 32. See also *id.* 64; House Hearing 18; 78 *Cong. Rec.* 11729 (15 June 1934).
57. Senate Hearing 107.
58. *Id.* 65.
59. *Id.* 32; House Hearing 42.
60. *Id.* 23, 43.
61. *Id.* 23, 24, 25, 67, 90, 117; Senate Hearing 268−69.
62. *Id.* 65, 66, 68, 69, 70, 71, 154, 157.
63. House Hearing 123, 324−25.
64. Senate Hearing 177−80.
65. House Hearing 22; Senate Hearing 32.

committee that the bureau would not review individual tribal ordinances,[66] Interior Solicitor Fahy conceded to the House committee that charters might well "require that ordinances of certain types should be subject to the approval of the Secretary of the Interior" in accordance with the previous custom of the government.[67] Chairman Howard agreed. "It is obvious that, in their initial stages at any rate, Indian corporations should have careful supervision by the Government to protect their members from unwise enterprises."[68]

Would the bill, then, "reduce and decentralize" the bureau as Chairman Howard promised?[69] Representative Kelly of Pennsylvania concluded that "it tends to make the Bureau domination more complete and secure," resulting in nothing more than a "bigger and better Bureau."[70] Bureau discretion was not eliminated, but paradoxically made "more absolute."[71] Chairman Wheeler was joined by tribal leaders and "friends of the Indian" in predicting an increase in the staff, cost and power of the bureau should the bill pass. In the end, Collier was forced to admit that his office would retain significant power, but "only a tithe" of what it already enjoyed and only what was necessary to provide some degree of "flexibility."[72] He pointed out that the bill created a special federal court of Indian affairs with authority to review the actions of the Bureau of Indian Affairs.[73]

Even the long-range goal of the program was in question. Commissioner Collier pointed out the "advantages of community action" by analogy to economic cooperatives.[74] He was also prepared to ascribe a nobler, political purpose to his proposal: to "extend to all Indians that minimum of home-rule in domestic and cultural matters which is basic to

66. As did Collier (*id.* 106−7):

"SEN. WHEELER. If you give them a charter you want to give them one so that they can do these things subject to the approval of the Secretary of the Interior.
    MR. COLLIER. No. . . ."
67. House Hearing 327−28. Everyone agreed that tribes' choice of legal counsel should be supervised (Senate Hearing 244).
68. 78 *Cong. Rec.* 11731 (15 June 1934). See also Collier's remarks in Senate Hearing 323−24.
69. 78 *Congressional Record* 11732 (15 June 1934).
70. *Id.* 11733−4.
71. Senate Hearing 56, 66−67, 163−64, 175−76, 215; House Hearing 47.
72. House Hearing 47.
73. *Id.* 52−53; Senate Hearing 137, 196−97. But this feature was deleted before the bill reached the floor.
74. *Id.* 75−76, 152.

American life.''[75] Bureaucratic absolutism had exceeded all tolerable levels. ''Any American community that was at the mercy of such things would move out or rise in rebellion.''[76] House Chairman Howard agreed that recognition of tribal governing bodies would end ''taxation without representation'' and give Indians ''what the white man has fought and died for over the centuries: The right to personal liberty and to a voice in the conduct of his daily life.''[77]

On the Senate side, Chairman Wheeler argued that tribes should be limited to the exercise of proprietary powers. In his opinion, Indians had already become largely assimilated. Giving them encouragement to make separate laws and create separate political agencies at this time would ''bring you into all kinds of conflict [with the states] and be a step backward.''[78] Collier was loathe to alienate the support of assimilationists, so he told them they would get what they wanted, too. In his prepared statement for the House committee, Collier observed of the bill,

> Does it contemplate for the Indian a permanent tribal status, isolation from the white man, collective as distinguished from individual enterprise, and nonassimilation into American civilization?
>   The answer is a clear-cut one: No.[79]

Of course, this promise is not inconsistent with permanent tribal status *without* isolation, or some idea of political, as opposed to cultural assimilation. Elsewhere Collier intimated that tribes might someday become state counties,[80] a form of political assimilation without loss of collective identity which would not perpetuate tribes as such. In any event, the assimilationists in Congress heard what they wanted to hear in this and other of Collier's statements.

So did the remaining paternalists. Collier told *them* that the program would give Indians ''experience'' in ''civic and business responsibility and

75. House Hearing 20.
76. ''I, in my town of Mill Valley, or you, in your town, if we had someone from Washington dictating to us about different things, how would we like it? We would not endure it'' (*id*. 40; also 64).
77. 78 *Congressional Record* 11727 (15 June 1934) (Howard). See also 11731.
78. Senate Hearing 249, 170–71, 177–78, 199–200, 208. Compare Collier's remarks (*id*. 251).
79. House Hearing 20.
80. *Id*. 69. ''Not until the chartered Indian Community is a complete autonomous governmental unit able to exist without special federal appropriations or special federal control will it be able to take a legal place within the State'' (*id*. 28). Collier also suggested that tribes be gradually subjected to state taxes (*id*. 50).

the opportunity to manage property and money," educating them for "real assimilation."[81] Indians would "gradually learn to administer their own affairs . . . thus making continuous progress in the exercise of citizenship."[82] Chairman Howard carried this perspective back to the full House, arguing that past policy had deprived Indians of "practice" in the arts of business and government.

The program of self-support and of business and civic experience in the management of their own affairs, combined with the program of education, will permit increasing numbers of Indians to enter the white world on a footing of equal competition.[83]

Collier gave every faction in Congress what it wanted, stood firm on nothing but the need to pass the bill, and was purposely vague throughout.[84] Whatever his real purpose—and he would later write that his real purpose was to guarantee Indians a measure of true self-government[85]—he created a situation in which the impact of the law would come out entirely in its discretionary implementation by the bureau. Was it a bureau bill? It appears that employees who criticized it while it was pending in Congress were threatened with dismissal.[86]

The self-government features of the bill were still so controversial that a compromise measure became necessary.[87] Most of the economic features of Collier's bill were preserved, but the new draft eliminated the enumeration of tribal governing powers, the authorization for secretarial review of the exercise of those powers, the provisions for transfer of administrative functions from the bureau to tribes, and the provisions for judicial review of administrative decisions. The original ten sections were trimmed to one, which provides in pertinent part that

Any Indian tribe, or tribes, residing on the same reservation, shall have the right to organize for its common welfare, and may adopt an appropriate constitution and

81. *Id.* 21.
82. *Id.* 63–64.
83. 78 *Congressional Record* 11729, 11732 (15 June 1934).
84. Representative Werner of South Dakota caught him at this and openly accused him of equivocating (*id.* 64).
85. John Collier, *The Indians of the Americas* 261–87 (New York: 1947). Compare another controversial Indian commissioner's memoirs: Francis E. Leupp, *The Indian and his Problem* (New York: 1910).
86. Letter of the Secretary of the Interior, 78 *Congressional Record* 11738 (15 June 1934).
87. *Id.* 11726–7, 11732; also Senate Hearing 237.

bylaws, which shall become effective when ratified . . . and approved by the Secretary of the Interior. . . .

In addition to all powers vested in any Indian tribe or tribal council by existing law, the constitution adopted by said tribe shall also vest in such tribe or its tribal council the following rights and powers: To employ legal counsel, the choice of counsel and fixing of fees to be subject to the approval of the Secretary of the Interior; to prevent the sale, disposition, lease, or encumbrance of tribal lands, interests in lands, or other tribal assets without the consent of the tribe; and to negotiate with the Federal, State, and local Governments.[88]

Unlike the original, the Indian Reorganization Act in its final form requires that certain *minimal* powers be provided in every constitution, but leaves the balance to the interpretation of "existing law." On its face, the act leaves unresolved the most elementary issues: tribal permanence, residual sovereignty, and continuing bureaucratic control of tribal activities.

Whether the new law operates as a grant or recognition of tribal powers turns on that ambiguous phrase, "all powers vested in any Indian tribe or tribal council by existing law." It was the product of hasty compromise, never debated or fully explained before the act's passage. So, ironically, Congress itself turned to the solicitor of the Interior Department four months later to interpret it. The solicitor's reply embraced a broad conceptualization of tribal status, much warmer to residual sovereignty than any of the testimony heard in committee earlier the same year.

"The question of what powers are vested in an Indian tribe or tribal council by existing law," Solicitor Nathan Margold reasoned cautiously in this crucial opinion, "cannot be answered in detail for each Indian tribe without reference to hundreds of special treaties and special acts of Congress."[89] "It is possible, however," he admitted, "on the basis of the reported cases, the written opinions of the various executive departments, and those statutes of Congress which are of general import, to define the powers which have heretofore been recognized as lawfully within the jurisdiction of an Indian tribe."

Margold characterized the Indian Reorganization Act as a recognition of tribes' original sovereignty rather than a codification of federal laws delegating tribes limited powers.

88. §16 of the act, 25 U.S.C. 476. Compare §17, 25 U.S.C. 477, which incorporates only business powers, consistent with Senator Wheeler's original proposal.
89. Op. Sol. M27781, 55 I.D. 14, 17 (25 October 1934). Felix Cohen's widely-read works followed Margold closely ("Indian Rights and the Federal Courts," 24 *Minnesota Law Review* 145 [1940]; *Federal Indian Law* [Washington, D.C.: 1942]).

I have no doubt that the phrase "powers vested in any Indian tribe or tribal council by existing law" does not refer merely to those powers which have been specifically granted by the express language of treaties or statutes, but refers rather to the whole body of tribal powers which the courts and Congress alike have recognized as properly wielded by Indian tribes, whether by virtue of specific statutory grants of power or by virtue of the original sovereignty of the tribe insofar as such sovereignty has not been curtailed by restrictive legislation or surrendered by treaties.[90]

If Congress had intended to limit the powers of the tribes to those granted in special legislation, it would not have used the broad phrase "existing law" when defining them. "[I]t was clearly not the purpose of Congress to narrow the body of tribal powers which have heretofore been recognized by the courts" to "express statutory grants of specific powers."[91]

From his survey of all "the judicial decisions, treaties, constitutional provisions and practices, and other sources controlling the decisions of courts," Margold announced what he conceived to be the "most basic principle of all Indian law":

[T]hose powers which are lawfully vested in an Indian tribe are not, in general, delegated powers granted by express acts of Congress, but rather inherent powers of a limited sovereignty which have never been extinguished. Each Indian tribe begins its relationship with the Federal Government as a sovereign power, recognized as such in treaty and legislation. The powers of sovereignty have been limited from time to time by special treaties and laws designed to take from the Indian tribes control of matters which in the judgment of Congress, these tribes could no longer be safely permitted to handle. The statutes of Congress, then, must be examined to determine the limitations of tribal sovereignty rather than to determine its sources or its positive content. What is not expressly limited remains with the domain of tribal sovereignty, and therefore properly falls within the statutory category, "powers vested in any Indian tribe or tribal council by existing law."[92]

"The legal powers of an Indian tribe, measured by the decisions of the highest courts," he advised Congress, "are far more extensive than the powers which most Indian tribes have been actually permitted by omnipresent officials to exercise in their own right."[93] Three basic principles

90. 55 I.D. 18–19.
91. *Id.* 19.
92. *Id.*
93. *Id.* 26.

mark "the whole course of judicial decision on the nature of Indian tribal powers."[94]

An Indian tribe possesses, in the first instance, all the powers of any sovereign State. Conquest renders the tribe subject to the legislative power of the United States and, in substance, terminates the external powers of sovereignty of the tribe, *e.g.*, its power to enter into treaties with foreign nations, but does not by itself affect the internal sovereignty of the tribe, *i.e.*, its powers of local self-government. These powers are subject to be qualified by treaties and by express legislation of Congress, but save as thus expressly qualified, full powers of internal sovereignty are vested in Indian tribes and in their duly constituted organs of government.[95]

Margold's opinion emphasized that judicial recognition of tribal sovereignty "has not been a matter of lip service to a venerable but outmoded theory," but was based on "a spirit of whole-hearted sympathy and respect." The Supreme Court had "opposed the efforts of lower courts and administrative officials to infringe upon tribal sovereignty."[96] As an illustration he cited the Court's doctrine that "Indian laws and statutes are to be interpreted not in accordance with the technical rules of the common law, but in the light of the traditions and circumstances of the Indian people."[97]

"The whole course of Congressional legislation with respect to the Indians has been based upon a recognition of tribal autonomy, qualified only where the need for other types of governmental control has become clearly manifested."[98]

Thus treaties and statutes of Congress have been looked to by the courts as limitations upon original tribal powers, or, at most, evidences of recognition of such powers, rather than as the direct source of tribal powers. This is but an application of the general principle that "It is only by positive enactments, even in the case of conquered and subdued nations that their laws are changed by the conqueror."[99]

To terminate tribal autonomy, then, "the provisions of a treaty or statute must be positive and unambiguous," not the product of "doubtful inference."[100] The political survival of the tribe is therefore to be pre-

94. *Id.* 22.
95. *Id.*
96. *Id.* 26.
97. *Id.* 27.
98. *Id.* 28.
99. *Id.* 20. As authority for this general principle, Margold cited *Wall v. Williamson*, 8 Ala. 45, 51 (1845), but *Wall* contains no such language and was decided on other grounds.
100. *Id.* 30; 20.

sumed. "[T]he internal sovereignty of the Indian tribes continues, unimpaired by the changes that have occurred in the manners and customs of Indian life, and, for the future, remains a most powerful vehicle for the movement of the Indian tribes toward a richer, social existence."

The problem was that tribal government had been suppressed or ignored to the point where, at the time the act passed, very little original sovereignty was left. Margold carefully argued that these encroachments were merely de facto.

It is a fact that State governments and administrative officials have frequently trespassed upon the realm of tribal autonomy, presuming to govern the Indian tribes through State law or departmental regulation or arbitrary administrative fiat, but these trespasses have not impaired the vested local powers of local self-government which have been recognized again and again when these trespasses have been challenged by an Indian tribe. "Power and authority rightfully conferred do not necessarily cease to exist in consequence of long nonuser." (*United States ex rel. Standing Bear v. Crook*, 5 Dill. 453, 460.) The Wheeler-Howard [Indian Reorganization] Act, by affording statutory recognition of these powers of local self-government and administrative assistance in developing adequate mechanisms for such government, may reasonably be expected to end the conditions that have in the past led the Interior Department and various State agencies to deal with matters that are properly within the legal competence of the Indian tribes themselves.[101]

Margold concluded by classifying as *inherent* all of those specific powers which the bureau's original bill had described as *granted*, including "power to adopt a form of government . . . through which the will of the tribe is to be executed," control of membership, domestic relations, probate, taxation, land use controls and business regulation. He distinguished from these powers tribal power over bureau employees, which exists only to the extent "expressly delegated by the Interior Department."[102]

This Interior Department opinion was not from the mouth of Congress, nor, it seems probable, would a majority of Congress have endorsed it. There was no official denial of its validity, however, and it had a virtue of clarity and conceptual consistency entirely absent in the legislative history of the Indian Reorganization Act. As a result it achieved greater influence than the act itself, and all subsequent developments in doctrine must be measured from this foundation.

101. *Id.* 28–29.
102. *Id.* 65–66.

10

The Triumph of the Doctrine of Plenary Power, 1934-1968

The administration's official interpretation of the Indian Reorganization Act proved to be a two-edged sword. It endorsed the principle of original or residual tribal sovereignty, reversing a fifty-year trend of describing tribal governments as mere instrumentalities of federal "tutelage." At the same time, by resurrecting the fiction of conquest, it dispelled any lingering hopes that congressional intervention in tribes' domestic affairs could be limited by treaties. What is the meaning of residual sovereignty if the residuum can be confiscated by Congress at any time without recourse? Congress continued to enjoy as much power over tribes as previously, but had been cautioned to exercise it, if at all, only in express acts.

With the publication by the Interior Department of Felix Cohen's *Handbook of Federal Indian Law* in 1942, the principles established in the Margold opinion became conventional dogma. Cohen's *Handbook* was the first work of its kind. In a field of law Commissioner Collier once described as "decidedly peculiar," it was welcomed by lawyers and quickly became a "litigation bible."[1]

---

1. "Hearings, 'Readjustment of Indian Affairs,' " 54. At this time Cohen was assistant solicitor of the Department of the Interior. "Felix S. Cohen: Biography," in his *Handbook of Federal Indian Law* ix (repr. of 1942 ed., Albuquerque: 1973).

It is, as Felix Frankfurter observed, the only book that has made sense and order from "the vast hodgepodge of treaties, statutes, judicial and administrative rulings, and unrecorded practice in which the intricacies and perplexities, confusion and injustices of the law governing Indians lay concealed."[2]

Because of its straightforwardness and generalization, it seduced many members of the legal profession into ignoring the warning of Secretary of the Interior Harold Ickes in his foreword to the original edition:

This work cannot have the legal force of an act of Congress or the decision of a court. Whatever legal force it will have must be derived from the original authorities which have been assiduously gathered and patiently analyzed. In publishing this work the Department of the Interior does not assume responsibility for every generalization, prediction, or inference that may be found in the volume. What is implicit, however, in the fact of publication is a considered judgment that this volume will prove a valuable aid in fulfilling the obligation which Congress has laid upon the Department of the Interior to protect and safeguard the rights of our oldest national minority.[3]

The *Handbook* did not purport to be a cyclopedia or the last word on federal Indian law.[4] It was, both in fact and in principle, an attempt by the Interior Department to reaffirm federal power over Indian tribes in a more conceptually consistent manner. It was a handbook for employees of the Interior Department, not for tribes.

Representative Werner remarked prophetically during the 1934 House hearings, "In regard to the promises that were made to the Indians in regard to this bill, that is something that no one can tell."[5] Collier admitted that "administration can defeat any law," yet he was prepared to predict that the Indian Reorganization Act would stabilize federal Indian policy and put it on a new footing.[6] He promised "the elimination of the Office of Indian Affairs in its present capacity as a nonrepresentative governing authority over the lives and property of Indians," and its eventual reduction to a "purely advisory and special service body."[7] When Felix Cohen compiled the *Handbook of Federal Indian Law* eight years later, the

2. *Id.* xviii.
3. *Id.* xiv−xx.
4. *Id.* xxviii.
5. "Hearing, 'Readjustment of Indian Affairs,' " 191.
6. *Id.* 62−63; 37.
7. *Id.* 22.

promise was renewed in the most vigorous terms.

The most basic of all Indian rights, the right of self-government, is the Indian's last defense against administrative oppression, for in a realm which the states are powerless to govern and where Congress, occupied with more pressing national affairs, cannot govern wisely and well, there remains a large no-man's land in which government can emanate only from officials of the Interior Department or from the Indians themselves. Self-government is thus the Indians' only alternative to rule by a government department.[8]

In 1947, the bureau officially took stock of the Indian Reorganization Act's first ten years in a publication evidently intended for general distribution. Written by Chief Counsel Theodore Haas, the report applauded a "new relation" between the agency and tribes, a "partnership" in which tribes that "proved capable and faithful to their trust . . . would be delegated additional powers by the Secretary."[9] Haas likened the *old* bureau to "a colonial administrator who feels a keen sense of duty as a superior over an inferior people whose lives he controls"; who unconsciously downplays Indian achievements and broadcasts their failures; and who resents, avoids, and even suppresses tribal governments.[10] Unfortunately the *new* bureau, he explained apologetically, was hampered by the survival of such attitudes among its employees. Other causes of failure were identified. Indians were inexperienced in administration and lacked leadership, and when confronted with disappointment, blamed their difficulties on the bureau and on IRA government.[11] Indians were also misinformed and swayed by rumors instigated by whites that the act was a plot to take away their land.[12] Indians and aging civil servants were responsible for the act's failures, not Congress or the Collier administration.

On the plus side, Haas stressed the economic impact of the act. The political accomplishments were left vague. In contrast to the Margold opinion, Haas described tribal powers as "delegated" rather than recognized, a reward for good behavior rather than a right. "The Department offers its assistance in the preparation of [tribal constitutions], "but only to the extent that such assistance is required," Haas explained defensively,

8. *Handbook of Federal Indian Law* 112.
9. Theodore H. Haas, "Ten Years of Tribal Government under I.R.A.," *Tribal Relations Pamphlet No. 11* (Washington, D.C.: 1947).
10. *Id.* 5−6.
11. *Id.* 6.
12. *Id.* 6−7.

"Scrupulous care is exercised to see that the document represents the wishes of the Indians."[13] Furthermore,

Many constitutional provisions are substantially the same, notably those designed to enable tribes to take advantage of the specific powers and benefits provided for in the Act. There are wide variations, however, in the provisions regarding tribal membership, the governmental organization, the safeguards available to individual members, the methods of handling tribal business and the extent of the supervision of the Secretary of the Interior.[14]

The secretary's dangerous power of vetoing ratified constitutions was soft peddled by emphasizing the tribes' right to hold ratification elections.[15]

Evidence of political change and its benefits was approached from the government's point of view, not the Indians'. Tribes now had their own office buildings and law and order codes, to be sure, Why were these things advantageous? Only three noneconomic payoffs were specifically addressed. Two of these were really payoffs for the bureau. Since "[o]ne of the major problems of local agency administration is to diffuse a knowledge of its policies and of other important facts to local personnel and others principally affected," tribal government afforded a valuable opportunity to delegate to Indian leaders "a responsibility of conveying the news to their people."[16] Moreover, tribal government "also furnishes a means whereby administrators may know the opinions, hopes and aspirations of the Indians," presumably so that this "insight" can be applied to the process of supervision.[17] In short, tribal governments would help the bureau assess Indian sentiment and communicate bureau orders. As a go-between, tribal government would assume apparent responsibility for the bureau's actions. The effect of the act, to this extent, was just what one of its critics predicted in 1934, "a bigger and better Bureau."

There was one more political consideration. "An ability to vocalize a complaint constitutes an emotional outlet of distinct social value."[18] Tribal government afforded Indians an opportunity to *feel* as if they were participating in the decisions that bound them, and thereby mitigated their sense of oppression.

13. *Id.* 2.
14. *Id.* 3.
15. *Id.* 2.
16. *Id.* 10–11.
17. *Id.* 11.
18. *Id.* 11.

There is no doubt that the gradual increase in self-government among the Indians during the last decade has contributed much toward overcoming historical bitterness and mistrust felt by some Indian groups against the United States. This has been evidenced by Indian leaders who frequently expressed their patriotism by speeches and deeds.[19]

The Sproul committee had resolved sixteen years earlier to *teach* historical resentment out of Indians. According to Haas, the same objective was being accomplished by giving Indians a carefully limited voice in their own affairs.

In fact Commissioner Collier described his own program when he said of the General Allotment Act, "[t]he very act intended to put them on their feet and make them . . . self-governing, developed paternalistic and bureaucratic restrictions."[20] He promised Congress that it would end arbitrary bureaucratic supervision of probate, selection of lawyers to represent tribes, and control of Indian contracts.[21] None of this changed.[22] He promised that tribes would be involved in the federal budgetary process, but in 1947 Haas admitted that this had not been done.[23]

The Margold opinion was explicit regarding the promise of tribal self-government.

Since any group of men, in order to act as a group, must act through forms which give the action, the character and authority of group action, an Indian tribe must, if it has any power at all, have the power to prescribe the forms through which its will may be registered. The first element of sovereignty, and the last which may survive successive statutory limitations of tribal power, is the power of the tribe to determine and define its own form of government.[24]

Section 16 of the Indian Reorganization Act requires secretarial approval before a tribal constitution can become effective.[25] Section 9 of the original bill also authorized secretarial vetoes of tribal legislation, but it was omitted in the act. Nevertheless, tribal constitutions were not approved

---

19. As evidenced by their giving up *some of their land* for the war effort: (*id.* 7−8). Similarly, *Report of the Secretary of the Interior, 1944* 238.

20. "Hearings, 'Readjustment of Indian Affairs,' " 33.

21. *Id.* 47−48.

22. R. L. Barsh and J. Y. Henderson, "Tribal Administration of Natural Resource Development," 52 *North Dakota Law Review* 307, 314−27 (1975).

23. Haas, "Ten Years of Tribal Government," 11.

24. Op. Sol. M27781, 55 I.D. 14, 30 (25 October 1934).

25. Act of 18 June 1934, c. 576 S16, 48 Stat. 984, 25 U.S.C. 476.

unless they delegated extensive veto powers to the secretary.[26] In 1964 the Senate Committee on the Judiciary could find no statutory authority for this practice and concluded that it "frustrates responsible tribal self-government."[27] "[T]he tribe's ability to govern its affairs had been sacrificed to bureaucratic control."

In the Indian Reorganization Act's first decade, ninety-one tribes adopted constitutions,[28] but frustration with the program was building. The cost-cutting pressures of a wartime economy gave Senator Wheeler's committee on Indian affairs, now chaired by Elmer Thomas of Oklahoma, another long-time critic of the bureau, an opportunity to launch a massive investigation of federal Indian policy. Senate Report No. 310, released in 1943 and cosigned by Wheeler, Thomas (another veteran of 1934), Dennis Chavez of New Mexico, and Henrik Shipstead of Minnesota, was a personal blast at Collier. Questioning Collier's "accuracy" and "motives,"[29] the report called for immediate abolition of the bureau and unrestricted citizenship for all Indians. Sometimes intimating that Collier had betrayed the Congress that passed the Indian Reorganization Act, the report also revealed a deeper, lingering dissatisfaction with the whole principle of that legislation.

While the original aim [of federal policy] was to make the Indian a citizen, the present aim appears to be to keep the Indian an Indian and to make him satisfied with all the limitations of a primitive life. We are striving mightily to help him recapture his ancient, worn-out cultures which are now hardly a vague memory to him and are absolutely unable to function in his present world. We non-Indians would not try, even, to recapture our glamorous pioneer culture though it might be done without great sacrifice, and though the adjustment in attitude and desires could be made with far less difficulty than the Indian would have in holding onto his rapidly receding past, to say nothing of his ancient past.[30]

26. A typical example is the Constitution and By-Laws of the Oglala Sioux Tribe of the Pine Ridge Reservation, which provides in Article IV "that the tribal council shall exercise, subject to review or approval of the Secretary of the Interior, the following powers. . . ." A detailed statistical study of 198 tribal governments, now underway for future publication, indicates that more than half of the specific powers granted in tribal constitutions are subject to approval. More significantly, these powers clauses are almost identical to one another *and to section 4 of the original reorganization bill supported by the bureau but not adopted by Congress.*
27. "Summary Report of Hearings and Investigations by the Subcommittee on Constitutional Rights," 1–4, Senate Committee on the Judiciary, 88th Congress, 2nd Session (1964).
28. Haas, "Ten Years of Tribal Government," 22.
29. Senate Report No. 310, 78th Congress, 1st Session (1943), at 1.
30. *Id.* 18.

Here the report made its first great error: identifying tribal self-government with cultural fossilization. White self-government does not depend upon the preservation of "pioneer culture." Like all government, it continues to provide a process for mediating social, economic and cultural *change*. Self-government transcends culture; it is the right to choose culture.

Unfortunately, the commissioner never explicitly made this distinction himself. A devotee of anthropology, he habitually overemphasized the value of traditional tribal governments instead of laying a conceptual foundation for tribes' right to govern themselves by any means they chose. In response to the Senate committee's criticisms, moreover, he attributed all tribal rights to the federal government's *moral obligation* to compensate and rehabilitate them for past wrongs.[31] Arguments from morality are always spongy, but in this case the reaction was not only to dismiss, but ridicule the position. "Why continue to bewail their lost lands which they never used," the report asked, facetiously directing the counterattack at the Indians rather than Collier, "while they are still not using millions of acres of what they do own?"[32] In complete reversal of the tone of the 1934 hearings, the report praised the General Allotment Act as a "simple act of justice" and bemoaned its passing.[33]

The report's second great error was to project the bureau's failings on the Indians themselves. The bureau was, the report admitted, the root evil.

The Bureau has been concerned with building up a system instead of a service, attempting to build self-perpetuating institutions, making material improvements for the Indian Service at the expense of Indian life; furnishing physical relief that was not needed nearly so much as economic and civic encouragement, breaking down assisting agencies, segregating the Indian from the general citizenry, condemning the Indian to perpetual wardship, making the Indian the guinea pig for experimentation, grouping the Indians for convenience of supervision for which they are presumed to exist, tieing him to the land in perpetuity, forcing a conventional type of education on him, attempting to compel all Indians to engage in agriculture and stock raising.[34]

Examine the subtle confusion of tribal and agency goals. Tribal government is made to appear only an agency objective—an institution that serves

31. *Id.* 13.
32. *Id.* 6–7.
33. *Id.* 4–5.
34. *Id.* 17. The report also criticized the agency's "survey habit" (*id.* 19). At least some congressmen perceived they were being led by the bureau's self-serving statistics.

agency convenience and permits "experimentation" by bureaucrats. Perhaps that explains why the bureau advocated reorganization. But the fact that an agency advocates a program for the wrong reason does not make the program itself wrong.

The report's third error was to assume that emancipation from bureau supervision necessarily implied absorption by the states. It recommended that bureau service functions be forthwith transferred to state agencies, and that tribal property be distributed and become taxable by the states.[35] The senators obviously did not conceive that one of the rights of citizenship is to choose one's local political allegiance. Most citizens make that choice when they purchase land. Indians were not going to be allowed to make that choice, because their land was to be granted to states without their consent. Western territories had always had the option of combining with existing, neighboring states or becoming separate states when they were emancipated from federal supervision.

Dramatic in its accusations and program, the report had no immediate effect on policy. A war was being fought, and national attention was on Europe and the Pacific. Parallel hearings were, however, conducted by the House in 1943 and 1944 pursuant to House Resolution 166, which praised Indians' educational achievements and proposed to "reward" them for their contribution to the war effort by emancipating them from the bureau.[36] Fifteen hundred pages of testimony were collected in field hearings around the country, from Indians, non-Indians, bureaucrats, even missionaries, with virtually no reference to tribal government. The committee was only interested in whether Indians were as a whole intellectually competent to manage their own property.

In response to growing charges of agency paternalism, Commissioner Collier tried to argue away the problem. In a lengthy statement submitted to the House, he offered to peel away the "layer upon layer of historical accident and administrative and legislative expediency" embodied in the legal doctrine of Indian wardship, and prove that Congress simply misunderstood the nature and scope of the bureau's power.[37] All wardship had ever meant, he argued, was that Indians were subject to congressional

35. *Id*. 20–22.
36. "Hearings, 'Investigate Indian Affairs,' " House Committee on Indian Affairs, 78th Congress, 2nd Session (1943–44).
37. *Id*. Part 1, 100–101.

legislation. "[T]he fact that Indians are subject to congressional legislation does not make them subject to administrative government." Wardship and citizenship are not mutually exclusive; the ward-citizen simply
has a right to compensation for lands taken in the form of continuing
services.

If we get rid, then, of the confusions which have clustered around the term "wardship," we come down to the basic fact that tribal Indians are citizens, who ought to
enjoy all the rights of citizenship but toward whom the Federal Government has
assumed certain additional obligations generally connected with the rendering of
public services. The basic job of the Indian Service is that of meeting these special
obligations without infringing upon the Indian's right of citizenship.[38]

Then, in his strongest language ever, he challenged Congress's assumption that full citizenship meant state citizenship. Federal courts had held,
he observed, that national citizenship is *not inconsistent* with tribal membership or federal supervision. If they chose, then, tribes could lawfully
retain their separate political identify without loss of national rights.

Some would argue that the facts of our national life and the facts of tribal existence
have changed greatly since John Marshall's day. And so they have. . . . Are we
then in a position where we dare not, as a matter of national safety, concede to
Indian tribes the status of limited municipal sovereignty? Not at all. There might
have been some danger, in John Marshall's day, in his invitation to Indian tribes to
prosper and grow strong according to their accustomed ways of doing. There is no
longer that danger.
    What, then, of the facts of tribal existence? Have the tribes so altered that it is
useless and impractical to consider them as going concerns, or to give thought to
ways of implementing their powers, if any remain, to increase their effectiveness? . . . Some tribes have vanished, granted; others are so soon to vanish that if
we help them at all it should be with the thought of helping them to get out of the
business. That decision, however, should be theirs, not Government's. But for
scores of tribes—without stopping to calculate I would say a hundred—the day is
still at the morning.[39]

At last, Collier's thinking was unified. He even described tribes as
"sovereign nations" that were growing and changing rather than remaining primitive.[40] But it was too late.

38. *Id*. Part 1, 102.
39. *Id*. Part 1, 103.
40. *Id*. Part 1, 106. "Indians are more themselves than they have been for a long time,
and they are certainly more assimilated than they ever were," Collier argued, suggesting that
for the future Indians should be encouraged to adapt constructively without giving up their
own heritage.

While Collier was defending tribal government in the House, the Senate committee was on the move again, this time entertaining a bill spearheaded by some members of Oklahoma tribes to immediately remove all restrictions from the use, sale and taxation of individually-owned property.[41] The committee's report vilified Collier and openly accused the bureau of coercing Indians into backing and participating in the working of the Indian Reorganization Act.[42] Passage of the reorganization act was attributed to a "Bureau-organized propaganda machine," implying that Congress had been deliberately misinformed. The tribes themselves would have opposed it if they had been fully informed.

The committee's one specific charge was new and serious.

The Indians were supposed to write their own constitutions, but they had no experience in such matters; besides they did not know what the Bureau wanted them to want. The only way to organize them was to offer them model constitutions acceptable to the Indian Bureau and to allow them to accept such drafts, revise them within limits set by the Indian Bureau, or else reject them. Using standard forms, a constitution could be pieced together in a conference with the Indians by allowing them to fill in the blank forms as suggested, between the items required by the Bureau. Some constitutions when completed contained more Bureau required or suggested matter than matter that was used to fit the actual situation.[43]

Included in the report was a particularly damning letter written by Assistant Solicitor Charlotte Westwood based on her review of Indian Reorganization Act implementation in the Great Lakes. "I have found an incredibly high degree of standardization of the constitutions drafted for the heterogeneous Wisconsin groups," she wrote, "all of which constitutions are almost exact copies of certain constitutions drawn up for the Indians of the Plains and informally approved by the Secretary. Such standardization cannot help but discredit the whole policy of Indian self-government and

41. "Hearings, 'Remove Restrictions on Indian Property,' " 2, Senate Committee on Indian Affairs, 78th Congress, 2nd Session (1944).
42. Senate Report. No. 1031, 78th Congress, 2nd Session (1944), at 1–2.
43. *Id.* 5. Compare Collier's glowing appraisal of reorganization in his annual reports to Congress, e.g., "Functioning self-government is the end we are seeking. . . . It may not be as varied as, historically, tribal governments were in their original growth, but it should be at least as varied in form and content as the needs of the Indian people, acted upon by living tradition, require, and that will permit of a considerable range" (*Report of the Secretary of the Interior, 1939* 24). In the *1937* report, at 200, Collier remarked on his employment of anthropologists to "see that the constitutions are really based on the contemporary social and economic life of the people concerned."

lead to the conclusion that these constitutions are nothing more than new Indian Office's regulations."[44] Her warning was prophetic.

This time the commissioner openly accused Congress of double-dealing, pointing out how generally it had supported the IRA in 1934.[45] He denied the Senate's charge that his agency had influenced tribes' choice of constitutional provisions, alleging that "no two of the 106 constitutions . . . are alike," and further denied that he had reserved veto powers in those constitutions.[46] In fact, many constitutions were identical, dozens differed in only a few sections, and all reserved veto powers.[47] But Collier insisted that the committee was prejudiced when it found no significant gain in "self-determination" since 1934.

Where did the authors of the report look? Where did they seek evidence? By what criteria did they judge attainment of self-determination? Did they attend any significant number of meetings of tribal councils throughout the Indian country? Did they confer with responsible tribal officials? Did they study the files of council minutes, or examine the numerous resolutions and ordinances enacted by these groups?[48]

Objectively analyzed, he argued, reorganization had "immeasurably hastened the day when complete integration of the Indian into the general population will have been achieved."

Collier failed, however, to separate the issues of bureau malfeasance and tribal self-government in the minds of key congressmen. In 1945 he was replaced as commissioner. Meanwhile, Senator Langer of North Dakota, a member of the Wheeler Indian affairs committee, became Chairman of the Senate civil service committee. In 1947 he launched an investigation of unnecessary federal employees which quickly became a rerun of the wartime Indian affairs hearings. This time, the bureau lacked its most zealous advocate.

44. *Id.*
45. "Hearings, 'Investigate Indian Affairs,' " Part 4, 18–19.
46. *Id.* 19–20.
47. Big Valley and Stewart's Point, both in California, are identical; Omaha, Ponca and Santee differ in only a few words; Grindstone and Alturas are almost identical. Certain parts of constitutions seem formulaic, e.g., bills of rights and provisions for regulation of trade, and the omnipresence of bizarre provisions for "charity" and "arts and crafts" suggest centralized drafting (George E. Fay, ed., *Charters, Constitutions and By-Laws of the Indian Tribes of North America*, University of Northern Colorado Museum of Anthropology, Occasional Publications in Anthropology, Ethnology Series [Greeley, Colo.: 1967–1971]).
48. "Hearings, 'Investigate Indian Affairs,' " Part 4, 27.

The committee agreed that if we "let those people handle their own lives we could save a little money."[49] "I think it is time we came to a show-down on this," Senator Langer harangued the bureau's spokesman, Acting Commissioner William Zimmerman, "Either Congress has to run this or you."[50] No one suggested that Indians remained incapable of intelligent self-management. Senator Chavez waxed ecstatic on this point.

Thousands upon thousands went into the war. They learned to fight. They learned to take care of themselves. They learned to brush their teeth. They learned to wash. They learned to eat and it is a shame the way the Indians are treated in the United States of America.[51]

I am very much upset at times because we treat them like a bunch of peons and slaves. That is our attitude, instead of letting them join us and be assimilated, they are good enough to go to war, but they cannot handle their own affairs, and they have been handling their own affairs from time immemorial. They have had their own courts and civil government within the pueblos—have had for hundreds of years.[52]

The bogey, as always, was the bureau, not tribes. "I am for abolishing it, and the more I see it the less I like it," Senator Langer confessed, "but I realize this Indian Bureau was terrifically well entrenched."[53] Zimmerman's counterattack was feeble. He tried to deny the existence of federal supervision. "They have all the rights of citizens," he argued, admitting, however, that "[t]here may be a restriction on some of their property."[54] The committee was unconvinced, and so was William Zimmerman. Further along in the hearings, Senator Buck asked him, "You pretty nearly supervise everything they do; is that not correct?" Zimmerman agreed.[55]

The acting commissioner also tried to pin the blame on Congress for program failure, depicting both the tribes and the bureau as mere pawns.

MR. ZIMMERMAN. . . . It looks to me as if you want to hang the patient, because the doctor gave the wrong prescription.
SEN. CHAVEZ. Who is the patient? The Indian, or the Indian Bureau?
MR. ZIMMERMAN. Either one; I do not care how you look at it.[56]

49. "Hearings, 'Officers and Employees of the Federal Government,' " 76, Senate Committee on Civil Service, 80th Congress, 1st Session (1947).
50. *Id.* 79.
51. *Id.* 95.
52. *Id.* 248.
53. *Id.* 591; also 721.
54. *Id.* 95; also 77. Compare Secretary of the Interior Krug's remarks (*id.* 218).
55. *Id.* 123.
56. *Id.* 91.

By this gambit he reinforced one of the most pernicious misconceptions in Indian affairs, that tribes and the bureau stand or fall together. Congress was increasingly solicitous of Indians' "freedom,"[57] but why should that entail anything more than termination of federal regulations?

The Langer committee had already agreed that emancipated tribes must become a part of the states; continued tribal government was not an alternative.[58] They took the extraordinary measure of placing Zimmerman under subpoena and offering him "protection" if he would draw up a plan for transferring tribes to state jurisdiction and control.[59] He did. Although he pleaded with the committee not to transfer tribes to states against their wishes, he made no mention of tribes' political rights. In fact, he casually remarked that there were only "some" organized tribes, and that the only reason they wanted to keep their charters was to avoid state taxation![60]

Zimmerman classified tribes into three groups. The first were, he believed, ready for immediate termination. The second might be ready in ten years, and the third might require as long as fifty years unless federal expenditures for education were increased.[61] His criteria were "degree of acculturation," i.e., the "admixture of white blood, the percentage of illiteracy, the business ability of the tribe, their acceptance of white institutions and their acceptance by whites in the community"; the ability of tribal members to earn a "reasonably decent living"; and the agreeableness of the tribe and state to a transfer of control.[62] He estimated that termination of the first group of ten tribes would save the United States about five million dollars annually, but declined to predict whether it would be good policy.[63]

One thing Zimmerman was careful to do was to protect the bureau. Budget savings from termination of the first group should be applied, he

57. See, for example, *id.* 94.
58. The only mention of tribal government in the hearings was when Chairman Langer asked Zimmerman why the bureau hadn't encouraged tribes to hire their own personnel to carry out federal functions. Zimmerman blamed this on Congress's failure to enact §8 of the original reorganization bill, which would have authorized tribal-federal contracting (*id.* 242). Langer was not uncomfortable with the idea of tribes becoming mere business corporations (*id.* 557–63).
59. *Id.* 256. When Zimmerman made his first appearance before the committee, the chairman asked him about the bureau's "overall plan" for transferring tribal areas to the states, and expressed astonishment at Zimmerman's reply that the bureau had no such plan (*id.* 79, 86).
60. *Id.* 254.
61. *Id.* 544, 569.
62. *Id.* 544–45.
63. *Id.* 544–55; 544–45, 577–78.

argued, to programs for the other two.[64] This way the bureau would lose no personnel or budget, at least for the time being. Senator Thye of Minnesota accused the agency of wanting to have its cake and eat it, too, and the chairman expressed profound disappointment with Zimmerman.[65] But in a strange way, it reprieved the Indian service. The Langer committee was so frustrated it took no further action.

It is striking how little Congress understood tribes. The Langer committee was so sure Indians really *wanted* to sever their tribal allegiance, they concluded that tribes survived because Indians *thought it was illegal to expatriate*. Accordingly, they introduced legislation that guaranteed Indians' right to leave the reservation.[66] It was totally duplicative, but illustrates how tribal survival mystified the national government. They scrounged for explanations. One was that Indians were afraid to foreswear their tribal allegiance lest they miss out on future claims judgments against the United States.[67] The Indian Claims Act was not passed just to make it possible for tribes to sue the United States; individual tribal claims had been heard in the Court of Claims since the turn of the century. It was hoped that the Indian Claims Commission would *accelerate* the process of liquidating claims and thereby remove as quickly as possible Indians' supposed incentive for retaining their tribal allegiances.

Termination did not come in 1947, but the bureau prepared for the inevitable. In 1946, its annual report noted "interest" in transferring jurisdiction to the states with tribal consent.[68] In 1949 the annual report explained that it was "not the intention of the Federal Government to continue in the role of trustee," and promised complete Indian assimilation and dispersal in the near future.[69] In 1950 the bureau promised to study federal withdrawal and expressed hopes that termination would be gradual.[70] Plans for a "step-by-step transfer of Bureau functions to the Indians themselves or to appropriate agencies of local, State, or Federal

64. *Id.* 567–68, 570–73. "Or, to put it differently, if Indian progress to freedom collides with Departmental solidarity, choose the latter!" (Professor Charles Black, quoted by Felix Cohen in "The Erosion of Indian Rights 1950–1953: A Case Study in Bureaucracy," 62 *Yale Law Journal* 348, 380 [1953]).
65. "Hearings, 'Officers and Employees,' " 574, 575.
66. *Id.* 564–65. See Cohen, "Erosion of Indian Rights," and *U.S. ex rel. Standing Bear v. Crook*, 5 Dill. 453, 25 Fed. Cas. 695, 699 (C.C.Neb. 1879), regarding the controversy over tribal members' right of "expatriation."
67. *Id.* 81.
68. *Report of the Secretary of the Interior, 1946* 375–76.
69. *Report of the Secretary of the Interior, 1949* 338, 366.
70. *Report of the Secretary of the Interior, 1950* 342–43.

Government'' were announced in 1951.[71] The following year the bureau placed "greatly increased emphasis" on state jurisdiction, and the year after it was "programming for termination."[72] At the same time, paradoxically, the bureau was actively preparing and approving new tribal laws and constitutions.[73]

The assault on the bureau continued. "In general terms of effectiveness of management," the House Committee on Appropriations concluded in 1951, while "[t]he Bureau has, for many years, given lip service to the principle that its activities were pointed toward the eventual withdrawal of federal supervision over Indian activities, the accomplishments have been nill."[74] The mood of termination in the late 1940s and early 1950s grew out of two convictions: that Indians should be subjected to no greater administrative regulation than other citizens, and that the Bureau of Indian Affairs had proved inefficient and selfish in its administration of services. Oppressive bureaucratic centralization tapped the roots of the "red scare" and led to increasingly more frequent comparisons between the bureau and the government of the Soviet Union. The rhetoric of cultural assimilation was abandoned for a new ideal of political freedom. Federal Indian policy set a people aside from the benefits of citizenship.

If the evil was a lack of freedom, however, the proposed cure was strangely inconsistent. Involuntary amalgamation of tribal communities with states, without even the guarantee of municipal self-government under state law, deprived Indians of political choice. It was a kind of political arrogance to match the cultural arrogance that motivated the allotment policy. If Indians were to enjoy liberty, they would enjoy it through non-Indian political institutions or not at all. The choice had always been there, in fact. Indians had always been free to abandon their tribal citizenship and live among state citizens. Termination would take away this choice. Here, again, Congress fundamentally misunderstood tribalism. Indians did not remain tribal because the bureau forced them to, but because they chose to.

71. *Report of the Secretary of the Interior, 1951* 377.
72. *Report of the Secretary of the Interior, 1952* 390−91; *Report of the Secretary of the Interior, 1953* 23.
73. *Report of the Secretary of the Interior, 1946* 376−77; *Report of the Secretary of the Interior, 1951* 377; *Report of the Secretary of the Interior, 1953* 42.
74. "Hearings, 'Interior Department Appropriations for 1952,' " 246, 248, House Committee on Appropriations, 82nd Congress, 1st Session (1951).

The irony was strongly felt by Felix Cohen, then a visiting professor at the Yale Law School, whose own argument that "the Commissioner of Indian Affairs is, for most practical purposes, a law unto himself who looks nowhere but to his own will and conscience for direction," had provided fuel for the terminationists' fire.[75] He warmly advocated tribalism and blamed Congress's failure to distinguish tribal political rights from the perpetuation of the bureau on the agency's own self-serving representations. Unfortunately, like his long-time associate, John Collier, Cohen saved his clearest reasoning for when he had left government service and it was too late for him to influence policy.

When the bureau requested a 70 percent increase in its 1953 budget and proposed legislation granting it "vastly enlarged powers," the axe fell.[76] House Concurrent Resolution 108 declared it to be "the policy of Congress, as rapidly as possible, to make the Indians . . . subject to the same laws and entitled to the same privileges and responsibilities as are applicable to other citizens of the United States, to end their status as wards of the United States, and to grant them all of the rights and prerogatives pertaining to American citizenship."[77] To accomplish this Congress proposed immediately to terminate federal services and administration for all tribes in California, Florida, New York and Texas, as well as five of the tribes Commissioner Zimmerman had proposed for termination in 1947. No provision was made for tribal consent.

Two weeks later Congress enacted Public Law 83−280,[78] which must remain as a monument to congressional ambiguity and indecision. Hearings were held on a narrow proposal applicable to California and were

75. *Id.* 374.
76. *Id.* 387−88.
77. H.C.R. 108, adopted 27 July 1953, 99 *Congressional Record* 9968. Its sponsor insisted it was "nothing more than an expression of the sense of Congress," in a move to curtail debate on its wisdom (99 *Congressional Record* 9262 [20 July 1953]).
78. Act of 15 August 1953, c. 505, 67 Stat. 588−90, originally codified as 18 U.S.C. 1162 and 28 U.S.C. 1360, as amended 25 U.S.C. 1321−22. Section 1360 delegated to the named states "jurisdiction over civil causes of action between Indians or to which Indians are parties," and provided that "civil laws . . . that are of general application to private persons or private property shall have the same force and effect within . . . Indian country as they have elsewhere within the State." Senator Ervin subsequently interpreted this to mean that "Public Law 280 relates primarily to the application of state civil and criminal law in court proceedings, and has no bearing on programs set up by the States to assist economic and environmental development in Indian territory." ("Hearings, 'Rights of Members of Indian Tribes,' " 136, House Committee on Interior and Insular Affairs, Subcommittee on Indian Affairs, 90th Congress, 2nd Session [1968]). A similar view was taken by the Supreme Court

never published.[79] In their report, however, the House and Senate recommended a sweeping general law automatically delegating reservation jurisdiction to six states not included in H.C.R. 108, and authorizing other states to assume jurisdiction at their option.[80] It is essential to understand that P.L. 280 was limited to jurisdiction. It did not repeal the Indian Reorganization Act. It did not terminate the powers or charters of any tribes. It did not abolish existing reservations or prevent the creation of new ones. Unlike H.C.R. 108 it did not propose to terminate federal services.

It is somewhat more difficult to understand what P.L. 280 did do, and courts continue to interpret it differently.[81] The identical committee reports offer little guidance. "As a practical matter," they observed,

the enforcement of law and order among the Indians in the Indian country has been largely left to the Indian groups themselves. In many States, tribes are not adequately organized to perform that function; consequently, there has been created a hiatus in law-enforcement authority that could best be remedied by conferring criminal jurisdiction on States indicating an ability and willingness to accept such responsibility.[82]

"Similarly," the reports agreed, "the Indians of several States have reached a stage of acculturation and development that makes desirable

---

two years later in *Kennerly v. District Court*, 400 U.S. 423, 428 (1970), and was recently confirmed in *Bryan* v. *Itasca County*, 96 S.Ct. 2102 (1976). Congress passed a number of similar laws of narrower scope just prior to Public Law 280, viz., Act of 8 June 1940, c. 276, 54 Stat. 249 (criminal jurisdiction, Devil's Lake Reservation, North Dakota); Act of 30 June 1948, c. 759, 62 Stat. 1161 (criminal jurisdiction, Sac and Fox Reservation, Iowa); Act of 2 July 1948, c. 809, 62 Stat. 1224 (criminal jurisdiction, New York); Act of 5 October 1949, c. 604. 63 Stat. 705 (civil and criminal jurisdiction, Agua Caliente Reservation, California); Act of 13 September 1950, c. 947, 64 Stat. 845 (civil jurisdiction, New York).

79. An unpublished transcript exists. The committee reports are not particularly illuminating, either (Senate Report. No. 699 and House Report. No. 848, 83rd Congress, 1st Session [1953]). Hearings on the subsequent termination of individual tribes, however ("Joint Hearings, 'Continued Tribal Supervision,' " House and Senate Committees on Indian Affairs, 83rd Congress, 2nd Session [1954]; Senate Report. No. 1218 and House Report. No. 1904, 83rd Congress, 2nd Session [1954]).

80. The "mandatory" P.L. 280 states were Alaska, California, Minnesota, Nebraska, Oregon, and Wisconsin.

81. See Carole E. Goldberg, "Public Law 280: The Limits of State Jurisdiction Over Reservation Indians," 22 *U.C.L.A. Law Review* 535 (1975).

82. House Report. No. 848, 6; Senate Report. No. 699, 5. Since federal law enforcement operations on reservations were typically neither well-financed nor vigorous, and tribal law and order programs were chronically underfunded as well, there had been, according to Representative D'Ewart of Montana, a "complete breakdown of law and order on many of the Indian reservations." D'Ewart emphasized "[t]he desire of all law abiding citizens living

extension of State civil jurisdiction to the Indian country within their borders.''[83]

Why, exactly, state jurisdiction was "best" or "desirable" was nowhere explained. Once again, Congress assumed only two alternatives: state government or federal government. The report-writers were not altogether insensitive to tribal political choice. "[T]he attitude of the various States and the Indian groups within those States . . . should be heavily weighed before effecting transfer.''[84] Curiously, for evidence of tribal consent in the six "mandatory" states both committees relied entirely on a letter written by Assistant Secretary of the Interior Orme Lewis, not on public hearings or tribal plebiscites.[85] Lewis's opinion appears to have been based on personal communications; its accuracy is still a subject of debate.

P.L. 280 may have gone ahead without direct tribal consent, but it did not contemplate dissolution of tribes. The reports recommended that jurisdictional transfers provide that tribal laws not inconsistent with state laws be binding on state courts.[86] By implication, tribes were to become as state municipalities, following John Collier's suggestion in 1934. Like municipalities, they would be subject to state constitutions but retain the power of internal legislation and all collective proprietary rights. Moreover, since their status would arise out of a conditional federal delegation, their

---

on or near Indian reservations for law and order" ("Hearings, 'State Legal Jurisdiction in Indian Country,' " 14, 16, 23–24, House Committee on Interior and Insular Affairs, Subcommittee on Indian Affairs, 82nd Congress, 2nd Session [1952]). Congress claimed to be principally concerned, then, for public safety. *Cf. In re Mayfield*, 141 U.S. 107, 115–16 (1891): "The policy of Congress has evidently been to vest in the inhabitants of the Indian country such power of self-government *as was thought consistent with the safety of the white population* with which they may come in contact, and to encourage them as far as possible in raising themselves to our standards of civilization" (emphasis ours). But if this were true, would it not have been better to improve tribal law enforcement? The irony is that P.L. 280 itself resulted in a "breakdown of law and order" ("Hearings, 'Indian Law Enforcement Improvement Act of 1975' " Senate Committee on Interior and Insular Affairs, Subcommittee on Indian Affairs, 94th Congress, 1st Session [1975]).

83. House Report. No. 848, 6; Senate Report. No. 699, 5. We note a certain inconsistency here. Extension of state criminal laws was justified by the argument of Indian lawlessness. Extension of civil laws was justified by the argument of Indian acculturation and progress. Could these be the same Indians?

84. *Id.* See also "Hearings, 'State Legal Jurisdiction,' " 25.

85. House Report No. 848, 5–6; Senate Report No. 699, 6–8. That the committees were concerned with tribes' wishes is demonstrated by the specific exception from the final bill of two tribes which had vigorously protested it, Warm Springs and Red Lake.

86. House Report No. 848, 5; Senate Report No. 699, 6.

self-governing charters would presumably not be subject to state repeal, protecting their original sovereignty.

In any event, P.L. 280 reflected a decision to make the states, rather than the bureau, change agents through what Professor Price has called the "civilizing function of law."[87] On their part, the states assumed that their greater responsibilities would entail commensurate federal financial assistance. The State of California, for example, vigorously advocated the law, and felt betrayed when federal services were subsequently withdrawn. A 1969 report to the governor blamed the "deterioration of Indian health, education, employment and economy" following transfer on the state's confusion and unpreparedness for assuming service activities.[88] Wisconsin had a similar experience. The Menominee, one of the nation's wealthiest tribes in 1953, were made a county, only to become the poorest county in the state. In 1975 Congress restored the Menominee to federal control.[89] P.L. 280 only specifically required continuing federal responsibility in one area, land management.[90] Ironically, this had been the one area of bureau responsibility most widely criticized by Congress and Indians.

The bureau itself had for some time emphasized states' reluctance to bear added service costs,[91] and opposed federal subsidies to states accepting transfers of responsibility, arguing that there would

be some tendency . . . for the Indian to be thought of and perhaps to think of himself because of the financial assistance which comes from the Federal Government as still somewhat a member of a race or group which is set apart from other citizens of the State. And it is desired to give him and the other citizens of the State the feeling of a conviction that he is in the same status and has access to the same services, including the court, as other citizens of the State who are not Indians.[92]

The bureau was not disturbed by arguments that continued tax exemptions and federal supervision of land management would constitute as much or

---

87. Monroe E. Price, *Law and the American Indian* (Indianapolis: 1973). At the same time, many bureau services, such as health care, were transferred to the Department of Health, Education and Welfare, further "normalizing" Indians' legal status (see, for example, the Act of 5 August 1954, C. 658, 68 Stat. 674, 42 U.S.C. 2001).

88. *Report of the California State Advisory Commission on Indian Affairs to the Governor and the Legislature* 9–10 (1967).

89. "Hearings, 'Menominee Restoration Act,'" House Committee on Interior and Insular Affairs, Subcommittee on Indian Affairs, 93rd Congress, 1st Session (1972).

90. 18 U.S.C. 1162(b); 28 U.S.C. 1360(b).

91. "Hearings, 'Officers and Employees,'" 243, 251–52.

92. H.R. 1063, 83rd Congress, 1st Session (1953); transcript of hearings on H.R. 1063 before the Subcommittee on Indian Affairs of the House Committee on Interior and Insular Affairs, 83rd Congress, 1st Session (1953), at 8.

more of a badge of second-class citizenship. "The Department has recommended, nevertheless, that no financial assistance be afforded to the State."[93]

The bureau's position can only be understood as an effort to derail the "termination" program in its own self-interest. Without federal subsidies or taxation, the mandatory states would either have to raise additional taxes on their non-Indian base, or else offer very limited services to Indians. "Optional" states would probably choose not to assume jurisdiction in the first place; this appears to have been the case in South Dakota. Other "optional" states avoided costs by assuming "piecemeal" jurisdiction. Washington, for example, extended only its social services, education and traffic laws to selected tribes.[94]

By itself, P.L. 280 was not really "termination" at all. It delegated federal "plenary power" to the states subject to conditions. Congress had long made laws for the internal governance of tribes superior to tribes' own laws; now the states were to have that power. But Congress reserved control of tribal property and responsibility for many services. Most important of all, Congress implicitly reserved the power to extinguish tribes' residual sovereignty. Since only state laws of *general application* were to be binding on P.L. 280 reservations,[95] a state could not preempt tribes' legislation without preempting municipalities' legislation on the same subject. To abolish tribes by degrees, i.e., by successive preemptions of power, states would have to abolish all municipalities by degrees.

Real "termination" in the sense of dissolving tribal governments was still on the drawing-board in 1953. The committee reports on P.L. 280 looked forward to future legislation eliminating "restrictions and disabilities applicable to Indians only" and repealing laws "which set Indians apart from other citizens."[96] Bureau supervision of individual and tribal business was a form of discrimination Indians were probably anxious to overcome. An argument could also be made that the existence of tribal government is a form of discrimination. That argument would have to rest, however, on a failure to distinguish between race and tribal membership,

---

93. *Id.* 9.
94. South Dakota Legislative Research Council, *Jurisdiction Over Indian Country in South Dakota* (1964). Another response was to challenge tribes' tax immunities. See also "Hearings, 'Rights of Members of Indian Tribes,' " 25, 28–29, 30, 110, 113, 116.
95. 28 U.S.C. 1360(a): "general application to private persons."
96. House Report No. 848, 3; Senate Report No. 699, 3.

or between choice and compulsion. Freedom to organize for local self-government is a right of national citizenship. A requirement that persons of one race live in demographically isolated units is discrimination. Since Indians were already free to relinquish tribal membership and live where they chose, no racial discrimination was involved.

Later Congresses read the mandate of P.L. 280 differently. Beginning in 1954, tribes were individually studied and, in accordance with the criteria suggested by Acting Commissioner Zimmerman in 1947, summarily liquidated.[97] In contrast to P.L. 280, these acts distributed the tribes' assets by analogy to corporate dissolution and afforded the states an opportunity to modify, merge or abolish the tribe's governmental functions. Formal tribal consent was not obtained. This phase of "termination" differed only superficially from allotment. Instead of allotting tribal lands and subjecting them to state governance after a "trust" period, individual termination acts allotted tribal capital and subjected it to state governance after a transition period of one or two years.[98]

It was a relatively short-lived experiment. In 1968, congress amended P.L. 280 to maximize political choice. No further transfers of jurisdiction were to be made without tribal plebiscites, and prior transfers were to be subject to "retrocession" if agreeable to the tribe and state.[99] Additional remedial legislation has since been introduced to permit tribes, with the inevitable secretarial approval, to retrocede *without* state consent.[100]

Negative reaction to the coercive features of P.L. 280 had been almost immediate. President Eisenhower signed the bill into law reluctantly, expressing his regret that Congress had failed to provide for "full consultation in order to ascertain the wishes and desires of the Indians," and urging

97. Act of 13 August 1954, c. 732, 68 Stat. 718 (Klamath); Act of 27 August 1954, c. 1009, 68 Stat. 868 (Uintah and Ouray); Act of 13 August 1954, c. 733, 68 Stat. 724 (Western Oregon); Act of 23 August 1954, c. 831, 68 Stat. 768 (Alabamas); Act of 1 September 1954, c. 1207, 68 Stat. 1099 (Paiutes); Act of 1 August 1956, c. 843, 70 Stat. 893 (Wyandottes); Act of 2 August 1956, c. 881, 70 Stat. 937 (Peorias); Act of 3 August 1956, c. 909, 70 Stat. 963 (Ottawas); Act of 17 June 1954, c. 303, 68 Stat. 250 (Menominees); P.L. 87–629, 76 Stat. 429 (1962) (Poncas).

98. E.g., Act of 17 June 1954, c. 303, §§8–9, 25 U.S.C. 897–98.

99. 25 U.S.C. 1321(a): "The consent of the United States is hereby given to any State . . . to assume, with the consent of the tribe. . . ." Identical language is found in section 1322(a). Also 25 U.S.C. 1323(a): "The United States is authorized to accept a retrocession by any State of all or any measure of the criminal or civil jurisdiction, or both, acquired by such State" in accordance with P.L. 280.

100. S. 2010, 94th Congress, 1st Session (1975). The 1968 repealer of P.L. 280 expressly saved all previous state assumptions of jurisdiction (25 U.S.C. 1323 [b]).

the adoption of an appropriate amendment in the next session.[101] Two bills were in fact introduced at his direction, but they died in committee.[102] Subsequent efforts also failed, until the matter came to the attention of Senator Ervin's judiciary committee, then launching a major study of Indians' constitutional rights.

The Ervin committee's main objective had been "to protect individual Indians from arbitrary and unjust actions of tribal governments."[103] Federal courts had uniformly held that tribes are sufficiently within the Constitution to be bound by federal legislation, but not enough to be bound or protected by the Bill of Rights. Although citizens, tribal members were thereby denied many of the basic rights of national citizenship so long as they resided on reservation. The committee responded by approving legislation to apply the "same" constitutional limitations to tribal and state government.[104] They did not see this as a further encroachment on tribal self-government, but merely a way of rationalizing tribal government into the federal system. Many tribes supported this view.[105]

The committee's indulgence of tribal members' civil rights would have seemed hypocritical had it excluded consideration of their political liberty. Indians may have been denied conventionally defined due process in tribal courts, but tribes themselves had been denied the right of political choice by Congress in 1953. Senator Ervin was not insensitive to this. He described P.L. 280 as a "blight." "Subjecting a reservation to state, criminal or civil jurisdiction without its consent runs counter to that basic tenet of our democracy that governmental power is derived from the consent of the governed."[106] Title III of the bill would therefore prohibit extensions of state jurisdiction without tribal consent. President Johnson strongly urged Congress to adopt this measure. "Fairness and basic

101. Letter of John Collier, 24 February 1954, 100 *Cong. Rec.* A1467.
102. S. 2790 and H.R. 7370, 83rd Congress, 2nd Session (1954). Among the "optional" states, North Dakota, Montana and Washington provided for tribal consent in their own legislation accepting P.L. 280; Washington subsequently reneged.
103. Senate Report No. 841, 90th Congress, 2nd Session, quoted in its entirety in "Hearings, 'Rights of Members of Indian Tribes,' " 14.
104. *Id.* 14, 17, 33. Why, then, did the bill only *paraphrase* the Constitution? The Justice Department described it as "patterned closely" on the Bill of Rights (*id.* 26). Further problems arise when tribes guarantee essentially the same substantive rights through use of culturally unique procedures. The Pueblos made an excellent presentation on this point in their opposition to the bill (*id.* 36–38, 51).
105. *Id.* 104 ff., 111 ff. (comments of Marvin Sonosky and Arthur Lazarus).
106. *Id.* 136.

democratic principles require that Indians . . . have a voice in deciding whether a state will assume legal jurisdiction on their land."[107]

The Indian Civil Rights Act has been applauded as a recognition of tribes' political rights. It must be remembered that the Indian Reorganization Act was similarly received in 1934. Legislative recognition of a fundamental right is inadequate. Congress denied tribal political choice in 1953 and could deny it again. The temporary loss of choice under P.L. 280 destroyed many tribes politically and economically. Tribes cannot rely on sympathetic legislators to protect their existence any more than the states, which refused to enter the Union without explicit, constitutional institutionalization of their governments.

Besides, what did tribes have after the Indian Civil Rights Act preserved the status quo? Non-P.L. 280 tribes and retroceded tribes alike continued to exercise their self-governing powers subject to the doctrine of unlimited congressional "plenary power," supervised and regulated by the bureau. All that had been decided was, for the time being, that only Congress may encroach upon the political liberties of tribes.

107. *Id*. 131. This feature of the bill was also strongly supported by all of the tribal representatives and, paradoxically, by the governor of New Mexico (*id*. 96, 104 ff, 111 ff.). The only negative voice heard was that of Mayor Tims of Scottsdale, Arizona, whose comments are such a parody of nineteenth-century assimilationist thinking they deserve quotation at length:

These fine Indian people are being embraced by America. There is a natural course of events which follows such contact. Groups which encounter the mainstream of our country, regardless of their customs, their lack of education, their strangeness, have in the past, millions of them, embraced our life because they recognized the opportunities it provided.

Now, it is proposed by men, by legislation, to cut the Indian off from the personal participation essential to his development. The opportunity for the average Indian to profit from contact with growing America for the growing America would again be eliminated through a continued policy of segregation which is a denial of everything most of us have been brought up to believe as America's. The privilege of leasing Indian lands in the path of oncoming urbanization of metropolitan Arizona offers one of the greatest opportunities for Americanization in the best sense of the word ever presented an emerging minority. It will teach them about ownership, management of property, about the relationship of maintenance cost to income, about the cost of a community and the costs of municipal life (*id*. 76).

Part Three

Tribal Sovereignty at the Bar

A Case Study of
Unprincipled Judicial Decision Making

11

A New Role for the Court

It just seems the writer and those who unite with him didn't care what was said, so long as the opinion seemed plausible on its face. . . . I can hardly see the use of writing judicial opinions unless they are to embody methods of analysis and of exposition which will serve the profession as a guide to the decision of future cases. If they are not better than an excursion ticket, good for this day and this trip only, they do not serve even as protective coloration for the writer of the opinion and would much better be left unsaid.[1]

In the mist which shrouded the tribes' future after 1953, federal courts were repeatedly called on to define the nature of tribal sovereignty. Rather than assume a position of leadership, they proved they could be just as ambiguous as Congress and even less prepared to accept responsibility. From the Civil War to the century's end they armed the national legislature with ideological weapons to advance its arrogations of power over tribes. For the past thirty years, however, they have confused the issues so thoroughly that case outcomes and congressional declarations of policy bear little relation to one another.

Under pressure to devise independent standards, courts seek shelter in the doctrine of congressional "plenary power" popularized by Felix Cohen, a doctrine that all issues of Indian law are to be resolved by reference to the supreme will of the national legislature.[2] They seem unaware that the essential principles of Indian law have in the past developed out of the gaps in federal legislation rather than its substance. Familiar and portentous phrases such as "inherent sovereignty," "Indian

1. Justice Harlan Stone, in Alpheus Thomas Mason, *The Supreme Court: Vehicle of Revealed Truth or Power Groups, 1930–1937* 14 (Boston: 1953).
2. 34 Op. A.G. 171, 180 (1924); *Stephens v. Cherokee Nation*, 174 U.S. 445, 478 (1899). This slogan was popularized by Felix Cohen in his *Handbook of Federal Indian Law* (Washington, D.C.: 1942).

title of occupancy," "guardianship," and "tribal sovereign immunity" have all been judicial inventions to flesh out the skeletal framework of federal acts and treaties.[3] Even the Indian Reorganization Act, the one statute expressly addressed to tribal status, described tribal governing powers by reference to "existing law," i.e., federal common law.

It is a case of mutual buck-passing. Congress relied on the judiciary to give substance to the Indian Reorganization Act, and the judiciary relied on Congress to explain what the act meant. The courts have had less of an excuse. Tribes are not represented directly in the legislative or executive branches. In our system of checks and balances, the ultimate security of a minority excluded from or too few to take advantage of majoritarian political processes lies in the Constitution and constitutional courts.[4] Judicial failure to construct general principles limiting federal "plenary power" is at least as much to blame for its abuse as Congress and the Interior Department.

Rather than grapple with broad philosophical issues, judges often retreat to the safety of conservative, case-by-case reasoning, emphasizing facts over rules, and uniqueness over generality. In dealing with tribes, the Warren and Burger Courts have drawn their conclusions wherever possible from the most exacting, isolated scrutiny of the peculiarities of each case. Where this has fortuitously led them back to explicit federal legislation, they have accepted it with relief, avoiding any consideration of its wisdom or merits.[5]

3. Cohen derived original or inherent tribal sovereignty from *Worcester v. Georgia*, 6 Pet. 515 (1832), and *Ex parte Crow Dog*, 109 U.S. 556 (1883); Indian title of occupancy from *Johnson v. M'Intosh*, 8 Wheat. 543 (1823). For guardianship, see *Cherokee Nation v. Georgia*, 5 Pet. 1, 17 (1831); *U.S. v. Kagama*, 118 U.S. 375, 383 (1886); *U.S. v. Rickert*, 188 U.S. 432 (1903); and *U.S. v. McGowan*, 302 U.S. 535, 538 (1938). For sovereign immunity the traditional sources are *Turner v. U.S.*, 248 U.S. 354 (1916), and *U.S. v. United States Fidelity & Guaranty Co.*, 309 U.S. 506, 512 (1940); but see now P.L. 93–638, §110(a), 88 Stat. 2213 (1975).

4. Martin M. Shapiro, *Freedom of Speech: The Supreme Court and Judicial Review* (Englewood Cliffs, N.J.: 1966). See also Herbert Wechsler, "Toward Neutral Principles of Constitutional Law," in his *Principles, Politics, and Fundamental Law* 35 (Cambridge, Mass.: 1961).

5. "[I]t is to be presumed [the United States] will be governed by such considerations of justice as will control a Christian people in their treatment of an ignorant and dependent race . . . however, . . . the propriety or justice of their action towards the Indians, with respect to their lands, is a question of governmental policy" (*Missouri, Kansas & Texas Ry. Co. v. Roberts*, 152 U.S. 114, 116–8 [1894]). See also, *Cherokee Nation v. Hitchcock*, 187 U.S. 294, 308 (1902): "The power existing in Congress to administer upon and guard the tribal property, and the power being political and administrative in nature, the manner of its exercise is a question within the province of the legislative branch to determine, and not one

The legislative history of federal Indian policy is so multifarious, however, that courts have no choice but to evolve arbitrary assumptions about congressional intent in the form of rules of construction. A reservation, for example, is "presumed" to exist unless and until Congress *expressly* surrenders its trusteeship.[6] Most contemporary Indian law can be reduced to a few of these doubt-resolving presumptions. If the federal judiciary in fact stood by any Indian policy of its own after 1953, it must be discovered hidden in the use of presumptions. Perhaps this was unconscious, perhaps a matter of political discretion. Since rules of statutory construction seem arbitrary, and deceptively devoid of policy significance, they tend to avoid criticism and survive normative transformations. Long after the Court suspected that Congress was anxious to terminate federal Indian services and transfer tribal affairs to the states, it continued to repeat Felix Cohen's formula that tribes are presumed to enjoy certain inherent powers until actually specifically prohibited by statute.[7]

At the same time, preoccupation with statutory construction can become a narcotic. Since Congress has frequently legislated for individual tribes,[8] each case can be made to rest on a different base, and the courts become intoxicated with novelty and detail. By denying the possibility of general

---

for the courts"; *Perrin v. U.S.*, 232 U.S. 467, 471 (1926): "it must be conceded that it does not go beyond what is reasonably essential to their protection. . . . On the other hand, it must also be conceded that . . . Congress is invested with a wide discretion, and its action, unless purely arbitrary, must be accepted and given full effect by the courts"; *U.S. v. McGowan*, 302 U.S. 535, 538 (1938): "Congress alone has the right to determine the manner in which the country's guardianship . . . shall be carried out"; *U.S. v. Santa Fe Pacific RR.*, 314 U.S. 339, 347 (1941): "whether [extinction of Indian title] be done by treaty, by the sword, by purchase, by the exercise of complete dominion adverse to the right of occupancy, or otherwise, its justness is not open to inquiry in the courts"; *Delaware Tribal Business Committee v. Weeks*, 97 S.Ct. 911, 919 (1977): "The general rule emerging from our decisions ordinarily requires the judiciary to defer to congressional determination of what is the best or most efficient use for which tribal funds should be employed. . . . [L]egislative judgment should not be disturbed 'as long as the special treatment can be tied rationally to the fulfillment of Congress' unique obligation toward the Indians.' "

6. *DeCouteau v. District Court*, 95 S.Ct. 1082, 1092 (1975); *Mattz v. Arnett*, 412 U.S. 481, 505 (1973).

7. *Williams v. Lee*, 358 U.S. 217, 219–21 (1958). The Court relied heavily on the self-government provisions of the Navajo-Hopi Rehabilitation Act, 64 Stat. 44 (1949), 25 U.S.C. 636, which are almost the same as those of the Indian Reorganization Act, 48 Stat. 984, 987, 25 U.S.C. 476 (1934).

8. There are special provisions for twenty-two individual tribes in the current edition of Title 25, U.S.C., as well as special collective provisions for Oregon and Oklahoma tribes. Many tribes also fall under special legislation not published as part of the U.S. Code but nevertheless still the source of Bureau of Indian Affairs regulations, e.g., 25 C.F.R. 122, authorized by 41 Stat. 751 (1920) and 46 Stat. 1495 (1931). More than thirty acts of Congress have been passed to date regarding the Crow tribe alone.

principles, judges liberate themselves from the constraints of precedent and rulemaking and are free to be arbitrary. Because Congress may legislate for them individually, and courts will not establish general limits, tribal citizens have less certainty in their personal and commercial affairs than other Americans. They face discriminatory high risks and remain at a competitive disadvantage in the economy.

Preoccupation with statutory construction tempts judges to view federal legislation as the source, rather than a limitation of tribal powers. In its application, Felix Cohen's theory of "plenary power" is turned inside out. Cohen intended it to limit state power over tribes to matters expressly delegated by Congress, protecting tribes by requiring congressional initiative to interfere with them. The more courts speak of "plenary power," however, the more they seem to require congressional initiative to *prevent* state encroachments.

Lawyers often speak of legal doctrine as "evolving." This evokes an image of adaptive improvement, a gradual progress from generalization to specialization. Legal concepts do not always "evolve." When a court is satisfied with the ramifications of a new rule, regardless of its validity, it entrenches it through the use of extensions: differentiation, specialization, evolution. However, a court repentant of an earlier position, and embarrassed to overrule it outright, may weaken it gradually by narrowing its application and rendering its meaning ambiguous, until it stands for everything and nothing at the same time. This is what we call "involution."

Worcester v. Georgia attributed all legitimate federal power over tribes to tribal consent expressed in treaties. Powers not expressly granted the United States by the tribe were treated as reserved. Congress enjoyed no power over Indians independent of the Treaty Clause. During Reconstruction, however, the courts began to test the legitimacy of federal Indian legislation against its putative *purpose*. Reservations were reconceptualized as schools for the civilization of Indians, and reservation activities supposed to benefit Indians were immunized from state interference as federal instrumentalities.[9] This permitted Congress to reach beyond the limits of tribal consent, even to the extent of regulating the domestic affairs of tribes that had never signed a treaty.

9. *U.S. v. Clapox*, 35 F. 575 (1888); *U.S. v. Kagama*, 118 U.S. 375, 383 (1886); *U.S. v. Rickert*, 188 U.S. 432 (1903). These and the cases contemporary with them contrast markedly with the tribal-sovereignty language of cases decided prior to the era of federal intervention, e.g., *The Kansas Indians*, 5 Wall. 737, 755–56 (1867); *The New York Indians*, 5 Wall. 761 (1867); *Mackey v. Coxe*, 18 How. 100, 103–4 (1855).

This federal-purpose idea logically entailed a strict adherence to expressed congressional policies. Here began the use of the phrase, "plenary power," which nineteenth-century courts construed to mean extraordinary congressional discretion to make policy, and lack of judicial authority to review it.[10] Courts were not deterred on this path by *Worcester*. They reconceived it. In its narrowest reading, *Worcester* held that as between a state and Congress, only the latter could have constitutional authority to deal with tribes. Marshall's broad principle of tribal consent was ignored. This left congressional preemption without residual tribal sovereignty.[11]

At the height of the "termination" policy, the Supreme Court brought this transformation to a head. In *Tee-Hit-Ton Indians v. United States*, it held that Alaskan native lands in tribal occupancy "since time immemorial," but never expressly *recognized* by Congress, can be confiscated *without compensation*.[12] Ever since *Lone Wolf* the Court had backed Congress's power to regulate tribes' domestic affairs without their consent, but it had never made the United States immune from the Fifth Amendment.[13]

"We have carefully examined [the] statutes and the pertinent legislative history," Justice Reed declared, "and find nothing to indicate any intention by Congress to grant to the Indians any permanent rights in the lands of Alaska occupied by them by permission of Congress."[14] "There is no

10. See note 5, above. Also, *U.S. v. Sandoval*, 231 U.S. 28, 46–47 (1913); *Tiger v. Western Investment Co.*, 221 U.S. 286, 315 (1911); *Lone Wolf v. Hitchcock*, 187 U.S. 553, 565, 568 (1903); *U.S. v. Holliday*, 3 Wall. 407, 419 (1865).
11. Some minimal regard for the preservation of tribal laws was seen as a matter of good federal policy, not tribal right. *U.S. v. Quiver*, 241 U.S. 602, 602–4 (1916). The Cherokee Nation continued to enjoy considerable autonomy to the end of the nineteenth century (see, for example, *Talton v. Mayes*, 163 U.S. 376 [1896]), but only as the product of unique historical and political factors. Even Fifth Amendment limitations on federal disposal of tribal land were not seriously considered until after the passage of the Indian Reorganization Act (*U.S. v. Creek Nation*, 295 U.S. 103, 110 [1935]; *Chippewa Indians v. U.S.*, 310 U.S. 358, 375–76 [1937]). This deference to federal supremacy did not deter courts from occasionally acquiescing in arrogations of power by the states where the safety of non-Indians was putatively at stake (*U.S. v. Draper*, 164 U.S. 240 [1895]; *U.S. v. McBratney*, 104 U.S. 622 [1882]). Nor from suppressing some of the more extreme forms of "civilizing" violence, e.g., *U.S. ex rel. Standing Bear v. Crook* (5 Dill. 453, 25 Fed. Cas. 695 [C.C. Neb. 1879]), denying the authority of the army to imprison *detribalized* Indians without charge or trial, and *John Bad Elk v. U.S.* (177 U.S. 529 [1900]), to the effect that U.S. Indian Police cannot make arrests without warrants.
12. 348 U.S. 272, 277 (1954). Recall the case of *Penn v. Lord Baltimore*, discussed in Chapter 4, note 27.
13. *U.S. v. Alcea Band of Tillamooks*, 392 U.S. 40 (1946); Felix S. Cohen, "Original Indian Title," 32 *Minnesota Law Review* 28 (1947).
14. 348 U.S. 278.

particular form of congressional recognition of Indian right of permanent occupancy," he admitted. "It may be established in a variety of ways but there must be the definite intention by congressional action or authority to accord legal rights, not merely permissive occupation."[15] Altogether ignoring the Court's own earlier decisions holding federal Indian policy to Fifth Amendment limitations, he concluded that Congress may confiscate Indian property for any reason at all without judicial review.[16] "Every schoolboy knows that the savage tribes of this continent were deprived of their ancestral ranges by force," and if Congress chooses to continue in that tradition, it is not for the Court to interfere.[17] This "leaves with Congress, where it belongs, the policy of Indian gratuities for the termination of Indian occupancy . . . rather than making compensation for its value a rigid constitutional principle."[18]

Tee-Hit-Ton was widely criticized and may be disregarded as precedent because it was tried on meagre, poorly presented facts.[19] Nevertheless it was a portent of things to come. It purports to be a property case, but the Court recognized that it involved "more a claim of sovereignty than of ownership."[20] Was the very existence of the Tee-Hit-Ton band as a body politic dependent upon congressional recognition, and extinguishable without compensation? Herein lies the real significance of the case. Decided only a year after the enactment of Public Law 280, it anticipates the need for a doctrine legitimizing termination.

The Court argued that unrecognized rights cannot be entitled to compensation, and described the compensable rights of recognized tribes as *privileges granted* by the United States to those communities.[21] Congress can surely take back the privileges it has granted, but are granted privileges entitled to *greater* security than unsurrendered original property? The paradox becomes more acute in the context of sovereignty. When a power is delegated for the time being, it can be revoked freely. The exercise of an original power is another matter. *Tee-Hit-Ton* implies that tribes with

15. *Id.* 278−79.
16. *Id.* 287.
17. *Id.* 289−90.
18. *Id.* 291.
19. *Id.* 285−87; "The Supreme Court: 1954 Term," 69 *Harvard Law Review* 119, 150 (1955). Within a few years, the holding of *Tee-Hit-Ton* had been considerably weakened. See, for example, *U.S. v. Seminole Indians*, 180 Ct.Cl. 315 (1967); *Whitefoot v. U.S.*, 155 Ct.Cl. 127 (1961); *Tlingit & Haida Indians v. U.S.*, 147 Ct.Cl. 315 (1959).
20. 349 U.S. 287.
21. *Id.* 280, 292 n. 15.

treaties enjoy mere privileges, an unsubstantiated historical hypothesis, and tribes without treaties have nothing. No tribe, therefore, could be safe from termination.

Tee-Hit-Ton attributed this remarkable power to "discovery and conquest," citing only *Johnson v. M'Intosh* in support.[22] But Chief Justice Marshall had rejected both of these "pretensions" in *Worcester*:

> It is difficult to comprehend the proposition that the inhabitants of either quarter of the globe could have rightful original claims of dominion over the inhabitants of the other, or over the lands they occupied; or that the discovery of either by the other should give the discoverer rights in the country discovered which annulled the pre-existing rights of its ancient possessors.[23]

In *M'Intosh* itself, Marshall refused to follow the rule of *Campbell v. Hall* that the laws of a conquered people remain in force only until the conqueror pleases to alter them, implicitly rejecting the existence, historically, of a "conquest."[24] As we have seen, *M'Intosh* held only that the United States could prohibit *its* citizens from accepting tribal conveyances of tribal land. It had nothing to do with Indians' right to enjoy their own land under their own laws, a right "as sacred as the fee-simple, absolute title of the whites."[25] The United States "came in the place of the former sovereign by compact, on stipulated terms, which bound them to respect all of the existing rights of the inhabitants."[26]

Carino v. Insular Government of the Philippine Islands, an obscure case decided in 1908, sustained the right of an Igorot "savage" to his traditional plot of land, notwithstanding he had no paper title from either the United States or its predecessor-in-interest, the Crown of Spain.[27] The Court refused to consider the military conquest of the Philippines sufficient authority for Congress to confiscate natives' property, and, entirely consistent with the federal-purpose idea then gaining popularity in Indian

---

22. *Id.* 280; 8 Wheat. 543 (1823).

23. 6 Pet. 542−43. Similarly, "The power of war is given only for defense, not for conquest" (8 Wheat. 587, 591).

24. 8 Wheat. 576−80, rejecting counsel's arguments from *Campbell v. Hall*, 1 Cowp. 204, 209, 98 Eng.Rep. 1045, 1047 (1774). *Campbell* itself remarked on what it called the "absurd exception as to pagans, mentioned in *Calvin's case*," which the empire had formerly advanced in the New World.

25. *Cherokee Nation v. Georgia*, 5 Pet. 1, 48 (1831) (Baldwin, concurring). See also *Mitchel v. U.S.*, 9 Pet. 711, 756ff (1835) (*per* Baldwin).

26. *Mitchel v. U.S.*, 755, speaking of the effect on Indians of the Treaty of Florida between the United States and Spain.

27. 212 U.S. 449 (1908).

law, referred the whole matter to congressional intent. The Court's reading of congressional intent, however, was totally at war with *Kagama, Lone Wolf*, and other contemporary Indian cases.

> Whatever consideration may have been shown to the North American Indians, the dominant purpose of the whites in America was to occupy the land. It is obvious that, however stated, the reason for our taking over the Philippines was different. No one, we suppose, would deny that, so far as consistent with paramount necessities, our first object in the internal administration of the islands is to do justice to the natives, not to exploit their country for private gain.[28]

The Court relied on the Organic Act for the Philippines, which declared its purpose to provide "for the benefit of the inhabitants,"[29] but cited no authority for its characterization of federal Indian policy. There is, in fact, no statute that declares Indian policy to be governed by considerations of "private profit"; several expressly refer to Indians' "benefit" or "best interest."[30] We have already seen how allotment and police regulation of tribes in the last quarter of the nineteenth century were justified as beneficial to Indians. On this point *Carino* is completely without foundation. Of course it may be argued that, regardless what the statutes *say*, Congress *actually* always intended to manage Indian lands for the good of the white population. But why should Congress's words be taken at face value in the Organic Act of the Philippines and not in Indian legislation? Besides, if *Carino* is right, then all nineteenth-century federal encroachments on tribal affairs, predicated on beneficial federal purpose, were illegitimate.

Perhaps this is why *Carino* attracted little attention when it was decided. *Tee-Hit-Ton* not only cited it with approval, but did *not* cite any of the early instrumentality cases, such as *Lone Wolf*, with which *Carino* is in conflict.[31] Strictly speaking, *Tee-Hit-Ton* has only *Carino* for precedent. Later cases would prove equally careless of legal history, albeit less consistent with contemporary congressional activities.

The first indication that this shift in theory would affect the scope of *state* power over tribes actually preceded *Tee-Hit-Ton* and the termination

28. *Id.* 458.
29. Act of 1 July 1902, c. 1369 §12, 32 Stat. 691.
30. E.g., 25 U.S.C. 13, 174, 331.
31. 348 U.S. 284 n. 18.

program, although it emanated from the same panel of justices. *New York ex rel. Ray v. Martin* challenged the power of New York State to extend its criminal laws to Seneca Indians residing on the Allegheny Reservation.[32] In writing the opinion of the Court, Justice Black relied on *U.S. v. McBratney*,[33] an 1882 decision,

> For that case and others which followed it all held that in the absence of a limiting treaty obligation or Congressional enactment each state had a right to exercise jurisdiction over Indian reservations within its boundaries.[34]

This presumption in favor of state jurisdiction seems entirely inconsistent with *Worcester v. Georgia*.

However, here as later, Black displayed a style of loose citation of precedent in support of his own idiosyncratic generalizations. Most western states' enabling acts reserved to the United States "absolute jurisdiction and control" of Indian lands.[35] Colorado's did not, a fact the *McBratney* Court found pregnant with significance. "Whenever, upon the admission of a State into the Union, Congress has intended to except out of it an Indian reservation, or the sole and exclusive jurisdiction over that reservation, it has done so by express words."[36] Unlike its neighbors, Colorado might therefore govern tribal Indians without limitation.

On the basis of *McBratney*, Black's rule must be reread, "in the absence of a reservation of jurisdiction in the state's enabling act," implicitly classifying all tribes into two groups. Those located in states like Colorado are subject to unlimited state control. Those located in other states are

32. 326 U.S. 496 (1946).

33. 104 U.S. 622 (1882); 326 U.S. 497−98.

34. The enabling acts of nine western states (Arizona, New Mexico, Oklahoma, Idaho, Montana, North Dakota, South Dakota, Utah and Washington) do reserve "absolute jurisdiction and control" of tribal territory to the United States (25 Stat. 676, 677 [1889]; 28 Stat. 107 [1894]; 34 Stat. 267, 270 [1906]; 34 Stat. 278, 279 [1906]; 36 Stat. 557, 558−59 [1910]; 36 Stat. 568, 569−70 [1910]; Idaho Constitution, Art. XX, Sec. 19 [1889]). About 60 percent of all tribal members in the United States are enrolled in reservations located within one of these states (estimated from data in Economic Development Administration, *Federal and State Indian Reservations* [Washington, D.C.: 1971]). Alaska's statehood act reserves "absolute jurisdiction and control" over fishing alone (72 Stat. 339, §4 [1959]). A number of territorial organic acts (Colorado, Wyoming, Iowa, Kansas, Nevada, and Wisconsin) guaranteed treaty rights and exclusive federal jurisdiction in somewhat different language, but only Kansas retained the proviso when it became a state (10 Stat. 277, 284 [1854]; 12 Stat. 172, 209, 244 [1861]; 12 Stat. 126, 127 [1861]).

35. 326 U.S. 499.

36. 104 U.S. 623−24.

subject to no state control. When the United States does not explicitly reserve exclusive jurisdiction over Indians, it implicitly grants it.[37]

In support of his claim that this rule "has not been modified," Black cited three earlier cases of dubious authority. *Hallowell v. U.S.*, decided in 1910, sustained the conviction of an Omaha Indian allottee for violation of federal laws prohibiting the sale of liquor in "Indian country."[38] Hallowell and the government *stipulated* that "state government extend[s] over said Omaha Indian Reservation, and over and upon the allotments."[39] The Court did not rule on this, nor was it material. The real question was not whether it was "Indian country" within the meaning of the applicable federal statute. The Court held that it was, but the fact that *Congress* has some power over a tract of land has nothing at all to do with the existence or nonexistence of concurrent state or local jurisdiction.

Black also relied on *Surplus Trading Co. v. Cook*, a 1929 decision involving a state tax on personalty located on a *military post*.[40] Without citation of any authority, *Surplus* remarked in dictum that Indian reservations "are part of the state within which they lie and her laws, civil and criminal, have the same force therein as elsewhere within her limits, save

37. In *Ray* there was no enabling act to construe because New York was one of the thirteen original states. Colorado's enabling act declared it to be admitted to the Union "on an equal footing" with the original states, and *McBratney* had sustained Colorado's jurisdiction over Indians, though not on this basis. Black concluded from this that the original thirteen states have jurisdiction over Indians (326 U.S. 499, citing 194 U.S. 623). This placed the conclusion of the argument before the premise. Besides, since all of the enabling acts which *do* include reservations of "absolute jurisdiction and control" of Indian lands *also* provide for admission "on an equal footing," the equal-footing provision *could not* have been determinative in *McBratney* to begin with. Congress may place special limitations in enabling acts. See *The Kansas Indians*, 5 Wall. 737, 756 (1867); *Langford v. Monteith*, 102 U.S. 145, 146 (1880); *U.S. v. Chavez*, 290 U.S. 357, 365 (1933); *Coyle v. Smith*, 221 U.S. 559, 574 (1911). Black also dismissed the significance of the Senecas' 1794 treaty with the United States as merely "one of peace and friendship" (326 U.S. 500–501). He did not explain how a treaty can *implicitly* deny the political existence of one of the parties. New York did, however, have prior, colonial-era treaties with the Senecas which could have been considered controlling.

38. 221 U.S. 317 (1910).

39. *Id.* 319–20. This much was at least consistent with *U.S. v. Draper*, 164 U.S. 240 (1895), cited by Black, 326 U.S. 498, which held that the General Allotment Act implicitly intended the complete allotment of a reservation to transfer jurisdiction to the state. The Omaha reservation was in fact completely allotted (326 U.S. 319). However, the General Allotment Act was repudiated by the Indian Reorganization Act in 1934, long before *Ray*. Section 16 of the IRA indicates that Congress contemplated not only restoring allotted land to tribal ownership, but restoring it to tribal control as well.

40. 281 U.S. 647.

that they can have only restricted application to the Indian wards."[41] This sweeping generalization went far beyond *McBratney*, ignoring the significance of individual states' enabling acts.

The third leg of Black's rule in *Ray* was *U.S. v. McGowan*, an opinion he himself had written seven years earlier.[42] The issue was similar to that in *Hallowell* and equally inapplicable to *Ray*, but Black paraphrased *Surplus* in dictum to the effect that "[e]nactments of the Federal Government passed to protect and guard its Indian wards only affect the operation . . . of such laws as conflict with [them]."[43] No new authority was cited. The "rule" of *Ray* therefore rested on a single precedent, *McBratney*, which by its terms could only be applied to certain states.

Notwithstanding *Tee-Hit-Ton*, *Ray*, and the progress of the termination program, federal judges were still confused over the nature and source of tribal self-governing powers. Twenty years late, the spirit of the reorganization policy was beginning to filter into judicial consciousness. In *Iron Crow v. Oglala Sioux Tribe*, the Eighth Circuit upheld a tribal court's sentence for adultery, reasoning that tribal sovereignty is not established, but merely recognized by the United States.[44] "This sovereignty," they explained, "is absolute excepting only as to such rights as are taken away by the paramount government, the United States." The source of their reasoning was Felix Cohen's *Handbook*, which they quoted at great length:

From the earliest years of the Republic the *Indian tribes have been recognized as "distinct, independent, political communities"* . . . and, *as such, qualified to exercise powers of self-government*, not by virtue of any delegation of powers from the Federal Government, but rather by reason of their original tribal sovereignty.[45]

They explicitly rejected the appellant's contention that tribal courts are creatures of federal law, holding that tribal governments retained "inherent jurisdiction over all matters not taken over by the federal government."[46] Federal statutes such as the Indian Reorganization Act merely "support" tribal authority. Among the retained powers of tribes, the circuit found "the power of taxation which is an inherent incident of its sovereignty"

41. *Id.* 651.
42. 302 U.S. 535 (1938).
43. *Id.* 539.
44. 231 F.2d 89, 94 (8th Cir. 1956), *rev'g* 129 F.Supp. 15 (S.D. 1955).
45. 231 F.2d 92−93 (Court's emphasis, quoting Cohen).
46. *Id.* 96.

and which ''has not been pretermitted by any federal statute or agency ruling thereunder, but to the contrary *implemented* by the Indian Reorganization Act.''[47] Two years later, in a case challenging the same tribe's discriminatory tax on non-Indians' reservation leaseholds, the Eighth Circuit reaffirmed *Iron Crow*.[48] The termination program was already under heavy attack when, in 1958, the Supreme Court finally accepted the task of reconciling its worship of federal despotism in *Tee-Hit-Ton* with the persistence of the idea of tribal sovereignty.

47. *Id.* 99.
48. 259 F.2d 553, 556–57 (8th Cir. 1958), *rev'g* 146 F.Supp. 916 (S.D. 1956).

12

The Illusion of the "Infringement Test"

> Judicial authority to select the most apt of several possible avenues of decision is a sensitive and a powerful weapon. Utilized with sophistication, it complements the Supreme Court's broad discretion as to which cases the Court will entertain, and in what sequence. It is a weapon which strengthens the wielder, but tests him as well.[1]

Denying *certiorari* to cases involving the political rights of tribes, the Warren Court waited five years for an acceptable vehicle to synthesize the shifting tide of decisional law and congressional policy. *Williams v. Lee* involved a non-Indian creditor whose Navajo debtors resisted a state civil action for recovery of the debt.[2] The Supreme Court of Arizona followed Black's formula in *Ray*; failing to find any specific congressional prohibition against the exercise of state judicial power, it sustained a judgment against the debtors.[3]

Writing for the Court, Justice Black completely reversed his previous position. "Congress has," he claimed, "acted consistently upon the assumption that the States have no power to regulate the affairs of Indians on a reservation."[4] Accordingly, "when Congress has wished the States to exercise this power it has expressly granted them the jurisdiction," as, for example, in Public Law 280, which Arizona had failed to take advantage of when it might have.[5]

---

1. Professor Louis H. Pollak, quoted by Alexander M. Bickel, *The Least Dangerous Branch* 172 (Indianapolis: 1962).
2. 358 U.S. 217 (1958).
3. 83 Ariz. 241, 319 P.2d 998 (1957).
4. 358 U.S. 220−21.
5. *Id.* 220−21, 222−23.

Although the Navajos' 1868 Treaty with the United States did not guarantee tribal sovereignty as such, it did establish and protect their territory, and "[i]mplicit in these treaty terms, as it was in the treaties with the Cherokees involved in *Worcester v. Georgia*, was the understanding that the internal affairs of the Indians remained exclusively within the jurisdiction of whatever tribal government existed."[6] Congress had, moreover, "encouraged tribal governments and courts to become stronger and more highly organized."[7]

What accounted for Black's transformation? The new justices on the Court would later write opinions closer in many respects to *Ray* than *Williams*,[8] and the only relevant federal legislation since *Ray* had been Public Law 280, a termination measure. Federal intent to perpetuate tribes was no stronger in 1958 than it had been in 1946, at least on the legislative record. Black himself assumed that tribes would eventually be terminated.

Congress has followed a policy calculated eventually to make all Indians full-fledged participants in American society. This policy contemplates criminal and civil jurisdiction over Indians by any State ready to assume the burdens that go with it as soon as the educational and economic status of the Indians permits the change without disadvantage to them.[9]

He merely believed it to be Congress's intent to retain exclusive control over this process of transition.

The question must then follow, whether Black conceived of tribal self-government as flowing from tribal consent or federal purpose. The idea of consent was at the heart of *Worcester*. Federal purpose would have been more consistent with post-*Kagama* decisions. Black acknowledged a conceptual debt to *Worcester*, but suggested that, "[o]ver the years this Court has modified these principles in cases *where essential tribal relations were not involved* and where the rights of Indians would not be jeopardized."[10] Rather than admit to the shift in philosophy that followed

6. *Id.* 221–22.
7. *Id.* 220. Black did not consider the narrower ground that Lee was a federally licensed Indian trader operating under preemptive federal commerce power. This theory would emerge seven years later in Black's opinion in *Warren Trading Post v. Arizona Tax Commission*, 380 U.S. 685 (1965).
8. Chapters 13 and 14, below. The Warren Court was better known for its dramatic reversal of *Plessy v. Ferguson* (163 U.S. 537 [1895]) in *Brown v. Board of Education* (347 U.S. 483 [1954]) a few years earlier.
9. 358 U.S. 220–21.
10. *Id.* 219 (emphasis ours). He may have been recalling his own opinion in *New York ex rel. Ray v. Martin* (326 U.S. 501), in which he observed that "[t]he entire emphasis in treaties and congressional enactments dealing with Indian affairs has always been focused upon

Kagama, he attempted to distinguish the cases on their facts. "[A]bsent governing Acts of Congress," he concluded confidently, "the question has always been whether the state action infringed on the right of reservation Indians to make their own laws and be ruled by them."[11]

The distinction lacked real substantiation.[12] Black relied in part on cases upholding the right of Indians to avail themselves of state process, but this right goes to states' lack of power to discriminate on the basis of race rather than their power to exercise jurisdiction within Indian reservations.[13] Another prop of his argument was the nineteenth-century case of *Utah & Northern Railway v. Fisher*. The *Fisher* Court was of the opinion that collection of a state railroad tax would not interfere with the tribe's ability to limit access to its reservation to federal employees, as guaranteed by its treaty. However, the same treaty empowered Congress to take rights-of-way through the reservation, and the railway in question was operating on lands withdrawn from the reservation by Congress.[14] The real question in *Fisher*, then, was the location of the railway, not the powers of states on reservation lands.

The only other case Black discussed was *Ray*, in which he had reached the opposite conclusion. Instead of openly reversing himself, he hinted that *Ray*, a criminal case, applied only to conflicts over criminal jurisdiction, although his own opinion in *Ray* had said nothing of the sort. Moreover, Black's use of *Ray* in this manner could only have shown what the rule of law in conflicts over civil jurisdiction is *not*. Thus among all of the cases Black cited in support of his argument, not one was in point.

Williams suggests that state jurisdiction is a function of subject matter,

---

the treatment of the Indians themselves and their property," rather than matters that "did not directly affect the Indians."

11. 358 U.S. 220.

12. Robert Ericson and D. Rebecca Snow, "The Indian Battle for Self-Determination," 58 *California Law Review* 445, 473 (1970), appears to have been instrumental in populariz- ing the idea of an "infringement test."

13. Neither case Black cited for this proposition actually held that Indians have a *federal* right of access to state courts. *Felix v. Patrick* (145 U.S. 317, 332 [1892]) relies on Kansas and Idaho decisions construing those states' laws, and *U.S. v. Candelaria* (271 U.S. 432, 442–43 [1926]) relies on New Mexico state law.

14. 116 U.S. 28, 31 (1885). The railroad argued that collection of a state railroad tax within the exterior boundaries of the reservation violated the tribe's express treaty right to limit entry on its lands to officers of the United States. However, its right-of-way had been legislatively withdrawn from the reservation; the tribe, if it had been a party, might have com- plained of this, but the railroad couldn't. The tribe's 1868 treaty authorized Congress to legislate on "all subjects connected with the government of the . . . reservations" (Charles Kappler, 2 *Indian Affairs: Laws and Treaties* 1020 [Washington, D.C.: 1904]).

not territory. Black assumed that tribal lands are not reservations of original sovereign territory but were acquired from and remain a "part" of the states.[15] Without precise enumeration, subject matter is a difficult standard to apply. Any "balancing" of state and tribal interests in a particular controversy must be subjective, and it is illusory to suppose that there are cases in which only one of the two has an interest. Anything that a state does, on or off a reservation, will probably affect that reservation to a greater or lesser extent. State and reservation economies are inextricably interlinked, and there is a considerable amount of population movement across their common borders. State action will always pose problems of degree rather than kind.

The states have always maintained the importance of their own territoriality. No state, least of all in the great Atlantic seaboard megalopolis, would dare advance a power to govern its transient citizens wherever they travel. The ability of each state to maintain environmental conditions, behavior, risks and opportunities consistent with its public policy declines in proportion to the number of persons within its territory that it cannot fully control. Concurrency of any kind weakens state power.

How, then, can states complain about federal regulation within their borders, and advance the "infringement test" in support of a power to regulate activities on reservations? Is not the fact that a tribe resists state regulation evidence that it constitutes an "infringement" of tribal interests? Unless its officers are irrational or poorly informed, tribes will not invest real money in redress of imaginary grievances. The question in jurisdictional litigation is the right of sovereignty, not whether the exercise of sovereignty is desirable or valuable.

It might be argued that certain state encroachments, albeit injurious, are *de minimus*, since in the past tribes have exercised relatively little of the jurisdiction they may have. This, however, ignores the possibility that tribes may wish to implement their jurisdiction in the future. Even if tribal inaction justifies vacuum-filling state action, state action should be ousted by subsequent tribal legislation. Otherwise the effect would be to convert the temporary non-exercise of governmental powers into a surrender of those powers, a novel proposition in the public law of non-Indian government.

"Implicit in this new 'infringement test,' " a commentator subsequently

15. 358 U.S. 218.

reasoned, "was the assumption that there were some Indian matters in which the states could assert their power without prior Federal permission."[16] But was it really meant to be a "test" at all? Justice Black was notoriously averse to "balancing tests" in constitutional adjudication,[17] and it is difficult to impute to him the intention to create one out of thin air and without compelling reason. The Court itself made no further use of this "test" for eighteen years, although in the meantime it fashioned several other equally innovative and inconsistent rules.

Properly understood, "infringement" actually had nothing to do with the facts in *Williams*. Black described it as applicable only "absent governing Acts of Congress," then turned around and identified the Navajo-Hopi Rehabilitation Act, Navajo Treaty, and Indian Reorganization Act[18] as "governing" the Navajos. No balancing was necessary. These laws ruled out state jurisdiction. But none of them specifically address civil jurisdiction. Hence Black could not have intended to apply "infringement" in every case in which the tribe's authority has not been specifically defined by Congress. "Infringement" must have been meant for tribes like the Senecas, in *Ray*, which are neither included in reorganization nor individually recognized by special legislation like the rehabilitation act.[19]

After all, Black's case for the Navajos was based on the *implications* he read into general federal laws. He never discussed or identified their precise terms. It is therefore reasonable to interpret *Williams* as holding that if a tribe is legislatively recognized by the United States, the states are presumed to lack authority over it. To rebut that presumption a state must demonstrate the existence of an express *delegation* of federal plenary power—such as Public Law 280.

16. Ericson and Snow, "The Indian Battle for Self-Determination," 473.
17. Bickel, *Least Dangerous Branch* 84–98.
18. The Navajo were never an IRA tribe; however, in 1949 the Navajo-Hopi Rehabilitation Act authorized the adoption of a Navajo constitution in language borrowed from, and as vague as, Section 16 of the IRA. Compare "Such constitution may provide for the exercise by the Navajo Tribe of *any powers vested in the tribe or any organ thereof by existing law*, together with such additional powers as the members of the tribe may, with the approval of the Secretary of the Interior, deem proper to include therein" (25 U.S.C. 636) with "In addition *to all powers vested in any Indian tribe or tribal council by existing law*, the constitution adopted by said tribe shall also vest in such tribe or its tribal council the following rights and powers," etc. (set out in full in Chapter 8, above, 25 U.S.C. 476). If the rehabilitation act suffices to preempt state jurisdiction generally, the reorganization act must do at least as much.
19. About 190 at this time, to judge from George E. Fay, *Charters, Constitutions and By-Laws of Indian Tribes of North America* (Greeley, Colo.: 1967–1971), or about 90 percent of the tribes serviced by the Bureau of Indian Affairs.

If the commentators were fooled, the Tenth Circuit wasn't. In *Native American Church v. Navajo Tribal Council*, decided a year later, they concluded that *Williams* had not materially deviated from the old rule of *Worcester v. Georgia*, that,

Indian tribes are not states. They have a status higher than that of states. They are subordinate and dependent nations possessed of all powers as such [limited] only to the extent that they have expressly been required to surrender them by the superior sovereign, the United States.[20]

Powers not expressly prohibited to tribes are usually also not expressly prohibited to the states. According to our narrow interpretation of *Williams*, the Tenth Circuit is correct that such powers are presumed to remain with the tribes themselves. According to the more expansive reading of *Williams*, as a general balancing test in the absence of *specific* federal legislation, such powers may be tribal *or* state, and are presumed to be state unless they "infringe" on tribal self-government. Paradoxically, the expansive view would permit states to enjoy greater power over tribes than either the tribes have surrendered or the United States has demanded: plenary state power.

Native American Church could not, of course, foreclose the possibility that the Supreme Court itself would eventually adopt the expansive view. *Williams* is fundamentally ambivalent, and because the resolution of that ambivalence requires a choice between two such fundamentally different rules, it made tribal affairs considerably more uncertain. Unfortunately, rather than endorse one interpretation of *Williams* or the other, the Court avoided the case altogether.

20. 272 F.2d 131, 133 (8th Cir. 1959).

13

The Bewildering Alaskan Connection

Although it made few references to *Williams v. Lee*, the Court became increasingly obsessed with historical and legislative facts, as if it secretly believed that the words "absent governing Acts of Congress" should be interpreted as "absent specific delegations of power to the tribes." Its penchant for detail was expressed in new rules bearing little apparent relationship to "infringement": rules of statutory construction, assumptions about history, overbroad generalizations about tribal organization and government. In all the Court shrank from principle into the refuge of interminable distinctions.

Metlakatla Indian Community v. Egan[1] and *Kake v. Egan*[2] both involved attempts by the State of Alaska to prevent the use of fish traps by Alaskan natives. Natives had always used traps, which are, for anadromous fish stocks, the most efficient harvest technology and afford the trapper considerable cost advantages in the wholesale market.[3] However, marine fishermen have often prevailed on state legislatures to prohibit

---

1. 369 U.S. 45 (1962).   2. 369 U.S. 60 (1962).
3. James A. Crutchfield and Giulio Pontecorvo, *The Pacific Salmon Fisheries: A Study of Irrational Conservation* 38–39 (Baltimore: 1969); R. L. Barsh, *The Washington Fishing Rights Controversy: An Economic Critique* 7–12 (Seattle: 1977).

trapping on the pretense of conservation, the underlying motivation being to eliminate trappers' ability to undersell marine fishermen to fish processors.[4]

The Metlakatlans' Annette Islands Reserve was established by an act of Congress in 1891. In 1916 it was extended three thousand feet out to sea by presidential proclamation, in connection with a federally sponsored tribal cannery development.[5] Both the act and proclamation expressly authorized federal regulation of the Metlakatlans' fishery. The secretary of the interior accordingly issued regulations for Metlakatlan trap fishing within the reserve, and the regulations were not amended after passage of the Alaska Anti-Fish Trap Conservation law in 1959, notwithstanding state threats to enforce it against natives.[6] Metlakatla sought an injunction against state interference with its traps, raising as alternative grounds lack of state jurisdiction over Indian reservations, and lack of state power over federal instrumentalities.

The facts in the companion case were substantially the same. The coplaintiffs, Organized Village of Kake and Angoon Community Association, were both Indian Reorganization Act tribes, and like Metlakatla both were dependent for their livelihood on trapfishing for salmon. Both had received federal financing for cannery construction before Alaska was admitted to statehood.[7] However, neither community was located within a federal Indian reservation or on trust land. The traps were operated in the Tongass National Forest under permits from the National Forest Service and Army Corps of Engineers. In 1959 the secretary of the interior issued regulations for the licensing of these traps, which he purported to have authority to do under the terms of the Alaska Statehood Act. The source of the secretary's regulatory authority was therefore the principal difference between *Metlakatla* and *Kake*.

The resolution of these cases could have been made a simple matter. Section 4 of the Alaska Statehood Act reserved to the United States "absolute jurisdiction and control" of "any land or other property (including fishing rights), the right . . . to which may be held by any

4. Alaskans reacted to the traps as "the symbol of exploitation of her resources by 'Stateside' colonialism" (369 U.S. 47–48). Since traps are so costly to build, trappers tend to be relatively well-capitalized firms rather than independent fishermen.
5. *Id.* 48, 52. In *Alaska Pacific Fisheries v. U.S.,* 248 U.S. 78 (1918), this was held to be an exclusively tribal fishery.
6. 369 U.S. 49–50.
7. *Id.* 61.

Indians.''[8] Moreover, the special act extending Public Law 280 to Alaska specified that it was not intended to "deprive any Indian or Indian tribe, band, or community of any right, privilege, or immunity afforded under Federal Treaty, agreement, or statute with respect to . . . fishing *or the control, licensing, or regulation thereof.*''[9] Metlakatla's 1916 presidential proclamation can be interpreted as establishing federal fishing rights. A case can also be made, if perhaps a somewhat weaker one, that the federal permits and regulations governing native trapfishing in the Tongass National Forest created rights or privileges on federal property under federal law. The issue was simply one of statutory construction.

Writing for a unanimous Court, Justice Frankfurter repeated Black's error of going too far with too little, leaving behind a trail of confused theories and ambiguous rules. He began by promising to distinguish Alaskan natives from all other native Americans. There had been, he argued, no Indian wars in Alaska; few reservations had been created; Alaskan natives had "substantially" adopted white culture; they had not resisted state taxation; they could vote and hold state office; and the state had "always . . . assumed" that natives were subject to state laws.[10]

That there were no Indian wars in Alaska is a matter of history, but are peaceful societies less entitled to political recognition than hostile ones as a matter of law? Similarly, must Indians remain culturally "pure" in order to retain their political rights and self-government? The fact that Alaskan natives vote and hold state office was scarcely a distinction, since all native Americans have had that right since 1924.[11] And the fact that the state had "assumed" it had jurisdiction is meaningless. We wonder how a court in an ordinary civil case would react to the defendant's claim that he had always assumed that he had a right to take his neighbor's property! Furthermore, the Navajos had prevailed in *Williams*, although they had

8. *Id.* 54–59.

9. 72 Stat. 545 (1958), incorporating 67 Stat. 588 (1953).

10. *Id.* 50–51. But in the companion case he turned around and argued that "[t]he power of Alaska over Indians . . . is the same as that of many other States" (369 U.S. 71). Several years later the Court implicitly approved of Frankfurter's original distinction, refusing to extend either *Metlakatla* or *Kake* to a non-Alaskan case (*McClanahan v. Arizona Tax Commission*, 411 U.S. 164, 168 [1973]).

11. Act of 2 June 1924, 43 Stat. 253; *Ely v Klahr*, 403 U.S. 108, 119 (1971); also *Harrison v. Laveen*, 67 Ariz. 337, 196 P. 2d 456 (1948). Citizenship is not inconsistent with continued tribal self-government (*U.S. v. Nice*, 241 U.S. 591, 598 [1916]; *Winton v. Amos*, 255 U.S. 373, 391–92 [1921]; *Bd. of Commissioners of Creek County v. Seber*, 318 U.S. 705 [1943]; *Hallowell v. U.S.*, 221 U.S. 317, 324 [1911]).

never collectively resisted state encroachments; *Williams* itself was brought by individual Indians, not the tribe. Not only were Frankfurter's "facts" of questionable relevance and his use of them peculiar, but his practice of generalizing about history without citations or evidence was a dangerous precedent.

However disputable, Frankfurter's "facts" were supposed to distinguish *Metlakatla* from *Kake*. The creation of the Annette Islands Reserve made Metlakatla uniquely similar, among Alaskan communities, to tribal reservations in the lower forty-eight states. The 1891 act specified that the Metlakatlans were to use the reserve subject to federal regulations, and organize a tribal government under federal supervision.[12] No subsequent legislation had modified the terms or evident purpose of that law, not even the Alaska Statehood Act, which preserved Congress's "absolute jurisdiction and control" of native fisheries. The only flaw Frankfurter could find was purely technical. After 1959 the secretary of the interior had promulgated Metlakatlan regulations under the purported authority of the statehood act, when in fact his authority derived from the 1891 act and 1916 proclamation. Accordingly, *Metlakatla* was remanded with the expectation that the secretary would correct the attribution of his authority in the Federal Register.[13]

How did *Kake* differ? Although not the subject of special federal enabling legislation, both Kake and Angoon enjoyed Indian Reorganization Act charters. And if federal agencies had authority to recognize native fishing rights before Alaska statehood, that authority would have survived, owing to the statutory saving of "fishing rights" and "the control, licensing, or regulation thereof."

Frankfurter never denied the exclusive authority of the secretary of the interior to issue fishing regulations *before* statehood, but suggested that the statehood act itself had terminated it. Based entirely on a few statements made during the House hearings on Alaskan statehood, he concluded that "[t]he disclaimer was intended to preserve unimpaired the right of any Indian claimant to assert his claim . . . against the Government" for this implied taking, and nothing more.[14] But if this were the purpose, why

12. 369 U.S. at 53. The Navajo tribe was originally governed under a very similar administrative arrangement (Mary Shepardson, "Navajo Ways in Government: A Study in Political Process," 65 *American Anthropologist*, no. 3, pt. 2 [1963]).
13. See 25 C.F.R. 88.3.   14. 369 U.S. 67.

didn't Congress simply say that native rights were extinguished subject to a right of compensation, rather than perpetuate federal "jurisdiction and control" of them?[15]

Frankfurter admitted that the "absolute jurisdiction and control" phrase actually "received little attention in Congress," but there was, to be sure, strong opposition in the Senate to any provision depriving Alaska of police power over Alaskan native areas.[16] The obvious expedient would have been to adopt language different from the familiar phraseology of earlier statehood acts. The Senate's version of the act accordingly deleted any reference to federal "jurisdiction," but the House version retained it. In conference the House text was adopted, with one opposition Senator, Jackson, expressing himself reasonably confident that the two versions of the act would have had the identical effect.

Frankfurter's use of these facts asks us to accept two novel principles of interpreting legislative history: that a political victory should be construed against the successful party, and that a single senator's legal interpretation of an act is representative of the intent of Congress as a whole. The texts of the House and Senate bills differed sufficiently to force the matter into conference. If they were so much alike in effect, it is difficult to understand why the difference in wording was not taken care of by the sponsors in committee. Nor can it be concluded from the adoption of the House text that a majority in Congress were indifferent to its "jurisdiction" language, only that opposition in the House to the Senate text was greater than opposition in the Senate to the House text. This cuts against Frankfurter's argument.

Ten statehood acts, including Arizona's, include similar language.[17] If "absolute jurisdiction and control" preempted all state jurisdiction, then why, Frankfurter asked, had not the Court in *Williams* deprived Arizona of jurisdiction over the Navajos on this basis, instead of discussing "infringement" of tribal self-government? The *Williams* Court's lack of reliance on the Arizona Enabling Act proved, according to Frankfurter, that " 'absolute' federal jurisdiction is not invariably exclusive jurisdiction."[18] It is unnecessary to criticize this as semantic nonsense. The Arizona Enabling

15. This is just what Congress finally did in the Alaska Native Claims Settlement Act, P.L. 92–203, 85 Stat. 688 (1971), 43 U.S.C. 1601 *et seq.*; especially Section 4.
16. *Id.* 69–71.   17. *Id.* 67–68.
18. *Id.* 68. He also reviewed much of Justice Black's historical argument (*id.* 71–76).

Act was never an issue in *Williams*. The Court nowhere discussed it. For that matter, *Williams* was not an "infringement" case to begin with, since Justice Black was convinced that federal statutes "governed" the Navajos' status completely. Yet Frankfurter would have us read *Williams* as if it said, "*even where there is* a governing Act of Congress."

Frankfurter also relied on *Draper*, which, as we have seen, concluded that the "absolute jurisdiction and control" language in Montana's Enabling Act had been superseded by the General Allotment Act. The "governing Act of Congress" there was the allotment act, but it was repudiated in 1934 by the Indian Reorganization Act, a fact Frankfurter admitted.[19] Besides, the facts in *Kake* were entirely different. The General Allotment Act had never applied to Alaska.

Undaunted, Frankfurter argued that state power over tribes had increased "concurrent" with the Indian Reorganization Act. He relied on sections 231 and 452 of Title 25; in fact, both were enacted prior to reorganization. Moreover section 452 merely authorizes the secretary of the interior to contract "in his discretion" with states for the administration of federally funded Indian programs; it does not delegate police powers.[20] Similarly, although Frankfurter described section 231 as empowering states to enforce their sanitation, health, and compulsory education laws within reservations, the statute actually provides that states *must first obtain tribal consent.*[21]

Less easily dismissed was Public Law 280, still in its heyday. Frankfurter suggested that termination had recreated a transitional climate similar to allotment and had restored the vitality of *Draper*. However, if Public Law 280 was controlling, so was its proviso that it not be construed to "deprive any Indian or Indian tribe, band, or community of any right, privilege, or immunity afforded under Federal Treaty, agreement, or statute with respect to . . . fishing or the control, licensing, or regulation thereof." Frankfurter carefully avoided quoting this part of the law. Instead he paraphrased it as "disclaim[ing] the intention to permit States to interfere with federally granted fishing privileges."[22] The law itself unambiguously

19. *Id.* 73.
20. The secretary was also required to give preference in procurement to *Indian* contractors (25 U.S.C. 47). Title I of the Indian Self-Determination and Education Assistance Act (88 Stat. 2203 [1975], 25 U.S.C. 450) has the effect of including tribes in the category of government agencies eligible to contract under 25 U.S.C. 452.
21. The text of the statute is quite clear on this point. See *State ex rel. Adams v. Superior Court,* 57 Wash.2d 181, 356 P.2d 985 (1960).
22. 369 U.S. 74.

reserves exclusive jurisdiction to the United States. Frankfurter's paraphrase implies that the state may regulate tribal fisheries as long as it does not "interfere" with them.

He proceeded to argue that "state regulation of off-reservation fishing certainly does not impinge on treaty-protected reservation self-government, the factor decisive in *Williams v. Lee*."[23] This alone is troublesome, for the tribe and its government were supported by the proceeds of the traps, and the kind of gear used in harvesting salmon determines the size and unit cost of the harvest. Any limitation on gear choice must affect the realizable value of the fishery. A prohibition against trapping, the most efficient technology, reduces resource value as surely as a tax or confiscation. If state regulation of tribal resource exploitation is not an "interference," neither is a tax levied on the tribe. Of course, state regulation also precludes the power of the tribe to adopt inconsistent regulations of its own, a direct infringement of tribal self-government.[24]

But is it appropriate to apply "infringement" criteria at all to the interpretation of an explicit statute? According to *Williams*, they only apply "absent governing Acts of Congress," a condition Frankfurter evidently forgot.[25] Thus while *Williams* assured tribes of at least as much power as Congress expressly recognizes, *Kake* suggests that even expressly recognized powers may be judicially limited. Is the Court competent to make its "infringement" standard superior to legislation?

Innovation was unnecessary. The real question was whether Kake's

---

23. *Id.* 75–76. He did cite *Tulee v. Washington*, 315 U.S. 681, 683 (1942), but that case's brief mention of off-reservation fishing appeared in the court's summary of the state's argument, not a ruling (see the discussion of *Tulee* in *U.S. v. Washington*, 384 F.Supp. 312, 336 [W.D. Wash. 1974]). In *Strom v. Com.* (6 T.C. 621, 627 [1946], *aff'd per curiam* 158 F.2d 520 [9th Cir. 1947]), not discussed by Frankfurter, the court reasoned that a state tax on Indian fishermen's net income was not a burden on the right to fish—protected by treaty—but only on proceeds from the exercise of that right. Obviously, however, a tax on income from a good reduces its value to the possessor, and discourages the possessor from exploiting it. After *Kake*, the Supreme Court did get around to expressly permitting state regulation of off-reservation fishing where that regulation is "reasonably necessary" for the survival of the species (*Dept. of Game v. Puyallup Tribe*, 414 U.S. 4 [1973]; *U.S. v. Washington*, 337–39).

24. Frankfurter insinuated that the state has a special interest here, "[b]ecause of the migratory habits of salmon" (369 U.S. 76). However, traps are always the terminal gear type, since they must be anchored in shallow estuarine and riparian waters. Salmon that reach traps have *already* passed the gauntlet of state-regulated marine gear; those that pass the traps spawn and die. Tribes operating traps have no interest in overfishing since to do so would decrease future runs and thereby devalue their traps (see Barsh, *Washington Fishing Rights Controversy*).

25. 358 U.S. 217, 220.

permits in the Tongass National Forest qualified as a "right, privilege, or immunity afforded under Federal Treaty, agreement, or statute," in accordance with law. Frankfurter observed in passing that he believed they did not;[26] he need have gone no further. It is moreover inexplicable why Frankfurter applied "infringement" to Public Law 280 in *Kake*, but did not apply it to the 1891 Annette Islands Reserve act in *Metlakatla*. If state regulation would not "impinge" on Kake's fishing, how much different could Metlakatla be? Frankfurter's point that Metlakatla was granted reservation land, unlike other Alaskan tribes, has nothing to do with the effect of state fishing regulation on native fishermen.

In the three years following *Metlakatla* and *Kake*, Justice Black guided the Court away from Frankfurter's heresy, not by repudiating it openly but by fashioning alternative rules. In *Arizona v. California* the United States, on behalf of five Indian tribes, asserted reserved rights to the waters of the Colorado River.[27] The State of Arizona argued that its enabling act evidenced no congressional intent to reserve water for tribes, but the Court found a reservation of sufficient water to meet both present and future tribal needs *implied* in the act's express reservation of *land*.

There was precedent for this result. In *Winters v. United States* nearly a century earlier, the Court had reasoned that a tribe's agreement to restrict itself to a smaller territory and take up agriculture implied a reservation of sufficient water for irrigation.[28] It could have been argued with equal plausibility that when a fishing tribe agreed to give up all of its land it implicitly reserved sufficient fish for its future needs, but the Court did not follow the general theory of *Winters* in *Kake*. *Arizona v. California* repudiated *Kake's* restrictive interpretation of statutes in favor of the liberal use of implications that characterized Black's opinion in *Williams*.

In *Warren Trading Post v. Arizona Tax Commission*,[29] the appellant sought immunity from an Arizona gross income tax on the alternative grounds of preemptive federal regulation of licensed traders on the Navajo reservation and preemptive federal regulation of commerce with Indian tribes. The real significance of the case is diminished considerably by the fact that the court limited itself to the narrower of these two arguments,

26. 369 U.S. 76: "Nor have appellants any fishing rights derived from federal laws." Although the determinative issue in the case, this remark is little more than an aside at the conclusion of Frankfurter's ruminations.
27. 373 U.S. 546, 595 (1963).
28. 207 U.S. 564 (1908).
29. 380 U.S. 685 (1965).

refusing to consider the jurisdictional status of reservation businesses generally.

Observing, as he had in *Williams*, that "from the first days of our Government, the Federal Government had been permitting the Indians largely to govern themselves, free from state interference,"[30] Black remarked on the degree to which Congress had nonetheless exercised direct control over the activities of non-Indians entering tribal areas for the purpose of trade.[31]

The Interior Department had promulgated special regulations for licensing traders to the Navajo, Hopi and Zuni.[32] "These apparently all-inclusive regulations . . . would seem in themselves sufficient to show that Congress has taken the business of Indian trading on reservations so fully in hand that no room remains for state laws imposing additional burdens on traders."[33]

Black also opined on the *purpose* of this federal preemption of Indian trading.[34] There was, he concluded, an "evident congressional purpose of ensuring that no burden shall be imposed upon Indian traders for trading with Indians on reservations . . . in order to protect Indians against prices deemed unfair or unreasonable by the Indian Commissioner." He did not consider the reasonableness of accomplishing this by limiting entry rather than imposing price ceilings. Several years later, the Federal Trade Commission reported that the licensed trading system actually increased prices by limiting competition.[35]

Was the tax invalid, then, because the regulation of Indian traders had been completely preempted by Congress, or only because its effect would have been to increase prices paid by Indian consumers? If preemption is limited to its *purpose*, taxes on sales to non-Indians would have to be upheld, but if preemption extends to the entire *activity* of trading, taxes on sales made to any consumers are equally invalid. Black's opinion failed to choose between purpose and activity; he expressly declined to discuss the

30. *Id.* 686.

31. *Id.* 686–87, quoted in *McClanahan*, 411 U.S. 165, 168; also 688–90. *Worcester v. Georgia* (6 Pet. 515, 554 [1832]) interpreted these regulations as being in the nature of foreign trade laws.

32. 25 C.F.R. 252; *cf.* 25 C.F.R. 251. The Court did not cite these regulations.

33. 380 U.S. 690.

34. In applying preemption elsewhere, the Court has not uncommonly examined the purposes of federal and state statutes to determine whether there is in fact any inconsistency of purpose (*Merrill, Lynch, Pierce, Fenner & Smith v. Ware*, 414 U.S. 117, 139 [1973]).

35. 380 U.S. 691; Federal Trade Commission, *The Trading Post System on the Navajo Reservation* (Washington, D.C.: 1973).

effect of *Warren* on non-Indian consumers. This ambiguity left as much uncertainty in its wake as Black's ambiguity in *Williams* over the scope of the phrase "governing Acts of Congress." It was strange behavior for a man committed to "absolutes" and "strict construction" in jurisprudence, but, as Professor Bickel has suggested, Black often thought he was making himself perfectly clear when in fact his arguments lacked a definite shape or foundation.[36]

Warren is not a significant case, not as precedent. It was limited to federal preemption of state laws under a unique statutory scheme. The power of tribes to preempt state laws was not an issue, nor was the effect of general federal legislation such as the Indian Reorganization Act. Black's use of preemption was routine.[37] The interesting question is why Black didn't use preemption more explicitly in *Williams*, and didn't refer to "infringement" in *Warren*. Both cases involved licensed traders. In neither case was the controversy with the trader specifically addressed by federal legislation: the Interior Department regulations do not provide for taxation or recovery of debts. Black could have argued in *Williams* that federal preemption of reservation trading ruled out state jurisdiction of traders' debt collections. In *Warren* he could have argued that state taxation of reservation businesses infringes on tribal self-government by reducing the available tribal tax base.

Black appears to vacillate only if we accept the popular view that *Williams* was an "infringement" case. If its real theory was that the Indian Reorganization Act and similar general federal laws, when applicable to a particular tribe, preempt all state jurisdiction, then the only difference between *Williams* and *Warren* was in the particular "governing Acts of Congress" they chose to examine. Far more statutes and regulations govern the activities of tribal governments than the business of licensed traders. Most of the applicable title of the Code of Federal Regulations governs tribal use of property and tribal budgets.[38] Everything regarding licensed traders falls within a subpart of a subchapter.[39]

36. Alexander M. Bickel, *The Least Dangerous Branch* 84−98 (Indianapolis: 1962).
37. See, generally, *Merrill, Lynch, Pierce, Fenner & Smith v. Ware* (414 U.S. 117, 139 [1973]) and cases cited therein; *Huron Portland Cement Co. v. Detroit* (362 U.S. 440, 443 [1960]); and *Pennsylvania v. Nelson* (350 U.S. 497, 500, 502 [1956]). Black cited *Rice v. Santa Fe Elevator Corp.* (331 U.S. 218 [1947]), which is referred to approvingly in *Merrill, Lynch*.
38. 25 C.F.R., subchapters K through Q. In addition, subchapters B, F, and G regulate tribal governing functions, and H through J regulate tribal fiscal management.
39. C.F.R., subchapter W ("Miscellaneous"), subparts 251−52.

In *Warren*, then, Black implicitly returned to *Williams* in its capacity as a preemption case. The mistake commentators have made is in reading *Warren* as a different rule requiring a showing of specific federal preemptive legislation.[40] Federal licensing of traders is no more all-inclusive, and no more material to taxation, than federal financing of tribal courts or federal power to veto proposed tribal constitutions and codes of law. If the power to forbid a trader to trade demonstrates an intention to preempt all the activities of traders, the power to tell a tribe how to govern itself demonstrates an intention to preempt all the activities of tribes.

40. Robert Ericson and D. Rebecca Snow, "The Indian Battle for Self-Determination," 58 *California Law Review* 445 (1970).

14

The Shadow of the "Infringement Test"

Black's emphasis on federal preemption made his intent in *Williams* unambiguous. The Indian Reorganization Act and correlative acts "governed" the exercise of state power, preempting state jurisdiction within tribal boundaries. Tribal power was limited only by subsequent legislative delegations to the states, such as P.L. 280, and by federal supervision. Only *Kake* had ever actually applied an infringement standard to a set of facts, and there Frankfurter applied it in the wrong context.

Nevertheless the shadow of infringement remained. Hopelessly confused between the illusion of infringement in *Williams* and Frankfurter's peculiar exaltation of infringement in *Kake*, the Court groped for some integration. The *Kake* heresy of subjecting explicit legislation to infringement scrutiny was never again followed,[1] but the Court was reluctant to admit error and overrule it expressly. Nor was the Court prepared expressly to overrule Frankfurter's identification of *Williams* as an infringement case, especially after the commentators came out in support of it. As a result, infringement returned to haunt each subsequent decision.

1. *Kake* was distinguished away as applicable only to communities "not possess[ing] the usual accoutrements of tribal self-government" in *McClanahan v. Arizona Tax Commission* (411 U.S. 164, 167−68 [1973]); *Mescalero Apache Tribe v. Jones* (411 U.S. 145, 153 [1973]) distinguished *Kake* as applicable only to landless tribes.

166

In *McClanahan v. Arizona Tax Commission*, a challenge to state taxation of Navajos' reservation income, the plaintiff complicated matters further by *conceding* that she was a resident of Arizona.[2] Strictly speaking, then, the Court was not called on to determine whether reservations are part of the territories of states, but only whether a person who admits to being a resident of a state may nevertheless enjoy certain *exceptions* to the state's plenary territorial power. By framing the issue in this manner, the plaintiff assumed the burden of proving the personal exception, whereas in both *Williams* and *Warren* the state bore the burden of demonstrating some source for its authority.

Justice Marshall, writing for the Court, failed to communicate the fact that Mrs. McClanahan's residency was determined by stipulation, asserting that, "This case requires us once again to reconcile the plenary power of the States over residents within their borders with the semi-autonomous status of Indians living on tribal reservations."[3] Put this way it sounds as if *all* Indians are state residents *by operation of law*, and that this moreover raises a presumption in favor of state jurisdiction.

Reviewing the history of state jurisdiction cases since *Worcester*,[4] Marshall concluded that "the trend has been away from the idea of inherent Indian sovereignty as a bar to state jurisdiction and toward reliance on federal preemption. . . . The modern cases thus tend to avoid reliance on Platonic notions of Indian sovereignty and look instead to the applicable treaties and statutes which define the limits of state power."[5] This is exactly what Justice Black concluded in *Williams*. The question becomes one of identifying the "governing" or "applicable" laws and construing them.

In *Williams*, Black found all he needed in the Navajo-Hopi Rehabilitation Act, a general congressional recognition of Navajo tribal self-government analogous to the Indian Reorganization Act. *McClanahan* involved the same tribe, but Marshall did not identify the rehabilitation act

2. 411 U.S. 164, 166 n.3 (1973). Compare Black's language in *Williams* to the effect that reservations are a "part" of the states (358 U.S. 218).
3. 411 U.S. 165.
4. "[I]t would vastly oversimplify the problem to say that nothing remains of the notion that reservation Indians are a separate people to whom state jurisdiction, and therefore state tax legislation, may not extend" (*id.* 169).
5. *Id.* 172. At one point Marshall characterized tribes as "*once* independent and sovereign nations," and elsewhere as "*semi*-independent" (*id.* 172–73, emphasis ours). Thurgood Marshall obviously shared John Marshall's problem with labelling tribes' political status (see *Cherokee Nation v. Georgia*, 5 Pet. 1, 17–18 [1831]).

as determinative. Was he looking for more specific authority? When he claimed that "[t]he question [of residual tribal sovereignty] is generally of little more than theoretical importance, *since in almost all cases*, federal treaties and statutes define the boundaries of federal and state jurisdiction,"[6] he could not have been thinking of specific laws. If not the rehabilitation act, what federal statute had defined the boundaries of state jurisdiction in *Williams*? There was never any *express* statutory reservation of exclusive Navajo tribal civil jurisdiction. Black read such a reservation into the general language of the rehabilitation act and other acts providing for the support and relief of the tribe. Why, then, didn't Marshall simply read a reservation of exclusive Navajo tribal taxing power into the same laws?

Marshall seemed stymied by the state's argument that *Williams* is limited in its application to cases of *infringement of tribal government activities*, not interference with individual Indians.[7] This is strange. After all, a state tax on individual Indians' income diminishes the tribe's tax base. It is, therefore, as much of an interference with tribal government as a tax on the tribe itself, or state adjudication of private reservation disputes. By the same token, the *Williams* case was no more "governmental" than Rosalind McClanahan's. The Williamses were individual Indians and they did not join the tribe as a party.

Marshall never raised these points, however. Instead he conceded that *Williams* stood for a rule of "infringement," not preemption, and summarily limited it to "situations involving non-Indians" in which both the tribe and state have an interest.[8] Apparently Marshall also felt that Black's use of the Navajo-Hopi Rehabilitation Act was limited to the facts in *Williams*, for he proceeded to search for some independent evidence of federal preemption applicable to Mrs. McClanahan.

He reached back to a pre-Indian Reorganization Act case, *Carpenter v. Shaw*, which in another context had ruled that "[d]oubtful expressions are to be resolved in favor of the weak and defenseless people who are the

6. 411 U.S. 172 n.8 (emphasis ours). See also *id.* 180, where Marshall describes *McClanahan* as a federal preemption case. But in the companion case Justice White took a different view of *McClanahan* (411 U.S. 145, 148).

7. 411 U.S. 170, 179.

8. Marshall cited only one case for this sweeping generalization: *Kake*, which at the beginning of his opinion (*id.* 167–68) he said was *inapplicable* to the Navajos. He may have been thinking of conflicts-of-laws, where "interest tests" abound. In conflicts, however, although the discovery of another state's interest in a controversy may result in the application of that state's substantive law, it does not ordinarily require a change of the forum.

wards of the nation, dependent upon its protection and good faith."[9] Marshall interpreted this to require that, in the absence of *any* federal legislation one way or the other, the tribe is presumed to remain completely self-governing. He had no choice if he were to find for Mrs. McClanahan. When he rejected the rehabilitation act argument from *Williams*, he rejected the broadest piece of federal legislation supporting Navajo tribal authority, and was forced to find preemption in the common law. Preemption by common law? Surely this was a curious twist for a Court committed to defining the boundaries of state jurisdiction out of "treaties and statutes."

Upon closer analysis, Marshall's use of *Carpenter* results in a much more expansive conception of tribal power than Black ever suggested. *Williams* implied tribal jurisdiction out of laws recognizing the legitimacy of tribal government. A tribe must be recognized to assert its power in conflict with state claims. Marshall's *McClanahan* finds tribal jurisdiction in the absence of federal laws, which is what the Margold opinion and Felix Cohen's *Handbook* had argued thirty years earlier: tribal sovereignty restricted only by express federal statutory limitations. Could this be the same Justice Marshall who wrote that the concept of tribal sovereignty is "of little more than theoretical importance"?

Marshall had responded to the state's personal-rights theory by distinguishing away *Williams*, abandoning Black's reliance on the rehabilitation act as blanket evidence of federal preemption, and "discovering" a new and broader, nonlegislative source of "preemption" in the common law. He proceeded to conclude his opinion by disposing of the state's personal-rights argument: "To be sure, when Congress has legislated on Indian matters, it has, most often, dealt with the tribes as collective entities. But those entities are, after all, composed of individual Indians, *and the legislation confers individual rights*."[10]

His reasoning had come around full circle. Why had it been necessary to avoid *Williams* and seek new sources of law in the first place if that case was not distinguishable? The aftermath of Marshall's perambulation is an opinion replete with apparently contradictory theories. Was infringement still the test of state jurisdiction in cases involving tribal government or "in

9. 280 U.S. 363, 367 (1930). 25 U.S.C. 194 must have been intended to have this effect: "In all trials about the right of property in which an Indian may be a party on one side, and a white person on the other, the burden of proof shall rest upon the white person," etc. See 34 Op. A.G. 439 (1925), construing this provision, which has since become neglected.
    10. 411 U.S. 181 (emphasis ours).

situations involving non-Indians''? Or was Marshall's sweeping interpretation of *Carpenter* to be the standard in all cases? Marshall nowhere suggested that Indians' individual rights are *greater* than the rights of their tribes; indeed, he derived both sets of rights from the same sources.

A companion case, *Mescalero Apache Tribe v. Jones*,[11] demonstrates how Marshall's resolution of *McClanahan* brought the Court no closer to consistent principles. *Mescalero* challenged New Mexico state taxation of a tribally owned, off-reservation business. Unlike *McClanahan, Warren, Williams,* and *Kake*, it divided the Court, Marshall joining in White's majority opinion, and Douglas writing for the dissent. If *McClanahan* suggested any expansion of the preemption idea, *Mescalero* put it to rest.[12]

At the outset White promised to take the same tack as Marshall had in *McClanahan*. ''Generalizations on this subject have become particularly treacherous,'' he warned, reviewing the Court's record.[13] Questions of Indian law require ''individualized treatment of particular treaties and specific federal statutes.'' Here, perhaps, was a subtle deviation. There were no ''specific'' statutes in either *McClanahan* or *Willaims*. White's rephrasing is also inherently ambiguous. Which party bears the burden of coming forward with ''specific'' statutes, the tribe or the state? If, as in the previous cases, neither party's jurisdiction is precisely defined by law, which prevails?

White never answered these questions. He was preoccupied with the tribe's argument that, *as a federal instrumentality*, it must be immune from taxation wherever it does business. This theory he dismissed as a historical relic,[14] but he had difficulty substantiating his conclusion. The cases he

---

11. 411 U.S. 145 (1973).

12. *Mescalero* has sometimes been read for a general distinction between on-reservation and off-reservation trust lands. Federal statutes do differentiate between trust status, conferred by the secretary of the interior under 25 U.S.C. 465, and reservation status, which the secretary may grant under 25 U.S.C. 467. However, the functional distinction between trust land and reservation trust land is nowhere defined legislatively, nor does *Mescalero*, which actually involved nontrust land leased from the U.S. Forest Service (411 U.S. 146, 155 n.11) serve as a standard. We suggest that trust status alone protects the land from state taxation and possibly from some forms of state land-use regulation, while reservation status places the land under exclusive tribal jurisdiction. This is by analogy to the distinction between extraterritorial land purchases and annexations by a municipality.

13. 411 U.S. 148.

14. *Id*. 150. In support of this generalization (*id*. 154–55) White quoted at length from *Shaw v. Gibson-Zahniser Oil Corp*. (276 U.S. 575, 578–81) [1928]). *Shaw* actually based its conclusion that leaseholds in off-reservation trust lands are taxable by the state on the theory that to ''hold them immune would be inconsistent with one of the very purposes of their creation, to educate Indians in responsibility.'' In other words, although tax immunity may

cited to support it had that very day been held inapplicable to tribes which "possess the usual accoutrements of tribal self-government" by Justice Marshall in *McClanahan*![15]

White also thought it relevant that individual Indians become subject to state laws when they travel off-reservation.[16] It is true, of course, that state citizens become subject to other states' laws when they travel abroad. But the controversy was over the extraterritorial status of the tribe itself, not its individual citizens. The fact that a federal agency's employees individually live under state law does not give the state power to regulate the agency itself.

Notwithstanding, we see no reason why tribes should seek greater extraterritorial sovereignty than the states, if it means advancing a theory inconsistent with tribes' enjoyment of as much domestic sovereignty as the states. The federal instrumentality idea limits tribal power to activities that serve federal objectives. It also justifies federal intervention in tribal matters when Indians' interests are putatively benefitted.

White's denigration of the instrumentality idea was not inconsistent with wider trends in tax law, and it is rare indeed when Indian cases square with general principles. As White observed, quoting from one of the Court's earlier decisions, the "mere fact that property is used, among others, by the United States as an instrument for effecting its purpose does not relieve it from state taxation."[17] Early in this century the Court began to appreciate the danger of immunizing from state jurisdiction everything even remotely connected with federal activities, for example, land purchased from the federal government, since "[t]heoretically, any tax imposed on the buyer with respect to the purchased property may have some effect on the price, and thus remotely and indirectly affect the selling government."[18] Increasingly, non-Indian tax cases have, therefore, limited intergovernmental immunities to the activities of public agencies themselves.[19]

---

stimulate Indian economic development, nonimmunity serves a *higher purpose* of teaching Indians about the civic duty to pay taxes! *Shaw* was therefore very much an instrumentality case, however unorthodox its interpretation of the nature of the federal purpose.

15. 411 U.S. 150; *McClanahan*, 411 U.S. 168.

16. 411 U.S. 149–50.

17. *Id.* 151, citing *Choctaw, Oklahoma & Gulf R. Co. v. Mackey* (256 U.S. 531, 536 [1921]).

18. 283 U.S. 279, 282 (1931). The same rule has been applied to state taxes on sales of property by the United States (*U.S. v. City of Detroit*, 355 U.S. 466, 469, 472 [1958]).

19. The original case on this principle was of course *McCulloch v. Maryland* (4 Wheat. 316 [1819]), which involved state taxation of federal bank notes. State taxation of the use of a

That is where our agreement with *Mescalero* ends, for White summarily described the legislative history of the Indian Reorganization Act as evidencing an intent to free, rather than further entangle tribes in the federal bureaucracy.[20] This may have been true, but tribes in fact continued to be regulated and supervised by the Bureau of Indian Affairs. The Tenth Circuit had just ruled that federal approval of tribal operations constitutes "major federal action" within the meaning of the National Environmental Policy Act.[21] Tribes must obtain approval for leasing and contracting, and for the expenditure of the proceeds of tribal business; the traders in *Warren* were only required to obtain a discretionary license and refrain from selling liquor on their premises. The United States has not only regulated, but subsidized tribal enterprises, such as the one at issue in *Mescalero*, with the intent that they should profit.[22]

Having devoted himself to a demonstration that tribes are not instrumentalities of the United States, White actually decided the case on the basis of the federal government's argument, *amicus curiae*, that the Mescaleros' tribal enterprise was *located on trust land*. Although the land was merely leased from the Forest Service, White agreed that the additional administrative formality of taking the lease in trust for the tribe would have been "meaningless." Is any lease of federal land to a tribe, therefore, automatically trust land, even if the secretary of the interior never processes it in accordance with the applicable statute? *Kake*, it will be recalled, attached no significance whatsoever to the fact that the tribal fishery there was conducted on sites leased from the same federal agency, the Forest Service.[23]

Trust "land" is expressly immunized from state taxation by statute.[24] The New Mexico taxes complained of were levied on income and the use of

---

federal subsidy frustrates federal policy just as much as state taxation of federal currency, although the latter has a more general or diffuse effect. The Court now takes the position that an activity, to be exempt as an instrumentality, must be "virtually . . . an arm of the Government" (*Dept. of Employment v. U.S.*, 385 U.S. 355, 359–60 [1966]). See also *U.S. v. Boyd* (378 U.S. 39 [1964]) (contractor's use of federal property subject to state tax).

20. 411 U.S. 154. Recall Frankfurter's contrary argument in *Metlakatla*.

21. *Davis v. Morton*, 469 F. 2d 593 (10th Cir. 1972), aff'g 335 F. Supp. 1258 (N.M. 1971).

22. The majority and dissent both agreed that Congress intended to foster tribal economic enterprise. The real issue was the extent to which tax immunities were implied in this general policy.

23. Interestingly, White never considered whether a state can tax *at all* within a national forest in the absence of express federal legislation (see *Collins v. Yosemite Park Co.*, 304 U.S. 518, 528–29, 530, 534–36 [1938]).

24. 25 U.S.C. 465.

personalty. Accordingly White turned to the question of whether a tax on income earned on a tract of land is a tax on the land itself. A state resident's outstate realty cannot ordinarily be taxed by his state, but his income, including income earned on or proceeds from his outstate realty, can be taxed.[25] This rule avoids extraterritorial tax sales in violation of the much-esteemed exclusive authority of each state over its own realty, without significantly impairing the power of each state to tax its own citizens' wealth wherever found.

The Court had previously sustained *federal* taxes on Indians' reservation incomes, including the proceeds of trust lands. Oil royalties and per capita shares in mineral development on trust lands, individual and tribal, are subject to federal income taxation.[26] However, capital gains taxes do not apply to liquidation of timber on trust land, on the theory that to do so would amount to a tax on the value of the land itself.[27] Since the land is federally supervised, federal taxation would put revenue policy and Indian policy in direct conflict.

White concluded from this that income earned on trust land is presumed taxable unless *specifically exempted* by statute. There are some serious difficulties with this reasoning. The existence of a power in the United States does not imply the existence of an identical power in the states. The cases simply indicate that *federal* taxation of trust proceeds and income is lawful. There is to be sure a certain paradox in permitting the United States to tax its own "wards" more than the states can. On the other hand, there is a certain rationality in federal *preemption* of Indian taxation to preserve the "guardian's" discretion over how and when Indians will be taxed, since taxes do affect behavior and economic development.[28]

25. *Alpha Portland Cement Co. v. Com.*, 268 U.S. 203 (1925); *Cohn v. Graves*, 300 U.S. 308 (1937).

26. *Choteau v. Burnet*, 283 U.S. 691 (1931); *Leahy v. State Treasurer*, 297 U.S. 420 (1936). The non-Indian lessee of trust land is also taxable by the state (*Oklahoma Tax Commission v. Texas Co.*, 336 U.S. 342 [1949]), with the result that the Indian lessor's income is indirectly taxed. These cases only superficially suggest a jurisdictional distinction based on race. The lessees were residents of the taxing state, not the reservation. By the rule of *Alpha Portland Cement* a state resident can be taxed by his own state on the proceeds of outstate land.

27. *Squire v. Capoeman*, 351 U.S. 1 (1956). See also *Holt v. Com.*, 364 F. 2d 38 (8th Cir. 1966), *cert. den'd* 386 U.S. 931 (1967) (Sioux Indian's income from cattle grazed on tribal trust land subject to federal income tax); *Sup't of 5 Civilized Tribes v. Com.*, 295 U.S. 418 (1935) (income from reinvestment of tribal trust funds taxable by U.S.). IRS Rev. Rul. 67–284 provides that proceeds of trust land are tax-exempt only if "directly" derived from the land itself.

28. In addition, since the United States pays for most reservation services, it can advance the stronger claim for indemnification through taxes.

Besides, it is debatable whether the United States itself should have been able to tax the Mescaleros' ski resort, since it was a federally financed and supervised operation. The theory barring federal capital gains taxation of Indian trust lands was that Congress could not have intended, through the general revenue laws, to tax back what it had given pursuant to specific subsidy laws. It is easily transposed to tribal economic development programs which, like the acquisition of trust land, give tribes enterprise capital. An income tax chills the use of property as much as an *ad valorem* property tax computed on the basis of developable value.

Douglas's dissent argued that the same rules of taxability should govern both reservation and off-reservation enterprises. "There is no magic in the word 'reservation.'"[29] In support, he cited a number of cases holding that the federal government has power to enforce legislation protective of Indians off-reservation, both on trust land and on state-governed fee land.[30] The majority had not suggested, however, that a distinction exists. It read the statutory provisions for tax immunity as equally applicable to reservation and off-reservation lands.[31] If anything, this is what made *Mescalero* a dangerous case. When Douglas argued for parity, he had in mind that the perfect immunity of tribal operations on tribal land should extend to tribal operations elsewhere. When the majority failed to reject parity, they left open the possibility of deducing, from tribes' less-than-perfect off-reservation tax immunity, a less-than-perfect on-reservation immunity.

Mescalero expressly disposed of the instrumentality idea as a source of tribal power and left preemption at least superficially intact. The difference between these two theories is not great, however. When Black reasoned in *Williams* that federal laws recognizing tribal government implied an intention to preempt state regulation, he was saying, in effect, that state regulation of tribes would interfere with a federal purpose. Preemption connotes statutory construction and limitation to subject matter. Instrumentality involves immunization of an organization as a whole. Which was closer to the Court's thinking in *Williams, Warren,* and *McClanahan?* In a subtle way, *Mescalero's* rejection of the instrumentality idea was sugges-

29. 411 U.S. 161.
30. *Perrin v. U.S.*, 232 U.S. 478 (1914); *U.S. v. McGowan*, 302 U.S. 535 (1938). Neither case is strictly in point for this sweeping principle. *McGowan* involved liquor sales within an executive-order reservation. In *Perrin* the tribe had stipulated in its treaty of cession that no liquor be sold within the ceded tract. Thus in both cases the particular *situs* remained under some degree of special residual, territorial federal control.
31. 411 U.S. 155.

tive of a withdrawal from Black's and Marshall's holism in the use of preemption. *Mescalero* sought more specific statutory evidence than either Black or Marshall had required. Suddenly the Court was moving away from generalities, away from *Williams*. Black's vision of tribes as whole governments, requiring only recognition to bring them into being, was fading. In its place, each tribe would be viewed more and more as a unique bundle of powers, immunities, and liabilities possessing no inherent sovereignty of its own.

15

Territorial Sovereignty
and the Shadow

Somewhere between *McClanahan* and *Mescalero* the ideal of residual tribal sovereignty expressed by the Eighth Circuit in *Iron Crow* was lost. Preemption is the common thread that makes all the decisions intelligible, but preemption supposes that all tribal powers emanate from federal grants, explicit or implicit. Consistent with the reasoning that surrounded implementation of Indian reorganization, Cohen's *Handbook*, and the Margold opinion, *Iron Crow* described tribal powers as plenary except where preempted by Congress. *Mescalero*, on the other hand, seemed to assume that state powers are plenary except where preempted by Congress and redelegated to tribes. In terms of a flow-of-power model, *Iron Crow* was exactly the reverse of the position the Court found itself in after *Mescalero*.

U.S. v. Mazurie challenged a federal statute governing sales of liquor in "Indian country."[1] The independent authority of the tribe itself was not an issue, only whether Congress had constitutionally delegated to it power to license liquor retailers. The Tenth Circuit ventured in dictum to characterize tribal self-government, however, and a unanimous Supreme Court responded in more dictum. In its awkward attempt to devise a theory of delegation, the Court briefly mentioned inherent tribal sovereignty, leading to speculation that indifference to that theory was about to come to an end.

1. 95 S. Ct. 692 (1975), *rev'g* 487 F. 2d 14 (10th Cir. 1973).

The Mazuries operated the Blue Bull bar on ten acres of fee land on Fort Washakie, within the borders of the Wind River Reservation. About one-fifth of the reservation is owned in fee, resulting in a characteristic "checkerboard" pattern of ownership.[2] Federal law prohibits the sale of liquor in "Indian country," which is defined as including "all land within the limits of any Indian reservation under the jurisdiction of the United States Government, notwithstanding the issuance of any patent," except on "fee-patented lands in non-Indian communities," or where the tribe itself has adopted licensing regulations not inconsistent with state law and approved by the secretary of the interior.[3] Wind River adopted a conforming ordinance and the Mazuries failed to obtain the necessary tribal license. Resisting criminal prosecution by the United States, the Mazuries argued that the phrase, "non-Indian communities," is unconstitutionally vague, and that Congress cannot delegate federal police powers to an Indian tribe. Reviewing the case, the Tenth Circuit complained,

There is no standard provided as to what percentage of Indians or non-Indians is contemplated. Thus if a given area can be selected as a "community," the statute does not indicate . . . what the "community" is if there are a greater or lesser comparative number of Indians.[4]

The Tenth Circuit argued that this vague exception poisons the entire rule. Without a valid statutory definition of "Indian country," they concluded, there could be no federal jurisdiction at all within the Wind River Reservation, except on federally owned trust lands.

Private land sales cannot ordinarily divest a government of jurisdiction. If a citizen of Arizona sells his estate to a citizen of New York, the territory of Arizona is not diminished, nor is the territory of New York enlarged. We have never, however, overcome the convenient pretense that sales of Indian land imply cessions of sovereignty. The *Draper* Court assumed that opening a reservation to white settlement implied a termination of tribal self-government. Of course, restricting the sphere of tribal government to tribally-owned land suggests that tribal powers are analogous to, and no greater than, the exclusionary powers of private landowners.[5]

2. 487 F. 2d 15–17; 95 S. Ct. 694—97.
3. 18 U.S.C. 1151, 1154(a) and (c), and 1161.
4. 487 F. 2d 17–18. Assignment of the burden of proof on this issue was hopelessly confused at trial (95 S. Ct. 696 n.8, 698 n.10).
5. The court buried this conclusion in an aside, as if it were embarrassed by its own bootstrapping: "if the Government has the power to regulate a business on the land it granted in

In *Seymour v. Superintendent*, Washington State tried to persuade the Court that the reference to "fee-patented lands" in the statutory definition of Indian country was intended to be limited to *Indian*-owned fee lands.[6] All concurred with Justice Black's rejection of this claim as unsubstantiated by legislative history. Black also observed that "checkerboarding" leads to difficulties in law enforcement, intimating the propriety of a presumption against construing any statute to have that effect.

The Tenth Circuit tried to distinguish *Mazurie* from *Seymour*. They argued that tribal and state officers at Wind River were cross-deputized, and that the boundaries of non-Indian-owned fee lands were well known,[7] but the distinction was immaterial. *Seymour* was not based on Black's observation that checkerboarding is bad policy but on the fact that the statute defining "Indian country" was unambiguous. Nor did the Supreme Court agree, when it reviewed *Mazurie*, that the phrase, "non-Indian community," is fatally vague. Interestingly, enough, however, it failed to explain what it was in "the nature of The Blue Bull's location and surrounding population" that made it so clearly part of an Indian community, as the district court had originally found.[8]

Writing for the Court, Justice Rehnquist took more seriously the Mazuries' contention that Congress lacks power to delegate regulatory authority to Indian tribes. The Tenth Circuit held that "[t]here is no theory of sovereignty or governmental subdivision which would support such a delegation,"[9] and proposed a broad reconceptualization of tribal self-government, consistent with its concern for land ownership:

The Tribes have the usual powers of an owner of land, to the extent of such ownership, over those using their lands. This power is often confused with some

---

fee without restrictions, *which we doubt.* . . ." (emphasis ours). It was transfixed on the idea that the Mazuries' original fee patent did not include language reserving jurisdiction to the tribe. But patents do not contain language reserving jurisdiction to states, either, and yet are subject to state law. The real question is who has jurisdiction of the place, not what the patent says.

6. 368 U.S. 351, 358 (1962).

7. 487 F. 2d 18.

8. 95 S. Ct. 698. Congress adopted a kind of demographic test of tribal jurisdiction in the Alaska Native Claims Settlement Act (43 U.S.C. 1610 [b] [2] [B]). As currently administered, the reservation system forces educated and skilled Indians to choose between unemployment and self-government on their own land, or self-imposed but more profitable exile in urban areas.

9. 487 F. 2d 18.

elements of sovereignty when large tracts are involved, and when only the relationship between a Tribe and the Government is examined.[10]

This rendered Wind River nothing more than a "voluntary association, which is obviously not a governmental agency," and is therefore incapable of accepting a delegation of police power from Congress or of exercising any authority at all over nonmembers.[11]

A landowner can exercise no power over enterers that is inconsistent with state law; no case had ever suggested such a limitation on tribal governments. However, the Court's avoidance of the term "sovereignty" since *Williams* had undoubtedly encouraged the Tenth Circuit to move boldly for a new rule. Case law provided little to support the Tenth Circuit's theory, but then case law provided Black little to work with in *Williams*.

Rehnquist counterattacked by emphasizing Congress's power to regulate the affairs of Indians wherever they may be found, on or off-reservation, regardless of the ownership status of the *situs*.[12] Specifically, the power to suppress the sale of liquor to Indians had been sustained without exception for over a century. If the United States has this power, and can regulate the Mazuries wherever they may be, it can be delegated, perhaps not to private associations, Rehnquist admitted, but "where the entity exercising the delegated authority itself possesses independent authority over the subject matter."[13] Tribes "are a good deal more than 'private, voluntary organization,' " he concluded, and "possess a certain degree of independent authority over matters that affect the internal and social relations of tribal life." Rehnquist never actually stated that tribes have power to regulate

10. *Id.* 19, citing *McClanahan* and *Mescalero*, which is difficult to understand. The court also cited *Iron Crow*, but disregarded *Barta*, in which the same circuit recognized the same tribe's power to tax non-Indians. They would only admit that "certain tribes" have attributes of sovereignty. Astoundingly, the Wind River tribe did not submit an *amicus* brief to the Supreme Court to challenge these remarkable theories.

11. *Carter v. Carter Coal Co.*, 298 U.S. 238 (1936); *Schecter Poultry Corp. v. U.S.*, 295 U.S. 495 (1935); *U.S. v. Rock Royal Coop.* 307 U.S. 353 (1939). The Tenth Circuit did not cite these cases.

12. 95 S. Ct. 698–99. There is no contrary Supreme Court authority.

13. *Id.* 699, citing *U.S. v. Curtiss-Wright Export Corp.* (299 U.S. 304, 319–22 [1936]), which is not in point. *Curtiss-Wright* questioned the power of Congress to delegate foreign trade authority *to the president*, not to a state or local government or private body. If Rehnquist was assuming that tribes are, like the president, parts of the federal government itself, he ignored the contrary ruling of *Mescalero*.

liquor *even in the absence* of a federal grant, but that implication might be drawn from his argument.[14]

As a practical matter, the Court upheld Wind River's licensing authority throughout its territory and regardless of race, but the facts were peculiar and Rehnquist studiously avoided generalization. He neither revived "inherent tribal sovereignty" nor expressly modified preemption, continuing the *McClanahan* and *Mescalero* tradition of denying the existence of general principles. In the final analysis, Rehnquist did no more than agree with Justice White's observation that "the notion that reservation Indians are a separate people" provides a convenient "backdrop" for the resolution of troublesome issues.[15]

At the same time that it decided *Mazurie*, the Court was considering a challenge to the very existence of a tribal government. *DeCouteau v. District Court* raised the question of whether Congress, in opening a reservation to non-Indian settlement, had intended a transfer of political jurisdiction to the state.[16] The real issue, unrecognized by the Court, was the effectiveness of the Indian Reorganization Act in reversing the political consequences of allotment. The result should have dispelled any illusion that *Mazurie* heralded a positive new direction.

A similar controversy had been before the Court when it was deliberating *McClanahan* and *Mescalero*. *Mattz v. Arnett* reversed the Supreme Court of California's ruling that an 1892 law opening the Klamath River Indian reservation to homesteading had implicitly terminated the tribe.[17] Following its newly established practice, the Court, by Justice Blackmun, engaged in an exhaustive review of history, law and anthropology to establish the unique facts of the case. Klamath River was originally set apart by executive order in 1855, but when Congress revised the president's authority to maintain Indian reservations in California in 1864, Klamath was not recognized. It thereafter had only a *"de facto* existence," and in 1889 a federal circuit court held that it was not "Indian country." However an 1891 executive order expanded the Hoopa Reservation to include the original boundaries of Klamath River.[18]

---

14. 95 S. Ct. 700, citing *Williams* and *McClanahan*. Many tribes have licensing powers enumerated in their constitutions. In a sample of sixty-four north Plains, northwestern and basin tribes, we found thirty-one that had such provisions.

15. 411 U.S. 169.

16. 95 S. Ct. 1082 (1975).

17. 412 U.S. 481 (1973).

18. *Id.* 487–94.

The following year Congress opened Klamath River to settlement, authorizing the secretary of the interior to reserve from entry individual Indian allotments and village lands.[19] Blackmun construed this by analogy to what he perceived to have been the policy of the General Allotment Act, but his understanding of allotment was in direct contradiction to *Draper*. "Its policy," he claimed, "was to continue the reservation system . . . [until] all the lands had been allotted and the trust expired."[20] If the opening of Klamath River was nothing more than a special allotment act, then the reservation remained in existence until the allotment process was complete, and of course further allotment had been generally suspended by the Indian Reorganization Act.

Blackmun relied on *Seymour* v. *Superintendent*.[21] In *Seymour* the state argued that a 1906 act, not unlike the 1892 act opening Klamath River, had terminated the Colville reservation. The Court there pointed out that some tribal land had been reserved, and the proceeds of the sale of the surplus land were required to be deposited to the tribe's account in the Treasury. Thus it concluded that the 1906 act merely made it possible for non-Indians "to own land on the reservation."[22] It is interesting how the Court follows *Draper* when it is expedient to its purpose, and contradicts that case when it is not.

California drew Blackmun's attention to the language of the 1892 act, which referred to the reservation in the past tense, and to numerous supportive comments in the legislative record. Recall how in *Kake*, Frankfurter relied entirely on a single comment by Senator Jackson and construed the compromise conference bill *against* the political visitors. In *Mattz*, Blackmun sensibly paid heed to the implications of political compromise.[23] Where the act was ambiguous, moreover, he was "not inclined to terminate the reservation," effectively a presumption against termination. "A congressional determination to termination must be expressed on the face of the Act or be clear from the surrounding circumstances and legislative history."[24]

Klamath River was not organized; the Sisseton tribe in *DeCouteau* was. It is therefore particularly disturbing that *DeCouteau* did imply

19. *Id.* 494–95.
20. *Id.* 496.
21. *Id.* 497. *Seymour v. Superintendent*, 386 U.S. 351 (1962).
22. 368 U.S. 355–56.
23. 412 U.S. 499–503.
24. *Id.* 504–5.

congressional intent to terminate in an 1891 agreement with the Sissetons opening the Lake Traverse reservation to homesteading. The bulk of Justice Stewart's majority opinion concentrated on the evidence offered at trial, especially contemporary non-Indian accounts suggestive that the Sissetons themselves were satisfied with, and anticipated, political dissolution as a consequence of the pact.[25] He cited *Mattz's* presumption against termination approvingly, and agreed that "[w]ith the benefit of hindsight, it may be argued that the Tribe and the Government would have been better advised to have carved out a diminished reservation," instead of ceding all unallotted territory, but concluded nevertheless that restoring the original reservation was simply too drastic a remedy for bad policy.[26] "Some might wish they had spoken differently, but we cannot remake history."[27]

Douglas's dissent did more than quibble with Stewart's evidence of tribal consent. "This tribe is a self-governing political community," he argued, "a status which is not lightly impaired."[28] The Sisseton community continued to govern itself after 1891 and up to the time of trial. In 1946 it adopted an Indian Reorganization Act constitution, and continued to be supervised and subsidized by the Bureau of Indian Affairs, which maintained an agency there. Tribal laws were enacted and enforced in tribal courts.[29] Even if Congress and the Indians had agreed to dissolve the tribe

25. For evidence of the tribe's willingness to part with its territory, the Court relied largely on statements of tribal members recorded by negotiators for the United States (95 S. Ct. 1088 n.16) and reported in the *Minneapolis Tribune* (*id.* 1088 n.12)—scarcely unbiased sources. The Court had evidence before it that the tribe was in a desperate economic state, which their "guardian," the United States, had failed to relieve. Rather than ask Congress for funds, the Interior Department, under pressure from non-Indian businessmen, persuaded the tribe to sell its reservation to finance essential services (*id.* 1086 n.8). The tribe obviously had little choice in the matter. Approximately 72 percent of the reservation was sold, the balance being allotted to individual tribal members (*id.* 1089 nn. 16, 19). In his dissent, moreover, Douglas matched the majority's legislative history with reasonably persuasive evidence cutting the other way, i.e., that Congress intended the sale to have no effect on tribal self-government (*id.* 1101–2, 1101 n.2).

26. *Id.* 1092–94. Remember that in *McClanahan* Stewart joined Douglas in chiding the majority for not construing the facts there liberally enough.

27. *Id.* 1095.

28. 95 S. Ct. 1102, citing *Williams* and *McClanahan*, neither of which however actually include comparable language.

29. Its 1946 constitution invoked jurisdiction only over "Indian-owned lands," a provision found in about one-fourth of all current tribal constitutions. In 1966 the secretary of the interior approved a new constitution conferring complete territorial jurisdiction (id. 1092, 1102–3, 1103 n.8). All but two of the other eleven tribes administered by the Bureau of Indian Affairs' Aberdeen area office already had such provisions (Fay, 1 & 2 *Charters, Constitutions and By-Laws of Indian Tribes of North America* [Greeley, Colorado: 1967– 1971]). Congress provided funds for the tribe's maintenance both by special acts (39 Stat. 988 [1917]; 42 Stat. 576 [1921]) and in annual appropriations for Indian affairs.

in 1891, the subsequent appropriation of federal funds for the support of the tribe's government implicitly worked a repeal. The majority was curiously silent regarding legislation after 1891.

The Sissetons' articles of cession promised to "cede, sell, relinquish, and convey to the United States all their claim, right, title, and interest in and to all the unallotted lands within the limits of the reservation," but no reference was made to any cession of jurisdiction of governance.[30] Reading implications into this language on the basis of fragmentary, collateral history is weak compared with the fact of uninterrupted political recognition by Congress and the executive for more than eighty years. Stewart claimed to follow the presumption against termination, the rule of *Carpenter v. Shaw*, the strict construction of applicable statutes, but it is hard to reconcile this with the result. Thurgood Marshall, who introduced the *Carpenter* rule in *McClanahan*, joined Douglas in criticizing Stewart's legislative history.

DeCouteau was decided three months after Congress, in its Indian Self-Determination and Education Assistance Act, recognized the legitimacy of Indians' "desire" for continued self-government.[31] Yet Stewart and the majority made no mention of the Indian Reorganization Act or of the existence of a Sisseton tribal government. Termination was over. Congress was increasing its subsidization of tribal activities. And the Court was construing legislative history more favorably to implied political dissolution!

After *Kake* erroneously applied it to the interpretation of statutes, the "infringement test," that misbegotten and possibly unintended by-product of *Williams*, appeared hopelessly lost in the proliferation of new rules and minute distinctions. *Williams*, if followed, was followed as a preemption case. But the shadow remained to haunt the law with uncertainty. However false or undesirable, a nice concept has a certain persistence once introduced into the law. Preserved in the record of precedent, it never ceases to tempt resurrection to help some court out of a hard case. Thus after thirteen years of oblivion, "infringement" reappeared, and the Court introduced it as if it had been the right rule all along.

Fisher v. District Court challenged a Montana state adoption action

---

30. Article I of the treaty (*id.* 1098) discussed by the majority (*id.* 1093 n.33) and by the dissent (*id.* 1102). Compare France's cession of Louisiana to the United States "forever and in full sovereignty" (quoted and discussed by Chief Justice John Marshall in *Foster & Elam v. Neilson*, 2 Pet. 253, 310 [1829]).

31. See §2 (a) (2) of the act (88 Stat. 2203 [1975], 25 U.S.C. 450).

involving a minor child, resident on the Northern Cheyenne reservation.[32] Relying on *Williams, McClanahan,* and *Mescalero,* the Court reasoned in a brief *per curiam* opinion that in the absence of a federal statute expressly conferring jurisdiction over adoption on the state, the case turned on whether state adoption jurisdiction might "infringe" on tribal self-government.[33] The Court believed it would.

For twenty years the Court had almost succeeded in involuting the "infringement" side of *Williams* out of existence; Fisher suddenly made it respectable. In *Williams,* Black considered the Navajo-Hopi Rehabilitation Act a "governing Act of Congress" which preempted all state civil jurisdiction. The Northern Cheyennes have an Indian Reorganization Act constitution authorizing them to regulate the domestic relations of their members. To be consistent with *Williams, Fisher* should have gone no further than the evidence of the tribe's constitutional and statutory authority. Instead, *Fisher* subjected the specific exercise of tribal power to a balancing test of legitimacy against state infringement.

In *McClanahan,* Marshall noted parenthetically that Arizona's enabling act, disclaiming jurisdiction over reservation territory, was *consistent with* the evidence of congressional intent to perpetuate Navajo tribal government.[34] *Fisher* similarly invoked Montana's enabling act, which includes an identical disclaimer. But the *Fisher* Court went one step further, claiming that Cheyenne sovereignty had been "unaffected" by the Montana enabling act, citing in support *McClanahan,* which said no such thing, and *Kake,* which unambiguously held the opposite.[35] This confirms the impression that the Court never fully appreciated the interaction of its various Indian decisions and took little time to reread them.

How the Cheyennes' sovereignty could have been "unaffected" by the Montana enabling act and at the same time subject to the "infringement test," is a mystery worthy of a Solomon. Presumably the Cheyennes had complete national sovereignty, subject only to federal regulation, before the State of Montana existed. According to *Fisher,* as soon as Montana existed, it had a power to regulate reservation activities up to the point that

32. *Fisher v. District Court,* 96 S. Ct. 943 (1976).
33. 96 S. Ct. at 946–47. Northern Cheyenne is not a Public Law 280 reservation.
34. 411 U.S. 175–76.
35. *Id.* 946. *Fisher* therefore implicitly overrules *Draper.* But *Fisher* relies on *Kake,* which itself purported to rely on *Draper.* The conclusion is the converse of one of the premises.

it "infringed" on Cheyenne government. Either everything Montana does on the reservation is an "infringement," in which case the "infringement test" has no applications and is meaningless, or the creation of Montana resulted in a limitation of tribal territoriality.

Any discussion of infringement was gratuitous, however, for the Court also analyzed *Fisher* completely as a *preemption* case. Montana argued that it had routinely exercised civil jurisdiction over the Cheyenne reservation (in accordance with *Draper*) before the tribal government was organized in 1935, and should be presumed to continue in the exercise of that jurisdiction until divested by federal law. The Court responded that the Indian Reorganization Act had "overridden" and "preempted" state jurisdiction completely.[36] Now, how can preemption, thus construed, apply to the same facts as infringement? How can the same issue be "governed" by acts of Congress, and "absent governing acts of Congress?" In its haste to boilerplate, the Court gave equal standing to two completely hostile rules.

Having resurrected one rule, *Fisher* laid another to rest, repudiating Thurgood Marshall's hint in *McClanahan* that immunities from state regulation are *personal* rights of individual Indians. Montana challenged the Northern Cheyenne tribal court as a racist institution in violation of the Fourteenth Amendment. Without hesitation, the Court replied that "[t]he exclusive jurisdiction of the tribal court does not derive from the race of the plaintiff but rather from the quasi-sovereign status of the Northern Cheyenne Tribe under federal law."[37] *Mazurie*, and before that, *Iron Crow*, had spoken this way. But if tribal jurisdiction flows from the tribe's "quasi" sovereignty, why was it necessary to consider either infringement or preemption? Was *Fisher* merely taking the same tack as *Mazurie*, i.e., that tribes' political character legitimizes delegations, if any, of federal power, but may not suffice as an independent source of power?[38]

In Chapter 11 we suggested that the involution of a legal doctrine occurs where judges confuse the grounds for its application. The appearance of *Fisher* was a symptom of involution. After *Williams* the Court embarked upon a program of inventing new rules and reinterpreting old ones to

---

36. Montana had originally acquired this jurisdiction through *Draper*, which was approvingly cited by the Court in *Williams, Kake* and *McClanahan*.

37. 96 S. Ct. 948.

38. The Court may not have been entirely confident in its conclusion that tribal jurisdiction is political, not racial. In the next paragraph it cited *Morton v. Mancari* (417 U.S. 535, 551–55 [1974]), as authority that reverse discrimination in Indians' favor is constitutional.

dispose of cases to which *Williams* could have been applied. Legislation was alternatively construed strictly and loosely, sought out, and avoided, even subordinated to judicial standards. The Court acquired the power to reach any result it wanted, since it had any number of different, inconsistent rules of varying scope to choose from, all of which could be traced to precedent. *Fisher* rendered the uncertainty perfect by applying inconsistent rules in the same case and offering no explanation for their relationship to one another.

16

Economic Self-Determination and the Return of the Idea of Personal Rights

In *Moe v. Confederated Salish and Kootenai Tribes*, the Court revived the personal-rights idea last seen in *McClanahan* and, curiously, the instrumentality idea rebuffed in *Mescalero*.[1] Thus, within two months of *Fisher*, the Court backed off from infringement once again, neglected preemption, and returned the future of tribal status to uncertainty.

Like most of the cases that followed *Williams, Moe* involved resistance to state taxation. The tribe sought immunity from state cigarette excise taxes for its members' retail establishments. When the economic effect of a transaction is an operative fact in the application of a federal law, state classification of the transaction is not dispositive. "State law may control only when the federal . . . act, by express language or necessary implication, makes its own operation dependent upon state law."[2] If the "infringement test" is to have any meaning at all, it must be applied objectively.

---

1. 96 S. Ct. 1634 (1976).
2. *Burnet v. Harmel*, 287 U.S. 103, 110 (1932). See also *Com. v. Hausen*, 360 U.S. 446 (1959); *Com. v. Court Holding*, 324 U.S. 331 (1945); *Gregory v. Helvering*, 293 U.S. 465 (1935); *Cubic Corp. v. U.S.*, 74–72 U.S.T.C. 9967 (S.D. Calif. 1974). Similarly, the "economic interest" test for distinguishing between leases and sales for federal tax purposes, *Palmer v. Bender*, 287 U.S. 551 (1933); *Wood et al. v. U.S.*, 377 F.2d. 300 (5th Cir. 1967); *Vest v. C.I.R.*, 481 F.2d 238 (5th Cir. 1973). See also *Resorts Int'l v. C.I.R.*, 511 F.2d 107 (5th Cir. 1975) (sale v. license, "proprietary right" rule). *Cf. Central Oil & Supply Corp. v. U.S.*, 75–71 U.S.T.C. 16184 (W.D. La. 1975) (sale v. consignment, referred to state law).

Who actually bears Montana's cigarette excise tax is a matter of economics. In *Moe* a Montana court relied uncritically on Montana state law, however, according to which the tax, although levied on the seller, is "conclusively presumed to be direct taxes upon the retail consumer precollected for the purpose of convenience and facility only."[3] The danger in this approach is that a state might avoid the effect of federal laws simply by writing fictions into its tax code. What a state calls its tax has nothing to do with whether it interferes with federal policy. Thus *Warren* concluded that Arizona's gross income tax, while levied on the seller and defined as a tax on the seller, might actually affect Indian consumers, and therefore frustrated federal Indian policy.

The Montana court recognized the significance of *Warren*, but tried to distinguish it on the basis that the legal taxpayer there was a federally licensed trader, and the retailers in *Moe* were not.[4] If anything, however, this distinction cuts the other way. The original purpose of the federal licensing scheme was to protect Indians from unscrupulous non-Indian traders by limiting entry.[5] Understandably, Indian entrepreneurs have not been required to obtain licenses, although they may own and manage their real property subject to federal supervision. Non-Indians' licenses cannot therefore mean that they were intended to be more protected from state regulation than unlicensed Indian retailers. *Moe* painstakingly avoided the fact that the sellers were Indian businesspeople. Congress has repeatedly declaimed its interest in reservation business development, to that end providing special loans and loan guarantees for Indian entrepreneurs.[6]

Consistent with its "economic" findings, the Supreme Court had no difficulty setting aside the tax as applied to sales to Indian consumers. It

3. 392 F. Supp. 1297, 1308 (1976), quoting from R.C.M. 84−5606 (1). The court referred to this statute as the "factual background" of the case.

4. *Id.* 1311. The nonapplicability of state cigarette sales taxes to Indian consumers was never seriously disputed. Montana assumed criminal and limited civil jurisdiction under P.L. 280, but the district court concluded that taxation is neither criminal in nature nor implied in Montana's P.L. 280 jurisdiction over schools, public welfare, domestic relations, mental health, or traffic (*id.* 1305, 1317). In other words, the power to tax is not implied in the power to serve. Compare *Tonasket v. State* (84 Wash.2d 164, 525 P.2d 744 [1974]), which relied on, of all things, *Kake* and *Draper* to reach the opposite rule. See also *Mahoney v. Idaho Tax Commission*, 96 Idaho 59, 524 P.2d 187 (1974), *cert. den'd* 419 U.S. 1089 (1974).

5. See *Rockbridge v. Lincoln*, 499 F.2d 567 (C.A. Ariz. 1971). The currently applicable statutes are 25 U.S.C. 261−62.

6. See especially the Indian Financing Act, P.L. 93−262, 88 Stat. 77 (1974), 25 U.S.C. 1451−1543; §10 of the Indian Reorganization Act, 48 Stat. 986 (1934), as amended 25 U.S.C. 470.

concluded that a tax on Indian consumers, like the tax on Indians' income in *McClanahan*, interferes with the personal rights of Indians. This was its first error. *McClanahan's* rationale was that exclusive tribal jurisdiction is presumed in the absence of federal delegations to the state. Its mention of personal rights was directed at Arizona's argument that no *tribal* right had been infringed by the income tax. There should have been no question in *Moe* regarding the tribal nature of the right; the tribe itself was the plaintiff.

Under a theory of preemption, *Moe* should have gone no further than the fact that the Flatheads enjoy an Indian Reorganization Act constitution in which they are expressly authorized to tax both Indians and non-Indians. No previous preemption case had ever distinguished between Indians and non-Indians. Subject matters, not classes of persons, are preempted. On the other hand, *Williams* and *McClanahan* actually involved only Indian taxpayers and might be distinguished, however inappropriately, on that basis. Based on its reading of Montana law, the court reasoned that

[i]n a sale to a non-Indian without payment of the tax, it is the non-Indian consumer or user who saves the tax and reaps the benefit of the tax exemption. It is of course recognized that the seller would have a competitive advantage over non-Indian sellers on the Reservation as well as both Indian and non-Indian sellers off the Reservation through selling at a lower price.[7]

This assumes that sellers pass on all tax savings to consumers. In a freely competitive market the extent to which sellers pass on tax savings to consumers depends on the effect they expect this will have on volume of sales. Consumers are more or less sensitive to changes in the prices of different products. Economists describe the demand for products as being more or less "elastic" with price. Evidence contemporary with *Moe* indicates that Indian cigarette vendors were passing on only from 55 percent to 80 percent of saved state taxes, a condition of relatively but not perfectly inelastic demand.[8]

Voluntary coordination and tribal regulation of reservation "smoke-shops" probably limited competition and increased Indian sellers' ability to retain tax savings without sacrificing sales. If tax-exempt Indian retailers are a perfect cartel, they can maximize their profits by offering goods at a

7. 392 F. Supp. 1308.
8. Mary Ellen McCaffree, "Who Must Pay to Puff?" Address to the Western States Association of Tax Administrators, 23 September 1975 (Offprint by State of Washington, Department of Revenue).

price *just below* the off-reservation retail price of the same goods after adjusting for the extra cost to consumers of going out of their way to patronize reservation establishments. The amount of saved tax passed on to consumers will be just a little more than what is necessary to compensate them for the added inconvenience of extra travel. The closer the reservations to population centers, the more tax savings Indian vendors will tend to retain.

As long as the court pretended that consumers bear all of the tax, it could persuade itself that state taxation, concurrent with tribal taxing authority, would have no effect on tribal self-government.

It is clear that the collection of the tax by the Indian seller would impose no tax burden on the Indians residing on the reservation; nor would it infringe in any way upon tribal self-government. It may reasonably be inferred that *the stores were not established primarily for the benefit of Indian customers* residing on the reservation, but rather to sell cigarettes to prospective customers passing on the highway. . . . *The Indian seller profits from increased sales*. The non-Indian purchasers avoid the payment of a tax legally imposed upon them.[9]

For whose benefit were these stores established? Presumably for the benefit of the owners! Since the owners are Indians, and the court admits, however obtusely, that the state tax depresses sales, reservation Indians do benefit from non-Indians' avoidance of the tax. Congress has been a great deal more explicit in recent years about promoting Indian business than about cutting prices to Indian consumers; that is a matter of legislative history. Moreover, if the tribe raises a tax on sales or income, the state tax will depress its yield, forcing the tribe to tax both Indians and non-Indians at higher rates. A state tax will not only affect the operation of tribal government, but *indirectly impose a higher tax burden on reservation Indians*.

The court avoided economic reality in its original findings, but in a supplemental opinion it approvingly reported Montana's claim that it deserved the tax to support services to Indians. Emphasizing its legal obligation to serve both Indians and non-Indians equally, and the fact that 27 percent of the children in its Flathead reservation schools are Indians, the state argued that the federal government contributes only about 10 percent to the support of these schools.[10] In fact, the state advised the court of only one of the three major sources of special federal "formula"

9. 392 F. Supp. 1311 (emphasis ours); repeated in substance, *id.* 1317.
10. *Id.* 1314 n.9, 1314–15.

financing it was receiving for its Indian school populations.[11] Two studies available at the time described these programs as "redundant" and concluded they were overcompensating the states.[12] In its reporting of the state contribution to these schools, Montana also failed to distinguish taxes collected on Indian-owned fee lands from non-Indian lessees of reservation trust land, and from reservation Indians in off-reservation transactions.[13] In fact, Congress had granted Montana school lands within Indian reservations almost fifty years earlier, and the state's revenue from this source was not identified.[14] It is entirely possible that the state was *gaining* money through its reservation school districts.

"Benefit-burden" arguments cut both ways. The Court recognized that the tribe and the United States expend "substantial" sums on reservation programs, and that at least some of this benefits the non-Indians who comprise about 81 percent of Flathead's resident population.[15] Although many tribal services, such as income maintenance, are limited to tribal members, others such as police and fire protection, some roads, and utilities are equally enjoyed by all residents. Since the state taxes non-Indian reservation residents the same as other non-Indians, they are overtaxed, and the state is overcompensated, to the extent of these tribal services. Unable or unwilling to untangle the net flow of wealth and services involved, the court drew no conclusion.[16] At the very least,

---

11. 20 U.S.C. 236 *et seq.* and 631 *et seq.*, commonly referred to as "Public Law 874," or "Impact," provides state districts with 100 percent of the federally estimated "per pupil cost" of children whose parents live and work on a federal reservation. The Johnson-O'Malley Act (25 U.S.C. 452) authorizes subcontracting with states for Indian education. The Elementary and Secondary Education Act (20 U.S.C. 241a and 20 U.S.C. 241aa−241 ff.) provides for the special needs of the "educationally deprived." Montana attributed $356,735 to "impact" aid for Flathead (392 F. Supp. 1314) but also received $1.1 million statewide from Johnson-O'Malley ("Hearings, 'Department of the Interior and Related Agencies Appropriations Fiscal Year 1976,' " 892−93, Senate Committee on Appropriations, 94th Congress, 1st Session [1975]). This works out to $186 per Indian pupil, or about $105,000 for Flathead.
12. NAACP Legal Defense & Education Fund, *An Even Chance: A Report on Federal Funds for Indian Children in Public School Districts* (1971); Sar A. Levitan and William B. Johnston, *Indian Giving: Federal Programs for Native Americans* 41 (Baltimore: 1975).
13. The lower court seemed aware of this (392 F. Supp. 1314 n.9).
14. E.g., Act of 4 June 1920, 41 Stat. 756, §16 (Crow).
15. 392 F. Supp. 1313 n.2. This is unusually high. Fort Peck is comparable with 65 percent but the other five Montana reservations have probably less than 10 percent non-Indian residents (Economic Development Administration, *Federal and State Indian Reservations* [Washington, D.C.: 1971]).
16. 392 F. Supp. 1314: "We are unable to determine with exactitude the net effect of the loss of tax revenues to the state."

perhaps, it should have required the state to bear the burden of proving some substantial net loss.[17]

On review, the Supreme Court affirmed. Writing for the Court, Justice Rehnquist did little to crystallize the issues. At the outset, he confused the grounds for federal jurisdiction to enjoin state collection of the tax with the basis for the claimed tax immunity.[18] Federal law prohibits enjoining the collection of a state tax "where a plain, speedy and efficient remedy may be had in the courts of such State."[19] The lower court disposed of this by reference to cases holding that the prohibition does not apply to cases brought *by the United States* "to protect itself and its instrumentalities from unconstitutional state exactions."[20] Relying on two early cases describing reservation activities as federal instrumentalities,[21] Rehnquist agreed that the United States has always had authority to protect its Indian programs in its own courts. On the basis of a single ambiguous sentence in a House report, he reasoned further that Congress had intended to extend this same authority to tribes when it accorded them standing to bring civil suits in federal district courts.[22]

Montana argued that *Mescalero* had ended characterization of tribes as federal instrumentalities.[23] In a judicious footnote, Rehnquist conceded his reliance on "the federal instrumentality doctrine," which *Mescalero* had "effectively eliminated . . . as a basis for immunizing Indians from state taxation," and admitted to "a certain inconsistency."[24] The only possible reconciliation was to distinguish between jurisdiction and substantive law: for jurisdictional purposes, tribes are federal instrumentalities, but once jurisdiction has been established, they are not and must specifically allege and prove each individual claimed tax immunity![25]

17. An interesting and vigorous dissent argued that the reservation no longer existed (*cf. DeCouteau*), that the tax immunity for Indians violates the Fourteenth Amendment (*cf. Fisher*), and that Indians, as state citizens, ought to be required to pay state taxes (*id.* 1319–24).

18. 96 S. Ct. 1639–42.

19. This issue was not raised in *McClanahan*, 411 U.S. 164 (1973).

20. 392 F. Supp. 1303, quoting from *Dept. of Employment v. U.S.*, 385 U.S. 355, 558 (1966).

21. *Heckman v. U.S.*, 224 U.S. 413 (1912); *U.S. v. Rickert*, 188 U.S. 432 (1903).

22. 96 S. Ct. 1641–42. The report merely said that §1362 would provide "the means whereby the tribes are assured of the same judicial determination whether the action is brought in their behalf by the Government or by their own attornies."

23. *Id.* 1640.

24. *Id.* 1641 n.13.

25. *Id.* 1640–41, especially n.13.

Recognizing that *McClanahan* can be read for a presumption against the existence of a state power to tax, Montana proposed that *McClanahan* be distinguished away as applicable only to tribes as autonomous, historically, as the Navajo. Rehnquist agreed with the lower court that Flathead is not "now so completely integrated with the non-Indians . . . that there is no longer any reason to accord them different treatment from other citizens,"[26] but in this way he implicitly conceded the appropriateness of a demographic or cultural test of tribal sovereignty. Nor did he indicate what evidence, if any, he would accept to prove that some tribe other than Flathead *is* substantially assimilated and therefore not entitled to a presumption in its favor.[27]

Rehnquist refused to reconsider the lower court's "economics," agreeing that Montana law is determinative.[28] He was evidently sensitive, however, to the contradiction between finding that the tax saving is enjoyed entirely by the consumer and conceding that it increases the volume of sales enjoyed by Indian retailers. Instead of reversing the holding that the tax does not affect Indians, Rehnquist tried to argue away the effect of the tax on retailers' profits—making the economic analysis even more absurd rather than correcting it.

Since nonpayment of the tax is a misdemeanor as to the retail purchaser, the competitive advantage which the Indian seller doing business on tribal land enjoys . . . is dependent on the extent to which the non-Indian purchaser is willing to flout *his* legal obligation to pay the tax. Without the simple expedient of having the retailer collect the sales tax from non-Indian purchasers, it is clear that wholesale violations of the law by the latter class will go virtually unchecked.[29]

In other words, since Indian retailers' competitive advantage arises solely from non-Indians' violation of state law, it is therefore not a *legitimate*

26. 96 S. Ct. 1642—43.

27. Consistent with *Mazurie*, however, Rehnquist rejected the state's contention that allotment of the reservation had the effect of checkerboarding tribal jurisdiction (*id.* 1643—44, citing *Mattz v. Arnett*, 412 U.S. 481, 491 [1973], *Mazurie*, 95 S. Ct. 692, 554—55 [1975] and *Seymour v. Superintendent*, 368 U.S. 351, 358 [1962] ["impractical pattern of checkerboard jurisdiction" contrary to federal purpose in creating reservations]).

28. 96 S. Ct. 1645, where he says the fact that the burden falls on the consumer "necessarily follows" from the *wording* of the statute. Four years earlier the Court had held that a Connecticut sales tax was borne entirely by purchasers, relying entirely on the fact that Connecticut law required stores to ring the tax up separately (*Sullivan v. U.S.*, 395 U.S. 169, 171 [1969]). Cigarette taxes are included in the shelf price of the goods. Is the *Sullivan* rule reconcileable with *Moe*?

29. 96 S. Ct. 1645 (emphasis is the Court's).

Indian interest for infringement purposes. Of course, the whole issue in the case was *whether* reservation purchases of unstamped cigarettes are in violation of Montana law. Rehnquist's argument is perfectly circular.

It may have been possible to disregard the indirect effects of the tax on Indian retailers' income, but there was no way to avoid the administrative inconvenience of precollection. The lower court did not even attempt to argue away the effect of precollection on Indian retailers, but invented the novel theory that they are "involved with non-Indians to [such] a degree" they cannot justly complain.[30] This implies that by engaging in commerce with non-Indians, Indians lose their political rights; tribes must remain poor if they wish to be self-governing. Only transactions in which all parties, immediate and remote, are Indians, are safe from classification as "involving" non-Indians.

State enforcement of its tax entails the possibility of suing Indian retailers for an accounting of taxes received. *Williams* rejected the power of a state court to assume civil jurisdiction over an unwilling reservation Indian, and *Fisher* agreed. Rehnquist's matter-of-fact remark that there is "nothing in this burden [of precollection] which frustrates tribal self-government"[31] is therefore strange. What was it in *Williams* and *Fisher* that did frustrate tribal self-government? Besides, *Williams* was really a preemption case. The state there lacked jurisdiction altogether, not simply because its exercise of jurisdiction would burden Navajo government. Like the Navajo, the Flatheads are an organized tribe with courts of their own.[32]

As a whole, *Moe* intimates that *Williams* should be read for the right of reservation *Indians* to be governed by *their* own laws, the corollary being that there is no right of reservation *non*-Indians to be governed by Indian laws. None of the earlier decisions is necessarily inconsistent with this reading. All involved burdens on Indians, even *Warren*, where the Court identified Indian consumers as the ultimate taxpayers. *Moe* does not rule

30. 392 F. Supp. 1311, 1317. We wonder how the court would propose to measure "involvement."

31. 96 S. Ct. 1646. On exclusive tribal jurisdiction, *State ex rel. Merrill v. Turtle*, 413 F. 2d 683 (9th Cir. 1969); *Kennerly v. District Court*, 400 U.S. 423 (1971); *Crow Tribe v. Deernose*, 487 P. 2d 1133 (Mt. 1971); *Blackwolf v. District Court*, 493 P. 2d 1293 (Mt. 1972).

32. The Supreme Court did not rule on the lower court's theory that any other remedy would intolerably inconvenience state tax collection (392 F. Supp. 1311, 96 S. Ct. 1638 n.6). Convenience has never been a test of political power between sovereigns. New York cannot enforce its nonresident income tax within New Jersey just because it would be more convenient than enforcing it within New York. Most political rights, whether individual or collective, are costly in administrative inefficiency (M. W. Reder, "Citizens' Rights and the Cost of Law Enforcement," 3 *Journal of Legal Studies* 435 [1974]).

that tribes lack power to regulate reservation non-Indians, a power already well established in the tax area, and not otherwise precluded.[33] It embraces a notion of *concurrent* tribal-state jurisdiction over non-Indians where their activities do not directly affect Indians, and appears to reject that elusive thread of preemption in *Williams, Warren* and *McClanahan*, that federal recognition of tribal government by itself ousts the state of all reservation power. *Fisher* used preemption and infringement interchangeably. It was the transition, *Moe* the product.

Moe left the Court even more room to equivocate in future cases. In particular cases the test was to be whether the beneficiary of the transaction is an Indian, but the concept of "benefit," as applied in *Moe*, lacks economic sense or objectivity. Bilateral transactions necessarily affect both parties to a greater or lesser degree. What the Court means by "benefit," as something different from "effect," is mysterious. Is it looking for positive effects, or for substantial effects? And how will it assure reliability in making these judgments of degree, rather than of kind?

Only a year earlier, in *Mazurie*, Rehnquist had rejected the Tenth Circuit's theory that tribes are mere voluntary associations, analogous to private landowners. A private association of tenants in common has more power over its own members than over nonmembers, although it may have limited power to control nonmembers' activities while they remain on its land and to the extent that their activities may be injurious. This is about what tribes have, in principle, after *Moe*, if Rehnquist's new theories are carried to their logical conclusion.

Moe is also, paradoxically, exactly what Rehnquist promised it would not be: an instrumentality case. It makes the race of the taxpayer dispositive, rather than the *situs* of the transaction, resuscitating the personal-rights idea in *McClanahan* that *Fisher* seemed to have repudiated. If the theory of the exemption is to *protect Indians* and not to respect tribal territoriality, it makes Indians federal instrumentalities. We have returned to *Surplus Trading Co. v. Cook* and the analogy to military enclaves, for the law then had been that individual military personnel on federal lands are federal instrumentalities, even when engaged in private transactions.[34]

33. *Oglalla Sioux Tribe v. Barta, op. cit.*; *Buster v. Wright*, 135 F. 947 (8th Cir. 1905), *app. dism'd* 203 U.S. 599 (1906); *Maxey v. Wright*, 105 F. 1003 (8th Cir. 1900). On tribal power over non-Indians, see, for example, *Quechan Tribe v. Rowe*, 531 F. 2d 408, 411 n.4 (C.A. Cal. 1976).

34. *Standard Oil Co. v. Johnson*, 316 U.S. 481 (1942), adopted this view between the time of these hearings and the eventual passage of the Buck Act in 1947. *Cf. Collins v. Yosemite*

However destructive of tribes' power to tax or exempt from taxation, *Moe* was at least doctrinally pure. "Infringement" was economically misapplied, but it was infringement nonetheless. The Court had come around, as *Fisher* indicated it might, to what the commentators said it had meant eighteen years earlier in *Williams*. For the first time, it had applied the same rule in two consecutive cases; but that was not to last for long. Scarcely a month passed before *Bryan v. Itasca County* announced that the *real* rule all along had been preemption.[35]

Writing for a unanimous Court, Justice Brennan explained that *McClanahan* had "clarified" the law of state taxation, and *Moe* had followed it.[36] Read together, he argued, those two cases "preclude any authority in respondent County to levy a personal property tax" on the Indian petitioner "in the absence of congressional consent."[37] The only real similarity between them was in their result: invalidation of direct state taxes on Indians. In *McClanahan* it was because there was no evidence of a congressional grant, but in *Moe* because the taxpayer was Indian. In effect, Brennan amalgamated the rules: no state taxing power over Indians without congressional consent. He justified this racial distinction, as *Moe* had justified its racial distinction, by recourse to instrumentality thinking. Since Congress's plenary power extends only to the protection of Indians, federal preemption only affects state laws insofar as they apply to Indians.[38] But the Constitution speaks of "tribes," not "Indians," and any exercise of state taxing power within the taxable territory of a tribe detracts from that tribe's tax base, although it may have no direct effect on any individual Indians.

Brennan's rephrasing of the law was peripheral to *Bryan* itself, since the state claimed to enjoy delegated taxing authority under Public Law 280. Although the law itself does not expressly authorize state taxation, it expressly forbids state taxation of trust property. The Minnesota supreme court concluded that the prohibition was meaningless unless Congress had intended the states to have an otherwise unlimited power of taxation.[39]

Park Co., 304 U.S. 518, 528–29, 530, 534–36 (1938), and *Surplus Trading Co. v. Cook*, 281 U.S. 647 (1930). In Collins, the state reserved its power of taxation when it ceded the parkland to the United States.

35. 96 S. Ct. 2102 (1976).
36. *Id.* 2105.
37. *Id.* 2106.
38. *Id.* 2105 n.2.
39. *Id.* 2106.

Legislative history, however, indicated that taxation was not intended to be included in the law's grant of "civil jurisdiction," only a power to try civil causes.[40] Brennan simply followed the narrower version of the rule of "liberal construction" as it was understood in *Mattz* and *DeCouteau*,[41] without any consideration of "infringement" or tribal sovereignty.

Bryan is replete with interesting historical contradictions. Frankfurter read Public Law 280 to be a termination measure; Brennan made no reference to *Kake* and concluded that it was not.[42] *Moe* disregarded the effect of state taxes on tribal tax base; Brennan seems to have discovered that problem, at least in a cautious footnote.[43] Moreover, although every case since *Williams*, including *Bryan*, had narrowed tribal powers down to the point where they remained exclusive only over Indians, Brennan recognized that "[p]resent federal policy appears to be returning to a focus upon strengthening tribal self-government,"[44] an inadvertent admission that the Court had been following the wrong star.

The most interesting thing about *Bryan* is its flirtation with Frankfurter's conceit that in Indian affairs, judicial interpretations take precedence over statutes.

> The absence of more precise language respecting state taxation of reservation Indians is entirely consistent with a general uncertainty in 1953 of the precise limits of state power to tax reservation Indians respecting other than their trust property, and a congressional intent merely to reaffirm the existing law whatever subsequent litigation might determine it to be.[45]

This was "justified," Brennan continued, because in 1953 there was only one extant precedent, *Rickert*, decided in 1903. According to this reasoning the Court is the ultimate source of authority in Indian affairs, and it is necessary for Congress itself to wait until the Court has spoken before legislating. What prevented Congress from allocating taxing power any way it pleased in 1953? Certainly not the fact that the Supreme Court had not yet decided many tax cases! Besides, Brennan's theory is circular. If the role of the Court is merely to "liberally construe" congressional intent,

---

40. *Id.* 2107–10. The Court relied heavily on Carole E. Goldberg, "Public Law 280: The Limits of State Jurisdiction over Reservation Indians," 22 *U.C.L.A. Law Review* 535 (1975).
41. 96 S. Ct. 2113.
42. *Id.* 2111.
43. *Id.* 2111 n.14.
44. *Id.*
45. *Id.* 2112–13, 2113 n.16.

but Congress depends on the Court to tell it what the law is, who bears ultimate responsibility?

The marvelous irony of *Moe* and *Bryan* is that Congress *had* spoken more directly to the issue in a piece of legislation neither opinion cited. The Buck Act authorizes state motor fuels taxes, sales taxes, use taxes, and income taxes in "Federal Areas," exempting only "federal instrumentalities" and "Indian[s] not otherwise taxed."[46] The question should therefore have been whether either of the exemptions applied to the taxpayers.[47] The original bill referred only to "national parks, military and other reservations," without further clarification, but was vigorously supported by Arizona, New Mexico and Washington in the expectation, never dispelled by any member of Congress, that Indian reservations were "other reservations."[48] Senator LaFollette of Wisconsin proposed a specific amendment to render the Buck Act inapplicable to "any transaction" occurring on an Indian reservation, but despite support from the Interior Department, it failed.[49] Since the major source of friction was evidently taxation of non-Indians, no one opposed the "Indian[s] not otherwise taxed" clause as a substitute.[50]

It appears, then, that the Court could have reached the same result as *Moe* and *Bryan* thirty years earlier by reading the Buck Act. The Court did acknowledge the act briefly in *Warren* and again in *McClanahan*, but accorded it no significance.[51] Marshall observed in *McClanahan* that "[w]hile the Buck Act itself cannot be read as an affirmative grant of tax-exempt status to reservation Indians, it should be obvious that Congress would not have jealously protected the immunity of reservation Indians

46. Act of 30 June 1947, 61 Stat. 644, 4 U.S.C. 104−10 as amended.

47. There is also a question whether Indian reservations are "Federal Areas" in the first place. They are set apart for tribal use, not federal use (§§5 and 7 of the Indian Reorganization Act, 25 U.S.C. 465, 467; *U.S. v. Kagama*, 118 U.S. 375, 383 [1886] ["'set apart for the residence of the tribe'"]). Although lands may now be acquired in trust for tribes (25 U.S.C. 465, 465a, 488, 489, 501, 574, 608a, 621−22, 624[d], 640d−9) most reservations consist of original tribal territory. See the distinction between original reservations and those "bought and paid for" by Indians (25 U.S.C. 397, *Strawberry Valley Cattle Co. v. Chipman*, 13 Utah 454, 45 P. 348 [1896]). The definition of "Federal Area," however, is lands "held or acquired by or for the use of the United States" (4 U.S.C. 110[e]).

48. "Hearings, 'Application of State Sales and Use Taxes to Transactions in Federal Areas,' " 1, 2, 11−12, 18−19, Senate Committee on Finance, 76th Congress, 3rd Session (1940).

49. *Id*. 2, 18−19, 37; 84 *Cong. Rec*. 10907 (3 August 1939).

50. *Id*. 18. The Governor of New Mexico told Senator Buck that the LaFollette amendment, by comparison, "practically nullifies the purpose of your bill insofar as New Mexico is concerned" (*id*. 2, 6). See also *id*. 12, 18−19, 22, 38−39; 84 *Cong. Rec*. 10685 (2 August 1939).

51. 380 U.S. 690 n. 18; 411 U.S. 176−77.

from state income taxation had it thought that the States had residual power to impose such taxes.'' However, he said this to boilerplate his principal argument that the immunity is presumed in the *absence* of legislation. He placed the gap-filling cart before the legislative horse.

By ignoring the full significance of the Buck Act, the Court once again established itself as superior to Congress. The act is a concession of certain reservation tax revenues to states. Under judicial guidance, tribes avoided that result, and avoided the inevitable necessity of demanding legislative rectification for almost thirty years, until *Moe*. In getting around to the Buck Act result, however, the Court has unfortunately created a theory of the tribe-state boundary palpably more dangerous to tribal self-government. *Moe* and *Bryan* intimate that tribal power as a whole is a function of individual Indians' personal rights. Unless they are restricted to tax matters, they will give the states far greater reservation authority than Congress intended in the Buck Act.

Title 25 of the United States Code is a maze of innuendoes and negative implications respecting reservation taxation, many never discovered by the Court. The rules for granting rights-of-way for pipelines and telephones across trust lands provide that ''nothing herein contained shall be so construed as to exempt the owners of such lines from the payment of any tax that may be lawfully assessed against them by either State, Territorial, or municipal authority,'' and then refer mysteriously to lines that are ''not subject to State or Territorial taxation.''[52] Which lines did Congress assume were exempt, and why? No comparable tax-saving clauses appear in right-of-way legislation for railroads enacted at about the same time.[53] As in its classic ambiguity over tribal powers recognized by ''existing law'' in the Indian Reorganization Act, Congress deferred the important questions to the Court. The Court responded, characteristically, by striking off on its own, irrespective even of the few specific directions in the legislative record.

Congress was unambiguous in authorizing state taxation of oil, gas and minerals severed from tribal lands, and in empowering states to tax the property of lessees of tribal lands within executive order reservations.[54] When it provided for the sale or lease of timber and other reservation

52. 25 U.S.C. 319, 321.
53. 25 U.S.C. 312, 320.
54. 25 U.S.C. 398, 298c. After the Act of 3 March 1871 (as amended 25 U.S.C. 71) forbade the further making of treaties with tribes, reservations could only be established by act of Congress or by executive order.

resources, however, Congress was silent on the issue of state taxes.[55] By implication, the states can *only* tax developers of tribal oil, gas, minerals, and developers of executive order lands. Yet in recent years the Court has sustained a broader range of state taxes without reference to these applicable statutes.[56] The Indian Reorganization Act postdates all of the statutes delegating specific taxing powers to the states, and provides that "lands or rights acquired" for tribes pursuant to its authority "be exempt from State and local taxation."[57] It seems reasonable to assume that lands acquired after 1934 are not subject to the earlier delegations, but the Court has not made these distinctions.

Congress has rarely addressed state jurisdiction squarely. Perhaps the only genuine example of a general jurisdictional provision is the act of 1901 authorizing state condemnation of allotted lands.[58] A few tribes are expressly subject to peculiar applications of state probate laws[59]—implying, of course, that others are not. In some cases Congress has been quite explicit. Individually tailored legislation for the distribution of tribal claims funds or tribal assets usually specifies the scope of tax immunity to be afforded the beneficiaries.[60] It is understandable that the Court avoids the

55. 25 U.S.C. 406, 407; see also 25 U.S.C. 466, 403b, 415, 416.

56. Jay Vincent White, *Taxing Those They Found Here* (Washington, D.C.: 1972) includes a detailed review of the pre-*Williams* tax cases.

57. 25 U.S.C. 465; see also 25 U.S.C. 1466, added in 1973. Taking "in trust" has become synonymous with tax exemption in administrative practice and congressional draftsmanship. Compare the Oklahoma Welfare Act, §1, 49 Stat. 1967 (1936), 25 U.S.C. 501, which limits this general exemption.

58. 25 U.S.C. 357.

59. Probate: 25 U.S.C. 375 (Five Civilized Tribes), 564h (Klamath), 697(b) (Oregon Tribes), 747 (Paiutes), 797 (Wyandotte), 843(b) (Ottawa). *Cf.* 25 U.S.C. 416i(b). See 25 U.S.C. 348 regarding extension of state jurisdiction to allottees (*in personam*) after issuance of a fee patent; on mortgages for the Hopi Industrial Park, 25 U.S.C. 642(b). Also 25 U.S.C. 491 (mortgages to secure F.H.A. loans) and 695(d), 745(c) (trustees for Oregon Tribes and Paiute asset distributions to be appointed consistent with state law).

60. 25 U.S.C. 608(c) (Yakima); 25 U.S.C. 487(c) (Spokane); 574 (Shoshone); 610b (Swinomish); 565f (Klamath); 589, 590c (Shoshone); 594 (Chippewa); 609a, 609b−1 (Yakima); 648 (Hualapai); 662 (California); 676a, 677p (Ute); 690 (Red Lake); 749 (Paiute); 788b, 788f (Creek); 798 (Wyandotte); 853(b) (Ottawa); 876 (Otoe); 881 (Potawatomi); 882a (Sac & Fox); 883c (Osage); 912 (Quapaw); 937 (Catawba); 955 (Aqua Caliente); 963, 967c (Omaha); 978 (Ponca); 994 (Cherokee); 1013 (Snake); 1036 (Shawnee); 1058 (Tillamook); 1071, 1073 (Colville); 1087 (Quileute); 1104 (Nooksack); 1120, 1129 (Miami); 1134 (Duwamish); 1146 (Emigrant N.Y. Indians); 1154 (Chehalis); 1165 (Cheyenne-Arapaho); 1171 (Iowa); 1185 (Delaware); 1194 (Umatilla); 1204 (Sioux); 1211 (Tlingit & Haida); 1225 (Confederated Weas, Piankeshaws); 1234 (Chemahuevi); 1246 (Pembina Chippewa); 1252 (Flathead); 1273 (Jicarilla); 1282 (Havasupai); 1296 (Delaware); 1300a−3 (Yavapai); 1300b−4 (Kickapoo); 1300c−4 (Yankton Sioux); 1330d−8 (Mississippi Sioux); 1300e−6 (Assiniboine); 674 (Ute Mountain); 683, 686, 689 (Chippewa); 772 (Oregon Indians): 572

complete legislative record; it is full of traps and contradictions. But the Court might at least refrain from shielding its decisions behind the fiction of congressional intent.

With *Bryan* the judicial record, at the time of this writing, draws to a close. It is a record of fluctuation, involution, and inconsistency. Clear, consistent principles are prerequisite to order, and order is one of the paramount demands society makes on the judiciary. As a concession to individualism we institutionalize a greater degree of conflict in our courts than non-English-speaking Western European nations. However, that conflict is given narrow boundaries by our reliance on rules of judicial continuity: precedent, reasoned elaboration, clear and precise standards.

The key to order in the common law is time—time in which courts can develop a pattern of decision the significance of which will be accessible to hindsight, time to accommodate a changing social environment without sudden jolts. Federal Indian law is fortunate to have had the benefit of a major conceptual decision, *Worcester v. Georgia*, since 1832, but the Court has drifted away from it and abandoned precedent and order. Under *Worcester*, tribes' immunity from federal arrogations was left unsettled, but at least their immunity from the states was absolute and secure. Today it is incumbent on the Court to develop a new conceptualization of the tribal-federal relationship, one with sharp boundaries, and one it will be committed to uphold.

Herbert Wechsler called for "neutral principles" in constitutional adjudication more than a decade ago, arguing that value-neutrality and generality are essential to distinguish adjudication from politics.[61] His critics responded that the Court itself is, in reality, a power organ, notwithstanding its idealization as anti-majoritarian.[62] The Court's counterweight role *is* political, but it is a counterweight only if it is motivated by *different* political forces than the executive and the national legislature. Its principal

---

(Shoshone); 656, 658 (California Indians); 894 (Menominee); 564a, 564j (Klamath); 898 (Otoe); 1264 (Blackfeet). See also 25 U.S.C. 903d(c) (transfer of assets, Menominee restoration).

61. Herbert Wechsler, "Toward Neutral Principles of Constitutional Law," in his *Principles, Politics, and Fundamental Law* 21, 27–28 (Cambridge, Mass.: 1961).

62. Arthur S. Miller & Ronald F. Howell, "The Myth of Neutrality in Constitutional Adjudication," 27 *University of Chicago Law Review* 661 (1950); *cf.* Addison Mueller & Murray L. Schwartz, "The Principle of Neutral Principles," 7 *U.C.L.A. Law Review* 571 (1960); and Jan G. Deutsch, "Neutrality, Legitimacy, and the Supreme Court: Some Intersections Between Law and Political Science," 20 *Stanford Law Review* 169, 178–97 (1967).

motivation is maintaining its authority,[63] and as long as our national ideology assimilates judicial legitimacy to order and continuity, the maintenance of the Court's authority must remain a function of its ability to demonstrate consistency irrespective of majoritarian fashions. This it has failed to do in Indian law. Which is more important, the perceived advantage of a dozen states in challenging the existence of tribes, or the loss of credibility attendant upon more widespread discovery of the Court's abandonment of principled decision making? Even the majority has an interest in a consistent Court.

Martin Shapiro characterized the Court's function in First Amendment cases as protecting groups of citizens not adequately represented in the democratic process.[64] Wechsler and Learned Hand have agreed that the Court should accord a "preferred position" to such groups.[65] If this is true, tribes qualify for special attention. Not directly represented, too small to be effectively represented indirectly, and stripped of most powers of political and economic self-protection, they exemplify the problem of exclusion by a powerful and indifferent majority. What remains is to devise a conceptual vehicle that integrates tribal sovereignty and neutral principles, and is of a nature tractable by courts.

63. Alexander M. Bickel, *The Least Dangerous Branch* 235–43 (Indianapolis: 1962).
64. Martin M. Shapiro, *Freedom of Speech: The Supreme Court and Judicial Review* 2, 34–39, 111–15 (Englewood Cliffs, N.J.: 1966).
65. Learned Hand, *The Bill of Rights* 56 (Cambridge, Mass.: 1958); Wechsler, *Principles* 35.

Part Four

Towards a Theory of the Tribe
in the American Nation

17

Tribes, Territories, and Colonies

The essential political reality against which the American colonies rebelled was the power of the empire, by initiative and veto, to bend American wealth to its will without an American voice or consent. This arose in three ways. Parliament enjoyed a prerogative of legislation for the colonies although they sent no delegates and exercised no votes. The royal executive furthermore enjoyed the power of appointing colonial governors, judges and members of legislative upper houses, and removing them at pleasure. Through them, the king was potentially able to negative local acts at the time they were considered by any of the three branches of the colonial government. Finally, acts which succeeded in passing this royal test were returned to Parliament for approval.

It would be natural to assume that the founders of the American Republic sought to avoid in their own government the opportunities for tyranny they had fought to overthrow. This was at first the case. Members of the Continental Congress generally assumed that settlers on western lands were entitled to consensual government on republican principles. The conceptual problem was to guarantee republicanism and public safety without encroaching upon western communities' sovereignty. Some argued that these settlements were *sua sponte* sovereign.[1] The prevalent

1. Only this position could be completely consistent with the Lockeian conception of sovereignty embraced by the rebellious colonies.

view, however, was that some temporary form of administration would have to be exercised, by the states or by the United States, until the settlers were prepared to organize themselves, or until there were a sufficient number of freeholders to support a separate government.[2]

It was also generally agreed that these new republics were entitled to join the confederation on an equal footing, although the Articles of Confederation did not specify any procedure for the admission of new states.[3] Jefferson's Ordinance of 1784 promised automatic admission, as did the Ordinance of 1787.[4] Both laws were described as *compacts*, rather than mere legislative acts, to avoid any argument that they exceeded Congress's authority under the articles.[5] As such, they were supposed to be irrevocably binding on the nation.

Jefferson's ordinance anticipated that the territories would be wholly self-governing prior to admission. It even referred to them as "states."[6] The Ordinance of 1787 introduced some elements of colonial administration to limit that sovereignty. The territories were to receive congressionally appointed governors and judges and a congressionally appointed upper house of assembly. Only the lower house of assembly was to be popularly

2. Arthur Bestor, "Constitutionalism and the Settlement of the West: The Attainment of Consensus, 1754–1784," in John Porter Bloom, ed., *The American Territorial System* 13, 22–24, 27–28 (Athens, Ohio: 1969).

3. The absence of such an article was criticized in *The Federalist*, No. 43. Jefferson had proposed one, but it was never adopted, (Bestor, "Constitutionalism," 18). Congress's resolution of 10 October 1780 declared its policy that the West "be settled and formed into distinct republican states" to "become members of the federal Union and have the same rights of sovereignty, freedom and independence as the other states" (*id.* 21). New York State also passed a resolution endorsing equal footing for new states (George Ticknor Curtis, 1 *History of the Origin, Formation, and Adoption of the Constitution of the United States* 292 [New York: 1859]). Monroe was ambivalent, indicating to Jefferson in 1786 that he favored "a Colonial Govt. similar to that wh. prevail'd in these States previous to the revolution, with this remarkable difference that . . . they shall [eventually] be admitted into the confederacy" Earl S. Pomeroy, *The Territories and the United States. 1861–1890* 6 [Seattle: 1969]). Jefferson rebuked him, warning that to "treat them as subjects" for any time would cause them to "abhor us as masters, and break from us in defiance" (Bestor, "Constitutionalism," 32, n.103). The only outspoken dissenter was Gouverneur Morris, who advocated a baldly colonial system (5 *Elliots' Debates on the Confederation and Constitution* 492 [Washington, D.C.: 1830–1845]; letter quoted in *Scott v. Sanford*, 19 How. 393, 507).

4. 9 *Journals of Congress* 153 (23 April 1784); "An Ordinance for the Government of the Territory of the United States Northwest of the River Ohio," 13 July 1787, in Clarence E. Carter and John Porter Bloom, eds., 2 *The Territorial Papers of the United States* 37–50 (Washington, D.C.: 1934–).

5. Curtis, 1 *History* 299; Bestor, "Constitutionalism," 24.

6. Bestor, "Constitutionalism," 30.

elected.[7] This gave Congress the veto power formerly enjoyed by the king. On the other hand, the territories were enabled to pass their own laws, provided they conformed to six articles of general compact and limitation, including a brief version of the English Bill of Rights.[8] The English Bill of Rights was not enumerated in the United States' own organic law until 1790.

This frame of territorial government was ratified by the Act of 7 August 1789 which delegated the appointment powers to the president.[9] Shortly thereafter the idea of appointing one house of assembly fell into disfavor as an excess of federal supervision. After 1829 no territorial organic acts provided for appointed territorial legislators.[10] Federal involvement was thereby limited to the executive and judicial branches of territorial government—enforcement but not legislation.

Congress, under the articles, had no express power to legislate for the territories, although many had recommended it.[11] The Constitution remedied that defect with the clause authorizing Congress to make all "Needful Rules and Regulations respecting the Territory" of the United States.[12] Gouverneur Morris sought to make this clause even more specific, to the point of permitting Congress to "govern them as provinces," if it so wished, but he could not induce a majority of the framers to this view. The vagueness of the Needful Rules clause, as Morris later explained it, was born of a compromise between those who abhorred the idea of anything more than a temporary federal domination of western districts, and those few like himself who believed in a new empire.[13]

Since the Needful Rules clause authorizes it to extend its laws to the organized territories without their consent, albeit subject to certain fundamental limitations, Congress has Parliament's former power of initiative.

7. "Ordinance" of 13 July 1787, in Carter and Bloom, eds., *Territorial Papers.*
8. *Id.* These were denoted "articles of compact," rather than "limitations" or some other term connoting United States supremacy.
9. 1 Stat. 50.
10. Pomeroy, *Territories and the United States* 3, 97.
11. Bestor, "Constitutionalism."
12. Originally, Madison proposed that the Constitution expressly authorize Congress "to institute temporary governments for new States arising therein" (5 *Elliot's Debates* 439). This was not popular. The Needful Rules clause was a suggestion of Gouverneur Morris, left intentionally vague to pacify the states retaining western land claims (5 *Elliot's Debates* 496–97).
13. See his letter quoted in *Scott v. Sanford*, 19 How. 393, 507.

However, the Ordinance of 1787 recognized a right never enjoyed by the colonies: the right to send non-voting delegates to Congress with a privilege of debate.[14] Congress, unlike Parliament, was compelled to listen to the grievances and protestations of its subjects *at its own expense*.[15] The third negative of the British colonial administration, the power of approving local legislation, was never made a part of the American territorial system. Local laws were sometimes required to be filed with the president or a member of the cabinet, but for purposes of information rather than approval.[16]

Jefferson and Paine believed so firmly in the superiority of republican principles they intended even this temporary federal overlordship to merely guarantee that new governments would start off on the proper ideological footing.[17] Others, however, feared that the social and economic conditions of the frontier were such that only strong, authoritarian rule could preserve peace and order.[18] The frontiersmen were characterized as *"white Indians"* whose nature *"revolts against the operation of laws,"* like Cooper's Natty Bumppo.[19] They would have to be controlled to pave the way for the industrious farmers who would otherwise not risk proximity to such rough company, and whose efforts would eventually transform the wilderness into productive property.

Philosophers like Dr. Rush assumed that the advent of the agrarian producer was inevitable, a feature of natural economic progress, but also anticipated that the process could be accelerated by federal tutelage and

14. The customary powers of delegates and their influence are described by Pomeroy, *Territories and the United States* 80, 83–87, and Jo Tice Bloom, "Early Delegates in the House of Representatives," in John Porter Bloom, ed., *The American Territorial System* 65 (Athens, Ohio: 1969). A constitutional amendment to give delegates votes was introduced unsuccessfully in the nineteenth century (Herman V. Ames, "The Proposed Amendments to the Constitution," 2 *Annual Report of the American Historical Association, 1896*). Assignment to the House was authorized by 3 Stat. 363 (1819).

15. Pomeroy, *Territories and the United States* 88. Congress also paid all territorial officers, including members of the assembly (*id.* 28).

16. *Id.* 1103, 19–24.

17. Bestor, "Constitutionalism," 23; Robert Berkhofer, Jr. "The Northwest Ordinance and the Principle of Territorial Evolution," in John Porter Bloom, ed.; *The American Territorial System* 45, 48 (Athens, Ohio: 1969).

18. Berkhofer, "Northwest Ordinance," 50–52. Monroe advocated the necessity of transitional government to "protect the persons and rights of those who may settle within such districts in the infancy of their settlement" (*id.* 49). The theory has modern supporters, e.g., Pomeroy, *Territories and the United States* xii–xiii.

19. Berkhofer, "Northwest Ordinance," 50. Miller's discussion of Cooper's work is enlightening. Perry Miller, *The Life of The Mind in America* 99–104 (New York: 1965).

supervision in its early stages without any considerable loss of freedom. There was arguably little danger in this as long as admission to statehood was automatic upon attaining some population quotient. Federal governorship would, if it actually improved law and order, speed up the emigration of easterners to the territories, and they would thus achieve complete self-government all the sooner.[20]

Frontier lawlessness was advanced in justification of the three-stage territorial scheme (plenary federal control, territorial government, statehood) throughout the nineteenth century. If anything, the conditions of the far west reinforced it. Scattered settlements of ranchers and miners were far less tractable than the middle-western farmers of the antebellum territories. As Pomeroy[21] has noted, a striking characteristic of territorial government after the Civil War is how long it lasted—twenty to sixty years compared with five or ten years in the days of Jefferson and Monroe.

Indian tribes have passed through two stages of federal overlordship. Between *Kagama* and the Indian Reorganization Act, tribes were wholly subject to Congress and the president, acting through the Bureau of Indian Affairs. No local laws or assemblies were recognized, and a special police force was established to maintain federal supremacy. Traditional leadership was deposed, prosecuted, and sometimes killed when in conflict with federal agency policy.[22]

Post-IRA reservation governments have assumed a less restricted status. No tribal leaders are appointed. All are popularly elected according to tribal constitutions and laws.[23] However, Congress exercises three powers over tribes that it has never exercised over the territories. First, Congress has delegated to the secretary of the interior the power to approve or reject tribal constitutions.[24] This was a feature of Charles Pickering's proposal

20. Berkhofer, ''Northwest ordinance,'' 51.
21. Pomeroy, *Territories and the United States* xii, 2.
22. See for example the *Report of the Commissioner of Indian Affairs, 1881* xvii–xviii; *1882*, 76, 78, 109, 132; *1883* 42, 48–49; and William T. Hagan, *Indian Police and Judges* (New Haven: 1966).
23. Most govern through small assemblies which combine legislative and executive functions (George E. Fay, *Charters, Constitutions and By-laws of Indian Tribes of North America* [Greeley, Colo.: 1967–1971]). Tribal judges are often paid directly by the United States, resulting in our experience in some degree of influence over their actions by federal law enforcement agencies. Tribes may, however, select and pay tribal judges as provided by federal rules (25 C.F.R. 11–1 *et seq.*) or by their own tribal constitutions.
24. 25 U.S.C. 476. Regulations governing this process are found at 25 U.S.C. 52. It may not be entitled to judicial review (*Twin Cities Chippewa Tribal Council v. Minnesota*

for territorial government under the Articles of Confederation, but it was never adopted by Congress.[25] The power to approve constitutions has frequently resulted in a power to veto individual laws and contracts: the secretary has ransomed approval of the constitutions for grants of greater powers to him by the tribes.[26] Even without tribal "consent," review power over *property matters* is given to agency by federal statute.[27] Finally, although tribes are subject to congressional legislation, they have neither voice nor vote *as tribes* in Congress. Congress therefore enjoys Parliament's initiative and veto powers, and does not pay the expenses of local delegates to lobby against their exercise.

Moreover, for nearly a century no one has maintained that tribes are entitled to eventual statehood. All recent policy statements by federal officials indicate that tribes are deemed transitional to assimilation into the existing states, rather than separate statehood.[28] This was not always the case. As late as the 1830s, members of both political parties advocated policies conducive to tribal statehood, and the Indian Territory came very

---

Chippewa Tribe, 370 F. 2d 529 [C.A. Minn. 1967]). The approval power establishes the solicitor's office of the Interior Department as a kind of supreme court for tribes. Just as the Supreme Court of the United States interprets the meaning of the United States Constitution, the solicitor frequently passes on the tribal constitutionality of tribal legislation, usurping the function of tribal checking institutions. In reviewing a bureau veto of a tribal attorney contract, the solicitor explained:

On one hand, there is the principle that the Department should foster local self-government among organized Indian tribes and, in dealing with such tribes in the exercise of the Department's power over them, should impose requirements on a tribe only when it seems necessary to do so in order to protect some important interest of the tribe or of the Government. On the other hand, there is the principle that, for the standpoint of stability of the administrative process, the head of a Department who has delegated authority and responsibility concerning a particular matter to a subordinate official ought not to overrule such official unless the latter has exceeded his authority, or has failed to conform to instructions issued by the head of the Department, or has made a grave error in judgment which is apt to have serious consequences. If the responsibility for deciding the present case rested upon me I believe that I should give the greater weight to the second of the two principles and affirm the Commissioner's action.

(Quoted by Felix X. Cohen, "The Erosion of Indian Rights 1950–1953: A Case Study in Bureaucracy," 62 *Yale Law Journal* 380 [1953]).

25. Bestor, "Constitutionalism," 23.

26. This attempt to imbue the practical administration of wardship with an appearance of tribal consent is fraught with inconsistency. If tribes are too helpless and ignorant to govern themselves, as the existence of "plenary power" presumes, then they must be incapable of giving informed consent to such a delegation of power. If the basis of the power is, however, a free delegation, it should be revocable at any time; but amendments of tribal constitutions must also receive federal approval (25 C.F.R. 52.3). Moreover, the power of review is of that nature deemed "inalienable" by our ideological forebears.

27. Chiefly 25 U.S.C. 331–415.

28. R. L. Barsh and R. L. Trosper, "Title I of The Indian Self-Determination Act," 3 *American Indian Law Review* 361 (1975).

close to achieving statehood at the close of the nineteenth century.[29] Jefferson was particularly anxious that tribes prepare themselves for eventual statehood.[30] Tribes' refusal to submit to federal supremacy was a greater factor in their remaining separate from the Union than any consensus in Congress that it would be either inexpedient or *ultra vires* to admit them.

All federal policy since 1887 has cut against this goal. Allotment would have permanently abolished tribes, had its economic failures not persuaded Congress to restore some degree of tribal government in 1934. Reorganization itself was only seen as a temporary measure. Nineteen years after it was begun, Congress resolved to begin the process of abolishing tribes once again. Termination was suspended in 1968, but no alternative road to statehood (or the equivalent) has been provided. In current practice, tribes are perpetual dependencies.

The justification for this practice, erroneously attributed to Chief Justice Marshall's remarks in *Cherokee Nation*, is analogous to the justification for federal supervision of the territories. Tribal Indians were and are still regarded as incompetent to govern themselves wisely. Nineteenth-century observers took Dr. Rush's position that tribes would evolve naturally into agrarian gentility.[31] The purpose of federal supervision, they argued, should therefore be to accelerate the process and thereby more rapidly free Indian hunting lands for Indian and white tillage. Allotment was a rather dramatic effort in this direction;[32] reorganization was regarded by many as a slower, more educational program with a better prospect for success.[33] However, while Congress protected white territorials from abuse of

29. Annie Heloise Abel, "Proposals for an Indian State, 1778–1878," *Annual Report of the American Historical Association, 1907.*
30. See particularly his letters to the Chiefs of the Upper Towns of the Cherokees, 4 May 1808 and 9 January 1809, and his letter to James Pemberton of 21 June 1808, in Andrew A. Lipscomb, ed., 12 *The Writings of Thomas Jefferson* 74–75, and 16 *Writings* 432, 455 (Washington, D.C.: 1903).
31. See, for example, the remarks collected in Francis Paul Prucha, *Americanizing the American Indian* 79–129 (Cambridge, Mass.: 1973); Stephen J. Kunitz, "Benjamin Rush on Savagism and Progress," 17 *Ethnohistory* 31 (1970); Roy Harvey Pearce, *The Savages of America: A Study of the Indian and the Idea of Civilization* (Baltimore: 1953).
32. D. S. Otis, *The Dawes Act and the Allotment of Indian Lands* (Norman, Okla.: 1972).
33. The transitional function of the Indian Reorganization Act is also discussed at length in R. L. Barsh and J. Y. Henderson, "Tribal Courts, the Model Code, and the Police Idea in American Indian Policy," 40 *Law and Contemporary Problems* 25 (1976). For a different view, see unsigned "Note 'Tribal Self-Government and The Indian Reorganization Act of 1934,' " 70 *Michigan Law Review* 955 (1972).

transitional supervision by specifying automatic admission criteria or by giving them a voice in Congress, Indian tribal members are subject to unlimited agency discretion in the determination of their individual and collective competency to choose for themselves.[34]

The most significant comparison between tribes and territories lies not in the degree of power held by the United States, but by whom it is actually exercised, for it is in the exercise that abuses appear in laws originated with reasonable purposes. Federal power over the territories, chiefly the power of appointment, was exercised by the president with the advice and consent of Congress. Federal powers of review and supervision of tribal legislation are exercised by a regulatory agency, the Bureau of Indian Affairs. An appointed official in a district destined for statehood may feel some interest in pleasing the president, but even more interest in preparing his local support for eventual state office.[35] If the district enjoys a voice in Congress, the appointee's incentive to curry local favor will be even greater, because popular complaints might result in his removal. Assuming that high appointive office is temporary, the appointee must also be concerned with the demands of business, because his future lies in the private sector.[36]

On the contrary, when a civil service agency governs, its principal interest is in perpetuating and expanding itself. Career officers see their future in the agency, and are thus motivated to increase its salary scale and promotional opportunities rather than respond to political or business sentiment. Government by bureaucracy implies perpetual dependency. Scholars did not begin to argue for a civil service administration of new territories until the first nonwhite insular possessions were acquired.[37]

Territorial government was increasingly responsive to territorial resi-

34. One vice-president of the United States never received his "C.C."—certificate of competency—from the Bureau. "Hearings, 'To Grant Indians . . . Freedom to Organize,'" 132, 150, 264−65.

35. Territorial officials were also influenced by territorial business interests (Pomeroy, *Territories and the United States* 70). Social ties to the East ameliorated the territories' position (*id.* 106−7).

36. See Richard A. Posner, "Theories of Economic Regulation," 5 *Bell Journal of Economics* 335 (1974).

37. Pomeroy, *Territories and the United States* xiii, 1, 97; Edward Gaylord Bourne, "A Trained Colonial Civil Service," 169 *North American Review* 528−29 (1899): "Our previous annexations of territory . . . have never involved questions of administration essentially different from those with which our public men have been familiar." See also Alpheus Henry Snow, *The Administration of Dependencies* (New York: 1902); William Franklin Willoughby, *Territories and Dependencies of the United States, their Government and Administration* (New York: 1905).

dents in the nineteenth century.[38] To be sure, appointments were almost purely motivated by political patronage. However, the average appointee was inexperienced, ineffective, not a resident of the territory, and lasted less than four years before resigning or being removed. Appointees received few instructions from Washington. Underpaid, they frequently grew dependent upon compensation from the territorial assemblies, which manipulated the power of salary to great effect, as had the American colonial assemblies. Consequently, the appointed Governor's veto was exercised unsystematically, if at all.

Tribes have no institutional control over federal bureaucrats. They do not even have the right to grant them additional income.[39] The record of the bureau has been one of extensive intervention in local affairs, often guided by a policy of frustrating any local initiative that might suggest to Congress that the period of "dependency" has ended.[40] Although tribal status is supposed to be transitional, the budget of the bureau has increased tenfold since 1900, and now exceeds eight hundred million dollars.[41]

It was the experience of the territories that a federally-subsidized delegation to Congress helped to offset congressional legislative supremacy. Persuasion has far less weight than a vote, of course. Territorial delegates were essentially lobbyists with federal expense accounts and special privileges on the floor of the House. They were assisted by the fact that their constituents were emigrants from the states and retained social and business ties with the East. Most tribes, by comparison, cannot afford lobbyists; nor are they allowed to appear and debate in the House. Most grievous of all, territorial delegates have been given routine committee assignments since 1879, one of the first being on the Indian Affairs Committee.[42] This made more sense in 1879, when the territories engulfed

38. Pomeroy, *Territories and the United States* 11–13, 19–20, 24–25, 27, 38–40, 48, 62–64, 66, 98–99. If Congress had plenary power over the territories, it rarely exercised it before 1890 (*id*. 2, 92). See, for example, House Report No. 440, 48th Congress, 1st Session (1884), quoted by Pomeroy 92–93: "Congress ought not to interpose in subjects of local legislation unless it is manifest there has been an abuse of power by the Territorial legislature."
39. See 25 U.S.C. 68; 28 U.S.C. 437; 39 Op. Atty. Gen. 414 (1940).
40. Barsh and Trosper, "Title I of the Indian Self-Determination Act."
41. Sar A. Levitan and William B. Johnston, *Indian Giving*.
42. Delegates were assigned to the Territories Committee as well, beginning in 1876 Pomeroy, *Territories and the United States* 81. Territorial governors also frequently served as Indian agents, albeit reluctantly, leading to considerable misapplication of funds designated for the tribes (*id*. 67–70, 96).

Indian populations, than today. When tribal leaders appear before Congress, they often find that a member of the controlling subcommittee is the delegate from the Virgin Islands, for example, whereas as they have no delegates of their own.

The contemporary political status of tribes reflects the decline in Jeffersonian ideology that has accompanied the United States' growing imperial ambitions. Imperialists urged that nonwhite races be governed by the sword, unlike the white settlers of the old territories. Ironically, the insular possessions, which served as the focus of this argument, emerged by the middle of this century as completely self-governing as the old territories, if not as states or independent nations.[43] Tribes seem to have borne the brunt of imperialist ideology.

Imperialists argued from expediency. So had the westward expansionists of Jefferson's day who designed the three-stage system of territorial government. But imperialists were not simply concerned with temporary lawlessness. They revealed an abiding belief that nonwhites would be unfamiliar with American civics, rendering self-government a useless charade. Dean Langdell of Harvard Law School feared that extending the fundamental freedoms of American citizenship to "alien races" would "furnish as striking a proof of our unfitness to govern dependencies . . . as our bitterest enemies could desire."[44] Governor Baldwin of Connecticut was persuaded that the Constitution guaranteed the Bill of Rights to insular possessions, but considered it an "embarrassment."[45] His solution was legally to classify the "savage tribes" of the Pacific *as Indians* so that they could be denied citizenship pursuant to *Elk* and held in a similar state of perpetual "pupilage."[46] He was confident that this power would not be abused. An enlightened nation such as ours would establish "some system . . . for the interest of all concerned, and administered by their

43. Cuba and the Philippines were granted independence; Hawaii became a state; Puerto Rico calls itself a "commonwealth" and remains essentially a territory with certain additional unconventional privileges such as that of electing its own governor; Guam, Micronesia and American Samoa are old-style territories for all practical purposes. See Robert R. Robbins, "United States Territories in Mid-Century," in John Porter Bloom, ed., *The American Territorial System* 200 (Athens, Ohio: 1969).

44. C. C. Langdell, "The Status of Our New Territories," 12 *Harvard Law Review* 365 (1899).

45. Simeon E. Baldwin, "The Constitutional Questions Incident to the Acquisition and Government by the United States of Island Territory," 12 *Harvard Law Review* 393 (1899).

46. *Id.* See *People v. Hall*, 4 Cal. 399 (1854).

own inhabitants, so far as they may show a capacity for self-government."[47]

It was also popularly believed that alien populations were accustomed to autocracy and would therefore applaud autocratic colonialism. This theory was first advanced, in fact, in justification of the temporary military government of New Orleans by Thomas Jefferson.[48] Alternatively, scholars warned that tropical nations were submerged in anarchy, and that the "suppression of tribal feuds and of exploitation, as well as the suppression of local superstitions, does not seem possible" without American imperial dominance.[49] Radical imperialists like Professor Simon Patten of the University of Pennsylvania argued that the profit motive and technological progress take precedence over the Constitution, which he referred to as archaic and dispensable.[50] He justified colonialism as providing a "social uplift" to ignorant races.

The Bureau of Indian Affairs still refers to federal "trust responsibility"—the power of that agency to regulate all transactions in tribal property—as a duty to a helpless people rather than as a valuable commercial power of the United States.[51] Bureau officials continue to insist that this is not "paternalism."[52] Restraints on the power of tribal governments continue to be justified to Congress as necessitated to protect individual Indians.[53] Although both Congress and the agency have sponsored extensive studies of the social and economic condition of tribes, not one in

47. Simeon E. Baldwin, "The Historic Policy of the United States as to Annexation," *Annual Report of the American Historical Association, 1893* 369, 390.

48. *Id.*

49. Simon N. Patten, "Territorial Expansion of the United States," *University of Pennsylvania University Lectures* 197, 201 (Philadelphia: 1915). Baldwin's "Historic Policy" warned of the need for "a strong hand." Compare Senator Albert Beveridge's remarks to a Philadelphia audience in 1907, quoted by Robbins, "United States Territories," 200: "Not sudden 'self-government' for peoples who have not yet learned the alphabet of liberty; not territorial independence for islands whose ignorant, suspicious and primitive inhabitants, left to themselves, would prey upon one another *until they become the inevitable spoil of other powers*" (emphasis ours). Senator Beveridge joined Governor Baldwin in the use of words such as "wardship" and "trust relationship" to describe insular administration.

50. Patten, "Territorial Expansion."

51. Barsh and Trosper, "Title I of the Indian Self-Determination Act."

52. *Id.* Interestingly, the bureau has no compunction about conceding paternalism when doing so may further its institutional objectives and perpetuate its existence. Thus when the bureau introduced the reorganization program in 1934, and the self-determination package in 1970, both of which tend to preserve tribes as its subagencies, its leadership begged Congress to join it in *ending* paternalism.

53. Donald L. Burnett, Jr., "An Historical Analysis of the 1968 'Indian Civil Rights Act,' " 9 *Harvard Journal on Legislation* 557 (1972).

this century has attempted to compare the level of skills, the desire for republican self-government, or the administrative or business success rate, of tribes and state or municipal governments of similar size and responsibilities. Indeed, if such a test were required for local self-government today, the many cities such as Fall River and New York that have collapsed financially, and the many cities and states that have committed egregious fiscal blunders or stooped to the temptation of corruption, would surely qualify for perpetual federal supervision.[54] Only one conclusion can fairly be drawn: tribal Indians are denied effective self-government because they are Indians.

54. This suggests a fascinating question, whether Title IX of the Federal Bankruptcy Act (11 U.S.C. 401–43) is inconsistent with the Tenth Amendment. Title IX may result in a transitional period of direct federal receivership or trusteeship for a bankrupt municipality, bypassing the state legislature. It also prohibits the states from enforcing state municipal bankruptcy settlements on unwilling creditors (11 U.S.C. 403[i]). The only saving feature is the requirement that the city itself must request federal proceedings (11 U.S.C. 403[a]). Outcry in New York City against "Big Mac" (The Municipal Assistance Corporation), a creature of New York State law, was nevertheless accompanied by fears of such a federal receivership if "Big Mac" failed to restore the city's solvency. Whether the constitutional principle of federalism requires the United States to preserve local self-government under such circumstances is becoming increasingly relevant to national affairs. Perhaps Congress can offer financial assistance to cities conditional upon their consent to temporary receivership, but Congress's power to provide for involuntary municipal bankruptcy is a different matter.

18

Tribal Political Liberty in Contemporary Society

Although tribes have no guarantee against dissolution by Congress under existing law,[1] tribal members may vote in federal and state elections[2] and are subject to the burdens of federal taxation[3] and selective service.[4] Since a federal administrative agency and Congress itself periodically define what tribal governments may and may not do, the Indian vote should in principle have some impact on policies affecting tribal existence.

1. Indeed, one circuit has upheld that power (*Crain v. First Nat. Bank of Oregon*, 324 F. 2d 532, 535–37 [C.A. Ore. 1963]; followed, *U.S. v. Heath*, 509 F. 2d 16 [C.A. Ore. 1974]; see also *Bd. of Commissioners of Creek County v. Seber*, 318 U.S. 705, 718 [1943], *reh. den'd* 319 U.S. 782).

2. In several states tribal members were denied suffrage until the enforcement of federal voting rights legislation in the 1960s (see, for example, *Allen v. Merrell*, 305 P. 2d 490 [Utah 1957]; *cf. Montoya v. Bolack*, 70 N.M. 332, 364 P. 2d 974 [1962]). Recently challenges to state legislative apportionment schemes have been brought on the basis that they violate one-man, one-vote requirements (*Klahr v. Williams*, 339 F. Supp. 922 [D.C. Ariz. 1972]). Ironically, the prevalent objection of states to granting Indians suffrage was, to use the words of the *Merrell* court, "that Indians living on reservations are extremely limited in their contact with state government and its units and, for this reason also, have much less interest in or concern with it than do other citizens," a very good argument against further extensions of state power and in favor of tribal political autonomy.

3. For the evolution of tribes' susceptibility to federal taxation see Jay Vincent White, *Taxing Those They Found Here* (Washington, D.C.: 1972).

4. *U.S. v. Neptune*, 337 F. Supp. 1028 (D. Conn. 1972); *Ex Parte Green*, 123 F. 2d 862 (2d Cir. 1941), *cert. den'd sub nom. Green v. McLaren*, 316 U.S. 668 (1942).

The key fact is the small size of tribes, relative to the states. Reservations range in population from a score to over 100,000. Only about ten exceed 5,000.[5] The original draft of the Constitution provided that no member of the House represent fewer than 30,000 persons, and the first Congress of sixty five representatives closely approximated that ratio.[6] Only one recognized tribe today could have qualified to elect a member of the 1789 House. The current ratio is so high that no recognized tribe would qualify as a congressional district. It may be true that a determined bloc of as few as 10 percent of the voters in a congressional district has a reasonable certainty of determining the outcome of any House race; only one reservation tribe today can achieve such a turnout.[7] This would still be true if the population of reservation tribes, which is growing much faster than the rest of the American population, were to double in the next ten years, while the rest of the population remained the same.[8] If by some miracle of populist politics, the ratio of representation was reduced to 1:5,000, about ten tribes would qualify to elect a representative directly. However, the House would have 40,000 members, and fewer than forty of them would be elected by Indians.

Indians are nevertheless observed to enjoy some ostensible "clout" in Congress, if subsidy legislation is viewed to the exclusion of legislation affecting tribal self-government. This is susceptible to three interpretations. The simplest and probably least persuasive is that Indians are a sympathetic subject, like education and health, and that Indian clout reflects the large numbers of non-Indians who threaten to vote on Indian issues. An Indian sympathy vote probably does exist, but even if it is large and not as ephemeral as the black sympathy vote and other historical sympathy votes, it is *not* representation. There is no assurance whatever that it will be exercised in the real interests of Indians, rather than the goals perceived, perhaps in

5. Reservation tribes with 5000 or more enrolled members are the Gila River Pima-Maricopa, Hopi, Navajo, Papago, San Carlos Apache, White Mountain Apache, Red Lake Chippewa, Blackfeet, Flathead, Crow, Fort Peck, Standing Rock, Turtle Mountain, Osage, Cheyenne River, Oglala, Rosebud, Colville, and Yakima. In several of these cases, fewer than 5000 members actually reside on reservation. A number of tribes with populations greater than 5000 no longer have reservations, notably in Oklahoma.

6. See U.S. Bureau of Census, *Historical Statistics of the United States: Colonial Times to 1957* 692 (Washington, D.C.: 1960).

7. The Navajo, with a population of about 130,000, could constitute a quarter or more of a congressional district.

8. The Navajo would then have one-half of one district, but no other tribe would have more than one-tenth.

ignorance, by the non-Indians who exercise it. The American colonists were never satisfied by the English argument that there were many good people in England who *did* vote and who had the very best of wishes for the colonies. Nor is our system of government based upon the belief that any assortment of four hundred persons could sit in the House with the real interests of the nation equally at heart. If we believed that, we would choose our representatives at random. Direct election of representatives is essential to the ''new order'' of this republic.

A second explanation of Indian ''clout'' is lobbying; or, in other words, Indian ''loot'' produces Indian clout. This may also be true, in some degree, and it is enlightening how many tribal lawyers discover that lobbying constitutes a major part of their job. However, lobbying as a *sole* source of power has two drawbacks. It costs money, and the more money you have the more clout you have. Tribes are not rich. They cannot afford to divert funds from basic social and health maintenance programs, or from subsidies to economic development. Every dollar expended in lobbying is taken away from some already substandard welfare program. Tribes can, moreover, be outlobbied by wealthier, adverse commercial interests. The only justification for a democracy in a market society must be that it costs very little to vote. In a pure market world, any individual or group concerned enough about some issue or problem simply comes to terms with those in control of it and purchases a satisfactory solution. But in the imperfect world of reality, a market for issues and problems would result in a practical aristocracy. The rich would have more say about all things than the poor. A democratic government tempers the natural supremacy of wealth in the market with the supremacy of numbers in elections. Social choices are made both in the market and in politics, with the distribution of wealth *in principle* limited in effect to the former.

As long as representation is sufficiently accountable—elections are frequent, ratios or representation are small, and representatives hold real power over national policy—this will be true. In fact, lobbying and corruption combine with the attenuation of our modern national legislature to give ''loot'' great status in both arenas. Tribes suffer both ways. They have little power in the market, and the system of representation gives them *no* direct voice in Congress, limiting them to the power of money there as well.

The last possible interpretation of Indian clout is that it is, in fact, an illusion. This is strongly suggested by the pattern of federal Indian legislation since 1934, including reorganization, termination, the "Indian Bill of Rights," and the Indian Self-Determination and Education Assistance Act, none of which have liberated tribes from federal governorship.[9]

The position of tribes in the House is comparable to that of the small states. States, however, are represented in the Senate. Small states enjoy equality in the Senate regardless of their weight in the House. They refused to join the Union without this provision, for fear that they would be annihilated,[10] cogent evidence that small political units such as tribes should be more concerned with their right to Senate seats than their impact on House elections.

Territories of the United States were permitted to send nonvoting delegates to the House, but not to the Senate, where their numerical impact would have been greater.[11] Many of the opponents of eventual statehood for the insular possessions indicated that they feared nonwhite representation in the Senate far more than in the House.[12] Tribal members may vote for senators from the state in which their reservation is situated. This is more than territories had, but it is unlikely to be effective. Of the twenty-four continental states with federally recognized reservation tribes, Indians make up 1 percent or more of the population of ten, and 5 percent or more of the population of only one.[13] Not all are reservation residents, and in most states the reservation vote is divided among several tribes. Thus while states are assured representation in the Senate regardless of size, tribes influence the composition of the Senate *only* as a function of their size, and none are large enough to influence it considerably.

Effective tribal representation in the House is impossible, but representation in the Senate is based upon political status rather than the size of the unit, and is therefore a promising target for Indian control over tribal destinies. It

---

9. Termination is subjected to a useful analysis in Gary Orfield, "A Study of the Termination Policy," in *The Organization Question* 673, Committee Print, Senate Committee on Labor and Public Welfare, Subcommittee on Indian Education, 91st Congress, 1st Session (1969). The Indian Bill of Rights is 25 U.S.C. 1302 (1968), discussed in Donald L. Burnett, Jr., "The Indian Civil Rights Act," 9 *Harvard Journal of Legislation* 557 (1972).

10. E.g., see 5 *Elliot's Debates* 168–180; also *id.* 107 for Madison's frank estimation of the need for compromise.

11. All tribes combined for House enumeration would yield one representative, but there are over two hundred independent tribes.

12. E.g., see Langdell's remark regarding the insular possessions: "It is to be sincerely hoped that they never will . . . be permitted to share in the government of this country, and especially to be represented in the United States Senate."

13. Arizona, Idaho, Montana, Nevada, New Mexico, North and South Dakota, Oklahoma, Utah and Washington. Arizona, with about 5 percent, is the highest.

will not be politically feasible for each tribe to obtain a Senate seat, because tribes greatly outnumber the states; we assume the states will never consent to it. Perpetuation of tribes must therefore depend upon some other ratio of direct representation in the body that has constitutional power over their existence.

Tribal citizens cannot fully enjoy their political franchise unless they are separately enumerated and represented. Merging their votes with those of the states in which they are fortuitously located geographically reminds us of Dean Tucker's argument that the American colonists had nothing to complain about, because they could always move to England and vote there.[14] Geographical location has no bearing on the evolution of separate interests—the criterion of representation understood by the framers. To draw an analogy with another critical point of the revolutionary debate, it is no answer to say that state boundaries no longer meaningfully reflect separate interests. That merely proves that current state boundaries are inconsistent with the federalism envisioned by the draftsmen of the Constitution. It demonstrates that non-Indian citizens have lost or relinquished liberty, not that Indians ought not to have liberty.

The legislative reapportionment cases of recent years have read the first and second sections of the Fourteenth Amendment for a requirement of "one-man, one-vote."[15] Each voter must have an equal influence on the composition of the legislature to which he is subject. Congress is, however, apportioned so as to exclude tribal representation in the Senate, not because tribes are small, since size is irrelevant in the Senate, but because they are not states. They are not states because Congress will not recognize them as eligible for statehood.

14. Chap. 1, n.13.
15. *Baker v. Carr*, 369 U.S. 186 (1962). A review of apportionment cases is found in *Reynolds v. Sims*, 377 U.S. 533, 554 *et seq.* (1964). See also *Lucas v. 44th General Assembly*, 377 U.S. 713 (1964). Ironically, this rule is being applied to reapportion tribal councils (e.g., *Daly v. U.S.*, 483 F. 2d 700 [C.A.S.D. 1974]) but not to reapportion tribal representation in Congress.

19

The Politics of Tribal Influence

It is always hazardous to forecast political outcomes. Too often power is moved by combinations of subtle forces so numerous they defy accurate interpretation; it is probably correct to say that the number of variables in a political contest is at least equal to the number of members in the society. In the case of the federal-tribal compact, however, certain historical patterns emerge sufficiently clearly to warrant an exercise in prediction.

When we leave the realm of judicial decisions and explore statutory remedies, we confront a political triad of unusually durable and intractable nature. The points of this triad are Congress, the bureau, and the states.[1] Tribes are not a part of this system; they lobby all three of its divisions but have no independent power of their own to exact compromises. On the contrary, Congress, bureau and states each enjoy a certain degree of control, adequate to exact compromises from the others.

The parameters of congressional action are supremacy and responsibility. Under the Constitution, Congress has exclusive authority over tribes. This empowers it to assume, as "trustee," virtual control of tens of millions of

1. Some readers may object to separate treatment of Congress and the states. In the context of Indian affairs, the distinction is a practical political reality. A minority of states enclose the greatest part of the tribal world. Congress therefore effectively represents those states which do *not* enclose reservation areas.

acres throughout the country which it would be unable to acquire constitutionally for its own use. But the price of control is high: formal responsibility for services to tribal Indians. Although tribes cannot always legally enforce this duty,[2] Congress must bear it to some extent for political reasons. There has always been a constituency of idealistic non-Indians who expect to see some effort made to improve the condition of the tribes: the heirs of Jefferson who organized the Lake Mohonk Conferences, wrote books like *A Century of Dishonor*, and founded the Association for American Indian Affairs. However misguided their priorities, their votes count for something as a check on congressional irresponsibility. Congress's only ultimate escape from responsibility is, therefore, to delegate it to the states.

Federal responsibility is, and always has been costly. The relative isolation, poverty, and resistance of tribes has made it costlier to serve them than other citizens. A stopgap response is to serve them with less, but this is politically sensitive because it involves overt racial discrimination. Besides, it is an incomplete solution. Congress's final solution to the "Indian problem" has always been to abolish tribes and throw Indians willy-nilly upon the good offices of the states. Rapidly mounting costs, and strong internal political pressure to divert federal funds to other uses, have at least twice triggered this policy on a large scale. The hearings and debates on allotment and termination legislation reveal a Congress preoccupied with budgetary priorities, not with Indians.[3]

This only succeeds because the parameters of state action are revenue and responsibility. The states, like Congress, prefer to minimize their expenditures on Indians. Unlike Congress, the states can benefit directly from the sale, distribution and development of tribal lands: their aim is to obtain Indian resources without responsibility. A compromise they will accept is to assume some control of tribal resources and some responsibility for services where there is, in the balance, net gain. In other words, Congress can compensate the states for assuming responsibility by freeing its hold on trust lands.

This is why allotment worked to the states' satisfaction, but termination did not. The allotment program first liquidated most reservation land, and

2. *U.S.* v. *Mason*, 412 U.S. 391, 398 (1973); *Gila River Pima-Maricopa Indian Community* v. *U.S.* 427 F. 2d 1194 (9th Cir. 1970).

3. Francis Paul Prucha, *Americanizing the American Indian* 80, 85, 89, 95 (Cambridge, Mass.: 1973); "Hearings, 'Officers and Employees of the Federal Government,' " 77, 119, *et passim*, Senate Committee on Civil Service, 80th Congress, 1st Session (1947).

required the states to extend their laws later. Termination required them first to extend their laws, then to wait some indeterminate time until the bureau was prepared to terminate its trusteeship of tribal lands. When by the 1960s few reservations had actually been terminated, many states felt that their accumulated service costs were too high a price to pay for the ever-decreasing chance of termination.

Congress sometimes deliberately implements Indian programs to benefit the states—a happy marriage of interests. Many merely pass federal funds through tribes to state economies. Programs for Indian education in public schools candidly compensate state school districts for nontaxable reservation land. Programs for economic development often have little or no capital component, thus simply passing wages through Indian employees to non-Indian suppliers of consumer goods in border towns. Job training has been criticized for relocating Indians in urban areas, where their incomes have no impact on reservation economies.

As between Congress and the states, we should anticipate a shifting compromise. At each point in time, both responsibility and control of resources will be shared, each party struggling to move the balance to a more favorable ratio of the two. The situation is complicated by the mediating influence of the bureau, which since its establishment in the Department of the Interior in 1849 has led a somewhat independent political existence.

Federal indulgence of this bureaucracy costs tax dollars, but voters experience little direct discomfort from tax allocation to federal agencies. To this extent, Congress can afford to respond favorably to agency requests. Certain other aspects of Indian administration are, however, particularly obnoxious to the states. Reservations reduce tax bases already weakened by federal taxation, and create demands for uncompensated services. They tie up resources that could energize state economic growth. Indian programs are therefore especially vulnerable to attacks by state government. Policy seesaws between pleasing the bureau and not displeasing the states.

The parameters of the bureau's activity are supremacy and growth. Like any other bureaucracy, it seeks to expand its power and increase its payroll. Legally, it has no power over Indians independent of Congress; it depends upon delegations of power, just as the states do. Politically, however, it does enjoy a kind of power independent of both Congress and the states: control of information. With this it can influence decisions selectively, without openly advocating any particular choice, and without revealing its own interests.

In the past the Bureau of the Census did not routinely publish reservation data because it did not classify tribes as local governments. When the Economic Development Administration first published its handbook, *Federal and State Indian Reservations*, in 1971, it decried the misunderstandings incident in "the severe shortage of reliable historical and statistical information."[4] Nearly all published data has originated with the Indian bureau.[5]

The bureau's role as expert witness in its own case supports an effective strategy for avoiding reductions in agency strength. When Congress becomes anxious over increases in federal spending on tribes, the agency must strike first and propose a plan for phasing itself out. As expert witness, it can easily persuade Congress that its own plan is the best, and have it implemented promptly. The plan must have two elements. It must be designed to fail to achieve Indian self-sufficiency, and its implementation must require additional funds and staff. When the plan fails, the bureau, again as expert witness, must persuade Congress that the reason for failure was the incompetence and unpreparedness of Indians, i.e., their inferiority.[6] From this base the bureau complains that its own, prephaseout programs to *improve* Indian competence were underfunded and fragmentary, and calls upon Congress to restore and expand these programs. Combined with the usual ratchet effect of public tax and spending increases, this means that the agency wins a long-term increase in strength as the reward for offering to sacrifice itself for the good of the Indians. The bureau enthusiastically supported both termination plans—allotment and termination—for several years before they became law.[7] In each case the agency, at its own request, assumed additional administrative and fiscal responsibilities to phase itself out.

Why does Congress rely on the bureau for expertise? Why don't tribes contradict the bureau's data? It is possible, but unlikely, that the nation's

4. From the "Foreword." The *Handbook* itself is, apparently, drawn primarily from Bureau of Indian Affairs' data rather than independent research.

5. Census data when available, do not always square with the bureau's (e.g., "Hearings, 'Officers and Employees of the Federal Government,'" 223–24).

6. Precisely the kind of philosophy which William Ryan describes in a more general context as "blaming the victim" (*Blaming the Victim* [New York: 1971]).

7. E.g., *Report of the Commissioner of Indian Affairs, 1877* 1; *1882* xlii–xliv; *1889* 3–4; *Report of the Secretary of the Interior, 1946* 376; *1949* 338; *1950* 342; *1951* 353.

lawmakers have never really appreciated that the bureau is as much an interested party as the tribes, and is, accordingly, no more reliable as a witness. Perhaps congress prefers to believe the testimony of educated, professional white men, rather than hear the contradiction of Indians. As a well-financed agency, the bureau can also do more convincing, comprehensive research than tribes and package the results more attractively, regardless of actual validity.

There is a more powerful, and less readily overcome factor. Tribes themselves have been forced to become the bureau's best supporters. If tribes fail to contradict the bureau, it is more often by choice than out of an appreciation of futility. There are several causes. Tribal members themselves know little more about their economic or legal status than what they learn from the bureau. Congress hoped the agency would advise and educate the tribes, and it has, after its own philosophy. It is not unusual to hear older tribal representatives repeating with sincerity unsubstantiated beliefs such as that all Indians are idle, or genetically prone to alcoholism, or that Indian family structure is unhealthy for Indian children, all of which strengthen the bureau's position vis-à-vis Congress and all of which originate in official bureau publications of the late nineteenth and early twentieth centuries.

Even the unconverted have cause to support the bureau. Since tribes have no formal delegation in Congress, and lack the capital resources to maintain permanent lobbies, the bureau assumes the role of mediator and spokesman. What tribes do not pay in dollars for this service, they pay by way of the expectation that they will back the agency's requests. It is a marriage of convenience, born of necessity. If tribes were wealthier, or were subsidized, like the territories, to send their own delegates to the House, they would have far less interest in supporting bureau programs.

The bureau's position reminds us of the "undertakers" of eighteenth-century Ireland, who, for a price, interceded with the corrupt, crown-controlled Irish Parliament on behalf of private interests. According to contemporary accounts, these brokers eventually became more powerful than the Irish Parliament itself, and were the principal target of both the Irish and emigré English nationalists.[8]

When the bureau approaches tribal leaders for support on an issue, it may be an offer they cannot refuse. The agency has so much discretion in

8. Pauline Maier, *From Resistance to Revolution* 178 (New York: 1972).

the allocation of funds, authorization of tribal programs, and development of reservation resources, that it can if it chooses hold up on any one of a number of actions beneficial to a tribe until it agrees to pay a ransom in the form of public support. It is like the warden asking his prisoners to say good things to the inspection committee. The power of the agency to reward and punish cooperation deprives tribes of any free choice in the matter. Felix Cohen lampooned this elegantly, in a passage worthy of quotation at length:

Two excuses are generally given for the Indian Bureau's current refusal to surrender any of its powers. One is the "all or nothing" approach.

When this approach is used, Indians who want to take over control of their own funds, or credits, or cattle, or supervise their local extension service, or manage their own roads department are told by the Commissioner, in effect:

"We are very glad to have you do these things, but first you must learn how to run a hospital because we want you also to take over the reservation hospital."

To the Indians, this looks like going to a grocery store to buy cabbages and having the grocer say:

"Yes, we have some very nice cabbages and I'll be happy to sell them to you, but first you must buy a hospital."

This may be termed the Rebuff Courteous. On the reservation, if tribal lawyers are not present, Bureau employees are apt to use the Retort Churlish.

"Your councilmen are talking about doing away with the Indian Bureau. If that doesn't stop, we're going to close down your hospital."

Bureau employees whose jobs are at stake, and who are well supplied with gasoline and expense money, are able to bring terrific pressure upon an Indian community to see that protests against Bureau extravagance are discouraged or that councilmen who voice such protests are not re-elected.

The second Bureau reply to those who urge that it transfer its authorities to local agencies is the fast buck pass to Congress. "This we would like to do, but Congress won't let us; why don't you get a law through Congress?" This approach is particularly useful when Congress is not in session.[9]

Albeit a little cynical, these observations are about as apt today as when Cohen wrote them twenty years ago.

Finally, it is unfortunately true that many tribal leaders believe that dissolution of the bureau will unavoidably lead to termination of the tribes. There is a certain degree of plausibility to this, in the current state of the law. The bureau is the best insurance against termination tribes have. As long as it is around, it will strive to perpetuate its clients. Tribes pay a high price for this service, but they have no alternative. The agency is

9. Felix S. Cohen, "The Erosion of Indian Rights," 62 *Yale Law Journal* 378–79 (1953).

something like a protection racket. The less tribes invest in supporting it, the more likely it is that Congress will terminate their political existence.

Tribal termination is not a *legally* necessary consequence. Tribes are not legal creatures of the bureau, either historically or in law, as we have shown. The bureau regulates tribes the same way the Interstate Commerce Commission regulates railroads or the Federal Trade Commission regulates advertising. Each is an example of an administrative overlay on a pre-existing institution or activity. Dissolve the agency and the activity returns to its preregulation status. No one would suppose, for example, that dissolving the Securities and Exchange Commission would automatically disband the New York Stock Exchange.

Indeed the conceptual danger of the recent Indian Self-Determination and Education Assistance Act is in its scheme of assimilating tribes into the bureau's administrative network, rather than openly transferring power to tribes to exercise independently of the bureau. The organization and policy of bureau offices whose functions are transferred to tribes will remain the same; the tribe obtains little more than the power to hire and fire.[10] In this way, the act, which was supported by the bureau, makes tribes look and function more and more like creatures of the agency, as opposed to separate sovereignties. Nothing could be better calculated to convince Indians and the public that tribes are legally inextricable from the Bureau of Indian Affairs and must stand or fall with it.

If Congress were to repeal all but two provisions of Title 25, it would eliminate most bureau functions with no diminution of tribal powers. We would save sections 16 and 17 of the Indian Reorganization Act, striking out any reference to secretarial approval of tribal charters or constitutions; and the Indian Financing Act, which, although inadequately funded and poorly managed, is an acceptable temporary foundation for converting the bureau into an agency of limited domestic assistance. This is purely hypothetical, but illustrative of how much current law has no other function than to augment and clarify bureau regulatory authority.

The only feasible way for tribes to achieve such a legislative solution is to begin by convincing themselves that the costs of bureau regulation outweigh the benefits. Then they must convince Congress. Development of an independent data base and acquisition of public status by tribe-oriented

10. R. L. Barsh and R. L. Trosper, "Title I of the Indian Self-Determination and Education Assistance Act of 1975," 3 *American Indian Law Review* 361 (1975).

scholars will prove essential. Tribes cannot expect to move Congress without the support of congressmen from noninvolved states, and cannot expect to win the support of these congressmen without competing with the bureau for their attention.

Even a sufficiently aware Congress cannot proceed with changes of the magnitude we suggest without the acquiescence or indifference of its non-Indian constituency. As it will be impossible to empirically demonstrate the tribal position to tens of millions of electors who share hostile preconceptions and almost total ignorance, tribes must market themselves at an ideological level. It is much easier to demonstrate philosophically that one body of ideas is consistent with or more powerful than another, than to empirically demolish the first body of ideas and prove the truth of the second. Tribes will succeed if they can intellectually rationalize their position into familiar ideologies. They will fail if they ignore or challenge these ideologies and attempt to justify tribalism entirely on its own terms.

Let us for example consider the prevailing political ideologies. Laying aside Republicanism and Democratism as increasingly empty referents, we see that a new right is evolving around the tenets of decentralization, fiscal restraint, accountability of social programs, and Millsian libertarianism. President Carter might have lost the 1976 election had he not openly combined these principles with his advocacy of new social programs, thereby stemming the quadrennial defection of right-wing Democrats to the Republican candidate. The tribal position is entirely consistent with the new right, although there are pitfalls. Tribes need to disestablish a very expensive, self-perpetuating and nonaccountable federal agency. If the bureau were disestablished and only one-half of its budget distributed in direct revenue-sharing among tribes, both the tribes and taxpayers would benefit substantially. Tribes also agree with the principle of decentralization. They insist upon local control of domestic programs, without congressional or administrative interference. So do the states. Indeed, the states should be made to see in tribes an omen of their own fate should centralization of power in the United States continue unchecked.

Unfortunately, many states believe they have an interest in dispossessing tribes of their political rights and resources. Of course, we refer to the thirteen states which enclose substantial reservation areas.[11] Although they

11. Arizona, Idaho, Minnesota, Montana, Oregon, Nevada, New Mexico, North Dakota, South Dakota, Washington, Wisconsin, Wyoming, and Utah. Much smaller reservation

are a minority in both House and Senate, tribes cannot afford to risk ignoring them. Here, ideologies are in apparent conflict. For more than a century these states have viewed reservations as an undesirable federal intrusion into their domestic affairs. To them, decentralization therefore means absorption of tribal areas and jurisdiction.

Practically, states and tribes can and must be partially reconciled. Neither can successfully advance the principle of decentralization in its own interest without recognizing correlative rights in the other. When tribes and states do battle, it makes both appear irresponsible and hurts the cause of decentralization generally. Nonaligned states take this as evidence that the federal government must perpetually supervise both factions for their own good, a future neither desires.

Tribes have routinely employed the threat of federal intervention as a weapon against the states. In an era of increasing anti-Washington sentiment, tribal identification with the general government may prove dangerous. If tribes fail to form a coalition with the states before Congress is forced to thin the federal bureaucracy, it is probable that not only the bureau, but tribes themselves, will be among the casualties. Bureaucracy-trimming in the hands of a fiscally conservative, state-oriented Congress sympathetic to tribal self-government would prove beneficial to tribes. In the hands of a fiscally conservative, state-oriented Congress convinced that tribes are a mere tool of federal administration, bureaucracy-trimming would prove a disaster.

Tribes should anticipate danger from the liberal left. In general spirit, American liberalism is favorable to racial and ethnic minority interests. It is the method that counts, however, not good intentions. Liberals will tend to recoil from tribal government as "racist." This ideological barrier must be overcome. Even if it is overcome, tribes must beware the close historical association of liberalism and restrictive regulation of reservations. Bureau overlordship of tribal government was the brainchild of the "Quaker" or "Peace Party" in Grant's administration. Their intentions were idealistic and protective. Reconstruction had given them a unique opportunity to experiment with their theories of social engineering and

---

concentrations are located in California, Colorado, Florida, Iowa, Kansas and Nebraska. By contrast, there are major urban concentrations in New York City, Detroit, and "relocation" centers such as San Francisco/Oakland, Portland, Seattle, and Phoenix; and very large nonreservation but nonetheless tribal concentrations in North Carolina (Lumbees) and Oklahoma.

improvement. Like the disciples of a messianic cult, frustration and failure simply increased their fervor. Indians were their first target after the South; next, in the early years of our own century, were the laboring poor.

"Protective" laws limit choice and frequently impose higher economic burdens on the "protected" group. Sometimes they may be justified by the dangers or costs they protect against. Unfortunately, the liberal left is as dogmatically committed to protective legislation, for Indians and others, as the right is to deregulation. Tribes' opting for deregulation alienates them from the political sector that has traditionally sought to be their patron and benefactor, albeit through services and supervision rather than political emancipation. This will confuse liberals, and persuade many Indians and non-Indians alike that tribes are "selling out" to the states and big business. The acceleration of investment on reservations that will probably follow upon deregulation will confirm their suspicions. Tribes may therefore expect a "backlash" of protective sentiment following the enactment of deregulatory laws.

One final political dimension is worthy of consideration. Americans are far from abandoning their Cold War weltanschauung of a mortal struggle between democracy and communism, capitalism and socialism. Tribes stand in a peculiar relationship to this ideological contest. In the 1920s they were earnestly accused, by scholars, of being communistic, and this was described as being very bad.[12] When he assumed command of the bureau, John Collier produced a considerable amount of propaganda to rebut this; his reports during the Second World War were replete with examples of Indian patriotism and love of democracy.[13] But the fact remains that tribal economies are frequently socialized, not entirely without the encouragement of the bureau, and that many tribes believe this works quite well. Conditions of extreme poverty, and economies reliant on development of natural resources through environmentally-sensitive technologies, combine to make public ownership and control relatively desirable at the present time in many cases.[14] Tribes often share historical philosophies which

12. E.g., see "Hearings, 'Law and Order on Indian Reservations of the Northwest,' " 14173–75, 14188–89, Senate Committee on Indian Affairs, 82nd Congress, 1st Session (1932).

13. See the *Reports* of the secretary of the interior for the war years, e.g., the *1940* Report at 363, and the *1944* Report at 238.

14. R. L. Barsh and J. Y. Henderson, "Tribal Administration of Natural Resource Development," 52 *North Dakota Law Review* 307 (1975).

place a high value on distributive equity, and are consistent with, if not demanding of, a large public-wage sector. Can tribes admit this to the general public and still hope to win political support, especially from the conservative right?

The tribal position will seem contradictory to economic conservatives. On the one hand, tribes will seek deregulation of their governments and economies. This is consistent with free-market economic thinking. On the other hand, many tribes will propose to apply their emancipated political powers to the expansion and development of public industries and services much more ''socialized'' than any comparable state example. It would seem to be of no use in the long run for tribes to try to hide their theories of public policy from potential allies, lest the inevitable falling-out be more destructive than the current state of affairs. The alternative, then, must be for tribes to persuade economic conservatives that tribal policy is not fundamentally inconsistent with capitalism. We believe that it is possible to do this by demonstrating that tribes' distributive goals can be rationalized within the economic theory of public goods, and that their public operation of natural resource industries can be squared with the theory of environmental externalities. Tribal economists and spokesmen have their work cut out for them. At this time we can only identify the problem.

20

Wealth and Power

The Congress and the States have long neglected the rights of an American who has not been able to amass powerful lobby groups, large sums of money, and vast numbers of political crusaders.[1]

We have argued that Indian representation is inadequate because of federal electoral policy and apportionment. A second and possibly more powerful argument is that Indian representation fails because of Indian poverty. Poverty results in an inability to collect information, disseminate information, and monitor the political process, all apart from the fact that wealth is the wherewithal of political corruption. Effective participation in a procedurally egalitarian political system requires a continuous, largely non-recoverable investment in detecting the trend of the lawmakers and lobbying for their attentions.

Revolutionary patriots emphasized the relatively equal distribution of wealth in the new republic so often that it is fair to assume they regarded it as fundamental to the preservation of liberty. Noah Webster voiced their insight succinctly in a pamphlet urging adoption of the Constitution. Throughout history, he argued:

We observe that the power of the people has increased in an exact proportion to their acquisitions of property. Wherever the right of primogeniture is established, property must accumulate and remain in families. Thus the landed property in

1. Senator Ervin in "Hearings, 'Rights of Members of Indian Tribes,' " 136, House Committee on Interior and Insular Affairs, Subcommittee on Indian Affairs, 90th Congress, 2nd Session (1968).

England will never be sufficiently distributed, to give the powers of government wholly into the hands of the people. But to assist the struggle for liberty, commerce has interposed, and in conjunction with manufacturers, thrown a vast weight of property into the democratic scale. Wherever we cast our eyes, we see this truth, that *property* is the basis of *power*; and this, being established as a cardinal point, directs the means of preserving our freedom. Make laws, irrevocable laws in every state, destroying and barring entailments; leave real estates to revolve from hand to hand, as time and accident may direct; and no family influence can be acquired and established for a series of generations . . . the laborious and saving, who are generally the best citizens, will possess each his share of property and power, and thus the balance of wealth and power will continue where it is, in the *body of the people.*

A general and tolerably equal distribution of landed property is the whole basis of national freedom.[2]

The logic of this position is plain. If wealth is necessary to a voice in government, and land is (as it most definitely was in 1787) the chief source of wealth, then the policy of an enlightened republic should be to eliminate all legal obstacles to the free flow of agrarian commerce. In classical economic doctrine, commoditization of land and the eradication of dualistic and imperfect factor markets will result in a fairly uniform diffusion of wealth. Free enterprise will thus guarantee each individual his due influence in the councils of government.[3] "The only possible way of preserving public virtue," John Adams concluded, "is to make the acquisition of land easy to every member of society."[4]

Information, visibility and money were all part of the same process. Money buys information and visibility; therefore an alternative to equal-

2. Noah Webster, *An Examination into the leading principles of the Federal Constitution . . . By a Citizen of America* (Philadelphia: 1787); Charles Pinckney in 4 *Elliot's Debates on the Confederation and Constitution* 320−23 (Washington, D.C.: 1830−1845); George Logan, *Letter to the Citizens of Pennsylvania on the Necessity of Promoting Agriculture, Manufactures and the Useful Arts* (Philadelphia: 1800).

3. We recognize that eighteenth-century Americans' economic egalitarianism was capitalistic, i.e., an egalitarianism of access to the marketplace rather than literal equality of wealth (E.A.J. Johnson, "Federalism, Pluralism, and Public Policy," 22 *Journal of Economic History* 427 [1962]; Morton J. Horwitz, "The Legacy of 1776 in Legal and Economic Thought," 19 *Journal of Law & Economics* 621 [1976]).

4. Charles Francis Adams, ed., 9 *Works of John Adams* 376−77 (Boston: 1850−1856). For Jefferson's similar views see Alfred Whitney Griswold, *Farming and Democracy* 18−46 (New York: 1948). Also David Ramsay in *An Address to the Freemen of South Carolina, on the Subject of the Constitution* (Charlestown, S.C.: 1787): "In a country like our's [sic], abounding with free men all of one rank, where property is equally diffused, where estates are held in fee simple, the press free, and the means of information common, tyranny cannot reasonably find admission."

izing wealth is to equalize information. A free and independent press, in principle, reports all views and events equally, mitigating the visibility of wealth, and distributing information to the whole people. When Dr. Ramsay advocated adoption of the Federal Constitution, he professed his faith that with a tolerably even diffusion of land *and a free press*, America had nothing to fear from the defects of any republican frame of government. "[T]he people at large generally determine right," Oliver Ellsworth argued, "when they have had means of information."[5]

Many of Webster's and Ramsay's colleagues were less confident in the power of a free market to equalize wealth.[6] Madison and Hamilton reasoned that economic liberty would inevitably polarize men into competing economic interest groups, some characterized by wealth, and others by numbers. "In framing a system which we wish to last for ages," Madison warned the Convention, "we should not lose sight of the changes which ages will produce."

An increase of population will of necessity increase the proportion of those who will labor under all the hardships of life, and secretly sigh for a more equal distribution of its blessings. These may in time outnumber those who are placed above the feelings of indigence. According to the equal laws of suffrage, the power will slide into the hands of the former.[7]

Webster feared the power of wealth, Madison the power of numbers. Madison's remedy was to enshrine wealth in the Senate, according it a separate representation analogous to the separate representation of the states. He would have had the government reinforce the economy's tendency, as he saw it, to perpetuate inequality.

The failure of Madison's proposal did not make a majority of the Convention Websterites. They never went so far as expressly to provide in the Constitution for economic equalization or checks on the accumulation

5. "Letters of Landholder" (1787), Letter No. 1, reprinted in Paul Leicester Ford, *Essays on the Constitution of the United States* 139 (Brooklyn, N.Y.: 1892). Similarly, George Clinton's "Letters of Cato" (1787), Letter No. 5, reprinted in Ford, *Essays.*

6. Of individual men Madison deemed this true, but of the states collectively, "[a]lthough their climate varied considerably, yet, as the governments, laws, and the manners, of all, were nearly the same, and the intercourse between different parts perfectly free, population, industry, arts, and the value of labor, would constantly tend to equalize themselves" (5 *Elliot's Debates* 299–300).

7. 5 *Elliot's Debates* 242–43. Compare Yates's version of the same speech (1 *Elliot's Debates* 449–450); also the remarks of Hamilton (5 *Elliot's Debates* 244, 1 *Elliot's Debates* 450–51) and Johnson (1 *Elliot's Debates* 431).

or uses of wealth. If anything, the influence of wealth on power is a problem never fully resolved in our constitutional jurisprudence. The recent case of *Buckley v. Valeo* is illustrative.[8] The Supreme Court found itself caught between a contemporary legislative policy of equalizing political opportunities, and the apparent prohibition in the First Amendment against limiting the availability of political information.

"Discussion of public issues and debate on the qualifications of the candidates are integral to the operation of the system of government established by our Constitution," the Court agreed, and "virtually every means of communicating ideas in today's mass society requires an expenditure of money."[9] In the absence of any clear contrary direction in the Constitution, they felt compelled to read the First Amendment for a policy of maximizing political information regardless of its quality, reliability, or source.

The concept that government may restrict the speech of some elements of our society in order to enhance the relative voice of others is wholly foreign to the First Amendment, which was designed "to secure the 'widest possible dissemination of information from diverse and antagonistic sources.' "[10]

The Court purported to distinguish between a ceiling on contributions and a ceiling on candidates' own expenditures. Inherent in contributions was the added danger that they "will be given as a *quid pro quo* for improper commitments from the candidates," a practice by which "the integrity of our system of representative democracy is undermined."[11] It must be pointed out, notwithstanding, that a candidate's agreement with a direct contributor is no more enforceable than an agreement made with one who contributes indirectly by spending the money himself on campaign promotions. The ceiling on direct contributions will therefore have little effect on political contracts. While the Court sustained some parts of the law, the practical effect of its decision was to eliminate all limitations on the use of superior wealth in politics.

The Court expressed faith in the sufficiency of legislative apportionment to "assure that citizens are accorded an equal right to vote for their

8. 96 S. Ct. 612 (1976).
9. *Id.* 632–35, 638.
10. *Id.* 649. Also 649 n.55: "Democracy depends on a well-informed electorate." Evidently the Court was forced to squirm to avoid the implications of its previous decisions sustaining the F.C.C.'s "fairness doctrine" (*id.*).
11. *Id.* 638, 648.

representatives regardless of factors or wealth or geography,''[12] intimating that proportional representation obviates other means of "equalizing the relative ability of all voters to affect electoral outcomes.''[13] In a footnote, however, it conceded that incumbents, at least, benefitted from their "access to substantial resources provided by the government'' such as "local and Washington offices, staff support, and the franking privilege.''[14] The opinion as a whole vacillates between admissions and denials of the premise that wealth is an advantage in politics.

Supposing that we cannot limit the enjoyment of this advantage by those who have it, it becomes all the more important to guarantee universal economic mobility. If the poor cannot constitutionally equalize their voice by restricting the rich, they must have the opportunity to achieve political equality by acquiring riches. Any law that tends to keep the poor, poor, is necessarily a political law abridging liberty and the franchise.

It is evident from a review of Indian affairs that Indians are not only poor but have been systematically subjected to a dualistic market by federal law. Federal statutes establish an administrative hierarchy for validating and regulating the economic decisions of Indians and their communities.[15] Segregated markets are typically created by regulatory agencies with a view to *equalizing* factor prices, for example by increasing the costs of natural monopolies and decreasing the costs of the suppliers of public goods. On the contrary, federal law imposes higher costs on Indian businesses without a showing that some real-world imperfection would otherwise give Indians an advantage in trade. In fact, while all other regulation is directed at particular industries found to enjoy advantages or suffer from the disadvantages of market imperfections, only with regard to tribal Indians do we create a segregated market defined in terms of *political association*. The

12. *Id.* 649 n. 55.
13. *Id.* 638.
14. *Id.* 640 n.33.
15. R. L. Barsh and J. Y. Henderson, "Tribal Administration of Natural Resource Development,'' 52 *North Dakota Law Review* 307 (1975). A related point is that the territories were more often controlled (when at all) by the manipulation of federal financial aid than by direct regulation of their political affairs (Earl S. Pomeroy, *The Territories and the United States* 32–33 [Seattle: 1969]). Pomeroy's observation that federal aid to the territories was "small enough to be a chronic grievance, large enough to be a persistent deterrent to movements for statehood'' (*id.* 50) rings equally true for today's tribes. Sar A. Levitan and William B. Johnston, *Indian Giving* 9 (Baltimore: 1975), conclude that the "concentration of federal assistance . . . means that the economies and social structure of reservations are totally dominated by the federal presence.'' See, too, Alan L. Sorkin, *American Indians and Federal Aid* (Washington, D.C.: 1971).

nineteenth-century argument that these restraints are of a racial nature justified by Indians' infirmities is empirically insubstantial and repugnant to our Constitution.

Economic repression was at the heart of the American Revolution. "Is it not the avowed Policy of the whole Kingdom," Americans demanded, "that we are to be restrained . . . in every Exertion for our continental Interest, if it should be judged to interfere in the least with their Systems of Wealth?"[16] Most essential to liberty is man's "Right to enjoy the Fruit of his Labour, Art and Industry as far as by it he hurts not the Society."[17] In a free government, this right is preserved, but in the kingdom of a despot there are "perpetual Uncertainties, or rather certain Oppression, [and] no Men will embark large Stocks and extensive Talents for Business." Tribes well understand that condition. The uncertainties of discretionary administrative disposition have discouraged economic development and deprived tribes of the wealth prerequisite to effective political action.

The importance of effective political opportunities in our system of government cannot be overemphasized. The Bill of Rights is not a sufficient safeguard of citizens' liberties. James Iredell criticized it as a mere "paper limitation," of no more than ideological value.[18] After all, would an evil Congress be less bold to usurp power if there were a Bill of Rights? Would a patriotic Congress usurp the people's freedoms even if a strict construction of the Constitution might absolve it?

Iredell made much of the necessity of "confidence" in government. A realist, it was his position that the character of leaders would prove far more instrumental in preserving liberty than the Constitution itself. No written guarantees could fully immunize the country from clever scoundrels in the federal city. He was, perhaps, too optimistic. Responding to George Mason's fears that an unscrupulous president might contrive to manipulate the pardoning power to conceal criminal conspiracies to which he was a party, Iredell argued that the fear of such a man being placed in high office was "chimerical." History has vindicated Colonel Mason.

16. Silas Downer, quoted in Pauline Maier, *From Resistance to Revolution* (New York: 1972).

17. *Id*. 30; Thomas Pownall, 1 *The Administration of the British Colonies* 106 (5th ed. London: 1774).

18. James Iredell, *Answers to Mr. Mason's objections to the new Constitution*, reprinted in Paul Leicester Ford, *Pamphlets on the Constitution of the United States* 335 (Brooklyn, N.Y.: 1892).

At the first new Congress, Madison doggedly represented the state conventions that had ratified with the understanding that a Bill of Rights would be added by amendment. However, Madison must have shared Iredell's cynicism about "paper limitations," because he introduced a proposal of his own, that "the people have an indubitable, inalienable, and indefeasible right to reform or change their Government, whenever it may be found adverse or inadequate to the purposes of its institution."[19]

Where Iredell was prepared to rely upon the good faith of leaders, Madison would have left the way clear to revolutionary recommitments to fundamental principles in the spirit of the Declaration of Independence. Neither approach is truly satisfactory. If Iredell was correct about "paper limitations," then we should be no less secure by disposing of the Constitution altogether and relying upon a traditional frame of government, as does Great Britain. There is no reason to hold a mere paper limitation less potent than a mere paper enumeration of specific delegations of power. On the other hand, no one would suppose that a government can long exist that refers all demands for change to an "appeal to heaven."

It is very striking that no attention was paid during the ratification period to the possible role of the Supreme Court in utilizing the Bill of Rights to check federal excesses as a nonviolent alternative to popular resistance. It does not appear that the delegates were openly agreeable to lodging such a power in the Court.[20] The matter was only briefly touched upon during the Convention at Philadelphia and not at all in the state conventions. In truth, although the Court's legislative review power has grown into an institution of great weight in our national affairs, it depends, as legal scholars have so often pointed out, entirely upon public confidence in the Court and the execution of its decrees by the president.

The significance of the Constitution is, therefore, not so much in its declaration of what government will and will not do, as in its outlining of a *process* for constituting our governors. Our electoral franchise and equal representation assure us of control over those who have the sheer power to defy all of the "paper limitations" of the Constitution. Iredell's notion of

---

19. Herman V. Ames, "The Proposed Amendments to the Constitution of the United States," 185, 2 *Annual Report of the American Historical Association, 1896.*

20. E.g., see 5 *Elliot's Debates* 151, 164, 344, 429. Such a power was proposed to be lodged in a "Council of Revision," which never materialized. See also *The Federalist*, No. 78.

"confidence" makes sense, and the threat of insurrection is unnecessary, only as long as the people are enlightened, aggressive, *and have equal access to their representatives and to information about their representatives' activities.* Equal access depends upon at least some tolerably equal distribution of wealth. That is why Webster believed that the rights of persons in the first amendments were "all inferior" to the ability to acquire an equal share of the nation's wealth. Indeed, he described the right to acquire knowledge and the right of election as the two "auxiliary supports" that give practical significance to the "basic right" of security of property.[21] The Indian experience amply demonstrates the truth of his argument.

21. Noah Webster, *An Examination*. It might be fair to say that land ownership in a democratic society includes two general kinds of rights: the use of the land under law, and *participation in the process of changing the law*. If the latter is abridged, as it is for Indians, the value of land ownership decreases. That raises a substantial *Fifth* Amendment issue in challenge to federal supervision of tribal resources. On the extent to which the framers of the Constitution held the protection of property to be one of the most, if not the most important function of the new republican government, see 5 *Elliot's Debates* 243, 247, 260, 270, 275, 370–72, 386–89.

21

Tribal Political Liberty
and Social Forces

THE LIBERALS' DILEMMA

In the generation following *Brown v. Board of Education*,[1] political liberals and a liberal judiciary have labored for racial assimilation. Advocacy of racial equality has become synonymous with, and essential to, liberal political identity. In this context reservations are immediately assumed to be pernicious outposts of "ghettoization." Liberals' confusion of racial and political issues in the contemporary Indian movement persuades them that support for tribal government violates their past labors, their dreams, and their ideals.

Congress's "plenary power" is racially defined.[2] Title 25 of the United States Code is captioned "Indians," not "Tribes." Many tribal constitutions and the bureau's model penal code authorize tribal jurisdiction over "Indians" within their reservations, not "members" or "persons."[3] Even when the Bureau of "Indian" Affairs limits its services to "tribal members," non-Indians see this as limiting services to persons of one race *in effect*.

1. 347 U.S. 483 (1954).
2. See the approving reference to *U.S. v. Sandoval*, 231 U.S. 28 (1913), in *Baker v. Carr*, 369 U.S. 186, 215 (1962). See also 25 U.S.C. 2, 9, 13, establishing authority and appropriations for "Indian affairs" not "tribal" affairs.
3. 25 C.F.R. 11.2, 11.22, 11.38–11.74.

This confusion of racial and political categories is particularly striking in the recent case of *Morton v. Mancari*,[4] testing the constitutionality of federal laws and regulations according tribal members preference in hiring for the Bureau of Indian Affairs.[5] Writing for a unanimous Court, Justice Blackmun argued that the preference was not actually a racial one, but "an employment criterion reasonably designed to further the cause of tribal self-government and to make the BIA more responsive to the needs of its constituent groups."[6] The purpose of the Indian Reorganization Act, out of which Indian preference grew, was "to establish machinery whereby Indian tribes would be able to assume a greater degree of self-government, both politically and economically."[7] Since Indians had historically been undereducated and hence excluded from responsible leadership positions, hiring preference was a reasonable step in increasing their skills.[8] Indeed, Justice Blackmun expressed some concern that,

If these laws, derived from historical relationships and explicitly designed to help only Indians, were deemed invidious racial discrimination, an entire Title of the United States Code (25 U.S.C.) would be effectively erased.[9]

It should be kept in mind that the magnitude of an unconstitutional abuse of power is no justification of its continuance. The Court's use of an argument "from long usage" is eerily reminiscent of Chief Justice Marshall's argument that the doctrine of aboriginal title, albeit pretentious, could not be judicially abrogated on account of its pervasiveness and historical precedence.[10]

Justice Blackmun explained that Indian preference "is directed to participation by the governed in the governing agency,"[11] and is comparable to the requirement that elected officials be residents of the districts they represent. Why then, doesn't the law provide that each local branch of the bureau give preference to members of the particular tribes that branch serves? Or limit preference to persons actually residing on federally

4. 417 U.S. 535 (1974).
5. B.I.A.M. 335, 3.1, quoted at 417 U.S. 553 n.24. The original statutory authorization did not require tribal membership (25 U.S.C. 472).
6. 417 U.S. 554–55.
7. *Id.* 542.
8. *Id.* 543–44.
9. *Id.* 552.
10. Compare Justice Brennan's use of an argument from long usage in *DeCouteau v. District Court*, discussed in Chap. 14.
11. 417 U.S. 555.

supervised lands? The preference rule requires that an individual be a tribal member *and at least one-fourth Indian*. If Congress intended to promote a purely political objective, why did it not employ a purely political classification? And what about "participation by the governed in the governing agency?" We were under the impression that tribes governed, not the bureau. *Morton* is strongly suggestive of a disposition to regard the bureau as the true government of reservations, and concomitantly to look, perhaps, with skepticism at tribal claims of political liberty from arbitrary and discretionary agency supervision. Indeed, it may be described as holding that Indians' right to political liberty is satisfied through employment in the bureau. It is a strange thing indeed to suppose that a people's desire for self-government can be fulfilled by working for their governors. Would other Americans be satisfied to abolish the Congress, make the presidency perpetual, and submit their state governments to presidential veto, in return for an expansion in the number of federal administrative jobs?

THE TWO INDIAN MOVEMENTS

There are two Indian movements today, one ethnic and one political. Both are adaptive strategies by Indians to federal policy. They must be carefully separated in the public mind or both will fail. Indeed, they must also be separated in the minds of Indians.

The ethnic movement shares the same basic goals and strategies as contemporary civil rights movements. The constituency of the ethnic Indian movement are persons who identify themselves as Indians by ancestry and culture, but who are not now and do not anticipate being tribal citizens. Many are not members of extant tribes, and many cannot identify their tribe of origin with reasonable certainty. They are "Indian" in the same way a third-generation French-American is "French" or a Nisei is "Japanese." Their commonalty is not genuinely racial, because blood quantum varies from 100 percent to supposed. The ethnic movement has its power in the cities, especially those cities which, almost a generation ago now, served as the principal terminals for the federal relocation program.

The ethnic Indian movement is in agreement with the ideal of *procedural equality*. Two groups are procedurally equal if both are afforded the same range of alternatives and can choose among them in the same way. Procedural equality is fundamentally assimilationist. It assumes that all groups *want* to choose from among the same range of alternatives, the alternatives having been previously established by a dominant or oppressor group. A group becomes procedurally equal when it is assimilated to the dominant group's laws, and does not seek procedural equality unless already assimilated to its goals and values.

The tribal movement, on the other hand, seeks *political equality*, i.e., the right to establish goals and values, and make laws. Tribalists are active members of and, typically, residents of tribes. They may be as diverse racially as members of the ethnic movement, and as homogeneous culturally. But their rhetoric is the rhetoric of political liberty, not of civil rights. Their commonalty is political: they choose their own citizenship and system of government, and share the benefits and burdens of tribal citizenship.

Race is incidental to tribal citizenship. Before the reservation period, tribes freely naturalized nonmember Indians and non-Indians on the basis of their usefulness and willingness to respect tribal law.[12] They did this no differently than any other nation. It was Congress that limited new tribal "adoptions" to other Indians, as a way of limiting the United States' potential financial responsibilities.[13] "Obviously," Chairman Howard of the House Committee on Indian Affairs told Congress forty years ago, "the line must be drawn somewhere or the Government would take on

12. For example, the Chickasaw Constitution, Article II, sec. 3, simply referred to members "by birth or adoption" (*Constitution, Laws and Treaties of the Chickasaws* [1878]); the Cherokee Constitution, Article III, sec. 5 and Article IV, sec. 2, referred generally to "citizens," from which only blacks were excluded (*The Constitution and Laws of the Cherokee Nation* [1892]); Sac & Fox and Osage followed the Cherokee model exactly (*The Constitution and Laws of the Sac and Fox Nation* [1888], *The Constitution and Laws of the Osage Nation 1881–1882* [1888]); Muskogee referred to "citizens" without distinction as to race (*The Constitution and Laws of the Muskogee Nation* [1880]). The Chickasaw Constitution, under "General Provisions," sec. 7, provided that all naturalized Chickasaws shall enjoy equal rights. The only exception was the Choctaw Constitution, Article VII, sec. 2, which limited officeholding to lineal descendants of Choctaws; but voting or citizenship do not appear to have been so restricted (*The Constitution and Laws of the Choctaw Nation* [Folsom ed. 1869]). Among contemporary tribes, three Pueblos continue to exercise unrestricted powers of naturalization, at least on paper: the Isleta, Constitution, Article II(3); Laguna, Constitution, Article II(1) (f); Santa Clara, Constitution, Article II(2) George E. Fay, *Charters, Constitutions and By-Laws of Indian Tribes of North America* [Greeley, Colo.: 1967–1971]).

13. 25 U.S.C. 372a, 25 C.F.R. 11.29, and the tribal constitutions approved in accordance with the Indian Reorganization Act. The effectiveness of this device may be imagined by comparing the population characteristics of tribes like the Cherokees, which had been naturalizing non-Indians for generations before the era of intervention, and tribes like the Dakota Sioux, which were subjected to federal supervision before they came into regular contact with non-Indian populations.

impossible financial burdens."[14] In other words, the characteristic racial character of contemporary tribes is more a product of federal manipulation than tribal discrimination.

Unfortunately, the racial bias on tribal membership imposed by the United States has begun to impress itself on the ideology of tribalists, partly out of necessity, and partly from the lack of an appropriate alternative conceptualization of their identity. Federal laws setting forth the powers of the bureau, establishing reservations, and providing services for them, are essentially paternalistic. Most proceed from an assumption that "Indians" are ignorant and helpless, and require benevolent supervision removed from the contaminating influences of non-Indians. Paternalistic laws are repressive, but tribalists prefer a repressed tribal society to immediate political assimilation. They do what they can to perpetuate reservations and the laws that maintain them, and therefore also unavoidably the racial theories that justify the laws. If tribalists denied that reservations were necessary to protect "helpless Indians," they would deny, in most people's minds, the legitimate need for reservations at all.

At the same time, tribal Indians have been confronted in recent years with the necessity of distinguishing themselves from the urban ethnic movement. Since after a few generations of interspersal with the non-Indian population many "urban" Indians look less "Indian," race presents itself as a convenient, if not entirely appropriate discriminator. Indeed, race presents itself in this context for precisely the same reason it has always become a basis for making arbitrary social distinctions: it is easy to enforce and administer in a mass, impersonal society. It is much simpler merely to look at people, rather than examine political beliefs and allegiance, their values, and cultural affinity, before admitting them to membership in a common cause.

Tribalists accordingly try to defend the integrity of their movement by setting restrictive blood quotas on membership in their political organizations. This is potentially fatal. It bars many individuals who, though racially less "Indian," are deeply committed to the political goals of tribalists, and could prove serviceable. Similarly, it recognizes as a constituency racial Indians who have no desire to support the movement, no social bond with tribal society, and no real interest in its outcome. Most

14. 78 *Congressional Record* 11732 (15 June 1934); "Hearings, 'To Grant Indians . . . Freedom to Organize,' " 264, Senate Committee on Indian Affairs, 73rd Congress, 2nd Session (1934).

dangerously, it redefines the movement in the eyes of the majority as a struggle for racial segregation, rather than political self-determination—as an impermissible rather than a historically and constitutionally valid objective.[15]

It is extremely difficult to conceptualize a political movement so clearly that intellectual criteria for participation can be set. Yet Republicans are republican, Democrats democratic. Each political party sets standards for the commonalty which defines it. Tribalists cannot fail to do as much. When the self-identification of a party or movement becomes vague, the movement splinters and turns on itself, as recent national political party history so eminently demonstrates.

Even if tribalists succeed in defining their movement in political rather than racial terms, many people will still accuse them of being de facto racists. The evidence persists in the racial composition of tribal memberships. As long as this criticism presents itself to the public mind, tribalists will lose two potentially powerful coalitions: blacks and white liberals. Both groups are fundamentally committed against racism. Both see tribes as racist institutions, and understandably tend to be comfortable with federal efforts to assimilate Indians in urban areas. Since they see tribes as racist institutions, and believe that racist institutions are necessarily evil, they cannot conceive of any value in the perpetuation of tribal government.

The problem is one of misconception. Is Italy or Japan a racist nation? Almost everyone in the former is white, and almost everyone in the latter is Asian. These differences are not maintained by law, but result from historical demographic and socioeconomic patterns. The mere fact that a political unit has a racial characteristic does not render it racist. Similarly, if a city or state within the United States is predominantly white or black, it is not required to import families of the opposite color. Even the school busing program is a limited strategem; no serious thought has been given to moving the parents along with the children. If a city or state discourages immigration generally, without regard to race, it violates nothing in the Constitution. American demography is replete with examples of historical,

---

15. For an interesting empirical study of race as a boundary criterion see Ronald L. Trosper, "Case Study: Native American Boundary Maintenance," 3 *Ethnicity* 256 (1976). Professor Trosper concludes that property, not race, is the principal determinant of tribal boundaries. We disagree. In our judgment the special property rights attaching to tribal membership are insignificant compared with the value of the right of political participation, and the strength of belief in a common destiny.

de facto racial concentrations and enclaves at the local, city, state and regional levels.

Tribes are historical racial enclaves. Despite their own willingness to incorporate non-Indians in the nineteenth century, the federal government itself required the maintenance of a high degree of racial homogeneity. Most tribes are now loath to accept *any* new members, Indian or non-Indian, because of the scarcity of resources to service them. Is this a constitutionally compelling reason to deny tribal self-government?

The liberals' rejoinder might well be, "If tribes are sincerely nonracist, let them prove it now by removing all restrictions on immigration and land ownership, and allowing all residents, white or Indian, to vote." At this juncture in history, it would be extremely hazardous for any tribe to attempt this. It would destroy itself in the act of demonstrating its good faith. The reason is simple. Under federal supervision, development of tribal resources has languished. Reservations remain very poor, and very undeveloped. Altering land ownership and the franchise would attract immigration. Immigrants would demand services of a tribal government already incapable of serving its original population. If that did not succeed in bankrupting the tribe, the immigrants could use their votes to modify or abolish tribal law. After all, they would have no reason to prefer tribal law to the laws of their own states of origin.[16]

Besides, although it is true that the Constitution restricts the power of naturalization to Congress, tribes never ratified the Constitution and, as we have seen, have never been deemed entirely bound by it. If tribes reserved anything to themselves, it must have been this power of restricting their citizenship. Let us suppose that the power of a tribe to limit its citizenship is equal to the power of Congress to limit United States citizenship. Congress has frequently imposed immigration quotas of a racial, ethnic, or national character. Its power to do so is in conflict with, but apparently superior to, the Fourteenth Amendment. Rather than limiting the exercise of a similar

16. In melting-pot thinking, the United States needn't fear extending the franchise to *immigrants*. They have come here because they prefer our system of laws and government, and will support it. Even so, when large numbers of immigrants arrived simultaneously on these shores in the nineteenth century, xenophobic political paranoia spread through the "indigenous" white population as in the "Know-Nothing" movement against the Irish in mid-century. Because of their diminuitive size, most tribes could not even absorb a few hundred immigrants without serious political consequences. On the Cherokee experience, see Angie Debo, *And Still the Waters Run: The Betrayal of the Five Civilized Tribes* (Princeton, N.J.: 1940).

power by tribes, Congress has required it. The racial character of tribal membership, if preserved, is not necessarily either unconstitutional, or unusual, and ought not to alienate black and liberal support from the tribal movement.

Race is not the only issue that confuses and divides the ethnic and political Indian movements. Culture also poses problems. Ethnicity is self-defining in terms of origins. It is a rememberance of and reverence for roots. Moreover, "ethnic" groups tend to be defined by the state of the culture of origin at the time of separation, unless, as was the case for blacks, knowledge of that past culture has been lost. Italo-Americans preserve relics of a cultural setting they left, not modern Italy. Descendants of nineteenth-century Russian immigrants preserve some of the czarist Russia their ancestors knew, not the Soviet state.

All cultures change over time. Even ethnic cultures change. Russian Americans today are no more czarist Russians than they are Soviet Russians; Nisei are no more prewar Japanese than they are postwar Japanese. But there is an important difference between political and ethnic cultures. An ethnic cultural group adapts to integration into an alien society. It preserves its own institutions only to the extent that they do not conflict with those of the host society. Surrounded and dependent on alien institutions, it is forced to work out its ethnicity in media such as the arts that do not involve the use of power. A true political culture—a separate socioeconomic group with self-governing and self-defining powers—is not so limited. It adapts its culture freely in the process of shaping its own independent destiny. Japanese political culture today is a response to Japan's changing role as a nation in the world environment, while Japanese-American culture responds to immersion in the American national environment, and accepts most American institutions. Unavoidably, each has taken a different road.

On the one hand, Indians seek to define themselves by reference to the Indianness of long ago, looking nostalgically to origins rather than contemporary examples. Memories of origins tend to become almost mythological, and a self-definition drawn from origins is relatively static and idealistic. On the other hand, reservation Indians are experiencing a rapid transformation of original tribal institutions, and are searching for new, adaptive institutions to secure their political future. To this extent their Indianness is defined by reference to sovereignty, recognizing but not deifying origins. Their culture must be dynamic and accept of necessity both the legitimacy of dialogue and criticism, and the inevitability of experimentation and failure.

Not surprisingly, ideological confrontations occur. Young, formally educated Indians accuse older, tribal Indians of being (in substance) counterrevolutionary: the revolution is defined as a return to nineteenth-century institutions.[17] They are trying to validate their own noninstitutional, mythic self-identity by gaining tribal converts. Similarly, tribalists sometimes denigrate urban Indians and question their sincerity when they attempt, in the cities, to recreate lost institutions consistent with their mythic consciousness.

Each movement is still convinced that only one can be legitimate, because *non-Indians* do not yet understand how "Indians" can be two different groups with different objectives. To legitimize itself and gain power, each movement has two choices. It can enlighten non-Indians, so that they will see no inconsistency in the simultaneous existence of the ethnic and political movements. Or it can deny that the other group exists, avoiding confusing the public. The latter strategy is the cheaper.

Tribalists may feel they have more at stake—their lands, their communities, their political society—but both Indian movements share a common historical problem. The national government fails to accord all Indians the right to associate themselves with whatever political society they choose, a right assumed and defended by other Americans. It is an issue of political liberty no less important and no different than that which catalyzed the American Revolution.

BIG TRIBE, LITTLE TRIBE

Political obstacles to the full realization of tribal self-government are not limited to non-Indian institutions. We have already shown how each Indian movement, ethnic and political, must find some alternative form of self-definition that does not operate by negation of the other. Non-Indians see in Indians what appear to be two different and inconsistent sets of

17. See Points I and II of the Trail of Self-Determination Proposal (4 July 1976), prepared by the Sovereign Native Women's Conference. The proposal recommends "transition into a traditional Indian form of government," and assumes, falsely, that all traditional tribal governments were matriarchal like those of the Iroquois and eighteenth-century Cherokees. Everyone seems to have a different conception of "traditional" tribal government and the selection of "traditional" leadership (D'Arcy McNickle, *Native American Tribalism* [Oxford: 1973]).

ideals, and accordingly avoid commitment to either Indian cause. There are concrete political dangers within the national Indian community itself. They flow from competition for a very scarce supply of federal funds, and even more limited supply of federal recognition of political legitimacy. The lines of battle crosscut one another: large tribes against small tribes, national Indian organizations versus local tribal ones, and urban organizations versus reservation ones.

Scarcity is the key. When resources are scarce, institutions seek ways to distinguish themselves from one another because distinctions imply relative merit. Consider size. Larger, more populous tribes such as the Navajo can make a convincing case that they are potentially self-sufficient in resources, revenue and manpower. If it becomes clear that Congress will tolerate a few, but not many permament tribal states, larger tribes can advance potential self-sufficiency as a criterion of the right to statehood. This would exclude scores of small communities from consideration, thereby reducing competition and making Congress's task easier.

Some consideration of economic self-sufficiency is reasonable in choosing whether a community should, as a matter of *policy*, prefer autonomy or incorporation into a larger body. Cut off from sources of external revenue, a poor community will become poorer. Any community dependent upon external revenue is weak and of diminished value to its citizens. Smaller tribes may always require subsidy. Their interest lies in a perpetuation of federal responsibility.

The only way to completely satisfy both large and small tribes would be to offer them an option of political emancipation or continued supervision. Such a plan would probably divest Congress of power over the few prosperous tribes and leave it with the expense of maintaining all the impoverished tribes. Congress will therefore be tempted to make its getting out of the Indian business entirely the price for emancipating the most powerful tribes. In other words, the tribes' option, if any, will probably be between emancipation and assimilation. If such a plan becomes imminent, larger tribes will hurt their own interest by opposing it for the sake of smaller tribes. Congress may prefer to decide for itself which tribes will be offered emancipation and which must assimilate, as it did during termination. If that is the case, tribes will be forced to compete with one another for legislative recognition.

Large tribes already enjoy more influence in Congress because they can afford to do more lobbying and can promise more votes. This influence can be seen in the recent Indian Self-Determination Act. The act enables a tribe to assume the functions of the bureau employees assigned to it, and receive a commensurate share of the bureau's budget. This is all very well for a tribe served at the agency level by twenty or more bureau personnel, as would be the case for the twenty-five or so largest tribes, but has little meaning for the nearly two hundred tribes that share individual employees, i.e., one-tenth of a social worker's time, one-eighth of a realty specialist's, and so on.

If large tribes ever find it politically helpful to sacrifice small ones in the pursuit of greater autonomy, we would not expect any sentiment of pan-Indian unity to stay their hand. The Pueblos enjoy some of the most traditional tribal governments in the Indian world today. Yet when the representatives of Taos learned Congress was fearful of returning Blue Lake to them, lest it establish a precedent for other tribes to demand land restoration, they argued that their religious attachment to the land was unique among all Indians. This gave Congress a convenient criterion, however false, for distinguishing the Taos claim from all others.[18]

Decision makers always prefer to deal with people they know and understand. Business and politics develop social networks; persons who are on the network are relied on and given greater attention than those who are not. In the context of Indian affairs, it is difficult for decision makers to deal with nearly three hundred independent tribal groups. It is much easier for them to develop a network consisting of a handful of tribal leaders from large tribes, or deal with the leaders of a few national Indian organizations. The power of national Indian organizations is not in their size—they still represent less than one-half of one percent of the population—but in their fewness. This quality of fewness enables them to form stable networks with key politicians, and become brokers mediating between Congress and tribal leaders.

The danger lies in the fact that national Indian "brokers" can also insulate Congress from tribes. They increase their power both by obtaining federal favors for tribes, and by doing favors for Congress. They moreover develop their own networks for the distribution of favors. Since national organizations are loosely governed and unregulated, they need be less responsive to their constituents than tribal governments. National

18. "Hearings, 'Taos Indians—Blue Lake Amendments,'" 127, Senate Committee on Interior and Insular Affairs, Subcommittee on Indian Affairs, 91st Congress, 2nd Session (1970).

organizations are not immune from competition with one another. Since the broker role is valuable, each organization will seek a monopoly. Monopolizing Congress's attention increases an organization's ability to bestow favors on its constituents, thereby enhancing its power in the Indian world as well.

National groups do serve many useful functions. They can monitor and respond to new legislation without delay or duplication, and they can maintain effective united lobbying positions. They are also more likely to develop good press, because of fewness, visibility, and the prestige that comes with size and power. But to retain power they must avoid alienating the source of their power: Congress. If they become too irritating they will become ineffective as favor seekers and will lose influence among their constituents. Accordingly, they will tend to be no more aggressive as lobbyists than is necessary to avoid an internal coup among their members. They are safe so long as their membership is passive, even if it is passive and disenchanted. The older, more conservative black civil rights establishment, such as the NAACP and CORE, came under severe criticism in the late 1960s for lack of aggressiveness and overindulgence of Congress.

Politics inevitably involves a great measure of pandering to the idiosyncrasies of powerful men. The problem is that a national lobby soon becomes dependent for its daily bread on perpetuation rather than solution of problems. In this light, national Indian groups assume a role similar to that of the bureau. If Congress moves to definitive solutions, the lobbying role will become unimportant or obsolete, and the lobbyists will lose power. It is disappointing, but not surprising, then, that the National Congress of American Indians (NCAI) joined the bureau in supporting the Indian Self-Determination Act[19] and has taken a middle-of-the-road stand on retrocession of Public Law 280.[20]

One of the striking developments of the past decade in Indian affairs has been the rise of urban Indian centers. The most dramatic manifestation of this movement was probably the occupation of Fort Lawton and subsequent

19. "Hearings, 'Indian Self-Determination,' " 69–70, Senate Committee on Interior and Insular Affairs, Subcommittee on Indian Affairs, 92nd Congress, 2nd Session (1972).

20. After a glowing preamble, repeating in somewhat stronger terms the general policy ideal of the Indian Self-Determination and Education Assistance Act, S.2010 provides for the restoration—with the approval of the secretary of the interior—of such criminal and civil jurisdiction as a tribe *may have lost* in the wake of federal legislation (such as P.L. 280) or judicial decisions, without defining what these lost powers are, or *what other powers tribes may have had originally*. It therefore begs the question of tribes' inherent sovereignty, leaving that sovereignty as undefined and vulnerable as it was before. The original draft bill limited its effect to tribal jurisdiction lost through legislation; at our suggestion, the words "or court decisions" were added to Sec. 103(a) lines 24–25. Our further proposal to add a Title III

establishment of several Indian cultural centers in the Seattle-Tacoma area. Indians have discovered that they often represent a greater proportional force in city politics than in state politics, and can exact significant concessions—surely an unintended side effect of the relocation program! While this has been beneficial to urban Indians, it presents a certain danger to the aspirations of tribes.

Tribes and urban centers are now in competition with one another for federal Indian funding. The Indian Self-Determination Act makes no significant distinction between urban and tribal organizations.[21] Neither does the Indian Financing Act.[22] The Indian Health Care Improvement Act gives urban Indian organizations special, separate recognition.[23] As the urban component of the national Indian population increases, pressure to extend bureau services ordinarily limited to reservations will increase, and a net redistribution of federal subsidies from reservation to city will be the result. This should pose some immediate concern, because urban Indians are relatively less disadvantaged. They have greater access to state services and conventional job markets. Considerations of equity aside, however, urban pressure will draw public attention from the issue of tribal self-government. Not only is the urban-ethnic position more compatible with most Americans' conception of civil rights movements, it is gaining real political strength. Ironically, if it succeeds in significantly improving the conditions of urban Indian life, it will attract more Indians to emigrate from reservations and convince the general public that relocation was a success after all.

LAWYER, LAWYER!

There may exist yet a third class of obstacles to greater realization of tribal self-government. The legal profession itself, while it has

---

defining the residual powers of a tribe as power to ''regulate by civil and criminal laws all commerce and behavior throughout its territory; and . . . tax or exempt from taxation any person, property or activity within its territory,'' was rejected. The proposal for a Title III would also have guaranteed tribes' right to remove secretarial approval power from their constitutions and to make binding compacts with state and local governments. See, generally, ''Hearings, 'Indian Law Enforcement Improvement Act of 1975,' '' Senate Committee on Interior and Insular Affairs, Subcommittee on Indian Affairs, 94th Congress, 1st Session (1975).

21. An ''Indian organization'' need not be a tribe or group of tribes, just a group of tribal members (25 U.S.C. 450b[c]).

22. An eligible Indian-owned enterprise need not be chartered by or doing business within the territory of a tribe (25 U.S.C. 1452[e]).

23. 25 U.S.C. 1653 *et seq.*

frequently been an instrument of progress in Indian affairs, suffers from two problems which may abate its enthusiasm for the reconceptualization we are recommending. First, the bar as a whole is trained to a discipline of conceptual conservatism. Second, the Indian affairs bar depends upon the perpetuation of conflict and uncertainty for economic survival, just as the bureau depends upon the perpetuation of reservation poverty.

Tocqueville observed more than a century ago that the bar is a natural aristocracy.[24] Enjoying a virtual monopoly of access to the legal process, the bar is relatively immune from political and economic pressure and free to indulge its own independent objectives whether they be democratic or antidemocratic, progressive or conservative. In times of majoritarian excesses, it may become a citadel for the minority precisely because of this unresponsiveness to popular forces. Misguided, however, it is equally capable of considerable damage. Linda Medcalf has shown how the love affair between the War-on-Poverty bar and procedural civil rights was carried over to representation of individual Indian clients without a thought to the probable differences between tribal and white-liberal political cultures.[25] Civil rights lawyers, especially those in federal legal services programs, projected on their Indian clients the same political motivations and beliefs they held themselves, and urged them to legal action accordingly. This culminated in the passage of the Indian Civil Rights Act in 1968.

The lawyer's credo in the 1960s was that law serves to protect individual citizens from the government. It was assumed that all government is overpowerful and must be checked by periodic challenges in the courts. Lawyers failed to realize that *tribal* government is *too weak* to serve the basic welfare of Indians, much less to abuse their rights on the scale of state and national government. Persistent civil rights challenges against tribes unable to afford effective defenses further weakened tribal power.[26] In the

24. Alexis De Tocqueville, *Democracy in America* 267–69, ed. J. P. Mayer, trans. George Lawrence (Garden City, N.Y.: 1969). See, too, Anthony Trollope's *North America* (New York: 1862).
25. Linda Medcalf. "Law—Mirror or Miracle: A Study of Lawyers Who Represent Native Americans," Paper presented at the 1976 Annual Meeting of the American Political Science Association, Chicago.
26. It is historically significant that the OEO. financed legal services under an arrangement whereby lawyers could represent tribal members in suits against their tribes, but could not represent the tribes themselves. As a result, tribes were beset with litigation they often could not afford to defend, and were compelled by judgment or settlement to move rapidly in the direction of non-Indian institutions.

end, the bar's efforts to improve reservation Indians' condition actually made it worse.

Even if the lawyers who represent tribes lack preconceptions about what tribes really want, they will not ordinarily counsel their clients to demand more than the courts seem disposed to give. This is both an ethical and a practical matter. Familiar solutions are relatively easy and sure. New concepts are long shots, and require lawyers to forget what they were taught and already know for new and challenging theories. Lawyers will do what they feel they understand and can do well, and what will most probably result in *some gain* to the client. A lawyer who accomplishes something for his client using familiar theories has little to fear of malpractice. He can always attribute any shortfall in his client's expectations to the vagaries of the judges. But a lawyer who gambles on a new idea and loses everything, when a simple and familiar remedy would have produced some positive result, however small, will be held accountable for his own choice of strategies.

We have shown that the "infringement test" has no real legal basis upon close examination, and results in complete obfuscation of the tribe-state boundary. Why do lawyers continue to advance it on behalf of tribes, rather than challenge it? Their chance of success in any particular case cannot be hurt by challenging it in the alternative. However, that would take additional effort. Lawyers are not rewarded by their clients, in most instances, for establishing new principles of law, but for winning individual cases. Unless tribes insist that their legal representatives advance new theories—and reward them for their additional effort at it—cases will continue to be brought on the safest and narrowest grounds.

The law of tribes is today very uncertain. The courts have been unable to agree on any principle or hierarchy of principles to resolve this uncertainty. Do lawyers have an interest in resolving it? Litigation arises when people's expectations are in conflict. The more inflexible and unambiguous the rules, the less we need courts to interpret them. Lawyers often say that some flexibility is necessary for fairness, but flexibility is only fair to a party who misunderstands or chooses to avoid a rule, not to one who follows it. Flexibility adds to the sense of litigation as a great contest in which a party can by cunning persuade the judge to legislate ex post facto in his favor. Flexibility increases the prestige, influence and wealth of the bar.

The bar will tend to serve its self-interest by augmenting the power and discretion of courts as an alternative to legislation. In recent years there has been a tendency for courts to assume the role of administrative agencies with powers of continuing supervision and standard-setting.[27] This increases the demand for lawyers and does not decrease the uncertainty of outcomes in particular cases. Even where continuing remedies are indicated, it would be preferable to entrust their administration to expert agencies.

If the law is uncertain, it is also in lawyers' interests not to encourage clients to appreciate just how uncertain the law really is. The utility of prosecuting a case depends upon its expected value, i.e., the payoff discounted by the probability of succeeding. Clients will avoid taking action where the payoff is relatively less certain. They base their estimate of expected value on a lawyer's judgment of the probability of success. Besides, it is also in lawyers' interests to appear competent to their clients. A lawyer who says, "I really can't predict the outcome of your suit," will be less attractive to a potential client than one who confidently forecasts victory—and blames subsequent defeat on the judge.

Some areas of Indian law have proved to be goldmines. Of the $534 million awarded by the Indian Claims Commission from 1951 to 1974, $53 million went to lawyers' fees. Tribes probably pay more than a million dollars annually in retainers for general legal representation.[28] At that price tribes could organize a formidable lobbying force to address the basic instability and ambiguity of tribal status. We do not expect lawyers to spearhead a change in priorities.

27. See Abram Chayes, "The New Judiciary," *Harvard Law School Bulletin* (Fall 1976); R. L. Barsh, *The Washington Fishing Rights Controversy, An Economic Critique* 54–57 (Seattle: 1977).

28. Computed from data in "Hearing, 'Indian Claims Commission Appropriations for Fiscal Year 1976,'" Senate Committee on Interior and Insular Affairs, Subcommittee on Indian Affairs, 94th Congress, 1st Session (1975), and the 10 percent rule of 25 U.S.C. 70a. As early as 1934, moreover, there were complaints about "pet lawyers," i.e., lawyers who had ingratiated themselves with the Bureau of Indian Affairs and were favored for contract approval ("Hearings, 'To Grant Indians . . . Freedom to Organize,'" 244–46).

22

Constitutional Guarantees

Government, to an American, is the science of his political safety.[1]

The Constitution of the United States guarantees "States" proportional representation and local self-government. It was assumed in 1789, however, that tribes would join the Union, if at all, in the capacity of states.[2] A different category of local government was accordingly not described in Article I of the Constitution. Strict construction of this article to exclude tribes is not consistent with the general intent of its draftsmen, as made particularly clear by the Ninth and Tenth Amendments, and by examination of the use of the phrase "Indians not taxed."

STRICT CONSTRUCTION

Dean Langdell was persuaded that the use of the word "States" in the body of the Constitution and the Bill of Rights, along with the corresponding absence of reference to territories, is conclusive that political liberty does not extend to territorial residents.[3] Strict construction cuts both

1. George Clinton, "Letters of Cato" (1787), Letter No. 1, reprinted in Paul Leicester Ford, *Essays on the Constitution of the United States* (Brooklyn, N.Y.: 1892).
2. Annie Heloise Abel, "Proposals for an Indian State," *Annual Report of the American Historical Association, 1907.*
3. C. C. Langdell, "The Status of Our New Territories," 12 *Harvard Law Review* 365 (1899).

ways, however. For example, the only clause in Article I, Section 8 expressly limited in its application to states is the one that reserves state power to commission militia officers. Article I, Section 9, further limiting national powers, is often general in expression, e.g., "No Bill of Attainder or ex post facto Law shall be passed." The Bill of Rights mentions states only once: trial by jury in "the State and district where the crime shall have been committed." Elsewhere, its prohibitions are general, e.g., "Congress shall make no law," and "no Warrant shall issue."[4]

Strictly construed, the Constitution does grant Congress a few specific powers over nonstates which it is prohibited to exercise over states. It also exempts nonstates from Article I, Section 10: they could make treaties, grant letters of marque and reprisal, coin money, make ex post facto laws, confer titles of nobility, tax commerce, and maintain standing armies. Could this have been the framers' intent?

"INDIANS NOT TAXED"

The Fourteenth, Fifteenth, Nineteenth, and Twenty-Sixth Amendments guarantee all citizens eighteen years of age or older, regardless of sex or race, the right to vote. However, the Constitution's original provisions for the composition of the House, Senate, and electoral college, refer only to "States."

Article I, Section 2 of the Constitution and Section 2 of the Fourteenth Amendment exclude from the enumeration of state citizens for congressional apportionment all "Indians not taxed." Indians living on tribal land and under tribal jurisdiction, whether or not subject to some degree of federal protection, were "not taxed" by any state. Indians came to be taxed

4. The Full Faith and Credit and Privileges and Immunities Clauses refer to "States." Full Faith and Credit merely expresses the principle of coequality of constituent parts of the Union; Privileges and Immunities the coequality of citizens. Congress has expressly interpreted the former as also applicable to territories and possessions, but not to tribes (28 U.S.C. 1738–39). There is nothing in the use of the word "States" that necessitates exclusion of tribes. The opinion of the Court in *Cherokee Nation* that treaty tribes are not "States of the Union" is distinguishable because (1) that case arose under Article III, not Article IV of the Constitution, and was limited to a jurisdictional question; and (2) at that time the Cherokees expressly denied any role in the Union, and Congress vigorously eschewed any intervention in their domestic affairs, facts the Court itself considered dispositive of their status.

only by relinquishing their collective sovereignty or by individually emigrating to state lands.[5]

Even *Kagama* failed to interrupt a consistent line of decision, beginning with *Worcester*, that rejected the power of states to extend their jurisdiction to tribal territories without congressional consent.[6] On occasion the Court commented at length on the injustice of committing Indians to the authority of local governments avowedly adverse to their interests. Mr. Justice Miller observed of the tribes that, "They owe no allegiance to the states, and receive from them no protection. Because of the local ill feeling, the people of the States where they are found are often their deadliest enemies."[7] It seems inappropriate to combine, for apportionment purposes, communities that are mutually hostile and share no real economic interest or social kinship. Political diversity was, after all, as James Winthrop wrote in 1787, "the leading principle of the revolution."[8]

It is universally agreed that the object of every just government is to render the people happy, by securing their persons and possessions from wrong. To this end it is necessary that there should be local laws and institutions; for a people inhabiting various climates will unavoidably have local habits and different modes of life, and these must be consulted in making the laws. It is much easier to adapt the laws to the manners of the people, than to make manners conform to laws.[9]

Uniformity can only be established by the use of raw power, which breeds disaffection; Winthrop compared this to a procrustean bed.[10]

Besides, it was a fundamental maxim of the Revolution that governors should share in the same burdens as the governed. "The greatest security that a people can have for the enjoyment of their rights and liberties,"

---

5. See the historical reviews in Jay Vincent White, *Taxing Those They Found Here* (Washington, D.C.: 1972); 57 I.D. 195 (1940); and the dissent in *Elk v. Wilkins*, 112 U.S. 94, 114 (1884). Interestingly, the Articles of Confederation referred to some Indians as "members" of states, an explicitly political test (Article IX, cl. 4).

6. Federal consent is not to be implied (*Mattz v. Arnett*, 412 U.S. 481, 505 [1973]) but must be expressed on the face of a statute or treaty (*McClanahan v. Arizona Tax Commission*, 411 U.S. 164, 174–75 [1973]). It may be specific, e.g., 25 U.S.C. 357, authorizing states to condemn allotted lands within reservations, or general, e.g., Public Law 280, 67 Stat. 588 (1953), authorizing states to assume such civil and criminal jurisdiction as they choose.

7. *U.S. v. Kagama*, 118 U.S. 375, 385 (1886).

8. "Letters of Agrippa" (1787), Letter No. 4, reprinted in Ford, *Essays on the Constitution*.

9. *Id.*, Letter No. 12.

10. *Id.*, Letters No. 4 and 12. See, too, Roger Sherman's "Letters of a Citizen of New Haven" (1788), Letter No. 2, reprinted in Ford, *Essays on the Constitution*.

wrote Roger Sherman, "is that no law can be made to bind them . . . without their consent by representatives of their own chusing, *who will participate with them in the public burdens and benefits.*"[11] Officers elected from state districts have no more personal stake in the advocacy of tribal interests than the great majority of their constituents.

Nevertheless, the act conferring national citizenship on tribal Indians was uniformly interpreted in administrative practice as making Indians citizens *of the states.* Reservations were divided into existing state legislative and congressional districts, rather than established as new districts. Indians were permitted to vote for state legislators, and state delegates to the national legislature. However, the constitution, if it is to be given any meaning, requires that the members of tribes, where subject to federal power at all, be excluded from state apportionment. This necessarily implies that *the right of suffrage*, guaranteed to them as a fundamental right of national citizenship, *be exercised through separate representation* at the federal and local levels.

We are not aware of any constitutional requirement today that a citizen of the United States must be a citizen of any particular state. Territorial residents are United States citizens by birth, but are not citizens of any state. The law declares Indians "citizens of the United States," not "of the State in which they reside."[12] It provides expressly that "citizenship shall not in any manner impair or otherwise affect the right of any Indian to tribal or other property," a phrase that may be understood as a saving of tribal political sovereignty. If tribes, through citizenship, lose the limited independent legislative control of their property they now possess, their rights to that property are impaired.

Since the general policy of the Constitution is to maximize political liberty, Congress should read the words "or tribes" into the Constitution's references to "States."[13] There is precedent for this. The Full Faith and Credit Clause only refers to states, but Congress passed legislation some

11. Sherman, "Letters of a Countryman" (1787), Letter No. 4, reprinted in Ford, *Essays on the Constitution.*

12. Act of 2 June 1924, 43 Stat. 253, in relevant part: "all non-citizen Indians born within the territorial limits of the United States be, and they are hereby, declared to be citizens of the United States."

13. Except perhaps for the Fourteenth Amendment, Section 1. Strict application of the Equal Protection Clause would defeat the purpose of tribal membership, which we take to be preservation of an original political community of native ancestry. Tribes often established liberal naturalization procedures for non-Indians; they are now somewhat limited by federal law (25 U.S.C. 372a, and 25 U.S.C. 476). The latter provision, for discretionary secretarial approval of tribal constitutions, is relevant because tribal constitutions usually contain

years ago defining "State" in this context as including the territories and possessions of the United States.[14] In 1871, as we observed above, Congress passed legislation defining tribes *out* of the Treaty Clause of the Constitution. Congress thus asserts a power to redefine terms of the Constitution where necessary to execute its real intent. If Congress can determine that tribes are not foreign nations for the purposes of executive treaty making, surely Congress can determine that tribes are states for the purposes of political representation.[15]

THE TENTH AMENDMENT

The Tenth Amendment reserves all powers "not delegated to the United States, nor prohibited by it to the States . . . to the States respectively, *or to the people.*" This was Congress's response to the fears, voiced by Madison, that the contractual theory of our government might some day be forgotten or distorted. It provides express authority for tribal self-government, limited only by the powers Congress may exercise over the states.

If we consider a state, it is apparent that the people delegated some of their power to state government before entering into the federal compact. The people of Massachusetts first delegated police powers to the General Court of that Commonwealth; only later did they independently delegate police powers to the Congress. In fact, the language of the Constitution ("We the People") is highly significant in this regard. Congress did not accept a delegation of some of the state governments' powers, but a delegation of some of the *people's* powers, directly. The people delegated to Congress powers both previously enjoyed by their own local governments, and

membership criteria. See also 25 C.F.R. 11.29. Obviously the United States has a fiscal interest in limiting the number of persons enrolled in tribes and thereby eligible to receive special assistance; tribes often share this interest for similar reasons. At any rate, tribes also have cause to fear a loss of control over membership for purely political reasons. They have only to contemplate the fate of the Indian Territory, which was denied admission to statehood until it relinquished its restrictive naturalization criteria. The consequent influx of non-Indians utterly overwhelmed the tribal governments. Appropriately, federal law leaves membership criteria almost entirely in tribal hands, even after the enactment of special Due Process and Equal Protection requirements (25 U.S.C. 1302[8]; *Martinez v. Santa Clara Pueblo*, 402 F. Supp. 5 [D.C.N.M. 1975]; 98 S. Ct. 1670 [1978]).

14. 28 U.S.C. 1738–38.

15. If Congress chose to do so, would a challenge to that action be justiciable? See the recent discussion of justiciability in *Baker v. Carr*, 369 U.S. 186, 215 ff. (1962). The Court seems more disposed to rule on the constitutionality of a redistribution of power among the states, or among non-Indian citizens, than on the constitutionality of *any* policy directed solely at Indians.

previously denied them. The mediate source was irrelevant, because the ultimate choice rested with the people themselves.[16]

If the people had power to create local governing bodies *before* entering into the Union, they must have this power *afterwards* as well, unless it is expressly given up in the Constitution. We do not find any prohibition against the creation of local governing bodies in the Constitution. The people of the states generally relinquished the power of unlimited local incorporation in their *state* constitutions.[17] The members of tribes never gave up the right of local incorporation in their treaties or constitutions. Even if the right does not generally exist for state citizens, it may therefore exist for tribal members.

Tribes had their own local governing procedures before they entered into treaties with the United States. Otherwise, no Indian treaty can be valid, because all were made with putative leaders of tribal governments rather than with individual tribal members. If the treaty did not relinquish the right to self-government by express terms, then the people of the tribe must retain the right, enjoyed previously, of changing the form of their government. State citizens may adopt new constitutions without federal approval. They must only be careful to remain within the confines of the Constitution's express prohibitions on state powers. This state power is found nowhere expressly in the Constitution. It must therefore be a reserved power. Existence as a state is not necessary to enjoy reserved powers. They are reserved *to the people* themselves, and can therefore be exercised *by the people*, even when they owe allegiance to no state.

EXCLUSIVE LEGISLATION

Nothing in the Constitution should be regarded as superfluous, nor is any omission of words to be presumed meaningless.[18] In the penultimate

16. This aspect of the Constitution is elegantly discussed by John Marshall in *M'Culloch v. Maryland*, 4 Wheat. (17 U.S.) 316, 403 (1819).

17. The power of state citizens *under state law* to create and maintain local governments is defended in Amasa M. Eaton, "The Right to Local Self-Government," 13 *Harvard Law Review* 441, 570, 638 (1899–1900), and challenged in Howard Lee McBain, "The Doctrine of an Inherent Right to Local Self-Government," 16 *Columbia Law Review* 190, 299 (1916). Neither writer considered the status of American citizens not members of any state. See also "Note, 'The Right to Vote in Municipal Annexations,' " 88 *Harvard Law Review* 1571 (1975).

18. *Knowlton v. Moore*, 178 U.S. 41, 87 (1900). Moreover, "an exception of any particular case presupposes that those which are not excepted are embraced within the grant or prohibition" (*Rhode Island v. Massachusetts*, 12 Pet. 657, 722 [1838]; see also *Gibbons v.*

clause of Article I, Section 8, Congress is given the power of "exclusive Legislation in all Cases whatsoever" within the federal district. This raises two questions. First, why was it necessary to make this power "exclusive," when the District of Columbia had no legislature of its own, nor even existed yet as a territorial entity? *Perhaps because its residents would have had a right and power to create a legislature unless expressly forbidden by the Constitution.* If all power not delegated to the United States is reserved "to the people" in the absence of an intervening state government, the people must have as part of that power a capacity to delegate any or all of it to any form of local government not specifically forbidden by the Constitution. By the same token, why doesn't the Constitution appoint a power of "exclusive Legislation" over Indians, rather than a power to "regulate Commerce" with them? Congress has acted as if its power over tribes is as great as its power over the District of Columbia; even greater, to the extent Indian legislation disregards the Bill of Rights.

In the language originally proposed for the Constitution, Congress was to have power "To regulate affairs with the Indians."[19] The Committee of Detail suggested merely adding the word "and with the Indians" to the Commerce Clause, and the provision was enacted as "and with the Indian tribes."[20] There was no discussion or debate on this provision, and it was agreed to unanimously. For nearly one hundred years this was understood to authorize Congress only to regulate commercial intercourse with tribal Indians, and the conduct of American citizens in Indian territory.[21] It is difficult to justify stretching this into a grant of virtually despotic power, greater even than "exclusive Legislation in all Cases whatsoever."

The Northwest Ordinance has been described as an illustration of the revolutionary spirit of political liberty.[22] It extended a Bill of Rights and political franchise to territorial residents, and assured them automatic admission to statehood upon their meeting what was then a very minimal

---

Ogden, 9 Wheat. 1, 191 [1824]; *Brown v. Maryland*, 12 Wheat 438 [1927]). *A fortiori*, the grant of a limited power implies the lack of a general power. See Alexander M. Bickel's enlightening review of strict constructionism in *The Least Dangerous Branch* 84–98 (Indianapolis: 1962).

19. 5 *Elliott's Debates* 439.

20. 5 *Elliott's Debates* 462, 507.

21. Francis Paul Prucha, *American Indian Policy: The Formative Years* 139 ff. (Cambridge, Mass.: 1962).

22. Arthur Bestor, "Constitutionalism and the Settlement of the West," in John Porter Bloom, ed., *The American Territorial System* 13 (Athens, Ohio: 1969).

standard: population equal to that of the smallest state. If it did not afford the territories exactly as much political liberty as the states, there was a satisfactory explanation. The ordinance was a compact between the United States and its own citizens, pursuant to which they were authorized to emigrate westward with specified rights and specified liabilities.[23] It accordingly *did not* impose federal supremacy on tribes within the territories but on the contrary required that the "utmost good faith" with them be preserved. In fact, when Jefferson was considering the expediency of a constitutional amendment to expressly authorize the purchase of Louisiana, he showed his cabinet a draft in which "the rights of occupancy and of self-government [are] all confirmed to the Indian inhabitants as they now exist."[24] They advised him that the amendment as a whole was *unnecessary* and that ratification would merely delay the business of organizing the new territory. Jefferson persisted for several months, redrafting his proposal, but finally succumbed to their advice and never submitted it to Congress.[25]

THE NINTH AMENDMENT

Dean Pound has written that we should make "the natural law and natural rights as believed in by the founders of our polity effective political and legal instruments in the society of today."[26] General constitutional authority for this kind of flexibility is the explicit, original purpose of the Ninth Amendment.

A multitude of particular rights have been sought in the Ninth Amendment, mostly without success. The Supreme Court has been conservative, and appropriately so, because the amendment was not intended to hatch new principles but to guarantee the survival of original ones. Putative rights

23. Compare the theory of American political status advanced by British imperialists in the eighteenth century.

24. Herman V. Ames, "The Proposed Amendments to the Constitution of the United States During the First Century of its History," 2 *Annual Report of the American Historical Association, 1896* 178–79.

25. A later draft of this same proposal included the interesting provision that non-Indian residents of the new territories be citizens on an "equal footing" with resident of the states. It may be inferred from this that Jefferson feared that the revolutionary political spirit which pervaded his 1784 ordinance had begun to succumb to an imperialistic policy more like Gouverneur Morris's.

26. In his preface to Bennett Patterson, *The Forgotten Ninth Amendment* (Indianapolis: 1955).

to environmental quality,[27] public employment,[28] housing,[29] and political asylum,[30] for example, have been denied Ninth Amendment protection.

The core meaning of the Ninth Amendment was perhaps best summarized by Mr. Justice Chase almost two hundred years ago in the case of *Calder v. Bull*,[31] a challenge to Connecticut's adoption of the British practice of appeals from the highest court to the legislature. Rejecting the argument that this was fundamentally inconsistent with our form of government, he nevertheless agreed that:

There are certain vital principles in our free Republican governments, which will overrule an apparent and flagrant abuse of legislative power; as to authorize manifest injustice by positive law; or to take away that security for personal liberty, or private property, for the protection whereof the government was established. An act of the Legislature (for I cannot call it a law) contrary to the great first principles of the social compact, cannot be considered a rightful exercise of legislative authority.[32]

As examples of fundamentally bad law, Justice Chase suggested impairment of contracts, making men judges of their own causes, and laws permitting takings or taxes for private uses.

Successful Ninth Amendment challenges have generally been classified as having to do with "privacy," including abortion,[33] personal

27. *Environmental Defense Fund, Inc. v. Corps of Engineers*, 325 F. Supp. 728 (D.C. Ark. 1970), *reaff'd 342* F. Supp. 1211, *aff'd* 470 F. 2d 289. Similarly, *Ely v. Velde*, 321 F. Supp. 1088 (D.C. Va. 1971); *aff'd in part, rev'd in part on other grounds*, 451 F. 2d 1130; *Virginians for Dulles v. Volpe*, 344 F. Supp. 573 (D.C. Va. 1972); *Tanner v. Armco Steel Corp.*, 340 F. Supp. 532 (D.C. Tex. 1972).

28. *U.S. v. Zaugh*, 445 F. 2d 300 (C.A. Cal. 1971). See also *U.S. v. Farrell*, 443 F. 2d 355 (C.A. Cal. 1971), *cert. den'd* 404 U.S. 853; *U.S. v. Uhl*, 436 F. 2d 773 (C.A. Cal. 1970); *U.S. v. Cook*, 311 F. Supp. 618 (D.C. Pa. 1970).

29. *Velasquez v. Thompson*, 321 F. Supp. 34 (D.C. N.Y. 1970), *aff'd* 451 F. 2d 202; *cf. Colorado Anti-Discrimination Comm. v. Case*, 151 Colo. 235, 380 P.24 34 (1962).

30. *Ex parte Kurth*, 28 F. Supp. 258 (D.C. Cal. 1939), *app. dism'd* 106 F. 2d 1003.

31. 3 Dall. 386 (1798); cited approvingly in *Gunn v. Barry*, 82 U.S. 610, 623 (1872). A similar set of facts was recently at issue in *Seneca Constitutional Rights Organization v. George*, 348 F. Supp. 51 (D.C.N.Y. 1972), the district court holding in effect that separation of powers is not necessarily a requirement of due process as applied to tribal legal systems.

32. 3 Dall. 388. See also *Savings & Loan Ass'n v. Topeka*, 87 U.S. 655, 663 (1875), in which Justice Miller, the author of the *Kagama* opinion, wrote: "There are limitations on power which grow out of the essential nature of all free governments." In his dissent to *Topeka*, Judge Clifford challenged this standard as too vague—making an argument reminiscent of that levelled at the Americans who thought they had discovered the "spirit" of the British Constitution (*id.* 669).

33. *Roe v. Wade*, 314 F. Supp. 1217 (D.C. Tex. 1970), *jurisd. postponed*, 402 U.S. 941, *aff'd in part, rev'd in part on other grounds*, 410 U.S. 113 (1973), *reh. den'd*, 410 U.S. 959. The Court's formula in *Roe* has been followed in *Doe v. Rampton*, 366 F. Supp. 189 (D.C.

appearance,[34] and personal safety.[35] "Privacy" per se has no revolutionary precedent, and this may explain why the Supreme Court prefers to find it in the spirit or "penumbra" of the Fourth Amendment, relying on the Ninth Amendment merely for additional general authority.[36]

"Privacy" in the sense in which it is now understood bears its closest kinship to the philosophy of John Stuart Mill, expressed in his essay *On Liberty*.[37] This is ironic, because Mill was seeking to define the proper limits of power in a government of absolute supremacy (Great Britain) rather than a government of enumerated powers delegated by the people. He argued that no law should limit liberty (defined in the *Hobbesian* sense of unrestrained individual activity) without a corresponding social benefit. The converse of this is that government may make any law that does advance the general welfare. This is political heresy, at least in our traditions. *All* laws restrain Millsian liberty. The people's dearest right is to participate directly by their representatives in the process of making laws. That is their safety, not post hoc judicial evaluation of the laws' effect on them.

The only Ninth Amendment case on political liberty as we understand it challenged the Hatch Act as a restraint on the right to seek public office, a right with impressive roots in the revolutionary debate and the English Bill of Rights.[38] The Supreme Court conceded the existence of the right, although it sustained the Hatch Act by balancing the right to seek public

---

Utah 1973); *State v. Hodgson*, 204 N.W. 2d 199 (Minn. 1973); and *Doe v. Burk*, 513 P. 2d 643 (Wyo. 1973). The constitutional theory of *Roe* was also considered in *Doe v. Bolton*, 319 F. Supp. 1048 (D.C. Ga. 1970), *app. dism'd* 403 U.S. 936, *mod. on other grounds*, 410 U.S. 179, *reh. den'd* 410 U.S. 959.

34. *Stradley v. Anderson*, 349 F. Supp. 1120 (D.C. Neb. 1972), *aff'd* 478 F. 2d 188; *Berryman v. Hein*, 329 F. Supp. 616 (D.C. *Id.* 1971); *Dawson v. Hillsborough County School Bd*, 322 F. Supp. 286 (D.C. Fla. 1971), *aff'd* 445 F. 2d 308; *Dunham v. Pulsiver*, 312 F. Supp. 411 (D.C. Vt. 1970); *Reichenberg v. Nelson*, 310 F. Supp. 248 (D.C. Neb. 1970). But there is also contrary authority, e.g., *Kraus v. Board of Education*, 492 S.W. 2d 783 (Mo. 1973); *Pendley v. Mingus Union High School*, 504 P. 2d 919 (Ariz. 1972); *Miller v. Gillis*, 315 F. Supp. 94 (D.C. Ill. 1969).

35. *American Motorcycle Ass'n v. Davids*, 158 N.W. 2d 72 (Mich. 1968); *contra, State v. Albertson*, 93 Idaho 640, 470 P. 2d 300 (1970); *State v. Fetterly*, 254 Or. 47, 456 P. 2d 996 (1969).

36. *Griswold v. Connecticut*, 381 U.S. 479 (1965).

37. John Stuart Mill, *On Liberty* (London: 1859); see also his *Considerations on Representative Government* (London: 1861).

38. *United Public Workers v. Mitchell*, 330 U.S. 75 (1946). What about a "right" to make campaign contributions? See *U.S. v. Painters Local Union*, 79 F. Supp. 516 (D.C. Conn. 1948), *rev'd on other grounds*, 172 F. 2d 854. The Supreme Court's decision in *Buckley v. Valeo*, *op. cit.*, finds a right to contribute and spend money for political campaigns in the *First* Amendment, and does not discuss the Ninth at all.

office against dangers to the fairness of the electoral system posed by the participation of public employees.

The Court is apparently prepared to find political rights essential to our system of government in the Ninth Amendment. If tribes' demands for a full, fair representation in Congress and unsupervised local self-government were to be asserted as fundamental rights, what countervailing social interests could be arrayed against them? The historical justification, Indian ignorance and differentness, has been laid to rest by the Court's ruling that cultural differentness and technological simplicity cannot be suppressed unless injurious to public welfare,[39] if not as well by a century of federal investment in Indian education.

Although the Ninth Amendment itself has not proved a fertile source of new law, the Supreme Court has not been deterred from finding new law elsewhere in the Constitution. The rights of privacy and travel[40] are judicial constructions that have far less impressive historical roots than political liberty. Both are described as implied in other enumerated rights, although at least in the privacy area the implied right is far broader than the enumerated one. The Court has also moved to expand the definition of property in the Fifth Amendment so as to create rights in employment and public services, among other things.[41] If it can defend essentially new rights as responses to a changing world, reasoning from these tenuous analogies to the framers' intentions, certainly it has no excuse to deny the resurrection of so fundamental a principle as political liberty.

JUSTICIABILITY

Long acquiescence in some practice by the government does not render it constitutional.[42] Nor can the Supreme Court itself disregard its

39. *Wisconsin v. Yoder*, 406 U.S. 205 (1972). *Cf.* the interesting recent case of *State ex. rel. Swann v. Pack*, 527 S.W. 2d 99 (1975) (snake-handling cults).

40. See "Comment, 'The Right to Travel: Judicial Curiosity or Practical Tool?' " 52 *Journal of Urban Law* 749 (1975).

41. See *Bd. of Regents v. Roth*, 408 U.S. 564 (1972); *Wieman v. Updegraff*, 344 U.S. 183, 192 (1952); *Slochower v. Board of Education*, 350 U.S. 551, 556 (1956). See also *Hortonville Joint School District v. Hortonville Education Ass'n*, 66 Wis. 2d 469, 225 N.W. 2d 658 (1975), *app. for stay den'd* 96 S. Ct. 1 (1975). The rights of public employees to procedural due process are not entirely distinguishable from a right to employment on reasonable terms and conditions. See also *Goldberg v. Kelly*, 397 U.S. 254 (1970).

42. *Fairbank v. U.S.*, 181 U.S. 283, 307 (1901); *Marshall Field & Co. v. Clark*, 143 U.S. 649, 691 (1892). However, past practices are to be given great weight (*Cohens v. Virginia*, *op. cit.*, at 418; *The "Genessee Chief" v. Fitzhugh*, 12 How. 443, 458 [1852]; *Burrow Giles*

past errors. It is "the law of this court," Chief Justice Taney wrote in 1849, "that its opinion upon the construction of the Constitution is always open to discussion when it is supposed to have been founded in error, and that its judicial authority should hereafter depend altogether on the force of the reasoning by which it is supported."[43] Error may be sociological, as when the *Brown* Court reversed *Plessy v. Ferguson*, or historical, as when *Erie Railroad* reversed *Swift v. Tyson*.[44]

Cherokee Nation v. Georgia has long been misinterpreted as holding that the treatment of Indian tribes is a political question. In dictum, Chief Justice Marshall did express concern that the Court might exceed its authority if it issued and tried to enforce an injunction against the legislature of the State of Georgia.[45] In *Worcester v. Georgia*, however, Georgia's laws were declared unconstitutional, although counsel for the tribe never sought an injunction.[46] As Justice Brennan correctly observed in *Baker v.*

Litho. Co. v. Sarony, 111 U.S. 53, 57 [1884]; *Butte City Water Co. v. Baker*, 196 U.S. 119, 127 [1905]), especially where supported by numerous past decisions of the Court (*U.S. v. Curtiss-Wright*, 299 U.S. 304, 327 [1936]; *Missouri v. Illinois*, 180 U.S. 208, 219 [1901]; *McPherson v. Blacker*, 146 U.S. 1, 27 [1892]; *Kilbourn v. Thompson*, 103 U.S. 168, 204 [1881]; *Vezie Bank v. Fenno*, 8 Wall. 533, 541 [1860]; *Cooley v. Philadelphia*, 12 How. 299, 315 [1851]; *Wilkinson v. Leland*, 2 Pet. 627, 657 [1829]).

43. *Smith v. Turner* (The Passenger Cases), 17 How. 283, 470 (1849).

44. *Plessy v. Ferguson*, 163 U.S. 537 (1896); *Brown v. Board of Education*, 347 U.S. 483 (1954); *Erie RR. v. Tompkins*, 304 U.S. 64, 72−73 (1938); *Swift v. Tyson*, 16 Pet. 1 (1842). As Justice Story observed in *Prigg v. Pennsylvania* (16 Pet. 539, 610 [1842]), "perhaps the safest rule of interpretation after all will be found to look to the nature and objects of the particular powers, duties, and rights, with all the lights and aids of contemporary history." See also *Marshall v. Gordon*, 243 U.S. 521, 533 (1917) ("What went before the adoption of the Constitution may be resorted to for the purpose of throwing light on its provisions"); *Missouri v. Illinois*, 140 U.S. 208, 219 (1901); *U.S. v. Wong Kim Ark*, 169 U.S. 654 (1898). *The Federalist* is not conclusive but entitled to great weight in these investigations (*M'Culloch v. Maryland*, 4 Wheat 316, 433 [1819]; *Cohens v. Virginia*, 6 Wheat. 264, 419 [1821]; *Pollock v. Farmers' Loan & Trust Co.*, 158 U.S. 601, 627 [1895]). Debates in Convention are not, however, controlling of interpretation (*Legal Tender Cases*, 12 Wall. 457, 561 [1871]; *Maxwell v. Dow*, 176 U.S. 581, 601 [1900]; *Downes v. Bidwell*, 182 U.S. 244, 254 [1901]; *cf. Smith v. Turner*, 17 How. 283, 396 [1849]). A critical review of historical interpretations is to be found in Bickel, *The Least Dangerous Branch* 98−110, Brandeis exhaustively documented past Supreme Court reversals in his dissent to *Burnet v. Colorado Oil & Gas Co.* (285 U.S. 393, 407 n.2, 409 n.4 [1932]). The Court has always maintained that some provisions of the Constitution "may acquire meaning as public opinion becomes enlightened by a humane justice" (*Weems v. U.S.*, 217 U.S. 349, 378 [1910]), and that "the question respecting the extent of the powers actually granted [to Congress], is perpetually arising, and will probably continue to arise, so long as our system shall exist" (*M'Culloch v. Maryland*, 4 Wheat. 404).

45. 30 U.S. (5 Pet.) 1, 20.

46. See Joseph C. Burke, "The Cherokee Cases: A Study in Law, Politics, and Morality," 21 *Stanford Law Review* 500 (1969).

Carr, Cherokee Nation merely held that tribes lack standing to invoke the original jurisdiction of the Supreme Court.[47]

Reviewing past decisions of the Court, Brennan concluded that Congress enjoys an unreviewable power to determine what is good for Indians—but not to determine who *is* an Indian.[48] However, an issue is ordinarily justiciable if it involves alleged violations of the Constitution and does not require the Court to make policy judgments within the discretion of another branch of the national government. If standards have been established within which the Congress or president must act, the Court may examine obedience to those standards, as far as their meaning is reasonably clear.[49]

Whether Indians, who are citizens, are entitled to the same rights of local self-government and national representation as other citizens, is not a matter within executive or legislative discretion. The Constitution nowhere authorizes any branch of the national government to establish classifications of citizens for the purpose of limiting their political rights. It cannot be a political question whether Congress has any legitimate power to limit Indians' liberty, because Congress itself relies entirely upon a *judicial* doctrine for the exercise of that power.[50] If it struck down the "plenary" power of Congress, the Court would not be trespassing on a coequal branch, only recanting its own doctrines.

47. 369 U.S. 186, 215 (1962).
48. 369 U.S. 186, 215. He relied on the *Sandoval* case, discussed in ch. 5, seeming to approve of its rule that Congress should have unreviewable discretion over what is done to Indians, but not over who is an Indian.
49. 369 U.S. 186, 211 *et seq.*, 226.
50. In the recent case of *U.S. v. Antelope*, 523 F. 2d 400 (9th Cir. 1975), the court of appeals reasoned that a federal law prejudicial to Indians could be nullified judicially irregardless of "plenary power." Since the object of the power has always according to the courts, been the *protection* of Indians, all applications of it are to be measured by that standard. The case involved the Major Crimes Act. However, the United States Supreme Court reversed (97 S. Ct. 1395, 1399 [1977]), disagreeing that the law in question was prejudiced to Indians in fact, and citing *Morton v. Mancari* (417 U.S. 535 [1974]) to the effect that separate federal treatment of Indians is "not based upon impermissible [racial] classifications" but "rooted in the unique status of Indians as a 'separate people' with their own political institutions."

23

Treaty Federalism

Even if the Constitution itself did not guarantee certain inalienable political rights to all citizens, tribes would be entitled to political self-determination by virtue of their agreements with the United States. Intent, interpretation and practice combine to make these instruments something more than "treaties" as they are understood in international law. They are political compacts irrevocably annexing tribes to the federal system in a status parallel to, but not identical with, that of the states.

The significance of treaties lies not in their specific promises of so many blacksmiths, or so many schoolhouses, which have little contemporary relevance, nor in the proprietary arrangements for boundaries, fishing rights, and the like, which retain great economic value and are responsible for most recent treaty-rights litigation. Treaties are a form of political recognition and a measure of the consensual distribution of powers between tribes and the United States. In a national government of delegated and limited powers, it is not the tribe's responsibility to identify precise treaty authority for its continued political existence, but the task of the United States to rebut, using the evidence of express tribal consent, a presumption against its own authority to interfere.

Compact embodies all of our essential political ideas: the consent of the governed, the rational science of government in the service of political goals, the right of the people to remold their institutions in the common interest. How does a compact differ from a treaty? In *The Federalist*, Hamilton defined treaties as "CONTRACTS with foreign nations, which have the force of law, but derive it from the obligations of good faith."[1] Parties to a treaty have a right to revoke, and action inconsistent with its articles revokes a treaty de facto. An injured nation has no recourse but to war.[2]

Compacts differ in origin, nature and effect. Their object is to restructure the parties and create or enlarge some common, national sovereignty. Treaties are agreements between existing sovereigns; compacts create new sovereigns. Since compacts alter the fabric of government, they require the consent of the people themselves, the same as an internal amendment of either party's constitution. Once ratified by the people, a compact cannot be modified, dissolved or superseded except by the same process. It is not alliance, but the constitution of an amalgamated body politic.

The Constitutional Convention was embarrassed by the fact that while the Articles of Confederation had been unanimously ratified by the states, the proposed Constitution would become effective when ratified by only nine states. Would the ratification of the Constitution by any state dissolve the confederation, if opposed by the others? New Jersey's William Patterson argued that the confederation could only be dissolved by the unanimous consent of all the states. Madison disagreed.

Does this doctrine arise from the nature of compacts? Does it arise from any particular stipulation in the Articles of Confederation? If we consider the Federal Union [the Confederation] as analogous to the fundamental compact by which individuals compose one society, and which must, in its theoretic origin at least, have been the unanimous act of the component members, it cannot be said that no dissolution of the compact can be effected without unanimous consent. A breach of the fundamental principles of the compact, by a part of the society, would certainly absolve the other part from their obligations to it.[3]

He was obviously cautious not to imply that the American Revolution itself had been illegitimate. The articles had never been consented to by Great

1. No. 75.
2. This is how Justice Johnson originally interpreted the case of the *Cherokee Nation*, i.e., that the tribe's appeal "is to the sword and Almighty justice, and not to courts of law or equity" (30 U.S. [5 Pet.] 1, 29 [1831]).
3. 5 *Elliot's Debates on the Confederation and Constitution* 206 (Washington, D.C.: 1830–1845).

Britain, but the British compact had been broken by the Crown's disregard of "fundamental principles."

Madison did not suggest what comparable abuses justified a dissolution of the articles by a mere majority. Instead he intimated that the confederation was not a compact at all, since Congress could take no action except by unanimous consent. In practical effect, then, the confederation was nothing more than a "conventio[n] among individual states," i.e., a great treaty. If a treaty, then "[c]learly, according to the expositors of the law of nations . . . a breach of any one article, by any one party, leaves all the other parties at liberty to consider the whole convention as dissolved, unless they choose rather to compel the delinquent party to repair the breach."[4] The first state to ratify the Constitution would therefore render the whole confederation nugatory, unless the others preferred war.

If this theory was expedient in laying the old government to rest, it also concealed certain hazards for the new one. How was the Constitution different from the articles, such that it could endure the resistance of one or more disaffected states? The Constitution nowhere expressly provides that it is irrevocable, or forbids secession, although the procedure for amendment could have been intended to be exclusive. Express language was unnecessary, Madison contended.

If the breach of *any* article, by any of the parties, does not set the others at liberty, it is because the contrary is implied in the compact itself, and particularly by that law of it which gives an indefinite authority to the majority to bind the whole, in all cases.[5]

Later that year, Hamilton gave this germ of an idea further exposition in *The Federalist*.

It has not a little contributed to the infirmities of the existing federal system, that it never had a ratification by the PEOPLE. Resting on no better foundation than the consent of the several legislatures, it has been exposed to frequent and intricate questions concerning the validity of its powers, and has, in some instances, given birth to the enormous doctrine of a right of legislative repeal. Owing its ratification to the law of a State, it has been contended that the same authority might repeal the law by which it was ratified. However gross a heresy it may be to maintain that a *party* to a *compact* has a right to revoke that *compact*, the doctrine itself has had respectable advocates. The possibility of a question of this nature proves the necessity of laying the foundations of our national government deeper than in the

4. 5 *Elliot's Debates* 207.
5. 5 *Elliot's Debates* 206.

mere sanction of delegated authority. The fabric of American empire ought to rest on the solid basis of THE CONSENT OF THE PEOPLE.[6]

The special character of the Constitution is implied from its intent and from popular ratification. It is also implied in the structure of the political society established, a structure subordinating the constituents to a single, supreme national authority governing by the rule of the majority.

The Constitution is not, by its terms, exclusive of all other compacts. The principal difficulty in appreciating tribal treaties as compacts supplemental to the Constitution is conceptual. We are a nation of Constitution worshippers.[7]

The laws and the Constitution of our government ought to be regarded with reverence. Man must have an idol. And our political idol ought to be our Constitution and laws. They, like the ark of the covenant among the Jews, ought to be sacred.[8]

For Americans the Constitution is not merely a compact. It is imbued with an aura of uniqueness, and the history of its formation is the closest approximation to a myth of American national origin.

The first function of the founders of a nation, after founding itself, is to devise a set of true falsehoods about origins—a mythology—that will make it desirable for nationals to continue to live under common authority, and indeed, make it impossible for them to entertain contrary thoughts.[9]

The staunchest federalists freely admitted the Constitution's original defects in 1787. It was an instrument they fully expected to grow and be

6. No. 22. See also Madison in *The Federalist*, No. 40; Randolph in 5 *Elliot's Debates* 132. In *The Federalist*, No. 43, Madison observed that,

It has been heretofore noted among the defects of the Confederation, that in many of the States it had received no higher sanction than a mere legislative ratification. The principle of reciprocality seems to require that its obligation on the other States should be reduced to the same standard. A compact between independent sovereigns, founded on ordinary acts of legislative authority, can pretend to no higher validity than a league or treaty between the parties. It is an established doctrine on the subject of treaties, that all the articles are mutually conditions of each other; that a breach of any one article is a breach of the whole treaty; and that a breach, committed by either of the parties, absolves the others, and authorizes them, if they please, to pronounce the compact violated and void.

Madison's reasoning was incorporated by the Supreme Court in *M'Culloch v. Maryland*, 4 Wheat. (17 U.S.) 316, 403−4 (1819).

7. Frank I. Shechter, "The Early History of the Tradition of the Constitution," 9 *American Political Science Review* 707 (1915); H. Von Holst, "The Worship of the Constitution and its Real Character," 1 *The Constitutional and Political History of the United States* ch. 2 (Chicago: 1889).

8. From a 1791 jury charge related by Schechter, "Tradition of the Constitution," 733.

9. Forrest McDonald, *E Pluribus Unum: The Formation of the American Republic, 1776−1790* ix (Boston: 1965).

transformed as the condition of the country dictated.[10] The nature and future of Indian tribes was farthest from the thoughts of the Convention. None suspected the curious sequence of events that has isolated tribes from the rest of the federal system, and reduced them to a state of administrative trusteeship. The tribes they knew, like the Cherokees, Creeks, Miamis and Wyandottes were formidable military forces comprising tens of thousands of persons. The Constitution had almost reached its centennial before Congress was forced to face the inevitability of governing tribes within the federal system.

We must look behind the label to determine the real character of Indian "treaties."[11] In structure they resemble compacts, because they recognize the "supremacy" of Congress yet reserve local self-governing powers. Certain specific external powers, such as the power to make war, are relinquished. Boundaries are fixed and, not uncommonly, institutions are established for resolving disputes.[12] They are thus analagous to the Constitution itself and to the various state enabling acts. Regardless of their original intent, they have resulted in a complete political and economic integration of tribes into the federal system. Separation is practically impossible.

The United States today denies the power of tribes to revoke their treaties. A century ago, armed resistance by Indians placed them in a state of war.[13] Judging from the legal aftermath of the 1973 Wounded Knee confrontation, armed resistance is now regarded as merely criminal,

10. Especially *The Federalist*, Nos. 37 and 38.

11. When he first assumed office President Washington apparently had doubts whether treaties with tribes were treaties at all, i.e., whether they required the advice and consent of the Senate. William Maclay, *Sketches of Debate in the First Senate of the United States* 122–26 (Harrisburg, Pa.: 1880). Nevertheless, an extraordinary proportion of the first Senate's activity consisted of reviewing tribal treaties (1 *Senate Executive Journal* 3, 6, 17, 24–25, 28, 55–56, 58–59, 61, 85, 88, 98–99, 116, 134–36, 144–46, 168, 170, 220–21, 227, 229, 269–70, 306–7, 309–10, 312, 399–400, 405, 410, 423–24, 427–31, 442, 445, 473–75, 477–78, 481, 483.

12. It is fairly typical, for example, for treaties to give Indian agents quasi-judicial powers and to provide for mutual administrative extradition (discussed in *State ex. rel. Merrill v. Turtle*, 413 F.2d 683 [1969]).

13. There is an extensive literature on what constitutes an Indian war owing to the administration of the Indian Depredations Act (28 February 1859, c. 66 §8, R.S. 2156, 25 U.S.C. 229), which provides compensation for the acts of Indians belonging to tribes "in amity with the United States." See, for example, *Abrew v. U.S.*, 37 Ct. Cl. 510 (1902); *Leighton v. U.S.*, 161 U.S. 291 (1896); *Valk v. U.S.*, 29 Ct. Cl. 63 (1894).

perhaps treasonous.[14] The legitimacy of the treaty itself is no longer open to question in the courts. Evidence that a treaty was procured by fraud, or that tribal representatives lacked authority to treat, may support a claim for statutory compensation, but nothing more.[15] If tribes can no longer remove themselves from the Union, it is all the more essential that their political rights be secured on a fixed and certain basis. In an alliance of sovereigns, the ultimate relief from oppression is exit. In a national compact, the only safety is in the architecture of its constitution and laws.

We suggest there are *two* means of absorbing new subfederal sovereignties, *by compact*, into the Union. One is statehood, a procedure not defined in the Constitution but standardized in practice, requiring the consent of the people of the new state and a plurality of both Houses of Congress. The other is treaty federalism, a procedure also not defined in the Constitution but standardized in practice, requiring the consent of the tribal people by treaty and two-thirds of the Senate. This is a procedure for special cases, for the creative establishment of governments in circumstances where conventional statehood would be economically, socially or politically inappropriate, but where both sovereignties recognize the expediency of permanent union. It renders the Constitution adaptable to problems in political growth unanticipated by the framers.

Treaty federalism is not an entirely novel idea. It simply reinterprets the sources of federal Indian law to be more consistent with our general political and ideological heritage, and in a way reconcilable with the realities of tribal survival today. Why did John Marshall describe tribes as "domestic dependent nations" in *Cherokee Nation*? If they were truly nothing more than partners in federal treaties, would it not have been better to call them "allies?" What made them domestic was their permanent inclusion within the national territory of the United States, and what made them dependent was their recognition *by treaty* of federal supremacy. Marshall did not describe this as a transient condition, but one of permanence as against all the world.

Prior to 1921, all federal appropriations for tribes were keyed to

---

14. *U.S. v. Red Feather*, 393 F. Supp. 916, 921 (1975); *U.S. v. Consolidated Wounded Knee Cases*, 389 F. Supp, 235 (D.Neb. & W.D.S.D. 1975); *U.S. v. Banks and Means*, 383 F. Supp. 368, 371 (1974). *Red Feather* rejected a challenge to federal law enforcement officers' use of military equipment.

15. 25 U.S.C. 70a; *Buttz v. No. Pac. R.Co.*, 119 U.S. 55, 69 (1896).

fulfilling specific treaty obligations; in that year, the Snyder Act authorized general expenditures for Indian affairs.[16] Three years later, Indians were declared citizens.[17] Both acts suggest a policy of political integration. However, the idea of compact was not lost. The Indian Reorganization Act revitalized it in 1934 by establishing new tribal governments out of *mutual consent*: the consent of the United States manifested in the act, and the consent of participating tribes in referenda called for the purpose of adopting it.[18] In its application to individual tribes, the act embodies the principal criteria of compact. It restructures the governing of the parties, establishes a permanent political relationship, and flows from the consent of the people.

But, it will be argued, a compact can arise only from the consent of the people, and tribal treaties purport to be agreements between sovereigns. To begin with, tribes' authority to treat is an individual matter. Representatives of the large, hierarchically organized tribes such as the Cherokees bore specific instructions manifesting the consensus of the entire nation.[19] In some cases the United States assembled the whole tribe for the treaty conference, or representatives of each band, clan or family. Small tribes, if properly represented at all in the treaty councils, probably spoke from consensus, for "[w]ith them the whole authority of government is vested in the whole tribe. . . . Their government is genuinely democratical."[20] If the United States can assume, for its purposes, that all treaties were negotiated from proper authority, we can assume, from the structure and history of tribal governments, that that authority arose out of consensus.

Tribal consent to the Indian Reorganization Act was tested in federally supervised referenda.[21] Participation in the act realizes treaty sovereignty

16. Act of 2 November 1921, c. 115, 42 Stat. 208, 25 U.S.C. 13.
17. Act of 2 June 1924, 43 Stat. 253. Can a person be made a citizen without his consent? In *Elk v. Wilkins*, 112 U.S. 94 (1884), the majority reasoned that an Indian cannot become a citizen without the consent of the United States.
18. On referenda, 25 U.S.C. 478, 478a.
19. See, generally, John Phillip Reid, *Law of Blood: The Primitive Law of the Cherokee Nation* (New York: 1970); William N. Fenton, ed., *Parker on the Iroquois* (Syracuse, N.Y.: 1968).
20. James Winthrop, "Letters of Agrippa" (1787), Letter No. 17, reprinted in Paul Leicester Ford, *Essays on the Constitution of the United States* (Brooklyn, N.Y.: 1892). The *Report of the Commissioner of Indian Affairs, 1873* 4–5 considered it a *defect* of tribes that their authority proceeds entirely from the "consent of the governed!"
21. Congress provided that this be a one-time affair. Tribes which voted against reorganization were not given a second chance, and all were required to make a commitment one way or the other by 18 June 1936 (Act of 15 June 1935, c. 260 §2, 49 Stat. 378). Many

and, in accordance with its express terms, does not impair the obligation of preexisting compacts with the United States.[22] Any defect in treaty consent has been thereby repaired.[23]

It is true that the United States itself did not popularly consent to tribal treaties, but then the admission of a new state requires only a vote of Congress. Of course, Article IV of the Constitution provides that "New States may be admitted by the Congress," indicating a delegation or waiver of the right of popular consent. Is this right alienable by the people? Perhaps it is alienable in this case because of the peculiar nature of the transaction. The new state submits to supremacy of the nation, ceding a portion of its sovereignty. The general government is not altered, hence the whole people need not give their consent directly. How is it different with a tribe? The tribe in its treaty submits to federal supremacy, ceding a portion of its sovereignty. What it cedes is somewhat more or less than a new state, perhaps also somewhat different. In any event, the acceptance of the cession requires no compensatory alteration of the general government. Indeed, it may be harder to admit a tribe as a matter of treaty federalism, than to admit a new state. Ratifying a tribal treaty requires the consent of two-thirds of the states as they are represented in the Senate; admitting a state, only a plurality.

Since the United States can presume that tribal representatives had authority to cede, perhaps it is appropriate for tribes to presume that the United States had authority to accept. How were they to know the niceties of constitutional procedure? When they committed themselves to perpetual acts, they must have assumed that the United States had adequate authority to bind itself on the other side. For more than a century the general government has uniformly behaved as if its agreements with tribes were

---

tribes probably rejected reorganization under the impression that it would limit their original powers.

22. 25 U.S.C. 478b.

23. In *United States v. Mississippi Tax Commission*, now on review from the Fifth Circuit, the tribe is taking the opposite tack, i.e., that their 1831 treaty, in which they agreed to dissolve themselves as a body politic, was superseded by twentieth-century acts of Congress recognizing and subsidizing their community (541 F. 2d 469 [5th Cir. 1976]). Ironically the state of Mississippi rested its argument that the tribe no longer exists on the inviolability of Indian treaties—and won. According to the Fifth Circuit, the inviolability of treaties derives from the 1871 act prohibiting further treatymaking by the president. What, then, of the hundreds of pre-1871 treaties abrogated by Congress? "These cases, of course, were concerned with disputes between the government and Indian Tribes . . . *owing no allegiance to the States*" (*id.* 470).

permanent. Now that tribes ask for perpetual recognition, is there any equity in denying that tribal treaties were properly ratified by the American people?

The theory of treaty federalism replaces the mytho-historical notion of conquest that dominates Felix Cohen's *Handbook of Federal Indian Law*. According to the conquest myth, tribes possess, at first, all of the powers of a sovereign nation. Conquest by the United States renders the tribe subject to federal legislative powers, and effectively terminates the external sovereignty of the tribe. Finally, the balance of internal powers is subject to qualification by treaties and express legislation.

Conquest is an unnecessary and pernicious fiction. The Constitution suggests that federal overseas powers expand through the consent of foreign nations expressed in treaties and trade. The War Powers clause is silent about governing conquered peoples. The real root of the conquest myth is not in the Constitution at all, but in British common law, in *Campbell v. Hall*: "It is only by positive enactments, even in the cases of conquered and subdued nations, that their laws are changed by the conqueror."[24] Here is the whole substance of Cohen's formula. Once it is assumed that tribes are a conquered people, they have a right to retain all of their own laws and institutions until altered by positive—read for this "express"—acts of the conqueror, the United States. In this context, treaties are not *sources* of federal power, but *limitations* on its exercise.

Conquest is not only external to the Constitution, it has never been endorsed by the courts and has no historical foundation. *Johnson v. M'Intosh* laid it to rest one hundred and fifty years ago. As recently as 1973, in *McClanahan*, the Court observed that

The source of federal authority over Indian matters has been the subject of some confusion, but it is now generally recognized that the power derived from the federal responsibility for regulating commerce with Indian tribes and for treaty making.[25]

Not the war powers. If the constitutional source of the power is not in conquest, how can the law of conquest determine its scope and implementation?

24. 1 Cowp. 204, 209, 98 Eng. Rep. 1045, 1047 (1774).
25. 411 U.S. 172 n.7.

Conquest is the result of a just war and an unconditional surrender. Tribal wars with the United States ended in treaties filled with the language of mutual concession and mutual recognition. Many tribes were never at war at all with the United States, and many had treaties with the United States before they went to war, or went to war to redress federal treaty violations. If we wish to look for an example of conquest in American history there is none better than the Civil War. According to constitutional jurisprudence, the war was just, and the surrender was expressly unconditional. For a period of time the southern states were stripped of their political identity and governed in a manner that previewed the Indian reservation. Yet they were restored to their full sovereignty by Congress after a generation. Can tribes, which were never conquered, be entitled to less?

Although the courts have never spoken the language of conquest, they have often acted as if tribes were conquered people. How else can one explain the doctrine that Congress can unilaterally abrogate tribal treaties, but the tribes themselves cannot? It must be remembered that Cohen tailored his theory to the judicial facts as he saw them. His was an attempt to rationalize, not criticize, what came before. Unfortunately, his rationalization legitimizes practices apparently at war with the history, ideology, and objectives of the Constitution.

Treaty federalism rests on principles more consonant with American government: consent of the governed, representation, and political pluralism. "In point of form," Cohen observed a generation ago, "it is immaterial whether the powers of an Indian tribe are expressed and exercised through customs handed down by word of mouth or through a written constitution and statutes. In either case the laws of the Indian tribe owe their force to the will of the members of the tribe."[26] The will of the people is essential. It explains the survival of tribes. Treaty federalism makes it the test of political legitimacy.

THE REALIZATION OF TREATY FEDERALISM

There are two kinds of subfederal political relationships today. The relationship of each state to the general government is defined by the Constitution. The relationship of tribes to the United States is discernible only in the hundreds of treaties which link them and give authority to

26. *Handbook of Federal Indian Law* 122 (Washington, D.C.: 1942).

federal supremacy. To guarantee the security of tribes, it is incumbent on Congress and the people of the United States to resolve treaties into a single constitution of undisputed authority, presumably an amendment to our existing general Constitution. Congress has reversed itself so frequently in matters of tribal affairs that there is no reason to expect any greater constancy in the future. Mere legislative recognition of treaty federalism is inadequate.

A constitutional resolution of treaty federalism must above all clarify the reserved territorial powers of tribes, rejecting the authority of Congress to arrogate power unilaterally over tribes without denying tribe's authority to delegate additional powers to Congress. We suggest a standardization of tribal powers on the state model to avoid the prospect of endless judicial interpretations and tribe-by-tribe distinctions. The only exception would be to reserve tribes' power of naturalization, which has proved necessary, for the time being, to their political and economic stability. Once better established and able to support larger populations, tribes will probably conclude that traditional restrictions on entry and the political franchise tend to chill further growth, and will abolish them. We propose to begin with the following language:

Section 1. Except as provided by this amendment, Indian Tribes shall be deemed ''States'' for all purposes under this Constitution.

Section 2. All Constitutional powers of State self-government not hereafter expressly delegated to the United States by the vote of three-fourths of the members of an Indian Tribe are reserved by that tribe, and cannot be divested by Congress.

Section 3. The reserved powers of an Indian Tribe shall include, but not be limited to, the power to regulate behavior and tax persons and property within the exterior boundaries of its territory, concurrent only with the general Constitutional authority of the United States.

Section 4. Tribes shall have power to fix criteria for membership notwithstanding the second clause of the second section of the Fourteenth Amendment.

The future role of the Bureau of Indian Affairs is also a matter of great concern. There is no justification for a continuation of its ''protective'' powers, and if tribes can compete with states for federal domestic assistance on an equal footing, the bureau's subsidy functions will become redundant. However, at least in the short run, tribes' relative underdevelopment will necessitate substantial public expenditures beyond the scope of conventional subsidy programs. We propose to distribute an amount equal to the bureau's current budget directly to the tribes for ten years:

Section 5. For ten years from the date of ratification of this amendment, Congress shall appropriate $500 million to the use and for the benefit and economic development of Tribes, which fund shall be apportioned on the basis of membership and distributed directly to the respective Tribal governments without condition or limitation. Nothing in this amendment shall authorize the United States through any of its officers or agencies to supervise or regulate the use of this fund or the administration of tribal government generally.

By far the most crucial objective must be to secure tribes an adequate representation in the national government. Apportionment by existing formulae would result in an impractical and politically fatal absurdity: more than two hundred senators and no representatives. Since tribes are politically distinct from the states, it is reasonable to apportion them in a different manner, more suited to their circumstances and minimizing any disproportionate influence in either house:

Section 6. (a) For purposes of representation in Congress, there shall be two assemblies separate and apart from those established by Article I of this Constitution. The Tribal Senate Caucus shall consist of one Delegate from each Tribe. The Tribal House Caucus shall be apportioned by the membership of each Tribe, Tribes to have one Delegate for every five thousand members or part thereof.

(a) Delegates shall each serve for four years, one-fourth of the Delegates to be elected each year in such a manner as each Tribe shall respectively provide in its constitution.

(c) From year to year or at such times as each Caucus shall establish by rules, the Tribal Senate Caucus shall send two Senators to the Senate and the Tribal House Caucus shall send two Representatives to the House of Representatives, which Senators and Representatives shall serve and act in every way as any other members of Congress.

(d) The expenses of Delegates and the expenses of the respective Caucuses herein provided shall be paid by the United States.

Section 7. Henceforth no State shall exercise any power over the territory of any Tribe, except by the terms of a Compact approved by Congress, nor shall the resident members of any Tribe have the right of suffrage or election in any State.

Tribes would not gain complete control of legislation affecting them, nor would they significantly realign either house. Tribal representatives would nonetheless serve on committees, enjoy the privilege of debate, and, in common with territorial delegates, advocate their constituents' interests at public expense. The caucus procedure makes it likely that tribal congressmen would represent a broad consensus among tribes.

Not all tribes would volunteer to assume the burdens and responsibilities of a status tantamount to statehood. After the ten-year development period, they would have no choice but to make their own way by their own means. The concomitant loss of the state franchise is also an effective check on abuse of these provisions; no community already largely assimilated into a state or financially dependent on it will lightly trade its existing franchise for political autonomy. Of course, the principles behind this proposal require that each tribe choose for itself:

Section 8. This amendment shall apply only to those Indian Tribes which were incorporated by a constitution of their choosing for five years prior to the date of ratification, and which may consent to its application to them by the vote of two-thirds of their members in a plebiscite convened for that purpose.

Incorporating tribes into the federal system is not impossible. It can be accomplished without significantly altering the present state of affairs, and, if successful in realizing the full political and economic potential of tribal communities, it can reduce federal expenditures, conclude tribal-state hostility, and bring to an end the century-long struggle for power among the states, congress and the bureau. It is up to the American people to act consistently with the ideals of our political traditions.

Conclusion

The Road and the Chain

> The older people . . . expect their young people to have a home. From which place they can go out into the world, and if the world is too fast for them they will have a place to return when they seek refuge. That was the intention of the old chiefs.[1]

The Iroquois analogized the ideological and political integration of their federal republic to a chain—an interlinking of peoples and ideas. Tribal republics and the United States are part of a chain as yet little appreciated. Bernard Bailyn observes that the colonists held a cyclical view of history.[2] They saw in their mother country a repetition of the corruption and decline of the classical civilizations, and in their own struggle a resurgence of the virtues of the preconquest Anglo-Saxon yeomanry and the political idealism of the Restoration. "[C]auses and effects are things correlative," John Peter Zenger wrote in 1733, "and the same causes had and ever will have the same effects."[3] It is interesting, then, how considerable are the parallels between the situation and ideology of the colonial radicals, and of the tribal movement today. Now, as then, the "radicals" are in truth conservatives seeking recommitment to fundamental ideals, and the "conservative" defenders of the status quo are really the innovators.[4] Like their eighteenth-century counterparts, tribalists are "not attempting any change of Government—only a preservation of the Constitution."[5]

1. Peter Graves of Red Lake testifying in "Hearings, 'Readjustment of Indian Affairs,' " 219, House Committee on Indian Affairs, 73rd Congress, 2nd Session (1934).
2. Bernard Bailyn, *Ideological Origins of the American Revolution* 85 (Cambridge, Mass.: 1967).
3. Quoted in *id*. 85 n.31.
4. As Ambrose Bierce observed cynically, radicalism is often "[t]he conservatism of tomorrow injected into the affairs of today." Thus Tories viewed the principle of justified resistance against unjust magistrates as an antique of no surviving significance after the Restoration, inconsistent with "modern," enlightened political science (Pauline Maier, *From Resistance to Revolution* 139 [New York:1972]).
5. Quoted in Maier, *From Resistance to Revolution* 96, 101.

In common with the colonists, tribes hope to secure their political rights on legitimate historical and legal grounds, out of continuity rather than novelty.[6] The foundation of this approach is and was an appeal to charters. Colonial charters and tribal treaties both reconstitute the dependent government and subject it to the national legislature. If anything, the eighteenth-century argument from original charters was weaker, because the colonists had never existed in a state of autonomous sovereignty. Charters merely secured their rights as Britons, often subject to limitations and conditions.[7] In either case, however, the essential element in their argument was its emphasis on mutual consent.

Colonists' were aggrieved with executive veto of their laws, their lack of representation in a Parliament asserting the power to govern them and alter their laws, and their victimization and economic suppression by a corrupt bureaucracy. They demanded a permanent federal union with Britain which preserved their own independent internal sphere of sovereignty and in other ways accorded them all of the general rights of national citizenship. The position of tribes is no different.

The parallels are strong, but it has not been unknown for American practice to violate American principles. During the revolutionary struggle many on both sides of the Atlantic decried the hypocrisy of preserving black slavery in the midst of some of the most vociferously separatist colonies,[8] and slavery was to remain a problem for nearly a century. In the decade that followed this country's last centennial celebration, representatives of the western Territories criticized Congress for failing to fully realize the ideal of political liberty for all of its constituents. "The people of Dakota," the Bismarck *Tribune* explained in 1881, "feel that they are abundantly able to govern themselves and no matter how good and pure the man who is sent from the outside to govern them, a natural opposition to him springs up at once . . . very much as the governors sent from England

6. *Id*. 47–48; Bailyn, *Ideological Origins* 33.
7. Thomas Pownall, 1 *The Administration of the British Colonies* 74, 87–88, 287–88 (5th ed. London: 1774), and 2 *Administration* 16–30, 37–38, 91–92.
8. See Bailyn's review of this in *Ideological Origins* 232–45. It is particularly interesting that some New England theologians predicted the doom of the colonists' cause so long as they sinned by perpetuating slavery and thereby alienating divine Providence. Some Indian religious leaders have recently suggested that the moral corruption of contemporary America is an effect of the suppression of Indian freedom. Compare also Vine DeLoria's idea of white regeneration through Indian values and religion, *God Is Red* (New York: 1975), *We Talk, You Listen* (New York: 1970), with the colonists' idea of America as a refuge for uncorrupted Britons.

were regarded by our forefathers.''⁹ A few years later, Montana's delegate wrote, "It is a strange thing that the fathers of our Republic . . . established a colonial government as much worse than that which they revolted against as one form of government can be worse than another.''¹⁰ Within a generation, all of the contiguous continental territories had achieved statehood. When will the period of political subordination end for tribes?

Some have argued that since Congress by legislation created the "special federal relationship" with tribes, Congress can by legislation destroy it.¹¹ The problem arises in the interpretation of what this federally created relationship really is. The federal government did not, historically, create the sovereignty of tribes. Acts of Congress limited, modified, and channelled tribal powers, usually without tribal consent. The termination of what Congress created should therefore result in an *increase* in tribal self-governing powers. Instead, Congress has acted as if the termination of tribal dependency results in the dissolution rather than the emancipation of tribes.

Tribal incorporation into the federal system, and concomitant protection from coercive state encroachments, is not merely a product of congressional will. If that were entirely true and acted upon candidly, termination would restore tribes to their original international status, a result we believe neither practical nor desired by either party. The fact of the matter is that tribes' original submission to federal power was consensual. Unless that original consent expressly included some right in the United States to act without constraint, the presumption should be that any alteration of tribes' circumstances requires their fresh consent. Any other interpretation is inconsistent with our contractarian theory of government.

Treaties with tribes are admittedly vague. The general government has used this fact to argue that treaties are absolute delegations or cessions of territory and sovereignty. However, the United States' own agents drafted virtually all of the treaties. At least by the ordinary rules of construing instruments, they must be construed in favor of the tribes. If the United

9. Earl S. Pomeroy, *The Territories and the United States*, 103 (Seattle: 1969).

10. *Id*. 104. They also complained of "wardship" and of federal "tinkering" or "experimenting" with their governments, and branded the federal territorial service "a sort of Botany Bay . . . to banish broken-down politicians." Compare tribes' criticism of the Indian Reorganization Act as a bureau social experiment at the expense of their existing governments (78 *Cong. Rec.* 11735–36 [15 June 1934]). Perhaps it was: see John Collier's "The Indian Administration as a Laboratory in Ethnic Affairs," 12 *Social Research* 265 (1945).

11. *Crain v. First National Bank of Oregon*, 324 F. 2d 532, 535–37 (C.A. Ore. 1963).

States had wanted to obtain complete sovereignty and the tribes were willing to relinquish it, this should have been made plain in the documents themselves. The courts often construe tribal treaties against the federal government in land and resource matters,[12] but have never been asked to apply the same rule to the far more essential issue of political power. It is a fundamental principle of the American republic that political liberty is necessary in a free society—so necessary, in fact, that it is an "inalienable right." A vague document cannot be held to have conveyed an inalienable right.

If Indian treaties are compacts and therefore irrevocable, analogous to the state-federal compact (the Constitution), how are their ambiguities to be resolved? *Tribes must have no less political liberty than the states.* It is reasonable to infer that tribes would not knowingly have submitted their persons and property to Congress on substantially poorer terms than the states.

Congressional policy since the earliest days of the Republic has sought to answer the riddle of tribalism in a modern nation-state. It has refused to consider tribal statehood seriously. It has refused to afford tribal citizens the same liberties as the millions of immigrants who came to populate their country. Every tribe has been subjected to inconsistent and often unique requirements without constitutional recourse. The closest we have come to a general Indian policy is the recurrent rhetoric of "assimilation," "integration into the mainstream," and "Americanization," which challenges the ethnicity and lifestyle of individual Indians without addressing their political choice.

Americans persist in denying the existence of tribalism. It is a widespread assumption that no reasonable person would *choose* to live in a tribal community, therefore anyone who does must either be irrational or lack free will. Hence our national fascination with, and vacillation between, paternalistic supervision and compulsory termination of reservations. Indeed, the root of the conceptual problem may run even deeper. If most Americans no longer understand and agree with the Constitution and its sources, they cannot possibly appreciate the arguments for tribal political liberty.

The colonists thought of themselves as battling a corrupt, morally

12. *Carpenter v. Shaw*, 280 U.S. 363, 367 (1930); *Worcester v. Georgia*, 31 U.S. (6 Pet.) 515, 582 (1832).

degenerate society.[13] How apt is the parallel? Modern American society, the society Indians are supposed to emulate, has come a long way from its normative origins. Little is left of the ideals of family and community (a charge also levelled by the colonists at Great Britain), and order is maintained by power and interest instead of respect and moral unity.[14] Justice is represented by formal equality among strangers, by amorality, and generalization. The substantive justice and particularism of an organic community have disappeared. What will be accomplished by compelling tribes to follow the same road?

The corruption of modern society is political as well as social. Americans increasingly identify with political ideals antithetical to this nation's first principles: autocracy, passive obedience, political non-involvement, deliberate ignorance of events, and a consuming obsession with the maintenance of physical security at any political cost. Tribes cannot lose their struggle for political identity because their objectives and reasons are un-American, but only because contemporary America has departed from its original ideals of political liberty.

Two centuries ago, Dean Tucker warned the American rebels that adopting a republican government founded on political liberty would be dangerous.

New governments and new Commonwealths, half civilized and half savage, will start up in those distant Regions [in the West]: For every Topic and every Argument which the Sea Coast *Americans* now urge against the Mother Country, will be retorted with double Force against themselves.[15]

It was shortly after this country's first centennial that tribes were denied political liberty. It is appropriate as the bicentennial passes to renew the argument for political liberty in their behalf.

13. Bailyn, *Ideological Origins*, 25−26, 86−92, 132−37.
14. Roberto Mangabeira Unger, *Law in Modern Society: Toward a Criticism of Social Theory* 143−47 (New York: 1976).
15. Josiah Tucker, *A Series of Answers to certain popular objections, against Separating from the Rebellious Colonies* 24 (Gloucester, England: 1776).

Postscript

Cycles and Portents

It has been observed that Indian policy runs in cycles. After a generation of relative security comes a period of intolerance, confrontation, and confiscation. In time, the country confesses error and makes some small attempts at tribal reconstruction and preservation. Tribes regain a part of their former intellectual, political and technological strength. Then the cycle repeats.

Removal, allotment, reorganization, and termination coincided with significant historical trends in the demand for and availability of natural resources. The General Allotment Act (1887), for instance, came within a few years of the peak of homesteading (1884), just as the Indian Reorganization Act (1934) policy of repurchasing allotted reservation lands was adopted a year after the twentieth-century low point in the price of U.S. farmland (1933).[1] Policy cycles in Indian affairs are not as frequent as price fluctuations in the resource marketplace, however. Indian policy cycles reflect qualitative shifts in the public perception of Indians' place in our national system. Material interest may be the stimulus for some, but most non-Indian citizens derive no benefit from confiscations of

1. U.S. Bureau of the Census, *Historical Statistics of the United States, Colonial Times to 1957* 236−37, 278−79 (Washington, D.C.: 1960).

Indian rights and resources. The behavior of the majority must be sought in ideas, not profits.

When we completed this book in 1977 we were uncertain whether the 1980s would see another reversal in Indian policy. The Supreme Court had just dropped a hint that tribal jurisdiction would be limited by a race test.[2] On the other hand "self-determination" still showed support in Congress, and the elevation of the old Senate Subcommittee on Indian Affairs to select committee status under the leadership of Senator Abourezk, together with the release of the American Indian Policy Review Commission's pro-tribal, albeit somewhat confused final report, seemed hopeful signs.

The events of 1978 dispel all ambiguity. The Supreme Court has moved definitively in the direction of tribal termination. In *Oliphant v. Suquamish Indian Tribe*, an opinion fraught with errors of history, citation and logic,[3] the Court not only nailed down the racial standard of jurisdiction introduced by *Moe*, but announced a new theory of tribal powers. Solicitor Nathan Margold wrote in 1934 that

those powers which are lawfully vested in an Indian tribe are not, in general, delegated powers granted by express acts of Congress, but rather inherent powers of a limited sovereignty which has never been extinguished. . . . The statutes of Congress, then, must be examined to determine the limitations of tribal sovereignty rather than to determine its source or its positive content. What is not expressly limited remains within the domain of tribal sovereignty[.][4]

Compare this with the Court's assertion in 1978 that

Indian tribes still possess those aspects of sovereignty not withdrawn by treaty or statute, *or by implication as a necessary result of their dependent status.*[5]

No longer constrained by national legislation, the Supreme Court will henceforth embark upon an independent enumeration of powers tribes have supposedly lost "by implication."

Oliphant holds that tribes lack criminal jurisdiction over non-Indians.

---

2. As we argued in R. L. Barsh, "The Omen: *Three Affiliated Tribes v. Moe* and the Future of Tribal Self-Government," 5 *American Indian Law Review* 1 (1977).

3. A thorough review of the Court's reasoning in this case will appear in a 1979 issue of the *Minnesota Law Review* under the title "The Betrayal: *Oliphant v. Suquamish Indian Tribe* and the Hunting of the Snark."

4. 55 I.D. 14, 19 (1934).

5. *U.S. v. Wheeler*, 98 S.Ct. 1079, 1086 (1978), citing the month-old *Oliphant* decision as authority.

Oliphant's theory of power reaches much further. According to one federal district court, tribes now lack *civil* jurisdiction over non-Indians and non-Indian firms as well,[6] frustrating zoning, environmental regulation, and the enforcement of public health and safety standards on reservations. Without the power to protect reservation residents, tribes cannot long maintain political legitimacy. Ineffectual, they will die, and the tragedy is that tribal members themselves will be forced to call on state authority to preserve public safety and order.

Congress, for its part, has not been idle. In September 1977 Congressman Jack Cunningham introduced a frankly terminationist bill. Cleverly titled the "Native Americans Equal Opportunity Act," H.R. 9054 regrinds the grist of the Sproul and Langer committees, abrogating all treaties, abolishing BIA programs, promising Indians "full citizenship and equality under law" and "recognizing that in the United States no individual or group possesses subordinate or special rights." Like the General Allotment Act, H.R. 9054 would distribute all tribal assets among tribal members and subject them and their property to state jurisdiction.

Evidently some fundamental misconceptions of national principles persist. Political liberty as we have described it *is* a right of citizenship. To equalize political liberty all communities must be afforded an equal right of local self-government. The states are not equal in the sense of being identical, but in the sense of being equally free to differ. Nor are treaty fishing rights, the real target of H.R. 9054, "special" or unusual. Few resources are evenly distributed in our society, and we know of no constitutional principle requiring them to be. Some people own a great deal of land, others enjoy mineral rights; many possess little of anything. A few Indian tribes own a lot of fish. We thought that was capitalism. Jack Cunningham says it's un-American, at least when Indians have the upper hand.

Cunningham's defeat in his 1978 bid for reelection will dispose of H.R. 9054 but not of the resurgence of termination. So-called "backlash" organizations proliferate among non-Indians. The Interstate Congress for Equal Rights and Responsibilities is distributing nationally a booklet entitled *Are We Giving America Back to the Indians?*, in which Indians are depicted as the country's "most favored citizens" whose conceded poverty is due only to pampering and idleness.

6. *Trans-Canada Enterprises Ltd. v. Muckleshoot Indian Tribe*, District Court for the Western District of Washington, Civ. No. C77−882M (27 July 1978).

[T]he vast majority of Americans do not have the luxury of virtually unlimited sources of funding. Self-reliance is the strength of our nation, and it is grossly unfair to the Indians to deprive them the opportunity to gain that self-reliance. . . . [I]t is plain to close observers that these frequent doles have only increased the Indian people's ability to sit on the sidelines of activity with plenty of time to ask for more. This situation intensifies with each generation because they are born into and reared in an environment of inactivity with nothing to do but wait for another round of subsidization.[7]

Only Indians who have "broken away from this age-old system of inactivity" have become "happy, proud, and industrious." This perpetuates the tired old paradox of the past. Indians only *seem* to want to live together in their own communities. In his heart of hearts every Indian wants to be white, but the big, bad federal government pays him off to stay Indian.

Citizens justifiably resent the size and cost of government, especially when they feel they are deprived of its advantages. In the past couple of years we have witnessed tax revolts and a battle over "reverse discrimination" in higher education. Both have roots in the same fears. The problem we see is that a disgruntled public, in its zeal to strike out against government excess, will destroy government. Non-Indians complain of the high cost and negative benefits of federal Indian administration. So do Indians. Dissolving *tribal* government is no more a solution to this problem than dissolving *state* government will arrest federal overspending in nontribal activities.

State citizens appear blind to the implications of their own arguments. In 1971 white Alaskans celebrated the Alaska Native Claims Settlement Act, opening the way for the Alyeska pipeline at the expense of native self-government.[8] In 1978, the same people bitterly opposed "national interest lands" legislation that would have subordinated Alaska state development plans to the demands of out-of-state users of parklands. The morning the Supreme Court announced *Oliphant*, it also held that Washington State lacks power to impose environmental and safety controls on federally licensed oil tankers operating in Puget Sound. We find these coincidences prophetic. The states think they are protecting themselves from tribes when they demean the ideals of local self-government and political diversity, but

7. *Are We Giving America Back To the Indians?* 9–10 (Winner, S.D.: 1976).
8. The settlement act (P.L. 92–203, 85 Stat. 688) turns over the control of most native lands and funds to newly-created for-profit corporations that operate in accordance with state business laws and are scheduled to go public in 1991.

they are burying their own dreams. Inexorably they will demolish the political values that perpetuate federalism.

In the midst of this time of social and environmental reevaluation, in which Indian culture and Indian imagery have played so large a part, and in which a mixture of nostalgia and guilt over the passing of aboriginal America is so popular in the media, it is ironic that Indians are still not secure in the enjoyment of political liberty. The white Americans of the last century wept over Henry Sprague's romantic lectures on the vanishing red man while they put the architects of removal and allotment into public office. The white Americans of this decade consume an unprecedented number of books and films on Indian life and legends while they tolerate the legal dismemberment of tribal communities. It is not enough to mourn past misdeeds. It is necessary to challenge the power to repeat them.

Index

civil rights movement, 243–44; ethnic component, 243–44; political component, 244

Indian Police, U.S., 81

Indian Reorganization Act: and federal guardianship of Indian tribes, 99–100; economic program, 100; provisions for tribal self-government, 101–5, 107–8, 116–17; effect on Bureau of Indian Affairs, 105–6, 115; Margold opinion interpreting, 108–11; Haas report on results of, 114–17; as a compact with Indian tribes, 276–77

Indian Self-Determination and Education Assistance Act, 160*n*, 183, 228, 251, 253

Indian Trade and Intercourse Acts, 78–79

Indian treaties. *See* Treaties with Indian tribes

Indian tribes: reaction to American Revolution, 32–33; compared to territories, 209–14; statehood proposed, 210–11; size and political influence, 218, 220; interests compared to interests of the states, 229–30; financial manipulation by U.S., 237*n*; competition among, 250–51

Infringement test, 151–54, 166, 168, 183–85, 196, 255

Instrumentality, federal: used to describe Indian tribes, 170–72, 192, 195

Involution of legal doctrine, 140, 185–86

Iredell, James: views on Bill of Rights, 238

Iron Crow v. Oglala Sioux Tribe, 147–48

Jefferson, Thomas: Ordinance of 1784, 206–8; advocacy of tribal

statehood, 211; proposed amendment to the Constitution, 264

Johnson, Justice Thomas: on Indian tribes' status, 38–39

Johnson v. M'Intosh, 45–47, 65

Joseph, U.S. v., 73

Jurisdiction. *See* States

Kagama, U.S. v., 75, 82–83

Kake v. Egan, 155–58, 161–62, 166*n*, 168*n*

Knox, Henry: on state government, 22

Kuhn, Thomas: on paradigms, xi

Langdell, Dean C. C.: views on status of U.S. territories, 93–94, 214, 220*n*, 257

Langer Committee: criticism of Bureau of Indian Affairs, 124

Late Corporation Church of Jesus Christ v. U.S., 77–78

Lawyers: representation of Indian tribes criticized, 253–56

Lee, Richard Henry: on representations, 27

Legal reasoning: use of history, x–xiii; use of precedent, xi. *See also* Involution of legal doctrine

Liberalism: doctrinal conflicts with Indian movement, 241

Liberty. *See* Political liberty

Lincoln, James: definition of liberty, 20

Lobbying, Indian: impact on federal legislation, 218–20; by national Indian organizations, 251–52

Locke, John: on origins and purpose of government, 12–13

Lone Wolf v. Hitchcock, 92–93

Louisiana Purchase: power of U.S. to make questioned, 46

McBratney, U.S. v., 145–47

McClanahan v. Arizona Tax Commission, 167–70, 184, 193

Designer:	Al Burkhardt
Compositor:	Trend Western
Printer:	Thomson-Shore
Binder:	Thomson-Shore
Text:	Linocomp Times Roman
Display:	Linocomp Times Roman
Cloth:	Johanna Arrestox B 19990
Paper:	50 lb. P & S Offset Vellum